Queer Mobilizations

LGBT Activists Confront the Law

EDITED BY

Scott Barclay, Mary Bernstein,

and Anna-Maria Marshall

NEW YORK UNIVERSITY PRESS

New York and London

NEW YORK UNIVERSITY PRESS
New York and London
www.nyupress.org

© 2009 by New York University

Library of Congress Cataloging-in-Publication Data

Queer mobilizations : LGBT activists confront the law /
edited by Scott Barclay, Mary Bernstein, and Anna-Maria Marshall.
p. cm.
Includes bibliographical references and index.
ISBN-13: 978–0–8147–9130–1 (cl : alk. paper)
ISBN-10: 0–8147–9130–1 (cl : alk. paper)
ISBN-13: 978–0–8147–9131–8 (pb : alk. paper)
ISBN-10: 0–8147–9131–x (pb : alk. paper)
1. Homosexuality—Law and legislation—United States.
2. Gay rights—United States. I. Barclay, Scott. II. Bernstein, Mary.
III. Marshall, Anna-Maria.
KF4754.5.Q84   2009
342.7308'7—dc22   2009010118

New York University Press books are printed on acid-free paper,
and their binding materials are chosen for strength and durability.
We strive to use environmentally responsible suppliers and materials
to the greatest extent possible in publishing our books.

Manufactured in the United States of America
c 10 9 8 7 6 5 4 3 2 1
p 10 9 8 7 6 5 4 3 2 1

Queer Mobilizations

Contents

Acknowledgments

THIS BOOK REPRESENTS a professional, political, and personal achievement for the three of us who co-edited it. The three of us have devoted our professional lives to studying various dimensions of social movements. Over the course of our careers, we've been lucky enough to participate in networks of scholars who share our interests. Through those networks, we met the contributors to this volume, some of whose work we have admired for years, some of whom are new scholars who promise to make a lasting contribution to our respective fields. We are grateful to all of them. In addition, this volume would not have been possible without the inspiration and guidance of our friends and colleagues, including David Greenberg, Michael McCann, Gerald Rosenberg, Lynn Jones, Sandra Levitsky, Steven Boutcher, Richard McAdams, and Nancy Naples. We would also like to thank the Research Foundation of the University of Connecticut for awarding us a small faculty grant to support the production of this book. Finally, we would like to thank Ilene Kalish at New York University Press for her enthusiastic support of this project from the outset. We would also like to thank Aiden Amos of NYU Press for her assistance through the publication process.

The volume also speaks to the intersection between the personal and the political for all three of us. The following acknowledgements reflect our personal thanks.

To those select social scientists of the 1960s, 1970s, 1980s, and 1990s who toiled for many years to bring complex intellectual approaches and accurate data to the study of lesbian and gay rights. They often did these tasks amidst the veiled scorn of their academic counterparts in the larger discipline. The currently strong state of this field, as reflected in the extensive breadth of the ideas and research found in this edited volume, reflects their willingness to lay the necessary groundwork during difficult times.

—Scott Barclay

I would like to thank my life partner, Nancy Naples, for her consistent support through good times and bad. I would like to dedicate this book to my daughters, Alexandra and Samantha. I recently took them to the rally after the Connecticut Supreme Court legalized same-sex marriage. I didn't want to introduce the idea of homophobia into their four-year-old worlds, so I simply told them that we were going to a rally to celebrate families with two mommies or two daddies. I hope that my girls can grow up in a world where the legal and social disabilities associated with their moms' sexual orientation and relationship are quickly being relegated to the dustbin of history. I would also like to thank all of the activists who are working to make this transformation a reality.

—Mary Bernstein

My grandfather was a leader in the effort to unionize coal mines in northeastern Pennsylvania; my parents met at a union meeting; my sister went campaigning for Bobby Kennedy in 1968. I grew up in a household that was deeply concerned about social justice. I was lucky enough to find the political science department at Northwestern University, where they taught me the things I needed to know to study all the issues that have preoccupied me since childhood, and my friends and colleagues in the Law and Society Association have sustained those interests.

—Anna-Maria Marshall

1 The Challenge of Law

Sexual Orientation, Gender Identity, and Social Movements

Mary Bernstein, Anna-Maria Marshall, and Scott Barclay

THIS VOLUME EXAMINES the strategic ways in which the LGBT movement interacts with the law and the way those struggles, in turn, shape legal rules, public discourse, and the movement itself.[1] Through an in-depth study of the lesbian, gay, bisexual, and transgender movement, we examine empirically the relationships among social movements, social change, and the law. Many of the most important issues for the LGBT movement are represented in these pages, including struggles for same-sex marriage and family rights, for protection from discrimination in employment, education, and housing, and for criminal law reform. These chapters address three main themes: the ways in which social movements engage with the law; the relationship among activism, discourse, and legal change; and the contradictory impact of legal symbols on progressive movements and their opponents. Most importantly, *Queer Mobilizations* examines how the LGBT movement's engagement with the law configures and reconfigures the very meanings of sexuality, sex, gender, privacy, discrimination, and family in law and society more generally.

The lesbian, gay, bisexual, and transgendered movement has battled culturally and politically to reshape some of our most basic social institutions—the family, marriage, work. The LGBT movement's multidimensional legal, political, and cultural campaigns reflect the complex debates about the relationship between law and social change. On the one hand, legal reform by itself is unlikely to provide effective remedies for deep-seated structural oppression. In fact, many argue that engagement with legal institutions simply reifies the practices and ideologies that gave rise to oppression in the first place. Yet, concepts enshrined in legal institutions, such as rights, equality, and justice, represent persuasive and powerful symbols for movements for social change. These legal arguments can offer oppositional frames that may eventually resonate with the public in political debates and can have concrete material consequences, as well.

This collection of original essays draws on the expertise of contributors from the areas of law and society, sociology, political science, and legal studies to make several theoretical contributions to the existing literature on the relationships among law, social movements, and social change. The chapters in Part I, "Social

Movement Strategies and the Law," address a long-standing debate in the literature on law and social movements about the relative merits of legal strategies and other tactics. These chapters demonstrate the limits and possibilities of litigation and law reform for promoting structural and cultural transformation. The chapters also demonstrate that movements frequently call on legal symbols and frames when articulating their critiques of oppressive social conditions and formulating demands for change. In Part II, "Activism, Discourse, and Legal Change," the authors demonstrate that even conservative legal institutions are susceptible to discursive strategies that challenge and undermine existing sources of oppression. Finally, the chapters in Part III, "Legal Symbols: Constraints and Possibilities," show that law is at the center of fierce symbolic competitions where both movements and countermovements vie for the sympathies of the public and policymakers. By participating in these struggles over the meaning of law, social movements reinvent their vocabularies of harm, their theories of accountability, and their demands for redress.

While many have analyzed the diverse ways that social movements rely on legal symbols, these chapters emphasize the multiple meanings of law, both liberatory and repressive, that get deployed in struggles for social change. By showing how legal strategies can thus reshape movements themselves, the chapters in this book reveal the constitutive relationship between law and social movements. And, by focusing on the LGBT movement across issue domains, across organizational structures, and across national boundaries, this book also provides a rich contribution to existing studies of the LGBT movement. In the remainder of this chapter, we situate the contributions of this book within analyses of the relationship between law and social movements generally and between law and the LGBT movement more specifically.

The Politics of Naming

We use the broad term "LGBT" movement when referring to the panoply of organizations and activists that are seeking to improve the lot of lesbians, gay men, bisexuals, and transgendered people. Yet, references to a "lesbian, gay, bisexual, and transgender" (LGBT) movement have often been a case of wishful thinking or a hopeful gesture toward inclusivity for a movement in which there have been numerous divisions among these various subgroups (e.g., Bernstein 2002; Seidman 1993; Vaid 1995). Bisexuals and transgendered individuals in particular have often been excluded from the movement or have been hidden from public view during political campaigns (e.g, Bernstein 1997; Currah, Juang, and Mintner 2006; Randolph 2001). The LGBT movement is also composed of numerous organizations that differ starkly in terms of strategies and goals. Many of these differences are highlighted in the chapters that follow. When referring to the movement as a whole, we use the term "LGBT" so as not to leave out any self-defined group. Often, the presence of bisexuals and transgendered people within campaigns for "lesbian and gay" rights has gone unnoticed and unremarked. Instead, we prefer to err on the side of recognizing groups that have participated in various capacities in many, if not most, "lesbian and gay" organizations. In the chapters that follow, the authors sometimes use the more focused terms "lesbian" and "gay" when the legal campaigns discussed are really about strictly lesbian and gay rights, even though bisexuals and transgendered people may also benefit from those campaigns; otherwise, we use the more inclusive term "LGBT." Finally, although this book does not give equal attention to lesbian, gay, and bisexual issues on the one hand and transgendered issues on the other, we felt it important to highlight both in the title since, as several of the chapters in this book show, the legal issues regarding gender identity and sexual orientation sometimes overlap and sometimes do not (e.g., Stone, this volume).

Do Rights Matter for Social Movements?

For years, the research on law and social movements was dominated by a debate about whether rights matter for social movements. This debate emerged after the NAACP's successes in the judiciary in the 1950s, when courts delivered decisions that advanced the goals of the civil rights movement by dismantling Jim Crow laws that mandated racial segregation. Since then, many other social movements, such as the women's movement and movements for members of racial and ethnic minorities, have turned to the courts and have largely been successful in obtaining formal legal equality. Yet, the use of the courts to achieve broader goals of achieving more widespread structural change has met with increasingly mixed results as the political composition of the judicial branch has become more conservative. The courts have imposed serious limitations on the ability to prove sexual harassment claims (*Burlington Industries v. Ellerth* 1998); they have curtailed the rights of victims of wage discrimination who discover too late that they were underpaid for years (*Ledbetter v. Goodyear Tire & Rubber* 2007); courts have even tacitly endorsed school segregation by eliminating many of the remedies available for redressing the problem (*Parents Involved in Community Schools v. Seattle School District No. 1* 2007).

In the aftermath of these setbacks, skeptics have been deeply pessimistic about the possibility that law will create social change in controversial areas of public policy. Stuart Scheingold (2004 [1974]) argues that engagement with the law represents a significant distraction for social movements because it siphons off scarce resources—most notably, time and money—from more important political battles. In this view, judicial decisions rarely produce definitive results that generate structural change. Rather, protracted legal battles offer a series of legal victories and defeats. And, even when a social movement wins a favorable court order, that order rarely enforces itself. So, in *Brown v. Board of Education*, the Supreme Court ordered an end to school segregation. A year later, the Supreme Court had to issue another decision in which it ordered southern school districts to desegregate "with all deliberate speed." And now, fifty years later, American schoolchildren still attend racially segregated schools, and, because of a recent Supreme Court decision striking down a school desegregation plan, that condition is likely to get worse, despite the enormous investment of time and resources by civil rights organizations. Thus, even when a social movement wins a favorable judicial decision, the terms of the court order do not automatically take effect, and movements must continually reinvest in legal processes that are not particularly effective at rearranging structural inequalities.

For many, the very structure of legal institutions produces an environment that is inhospitable to social movements' claims. The critical legal studies movement noted that, over time, legal doctrines have developed in ways that protect the privileges of the powerful. By insisting on rights, movements depend on the state to validate their claims—a dependence that constrains the possibility of radical change. Moreover, rights claims are made *against* other social actors and institutions and therefore do not produce the inclusion and social connection sought by marginalized groups (Bauman 2002; Halley and Brown 2003; Kelman 1987; Unger 1983). Thus, in this view, rights-based strategies are doomed to recreate the relationships of power and domination that gave rise to oppression in the first place. These insights have been extended and elaborated by feminist and critical race scholars who have documented the ways that legal rules, narrowly construed by courts, support white male privilege. Legal rules may prohibit overt sexist or racist expression in some social relations but do nothing to redress the structural racism and sexism that resides in many institutions (Bell 1993; Crenshaw 1989; Crenshaw, Gotanda, Peller, and Thomas 1995; Delgado and Stefancic 2001; MacKinnon 1989).

Beyond legal doctrine, the mechanics of legal processes also support the powerful (Galanter 1974; Kritzer and Silbey 2003). Marc Galanter characterized powerful actors as "repeat players" who often engaged with the legal system and so felt more at home with its complexities. Because of their better access to rule-making institutions, "repeat players" can shape the legal rules that govern their affairs. Moreover, their superior resources ensure their access to the best legal talent and allow them to withstand the costs of delay so prevalent in the legal system. Galanter concluded, as have many others, that, because of repeat players' structural advantage, the legal system offers few opportunities for social change.

For critics, social movement strategies that rely on these legal institutions are therefore destined to produce outcomes that do not create social change. Judges operate under majoritarian constraints and so are unlikely to be far ahead of public sentiment. And, even when judges rule in favor of social movements, these marginal victories must be constantly monitored and enforced. Worst of all, some victories lead to severe backlash, thus harming progressive causes. As evidence, Rosenberg (2008 [1991]) cites the 1954 *Brown v. Board of Education* decision that desegregated public schools but that was not followed by the prompt desegregation of schools. Instead, it prompted a massive, often violent, countermobilization by white supremacists, which in turn emboldened southern segregationist politicians to resist federal efforts to integrate the schools or to promote other initiatives to advance civil rights (Klarman 2006). And, at their best, southern officials dragged their feet in taking the steps necessary to comply with the Supreme Court's decision (Rosenberg 2008 [1991]).[2]

Apart from unimpressive outcomes, social movement scholars have also been critical of the effects of legal strategies on social movements themselves (Barkan 1984; Benford 1993; Cable, Hastings, and Mix 2002; Handler 1978; Piven and Cloward 1977). Because they work within the confines of existing political and legal institutions rather than challenge them, legal strategies are often characterized by both scholars and activists as being too conservative. Litigation is dominated by lawyers and other experts who are often outsiders to the movement and who may be more willing than other activists to compromise on goals, ideals, and values. Moreover, this elite control over legal strategies is often blamed for demobilizing grassroots organizations whose participation in strategic decision making can be limited by their lack of expertise (Benford 1993; Cable, Hastings, and Mix 2002; Piven and Cloward 1977). Finally, activists who have recourse to the legal process might find that their own agenda narrows as they pursue a conventional "politics-as-usual" (Katzenstein 1998). The critics agree, then, that social movements ought to favor political mobilization over litigation.

In this tradition, queer legal theorists also see engagement with the law as detrimental to the advancement of social movements (e.g., Bower 1997; Stychin 2003). In the case of the LGBT movement, these theorists argue that the law normalizes some lifestyles and identities through legal recognition at the expense of others with less normative genders, sexualities, and family structures. In this view, advocating in the name of a lesbian and gay subject essentializes the categories gay, lesbian, and straight, obscuring the fluidity of sexuality. Thus, to queer legal theorists, rights based on gay and lesbian identities promote hierarchy, so that being lesbian or gay is still marked as "less than" or "other than" being heterosexual.

Although the risks of litigation have been well documented, social movements continue to articulate their grievances and to make demands for reform through legal processes. Given the extensive criticism of this approach, what explains social movements' continued attraction to the pursuit of legal rights? Rather than conclude that this strategic choice results from naiveté or false consciousness, many researchers explore the complexity of legal engagement in political campaigns for social change. Some go so far as to argue that legal strategies yield better results than political mobilization. For example, Pierceson (2005) fervently defends the use of legal tactics and goes so far as to claim that virtually every major lesbian and gay victory has been the result of legal campaigns (cf. Cain 2000). More common are studies emerging from the "legal mobilization" approach, which show that, even though litigation can be spectacularly unsuccessful, rights-based strategies nevertheless further important social movement goals (Handler 1978; McCann 1994; Milner 1989; Olson 1984; Silverstein 1996). Movements as diverse as the disability rights (Milner 1989; Olson 1984), animal rights (Silverstein 1996), Native American (Dudas 2005), and migrant farmworkers (Gordon 2005) have been examined using the legal mobilization perspective.

In these studies, activists are not naïvely puruing rights-based legal strategies; they are well aware of the limitations of litigation and legal processes and self-conscious about avoiding their pitfalls. Early studies of the disability rights movement, for example, demonstrated that social movement organizations used lawsuits to gain some leverage in ongoing negotiations with powerful institutions. Moreover, litigation generates media attention and can therefore be part of a public information campaign that can educate the public about the movement's grievances (Milner 1989; Olson 1984).

Beyond these pragmatic benefits of legal strategies, rights also perform important political work for social movements. The concept of rights is potent and salient in western political cultures and is spreading around the world (Frank, Boutcher, and Camp, this volume), so movements invoke rights to reframe long-standing grievances into new, collective injuries (McCann 1994; Polletta 2000). For example, Michael McCann showed that framing comparable worth as an example of sex discrimination helped activists explain the problem to working women who had not previously been politically active. In these ways, rights-based strategies can challenge hegemonic social arrangements (Hunt 1993; McCann 1994; Polletta 2000). Even when they lose in court—and some lose frequently—rights-based ideologies support ongoing resistance by mobilizing and empowering people to reimagine their lives. Thus, when part of a larger political strategy, rights play a significant role over the life of a movement.

The contributors to this volume build on this tradition of research on law and social movements. But, rather than asking whether litigation helps or hurts a movement, these authors situate their analyses of social movements' strategic choices within a broader inquiry about the complex and mutually constitutive relationship between law and social change. The chapters in this book take into account both the structural disadvantages social movements face in the legal system and the possibilities for resistance in rights-based strategies. And, pushing beyond this traditional debate, these chapters analyze how social movements deploy the law in their efforts to reshape their social, political, cultural, and economic environments.

Law, Social Movements, and Social Change

Beyond the confines of the courthouse, law also shapes social action (Ewick and Silbey 1998). Judicial decisions are important not only because they allocate material resources or because they set precedents but because they send broader symbolic messages to society about what is and is not acceptable (Bernstein 2003; Ewick and Silbey 1998; McCann 1994). Law and legal concepts are among the interpretive frameworks "that operate to define and pattern social life" (Ewick and Silbey 1998, 43; Sewell 1992):

> Through its organization, society provides us with specific opportunities for thought and action. Through language, society furnishes images of what those opportunities and resources are: how the world works, what is possible and what is not. These schemas . . . include cultural codes, vocabularies of motive, logics, hierarchies of values and conventions, as well as the binary oppositions that make up a society's "fundamental tools of thought." (Ewick and Silbey 1998, 39–40, quoting Sewell 1992)

Law can therefore help to construct commonsense understandings of how life should be organized.

Law's structural power is not isolated; instead, legal institutions are enmeshed with other powerful institutions and the discourses they produce. For example, medical and religious discourses on sex and gender influence legal categories and legal understandings. These sometimes conflicting systems of meaning can reinforce or contradict each other, creating dilemmas of interpretation and evidence and often setting powerful boundaries on the possibilities for change. Some scholars have shown that interactions with legal institutions (and with the state more generally) have a conservatizing effect on social movements (Naples 1998; Rosenberg 2008 [1991]), leading to cooptation of activists (Piven and Cloward 1977), to the abandonment of principles, or to the reframing of discourse and claims (Katzenstein 1990, 1995) so that the movement's transformative potential can be compromised. Moreover, legal scholars recognize that the structure of legal discourse transforms everyday problems into its own terms (Merry 1990; Smart 1989). So, for example, by privileging certain family forms and prescribing gender behavior, the law helps construct some identities, persons, and families as "normal," while others are deemed "deviant." Those who do not conform to cultural norms are denied basic rights to which others are entitled.

But, like all structures, law is susceptible to change and adapts to transformations in social and political conditions (Ewick and Silbey 1998; Sewell 1992). First, as an interpretive community, legal institutions and the discursive practices they foster are constantly changing and adapting to new demands and new forms of legal claims (Rosenblum, this volume; Sterett, this volume). Legal rules are, by necessity, abstract, and the legal community entertains continuing debates about their meaning. These debates provide for the fluidity and malleability that law needs to keep pace with dramatic changes in social life (McCann 1994; Herald, this volume; Pedriana, this volume; Stone, this volume).

But, more importantly, the discursive community responsible for shaping the law is not insulated from the pressure of changes in other social forces and cultural norms (Currier, this volume; Frank, Boutcher, and Camp, this volume; Stone, this volume). Rather, other structural systems of meaning anchored in particular institutions—family, work, sexuality, science—govern the way that power is organized, distributed, and experienced in our social lives (Armstrong and Bernstein 2008). Moreover, those institutions are themselves highly inscribed with law and legal meanings. Thus, as these structural systems are reorganized, they create pressure on the legal order, and law's malleability is reflected in the places where these normative systems interact and sometimes collide (Frank, Boutcher, and Camp, this volume).

Social movements are active contestants in this dynamic relationship between law and social change. They frame existing social conditions to point out injustice and generate grievances. Movements demand changes not just in policy but also in ways of thinking and living, thus generating new forms of legal demand (Currier, this volume; Fisher, this volume). Because legal rules often play a role in these struggles, social movements are also important participants in these discursive contests about the meaning of law often by filing lawsuits and amici briefs seeking to change legal rules (Daum, this volume; Pedriana, this volume). In these legal processes, social movements can translate the lived experience of their constituencies into legal theories whose indeterminacy makes them ripe for development, reinterpretation, and contradiction (Barclay and Marshall 2005; Daum, this volume). Many activists see the flexibility of legal categories as an opportunity to gain acceptance for new identities (Cohen 1985; Melucci 1985, 1989, 1996; Touraine 1981). Of course, movements do not dominate these discursive communities; legal institutions are highly competitive environments dominated by the powerful. Movements are constrained by the legal rules and by opponents with greater access to resources. Still, by participating in legal processes, social movements provide an ongoing challenge to make law more responsive to marginalized communities.

The LGBT movement has participated in this constitutive relationship between law and social change. Legal rules have long sustained the heteronormative order in the most intimate aspects of the lives of gay men, lesbians, bisexuals, and transgendered people. Hegemonic views of masculinity and femininity, with corresponding assumptions about appropriate (hetero)sexuality and family structures, are sustained by myriad laws that also discursively mark lesbian and gay sexuality and identity as deviant and inferior to heterosexuality (Bernstein 2001). During the past half century, laws against sodomy that were originally enacted to prohibit any nonprocreative sex (Greenberg 1988; Halley 1994) were increasingly used to control lesbians and gay men, who were targeted with undercover sting operations and who risked arrests in gay bars and cruising places, as well as in hotel rooms and in their own bedrooms. Historically, in the United States, these laws were used to justify denying employment or custody rights to lesbians and gay men (e.g., *Bottoms v. Bottoms* 1995; *Dallas v. England* 1993; *Shahar v. Bowers* 1995).

Yet, the law has also made it possible to challenge this heteronormative order. For example, legal conceptions of privacy have been central to the effort to decriminalize sodomy (Bernstein 2003). The U.S. Constitution does not specifically protect the right to privacy; rather, the Supreme Court recognized the right in a "penumbra" of other rights. Through the efforts of the women's and pro-choice movements, those rights have been inscribed with the experiences of heterosexual couples using birth control and women seeking to terminate pregnancies. Most recently, that penumbra of privacy rights has been used to protect same-sex couples who engage in consensual sex. However, many in the LGBT movement have debated the value and risks associated with the legal doctrine of privacy.

Privacy rights justify removal of sanctions on the basis that no one would have to know about the gender/sexual transgressions taking place. As Backer (1993) argues, "In return for removing the formal threat of severe criminal sanction for hidden and discrete acts (which society had rarely enforced in any case), dominant heterosexual society has sought the quiescence of sexual nonconformists—their tacit agreement to hide themselves from view and spare the beneficent dominant culture the disgust of any type of public presence" (759). In *Lawrence and Garner v. Texas* (2003), the Supreme Court declared sodomy laws unconstitutional on the basis of a legal recognition of the right to privacy (Pedriana, this volume). Yet, the movement has identified public repercussions faced by lesbians and gay men as a result of a lack of privacy rights that were reflected in *Lawrence and Garner* (Pedriana, this volume). Transgendered people have sometimes relied on privacy to prevent judicial scrutiny of their genitals as a way to determine their legal sex (Herald, this volume), while, other times, a lack of privacy rights has resulted in judicial determination of what constitutes adequate genitals (Coombs 2001). Ironically, organizations have used the developing theories of privacy to exclude sexual minorities from what can be considered to be public life, such as parades (Daum, this volume). Thus, the legal theory of privacy can have multiple and conflicting implications for lesbians, gay men, bisexuals, and transgendered people.

Cause lawyers are pivotal actors who often bridge the gap between the legal world and other fields of action in struggles for social change (Sterett, this volume). In representing movements in court, cause lawyers often assist in this delicate task of translation, molding movement demands into legally recognizable claims (Barclay and Marshall 2005). Yet, because of their professional obligations and identities, cause lawyers can sometimes appear to be double agents, subverting LGBT movement ideologies and values for the sake of winning narrowly defined victories. And when they have superior resources, cause lawyers may sometimes determine a movement's strategies and priorities (Levitsky 2006). Yet, recent studies have shown that cause lawyers can be as committed to movement goals and strategies (other than litigation) as any other activist (Barclay and Marshall 2005; L. C. Jones 2005, 2006). Their engagement with direct action and political tactics suggest that they can help rather than hurt movements that navigate the legal world without losing grassroots support or a more confrontational tactical repertoire.

But law does not simply change by virtue of changes in legal precedent and argumentation. The cultural and social practices of organizations and individuals outside courtrooms also influence the course of legal and social change. For example, Andersen (2005) explicitly highlights the relationship between social structure and political opportunities that affect the dynamics of legal opportunities. The current configuration of political elites and the path set by prior political organizing become structural features of the state that shape and are influenced by court decisions. Furthermore, Andersen (2005) points out that legal and political discourses may overlap but that they play to different audiences in different venues that have different rules for engagement. For example, Andersen shows how gay rights opponents in Colorado claimed that antidiscrimination laws to protect lesbians and gay men from discrimination would provide them with "special rights." While this discourse was politically persuasive as Coloradans passed the homophobic Amendment 2 overturning antidiscrimination protection based on sexual orientation, such arguments were effectively shown to be what Andersen calls the legal equivalent of "psychobabble"; Amendment 2 was overturned by the U.S. Supreme Court in *Romer v. Evans*. Thus, social movements encounter differing legal opportunity structures over time that interact in complex ways with political structures.

Legal norms codified in judicial decisions and statutes can, in themselves, generate potent political symbols that can be appropriated by activists in their political and cultural campaigns or that can be subsequently deployed by countermovements seeking to protect the status quo (Charles, this volume; Goldberg-Hiller, this volume). Concepts like "rights" and "privacy" and even "marriage" allow movements to claim the legitimacy associated with law in many regimes in their efforts to educate the public and to win support from the wider society. In the hands of social movement activists, law is a symbolic resource for advancing social change.

By participating in these struggles for social change in the context of law's discursive community, social movements may find that they too have changed. By confronting opponents on a legal terrain, movements must respond using the limited vocabulary of legal rules and regulation and must be prepared to accept compromise. These compromises may set the movement down a more conservative path that softens its more radical demands (Levitsky 2006). Yet, the law can also provide official ways of validating new identities, relationships, and family forms such as lesbian co-parenting (Andersen, this volume; Sterett, this volume). The ferocity of the public debates over same-sex marriage reveals the profound political, social and cultural significance of legal recognition. A valid marriage certificate exclusively grants a dizzying array of material benefits to heterosexual couples in fifty states in the United States, while in forty-five of those states also providing a marker of social inclusion and cultural capital unavailable to those who do not conform to the heteronormative ideal of "family."[3] Thus, public debates have addressed not just the legal status of same-sex partners but other issues, including the meaning of family and the role of religion in political and civic life. The constitutional principle of "equal protection" can help explain to the public why it is unfair to deny Social Security benefits to a surviving partner of a same-sex couple, even though it would be virtually useless to persuade a federal judge to change the Social Security system. Thus, legal discourse may be persuasive to the public in ways that it would not be in formal legal institutions.

In addition, the debates surrounding legal symbols can reach ordinary people whose social practices may generate further legal and social change. By articulating new identities and new types of relationships, individuals and/or social movements often turn to the law to reinforce their new arrangements (Andersen, this volume; Sterett, this volume). Thus, their altered values, expectations, choices, and demands can sustain new legal meanings. So when same-sex partners in the United States, in states other than Massachusetts, Connecticut, Iowa, Vermont, and Maine (as of this writing), want to comingle their lives, they can create wills, draft powers of attorney, open joint bank accounts, and buy property together. Of course, these options require a certain amount of class privilege, because only those with the economic resources can afford to pay for these privately negotiated legal arrangements (Boggis 2001). Nonethelesss, those lesbians and gay men with the resources who want to protect their families can seek new forms of adoption such as co- or second-parent adoption and subsequently advocate for recognition of those new relationships on revised birth certificates (Sterett, this volume). These social practices can mimic only a small fraction of the benefits of marriage and thus underscore the exclusion of same-sex partners from these legal privileges and emphasize—for some people—the need for civil marriage (Hull 2006).

In moving beyond the question of whether rights matter for social movements, the authors in this volume take on the larger project of exploring the many ways in which law both promotes and hinders social change. They recognize that law's role is complex and often contradictory, sometimes enabling the powerful and enshrining inequalities but sometimes offering the possibility of social and cultural transformation. The authors explore these theoretical developments through careful empirical studies of many different facets of the LGBT movement, creating an in-depth look at the way a single movement engages the law across many different issues.

Outline of Chapters

Part I: Social Movement Strategies and the Law

The authors of the chapters in this section place rights contests at the center of analysis by studying the LGBT movement's engagements with the law. But, in the tradition of legal mobilization research, they are careful to situate these tactical choices in the complex social, political and cultural environments where LGBT movements do their work. Yet, even in acknowledging the critical importance of institutions, norms, and values beyond the law, these authors nevertheless analyze the peculiar power of law to construct, define, limit, and empower social life. In these studies, legal rules can empower oppressed people even as they expose those people to danger; legal doctrines can reflect the lived experience and the aspirations of marginalized groups, or they can relegate them even further to the margins. And these active contests over the meaning of legal rules can affect the movement itself. Thus, the authors in this section ask what happens to movement claims once activists wage legal battles. How are they modified? What are the consequences of those modifications? In short, Part I examines the complexity of social movements' strategic choices in legal arenas.

The first two chapters in this section illustrate the risks of legal strategies, where radical challenges to existing social conditions are difficult to articulate through legal claims. In chapter 2, Currier examines the relationships among state policies, state repression, and social movements' strategic decisions in Namibia. In this case study, Currier explains how activists assessed the risks of seeking legal protection from discrimination that could both increase the visibility of lesbians and gay men and endanger their lives in a repressive political regime. In chapter 3, Rosenblum explores the limits of legal strategies by assessing the types of changes that the law can and cannot make by examining which groups and issues are best served by the law and which are not. While sympathetic to queer critiques of law, Rosenblum nonetheless concludes that the law has the potential to advance the radical goal of sexual liberation.

Despite the limits of legal change, in the course of litigation and law reform campaigns, social movements often articulate grievances and make public claims by drawing on legal rights and rules. Once movements opt for legal strategies, they still confront an array of choices about which legal rules to invoke. Law is an inherently contested terrain; the opposition almost always has a countervailing argument based on the same rules and doctrines. Moreover, like all tactical decisions, these choices vary in the way they resonate with movement constituencies. For example, in chapter 4, Pedriana examines the complex interplay between advocating for legal change based on a right to privacy and advocating for change based on a right to equal protection through analysis of the amicus briefs submitted in the U.S. Supreme Court's landmark decision, *Lawrence and Garner v. Texas*, that overturned the remaining sodomy statutes in the United States. Pedriana illustrates that, rather than deconstructing a lesbian and gay identity, lesbian and gay amicus curiae briefs stressed equal rights and equal protection for a lesbian and gay minority, reflecting a trend toward viewing sexual orientation as an identifiable and defining aspect of identity that separates gay/lesbian from straight. Challenging critiques of privacy arguments that assume that a right to privacy also entails secrecy and shame about same-sex sexuality and love, Pedriana claims that lesbian and gay amicus briefs and, more important, the *Lawrence* decision itself underscored the connections between a denial of privacy rights and the public consequences of that denial for lesbians and gay men.

Yet, even as some parts of the LGBT movement began to reclaim privacy doctrine, others have noted that privacy can be used to exclude sexual minorities from aspects of public life. In chapter 5, Daum examines trends in amicus curiae briefs submitted in all cases regarding gay rights that have been adjudicated by the U.S. Supreme Court. Daum finds that, collectively, these cases represent an expanding right to privacy, as well as a right to a civic presence in the public sphere, for lesbians and gay men. However, as privacy rights for individuals expand, Daum finds that privacy rights are also expanding for organizations and institutions such as the Boy Scouts and the Ancient Order of Hibernians (a sponsor of St. Patrick's Day parades), which are allowed to exclude persons (i.e., lesbians and gay men) and speech (related to being gay or lesbian) that they find distasteful. In short, privacy remains a tricky concept and a malleable legal theory whose contours both advance and restrict the rights of lesbians and gay men.

But not all legal strategy occurs in the courtroom. Rather, "law is all over" (Sarat 1990)—in the offices of lawyers and county clerks, as well as in hospital delivery rooms. In chapter 6, Susan Sterett shows that birth certificates are a terrain for social movement struggles. Birth certificates are yet another piece of paper with enormous social and legal significance; a parent's presence or absence from that piece of paper has material consequences in schools, physicians' offices, and playgrounds. Yet, this struggle often occurs at the margins of social movement activity—in the everyday lives of ordinary couples and in the offices of the sympathetic lawyers they hire.

Part II: Activism, Discourse, and Legal Change

Part II examines the interplay among social structure, legal meaning, and social change. Law exerts a structural force in society. Legal categories, rigid procedural rules, and resource-intensive judicial systems often reinforce already existing structural inequalities. Thus, law supports the heteronormative discourses in our culture and our politics that elevate and protect heterosexual social arrangements even as they cause hardship to those living outside those boundaries. Even while accounting for this structural power, the chapters in this section also demonstrate how law's indeterminacy provides the LGBT movement with opportunities for introducing novel interpretations and new meanings to established legal rules and symbols, thus creating the possibility for change. The chapters in this section ask how heteronormativity structures legal outcomes. How does dominant heteronormative discourse influence the ways in which legal change occurs? In what ways can law challenge and transform that discourse?

The chapters in this section explore different dimensions of law's structural power. The first two chapters demonstrate that the law often follows other societal forces and discursive regimes that are creating pressure for social change. In chapter 7, Frank, Boutcher, and Camp examine the global trend toward eliminating bans on consensual sex acts committed by adults in private. Adopting a world-society perspective, they illustrate the importance of global institutions and of changes in the symbolic meaning associated with sodomy to explain global patterns of legal change. In chapter 8, Stone takes a meso-level approach to understanding social movements and the law. She finds that, particularly in the context of local politics, the boundary between social movement activists and state officials is porous, thus exposing the local law to the demands of movement actors. In her study, social movements were crucial to constructing the discourse that established legal protection against discrimination for transgendered people in two towns in Michigan. Whether transgenderism is understood discursively as being "like sexual orientation" or "like gender" has

important implications for the nature of legal protection offered to the transgendered community.

While Stone shows that meaning is constructed through the process of social
movements' legal strategies, the law also contains and produces its own social and
cultural assumptions, from the proper sphere of governmental regulation to the
meaning of "female" and "male." These assumptions structure the types of changes
in law and meaning that are possible. In chapter 9, Gossett examines the legal
decisions that take place when antigay groups challenge city- and county-level
domestic-partnership ordinances for overstepping their policy-making authority. The legal powers of cities and counties are determined by Dillon's rule and
broadly structure the types of legislative activity that are permissible for cities and
counties. However, Gossett also finds that the extent to which these ordinances
adopt discursive constructions of family and dependence that challenge heteronormativity influences whether or not they are able to withstand judicial scrutiny. Finally, in chapter 10, Herald examines the ways in which discourse affects
the legal rights of transgendered people to marry and to be protected from discrimination. Like Gossett, Herald finds that rights are extended to the degree to
which heteronormativity, in this case, a binary understanding of sex as being male
and female and the family as being heterosexual, is upheld discursively. However,
through adopting legal theories that circumvent the challenge to heteronormativity, the law can extend rights to transgendered people while also undermining the
link between sex and gender. Taken together, these chapters show that, in the face
of law's structural power, challenges to heteronormativity—and sweeping social
change of any kind—will not be possible using legal means alone.

Part III: Legal Symbols: Constraints and Possibilities

Social movement scholarship has emphasized the importance of symbolism and
the struggle over meaning in movement campaigns for social change. Law provides
one set of symbols that is widely respected, particularly in the United States, but
is by no means the only symbolic resource that movements have at their disposal.
The LGBT movement vies over the meaning of family, work, and sex, for example.
Their opponents, including not just the state but also countermovements, work
with the same symbolic repertoire, and these engagements can shape and reshape
the movement's own message. In short, social movements are never fully in control of the symbols they choose. The chapters in Part III explore the ways in which
legal discourse and symbols impose political and cultural constraints on those who
use those symbols while simultaneously providing opportunities for opponents.

In chapter 11, Fisher examines how social movements deploy the law in order
to sway the discursive framing of same-sex marriage. Fisher finds that both exter-

nal events and countermovements influence how social movements frame their legal struggles in the domain of newspapers. As the LGBT movement struggles for the right to marry, opponents increasingly frame the issue in terms of abstract concepts such as democracy, rather than take on the actual forms of discrimination faced by lesbians, gay men, bisexuals, and transgendered people. For example, gay rights opponents frame same-sex marriage increasingly in terms of activist judges granting same-sex couples the right to marry and thus usurping the rights of the democratic majority to create public policy. This strategy deflects attention from the lesbian and gay movement's attempt to focus on the legal rights and benefits associated with marriage.

In chapter 12, Goldberg-Hiller also examines the political arguments about same-sex marriage but explores the aesthetics of opponents' strategies. He analyzes the images and texts that are circulated by those who insist on constitutional protection solely for heterosexual marriage. Through these images, opponents of same-sex marriage have developed an iconography that delegitimizes "civil rights" and promotes a picture of family life that relegates same-sex couples to the margins of society.

In chapter 13, Charles examines the ways in which legal meanings are taken up in dramatic representations of legal trials. By examining dramatic portrayals of the assassination of openly gay San Francisco supervisor Harvey Milk and the subsequent trial of Milk's killer, Charles illustrates how trials themselves are social drama and how homophobia in the courtroom can turn a homophobic murderer into a tragic hero. The trial itself can also be read as a microcosm that explains antigay activism more generally. In her ethnography of antigay activism in an Oregon town, for example, Arlene Stein (2001) argues that the decline of an economy based on timber has created a crisis in Timbertown (a pseudonym), undermining masculinity, the traditional division of labor within the family, and therefore the basis of community itself. Faced with these changes, Evangelical Christians have created a battle to prohibit gay rights, which is as much about the reconstitution of identity and community as it is about changing laws. Thus, Stein (2001, 4) shows "how sexuality became a resonant symbol upon which a group of citizens projected a host of anxieties about the changing world around them" and thus engaged in antigay activism. The trial of Harvey Milk's killer nearly twenty years earlier shares the same plot line.

In chapter 14, Andersen examines the difficulties that social movements face when sensible legal arguments create political liabilities. Andersen argues that the ability to divorce is an important benefit of marriage. However, the right to divorce is an unworkable political argument because of how divorce is culturally understood. The distinction between culturally sound arguments and legally sound ones thus limits the kinds of claims social movements can make. In this instance, same-sex couples are greatly disadvantaged by their inability to divorce but are not in a position to claim those harms as harms.

Collectively, the chapters in this volume enrich our understanding of social movements' strategic decisions to use legal tactics by situating those decisions in complex cultural, political, and legal environments. Moreover, they highlight the struggle to make law relevant and responsive to members of LGBT communities. These chapters also reject a simplistic approach to understanding law's structural power, opting instead for dynamic models that acknowledge both the constraints imposed by legal symbols and institutions and the liberatory opportunities they represent. Finally, these chapters analyze the symbolic power of law for social movements but also for their opponents in countermovements and the state.

PART I

Social Movement
Strategies and the Law

2 Deferral of Legal Tactics

A Global LGBT Social Movement Organization's Perspective

Ashley Currier

WHILE MANY LESBIAN, gay, bisexual, and transgender (LGBT) movements around the world employ legal tactics (Adam et al. 1999), for some LGBT movements in the global South, state repression, scarce resources, and diverse constituencies with complex needs can restrict and complicate their tactical repertoires, making legal tactics unimaginable or temporarily not viable.[1] Tactical choices that may be logical for LGBT social movement organizations in older democracies may not be so simple for LGBT social movement organizations in younger democracies in which the state is openly hostile to LGBT rights and organizing. How do LGBT social movement organizations come to regard legal tactics as viable or to eschew them? What makes legal tactics enticing to some LGBT social movement organizations and not to others? Legal tactics often require much time, money, expertise, and other organizational resources (Bob 2005; Burstein 1991). Convincing organizational members or LGBT constituencies that legal tactics are the best approach sometimes siphons additional practical and emotional energy. In this chapter, I explore how and why a Namibian LGBT social movement organization, The Rainbow Project (TRP), did not pursue legal tactics due to staff and members' fear of state repression and to internal organizational pressures. First, I outline The Rainbow Project's formation in response to Namibian state leaders' hostility toward sexual and gender diversity. Then, I situate my analysis within a conceptual framework of tactical repertoires before examining the external and internal conditions that led TRP to defer legal tactics.

The Emergence of the Namibian LGBT Movement

Movements that advocate for LGBT rights in southern Africa operate in sometimes-hostile political and social contexts (Epprecht 2004; Palmberg 1999). In Namibia, a former German colony and South African territory on southern Africa's west coast (Steinmetz 2007), state officials attempted to marginalize sexual and gender minorities and the LGBT movement by claiming they were un-African (L. Frank 2000; Melber 2003). For instance, elected officials from the South West African People's Organisation (SWAPO), which fought South Africa for Namibia's independence, perceived sexual minority rights as a threat to the liberation of Namibia; many officials equated homosexuality with Western culture and values (O. Phillips 2001). Some state leaders also treated LGBT organizing as a "straightforward product of Western cultural imperialism" because organizations used "Western-sounding language and Western-looking imagery" and received funding from Northern donors (Epprecht 2004, 226).

The Namibian LGBT movement emerged amid state leaders' hostility toward sexual and gender diversity and LGBT organizing (Lorway 2006). The movement coalesced in December 1996 after former Namibian president Sam Nujoma publicly denounced homosexuality at the SWAPO Women's League Congress in unrehearsed remarks. Horrified at Nujoma's comments, lesbians and gay men met at the office of Sister Namibia, a feminist social movement organization in Windhoek, to coordinate a response to Nujoma's statement, and they formed The Rainbow Project (TRP). Sister Namibia had earned a reputation for being a lesbian organization in 1995 because of its demand that state and SWAPO officials apologize for their homophobic comments in the state-run newspaper *New Era*. Countering a statement by Hadino Hishongwa, former Deputy Lands, Resettlement, and Rehabilitation Minister, that "he did not take up arms to fight for an immoral society" (*New Era*, October 5–11, 1995), members of Sister Namibia quipped, in a letter to *New Era* (November 2–8, 1995), "[H]omophobia (unlike homosexuality and lesbianism) can be cured!" Throughout the late 1990s, The Rainbow Project and Sister Namibia issued press releases that demanded apologies from Nujoma and other elected and SWAPO officials for their homophobic statements. Through their intolerant public comments, Nujoma and SWAPO unwittingly provided black, biracial, multiracial, and white sexual minorities with a politicized public identity around which to organize (HRW and IGLHRC 2003, 8).[2] Among TRP's priorities, as articulated in its constitution, was "[t]o lobby for equal rights and opportunities for gays, lesbians, bisexuals and transsexuals and any other group that suffers discrimination in public life and under the law."

LGBT activists' fears of a repressive backlash intensified when Nujoma and members of his government encouraged the police to "arrest, imprison, and deport" sexual minorities in Namibia in 2001 (*The Namibian*, March 20, 2001). Some police in Katutura, a Windhoek township, enforced Nujoma's order and singled out black men "wearing earrings, and tore them from at least two men's ears. One of the officers reportedly told his superior afterward that he was acting in response to the President's expressed will" (IGLHRC 2001, 15). Other Namibian human rights social movement organizations decried Nujoma's verbal attacks "as an indication of emerging authoritarianism in Namibia" (HRW and IGLHRC 2003, 5–6). Nujoma periodically made homophobic comments until he left office in March 2005, when Hifikepunye Pohamba succeeded him as the second president of Namibia. TRP staff regarded Pohamba as more tolerant than Nujoma of sexual and gender diversity, as evidenced by his administration's lack of public persecution of sexual and gender minorities, with the exception of Deputy Minister of Home Affairs and Immigration Theopolina Mushelenga's 2005 comments that Namibian gay men and lesbians were un-African (LaFont 2007; *The Namibian*, September 12, 2005).

Namibia has not always been inhospitable to sexual and gender diversity and equality. The Namibian constitution was one of "the first in the world" to feature "gender-neutral language," treating men and women as citizens and holders of rights (Diescho 1994, 63). In contrast, Namibian law has been gender-specific in criminalizing same-sex behavior; it criminalized only anal intercourse between men as sodomy and excluded sexual acts between women (Hubbard 2007). Thus, with regard to consensual sex, Namibian law does not treat same-sex and opposite-sex couples equally. Gay and lesbian activists, who eventually established The Rainbow Project, were able to persuade SWAPO officials quietly to prohibit employment discrimination on the basis of sexual orientation in the Labour Act of 1992 (Interview, TRP member, July 11, 2006).[3] After activists' work on the Labour Act, The Rainbow Project seemed set to pursue a legal campaign that clarified sexual and gender minority rights, yet the social movement organization did not take this path. Why did The Rainbow Project not mobilize broadly around legal rights for LGBT persons in Namibia?

LGBT Movement Tactical Repertoires

Scholars agree that the tactical repertoires available to activists are limited and change glacially, though exceptional historic "moments" may accelerate tactical innovation (Tarrow 1993; Tilly 1978). Acknowledging the flexibility of some tactics, Verta Taylor and Nella Van Dyke (2004, 266) modify the notion of repertoire of contention and adopt that of "tactical repertoires," which are "interactive episodes that link social movement actors to each other as well as to opponents and authorities for the intended purpose of challenging or resisting change in groups, organizations, or societies." This concept embraces a wider range of cultural and political forms of opposition that LGBT movements around the world have employed. "The struggle over cultural production and representation" has been a feature of LGBT movements in the global North and South (Seidman 1993, 109). Asserting control over how institutions and the public portray sexual and gender minorities has led some LGBT social movement organizations in the global South to contest public spaces in ways that resemble and differ from the tactics that predecessor or contemporaneous LGBT movements in the global North have used. Coming out publicly and announcing one's sexuality in hetero-sexualized spaces is a strategy that gay liberationist activists in North America pioneered and that LGBT social movement organizations in the global South have used (Armstrong 2002; Chabot and Duyvendak 2002). For instance, in 1995, the Gays and Lesbians of Zimbabwe (GALZ) contested the Zimbabwe International Book Fair's refusal to let them operate a booth because of opposition from President Robert Mugabe, a vocal critic of sexual diversity. Keith Goddard (2004, 96), the director of GALZ, contends, "[W]e had a right to exhibit and government had no right to ban us." GALZ's claim fundamentally questioned Mugabe's ability to define who could occupy public spaces in Zimbabwe. However, attempts at securing public space can be limiting. While the annual Lesbian and Gay Pride parade in Johannesburg, South Africa, reflects LGBT persons' appropriation and redefinition of public spaces, "it is no more than a surface manifestation of the aspirations of a small group of people, black and white, who have embraced a new liberationist politics" (Gevisser 1995, 64). South African sexual and gender minorities are largely "invisible to the public eye, still subject to their characterisation as 'unapprehended felons' by the law, sinners by the church, and deviants by society in general" (Gevisser 1995, 64).

State-social movement organizational interactions can also impact organizations' selection of tactics. In particular, a fear of repression may accompany and influence social movement organizations' selection of tactics. This specific anxiety can differ from a more generalized fear of repression that may induce individuals to stay in the "closet," as this specific anxiety emerges from specific state-social movement organization interactions (Brown 2000). For example, if state leaders encourage police to harass and arrest LGBT activists, an LGBT movement organization may postpone a march for sexual and gender minority rights or frame its response to such statements very carefully so as not to arouse further hostility. However, recent research on and theorizing about how repression dissuades activists from selecting certain protest tactics and results in demobilization overlooks LGBT movements as representing a particular moral or political threat to state authorities and social institutions (Earl 2003). Understanding the threat to states and state leaders that LGBT social movement organizations may pose can help researchers to apprehend how, when, and why organizations resignify such threats as mobilizing opportunities (Kulick and Klein 2003). The avoidance or deferral of tactics also remains understudied in social movement research. A place from which to begin examining why organizations shun certain tactics is how actors evaluate tactics. "To account for movement groups' strategic decisions, scholars must pay attention to the cultural beliefs that make some tactical options attractive or unattractive regardless of how effective those options are likely to be" (Polletta 2006, 54). For instance, the director of the Gays and Lesbians of Zimbabwe (GALZ) wonders whether his organization should have pursued legal tactics in addition to fighting for public space at the Zimbabwe International Book Fair (Goddard 2004, 97). In this sense, pursuing multiple tactics concurrently might have allowed GALZ to advance its goals in different arenas.

Like other influential social movement concepts and imagery, tactical repertoires originated in case studies of social movements in the global North. I am mindful of the possible implications and limitations of applying such concepts to the Namibian LGBT social movement organization, The Rainbow Project (TRP), that I examine in this chapter. In particular, I refrain from judging the effectiveness or development of TRP's tactical selection on the basis of the tactical decisions of LGBT social movement organizations in the global North and elsewhere in the global South. In so doing, I try not to essentialize the evolution of sexual and gender identities on the basis of a Northern model. I also do not assume that LGBT social movement organizations develop in a predetermined way across temporal and spatial boundaries (Adam 2002; Spurlin 2001). Instead, I am sensitive to the idea that LGBT movements in the global South are not merely mimicking Northern sexual and gender politics but are responding to local and national sociopolitical concerns and "global economic and social developments" (Drucker 1996, 92–93). Thus, I use gender and sexual identity terminology favored by Namibian LGBT activists, namely "lesbian," "gay," "bisexual," and "transgender."[4]

The Deferral of Legal Tactics

Why did a Namibian LGBT social movement organization, The Rainbow Project (TRP), eschew legal tactics when it seemed inclined to favor them? Did TRP shy away from pursuing a public law reform campaign because of state leaders' repressive rhetoric? A related question is why some black, biracial, and multiracial members of TRP regarded law reform as a white, middle-class tactic and pushed for tactics that addressed "bread-and-butter" issues (Interview, TRP member, July 11, 2006). These activists did not view law reform as compatible with social-service provision; they claimed that catering to the material needs of LGBT persons was more immediate than a legal campaign. Why did they not view law reform and social services as complementary or coexistent?

Using data from interviews I conducted with Namibian LGBT social movement organizational staff and members between April and July 2006 and organizational historical documents and newspaper articles, I explore two factors that led The Rainbow Project (TRP) to defer legal tactics. First, a fear of state repression kept TRP from pursuing legal tactics. Second, the organization's attempt to promote democratization within and outside TRP resulted in disagreements about what tactics the organization should pursue, disagreements that were rooted in members' differing class and racial identities.

Fear of Repression

Before gaining independence from South Africa, in 1990, Namibia was a haven for interracial and same-sex couples fleeing South African apartheid laws, policies, and authorities (Frank and Khaxas 1996; *The Sunday Independent*, May 20, 2001). Between 1990 and 1995, law reform seemed possible, especially given gay and lesbian activists' success in persuading lawmakers to include a sexual-orientation nondiscrimination clause in the Labour Act of 1992 Additionally, the state's refusal to prosecute consensual same-sex sexual behavior suggests that state leaders were not interested in harassing lesbian, gay, and bisexual persons (Hubbard 2000, 11).

Elected and SWAPO officials reversed the state's position on homosexuality in 1995 and 1996, creating confusion among Namibian sexual minorities about their legal position. Late in 1996, President Nujoma encouraged the "police and public to work hand in hand and arrest anyone caught practising homosexuality, which he likened to a criminal offence like theft" (*The Windhoek Advertiser*, December 12, 1996). Nujoma's statements generated uncertainty among TRP members, who had organized in response to these antigay remarks, about whether the state would criminalize all same-sex sexual behavior and/or enforce the existing sodomy law, even though then-ombudsman Bience Gawanas had informed TRP that "sodomy [would] be decriminalized" by the state; TRP members were not sure which officials would initiate this process (TRP meeting minutes, March 18, 1997). To resolve the legal limbo in which sexual minorities found themselves, Laurencia Davids and Sakeus Shanghala, law school students at the University of Namibia, demanded a public discussion about the legal position of gay men and lesbians early in 1997 in a letter to the editor (*The Namibian*, February 14, 1997).

In 1997, The Rainbow Project appeared poised to use legal tactics as a means to respond to the state leaders' attack on LGBT persons and threat to criminalize same-sex sexualities. In June 1997, the organization filed a legal complaint with the Office of the Ombudsman objecting to homophobic remarks made by President Nujoma in December 1996 and by SWAPO leaders in January 1997 and then disclosed this action to the Namibian media (*The Namibian*, June 6, 1997). Different civil society organizations had conventionally filed "complaints relating to maladministration by public officials" with the Namibian Office of the Ombudsman (Gomez 1995, 157). But these organizations had increasingly requested the

Office of the Ombudsman "to investigate violations of human rights as well. . . . In the Namibian case, the ombudsman [could] also give legal assistance or advice to those seeking enforcement of fundamental rights through the courts" (Gomez 1995, 157). TRP requested that the Office of the Ombudsman treat Nujoma's statement as a human rights violation because state intolerance of sexual diversity could provoke "violence and discrimination against law-abiding citizens" (TRP Submission to the Ombudsperson, June 4, 1997). However, the Office of the Ombudsman declined to investigate the matter for two reasons. First, the Office of the Ombudsman stated that it could investigate only claims of employment discrimination based on sexual orientation in accordance with the Labour Act of 1992, and TRP's complaint did not allege workplace discrimination because of an employee's sexual orientation. Second, it rejected the complaint because TRP publicized its filing, which violated the principle of confidentiality under which the Office of the Ombudsman operated, such "that it would seem that the Office was used as a stepping stone to raise publicity for your cause" (Office of the Ombudsman letter, September 30, 1997). Thus, TRP's pursuit of publicity related to the investigation resulted in negative sanctions and limited the redress that the organization could seek with respect to state and SWAPO leaders' homophobic remarks. Unless the Namibian Parliament prohibited discrimination on the basis of sexual orientation in the Constitution, as the South African Parliament had done one year earlier, in 1996, Namibian sexual and gender minorities would not be able to pursue legal redress of state leaders' antigay remarks through the Office of the Ombudsman (Croucher 2002).

The following year, in 1998, TRP members further deliberated about how to proceed with a public legal campaign. After soliciting and receiving guidance from experienced South African LGBT activists about how to run a legal campaign, TRP members decided to commit some resources to a public legal campaign. At its yearly strategic planning meeting in 1998, moderated by the South African National Coalition for Gay and Lesbian Equality, TRP members agreed to give priority to the decriminalization of sodomy, "employment benefits, immigration cases, and gay-bashing" as pressing legal concerns (TRP 1998, 16). Members of the Coalition shared their experiences organizing around sodomy, which was decriminalized in South Africa in 1998, and advised TRP to pursue this issue very carefully, given the increasingly hostile sociopolitical environment in Namibia. Possible legal tactics included "going to court" and "lobbying political leaders" and the public (TRP 1998, 17). However, TRP members agreed that amending "the Constitution to include sexual orientation"—to prohibit discrimination on the basis of sexual orientation—as South African LGBT social movement organizations had favored was "not ideal" because state and SWAPO leaders might interpret suggested constitutional amendments as a threat to their authority (TRP

1998, 17). Instead, members seemed satisfied with trying to ensure that LGBT persons'"[b]asic rights [were] covered" and decided to work within existing legal frameworks (TRP 1998, 17).

TRP staff and members decided to pursue the decriminalization of sodomy through a public legal campaign. They understood sodomy as sex between men, a law "inherited from the colonial regime" (*New Era*, February 13–15, 1998; see Frank et al., this volume).[5] Decriminalizing sodomy could have been an important step in decolonizing and democratizing Namibian laws, policies, and state structures. In 1998, the Legal Assistance Centre (LAC), a human rights organization, requested clarification about the sodomy law on behalf of TRP and asked if the Prosecutor General "would . . . prosecute charges of sodomy where the sexual act has taken place in private between two consenting adult males" (LAC letter, April 24, 1998). Such an inquiry could have reduced the uncertainty that some LGBT persons experienced; they feared state leaders would actualize their promise to criminalize and prosecute homosexuality. However, the Prosecutor General declined to discuss the issue (TRP meeting minutes, May 6, 1998, June 3, 1998). The Attorney General, in contrast, asserted that "the sodomy law [was] unconstitutional and [had] to be challenged" (TRP meeting minutes, June 3, 1998). Yet the Attorney General apparently did not push this constitutional inquiry further by introducing the issue before Parliament, which could have considered the constitutionality of the sodomy law.[6] The failure of the Attorney General to institute the promised challenge constituted another institutional obstacle to TRP's effort to decriminalize sodomy.

State leaders' opposition to homosexuality and to sexual minority rights intensified in 1998, transforming the political environment in which TRP operated. Late in 1998, the Minister of Home Affairs Jerry Ekandjo threatened to stiffen penalties for same-sex sexual conduct (*Windhoek Observer*, November 14, 1998). TRP and other human rights organizations, such as the Legal Assistance Centre, publicly demanded that Ekandjo withdraw his statement and asserted that such legislation would violate the Constitution (*Business Day*, November 9, 1998). In 1999, when discussing the national budget, which had little to do with sexual minority rights, Ekandjo's deputy minister, Jeremiah Nambinga, reissued Ekandjo's threat to increase penalties for same-sex sexual conduct (*The Namibian*, April 21, 1999). Prime Minister Hage Geingob intervened and stated that the state would not criminalize homosexuality, temporarily defusing the tense political environment (*The Namibian*, May 3, 2000).[7]

Amid state officials' increasing antagonism toward sexual and gender minorities in 1998 and 1999, TRP decided to switch strategies. The organization decided to pursue the decriminalization of sodomy less publicly with the help of the Legal Assistance Centre. The Legal Assistance Centre provided research support and litigated cases related to Namibian human rights; seeking the decriminalization of sodomy fell within the organization's mandate. TRP met behind closed doors with lawyers and researchers at the Legal Assistance Centre, who, in turn, would publicly mount a legal challenge to the sodomy laws. But, by the end of 1999, it was not clear how the organization would proceed with this campaign with the Legal Assistance Centre, as members and staff spoke vaguely about moving forward with a legal challenge (TRP meeting minutes, June 20, 1999, December 1, 1999). In 2000, the option to pursue the decriminalization of sodomy seemed to disappear when state leaders resumed their antigay vituperation. President Nujoma renewed his earlier homophobic remarks, and Home Affairs Minister Jerry Ekandjo who was "in charge of the police . . . commandeered 800 newly recruited police officers to 'eliminate' gay men and lesbians 'from the face of Namibia'" (*Mail and Guardian*, October 6, 2000). Such statements put TRP on the defensive in a "general climate of persecution," especially in light of Ekandjo's incitement of police violence against sexual minorities (Legal Assistance Centre Annual Report 2001, 2).[8] In a press release condemning these remarks, TRP demanded that the state snub Ekandjo's call for police to arrest gay men and lesbians and "repeal or amend all laws that discriminate against lesbian, gay, bisexual and transgender people in Namibia" (*The Namibian*, July 14, 2000). Responding to state leaders' escalating antigay statements kept TRP busy crafting responses and forced the organization to take a consistently defensive posture when fending off antigay remarks, preventing the organization from moving forward with a proactive legal reform agenda. The organization occasionally discussed launching a public campaign to decriminalize sodomy in 2000 and 2001, but these discussions did not lead to action (TRP meeting minutes, May 9, 2001).

In light of state leaders' opposition to LGBT persons and organizing in the late 1990s and early 2000s, TRP staff and members feared provoking a repressive state backlash (HRW and IGLHRC 2003). In particular, several TRP members and staff I interviewed between April and July 2006 believed that any attempt to overturn the sodomy law while Nujoma had held office would have failed. State leaders' homophobia and the Ovambo ruling ethnic majority's patriarchal practices, exemplified by Nujoma's frequent justifications for why lesbians and gay men did not deserve equal rights, constrained "the space available to the LGBT community to push the boundaries of the interpretation of the constitution in a more liberal direction" (Isaacks 2005, 79; LaFont 2007, 254).

Between 1998 and 2001, during a period of increasing state opposition to sexual minority rights, immigration rights for same-sex couples emerged as a campaign that TRP could support. But the organization opted not to mount a large-scale campaign in support of immigration rights for same-sex couples or to launch a public antisodomy legal campaign. TRP feared growing state hostility and did not want to jeopardize the immigration case of one of its members. In 1998, Liz Frank, a German lesbian, a member of Sister Namibia, and a founding member of TRP, filed for permanent residence on the basis of her long-term partnership with a Namibian woman with whom she was raising a child and who also belonged to both organizations (Hubbard 2007). In 1999, to avoid incurring state leaders' wrath, TRP staff and members recommended approaching an international LGBT social movement organization, the International Lesbian and Gay Association, for assistance in pressuring the Namibian state about Frank's immigration case when it held its yearly world conference in Johannesburg, South Africa (Bob 2005; Keck and Sikkink 1998). The organization could have used Frank's immigration case to launch a public law reform campaign, but staff and members did not want to aggravate antigay state leaders. If an international third party had pressured the state about the case, state leaders might have singled out Sister Namibia and TRP for verbal harassment.

As the case unfolded amid state leaders' hostility toward LGBT rights and persons, The Rainbow Project publicly endorsed only immigration rights for same-sex couples in press releases that pertained directly to the Frank case and did not mobilize broadly around securing immigration rights for all LGBT persons. Home Affairs Minister Jerry Ekandjo specifically opposed granting Frank permanent residence, stating that "homosexuality [was] a crime," even though the law did not criminalize sex between women (*The Namibian*, November 3, 2000). State opposition to sexual minority rights was in evidence in 2001, when the Supreme Court overturned a lower court's ruling granting Frank permanent residence. The Supreme Court refused to consider Frank's long-term, committed lesbian partnership with a Namibian woman as a "factor that should count in her favour when her permanent residence application" was reviewed, but the Court did direct the Immigration Selection Board, which was housed in the Ministry of Home Affairs, to reconsider Frank's application (*The Namibian*, March 6, 2001). TRP members construed the Supreme Court's ruling as "extremely homophobic (even questioning [Frank and her partner's] ability as parents) and puts TRP back even farther" (TRP meeting minutes, March 7, 2001).

After the Supreme Court ruling was issued in 2001, TRP staff and members questioned whether they should scrap legal tactics altogether. Members asked, "Regarding the sodomy law, we must now decide whether any attempts to change it, in the present climate, [are] advisable" (TRP meeting minutes, March 7, 2001). Staff and members recognized that the organization had not followed through with serious legal lobbying (TRP meeting minutes, March 7, 2001). Despite members' concerns about state leaders publicly attacking the organization and actualizing their promises to stiffen penalties and laws related to same-sex sexual acts, the organization ultimately downplayed the gravity of the public portrayal of this setback because "Namibians on the average [did] not read newspapers and news coverage [about an issue was] usually very brief" (TRP meeting minutes, March 7, 2001). In 2001, Frank succeeded in obtaining permanent residence in Namibia (*The Namibian*, June 28, 2001).

The Rainbow Project decided that, as long as state leaders persisted in issuing homophobic threats, it would be best to postpone a public legal campaign centered on sexual and gender minority rights. Instead, the organization decided to develop an inclusionary orientation centered on human rights and to cast sexual and gender minority rights as human rights. To thwart state repression and to cultivate support from other civil society organizations, TRP styled itself as a broad-based Namibian human rights organization. For instance, TRP members coached key political or religious readers to denounce antigay rhetoric by voicing their support for all human rights, instead of specifically singling out sexual and gender minority rights. TRP's broad embrace of human rights prevented it from pursuing a legal campaign because it became entangled in antigay hostility within the human rights sector. When TRP first applied to become a member of the Namibian Non-Governmental Organisation Forum in 1999, the Forum demanded that TRP representatives deliver an oral presentation about the merits of the group's application. Prior to TRP's application, no other prospective member organization had had to make an oral presentation. Presumably because The Rainbow Project represented LGBT rights, persons, and interests at a time when Nujoma's antigay speeches were frequent, the Forum may have attempted to intimidate TRP representatives by requiring them to make a formal presentation about their work. The Forum's special treatment of TRP's application provoked outraged responses from Sister Namibia and from the National Society for Human Rights, both of which stated that they would consider withdrawing their Forum membership because they did not want to belong to a coalition that created special criteria for joining. TRP soon received full Forum membership and played a significant role in rejuvenating the Forum's Human Rights and Democracy Sector.

Antigay antagonism within the Forum toward TRP persisted, siphoning TRP's attention, energy, and resources. In 2002, The Rainbow Project rescued the Forum from financial ruin when TRP staff sponsored a successful national HIV/AIDS conference to keep the Forum from having to repay an international pharmaceutical company for funds the Forum had misused. With TRP's support, the Forum arranged with the pharmaceutical company to use the funds remaining from its donation to host an HIV/AIDS conference. After the conference, The Rainbow Project received flak from some hostile Forum members because TRP conference planners included a session that addressed how HIV/AIDS affects men who have sex with men. Critics interpreted this issue as a symptom of The Rainbow Project's "hijacking" the Forum to advance LGBT rights, as in the case of TRP's role as leader of the Forum's Human Rights and Democracy Sector. "'Why were LGBT issues suddenly so prominent in [the Forum]?' they [Forum critics of TRP] asked" (Fieldnotes, May 31, 2006). A TRP staff member suspected that the organization's opponents within the Forum hoped that TRP conference planners would "fall flat on our faces" when organizing the HIV/AIDS conference (Fieldnotes, May 31, 2006).[9] Continuing hostility from Forum members triggered TRP's eventual withdrawal from a leadership role in the Forum's Human Rights and Democracy Sector. TRP's continued participation in the human rights sector between 1999 and 2003 also kept the organization from mounting a legal challenge because leaders directed staff support and energy toward human rights mobilization, instead of toward specific LGBT rights legal challenges.

Promoting Democracy Within The Rainbow Project

As TRP reinvented itself as a promoter of human rights and democracy in Namibia, core members tried to instill democratic practices in the organization and to encourage participation from underrepresented groups, specifically poor, working-class, black, biracial, and multiracial LGBT Namibians. TRP's founding members in 1996 resembled their South African counterparts, who were "privileged mostly white, mostly middle-class, mostly urbanized lesbians and gays, who [were] safe enough to come out and identify as lesbian or gay, [and] fight for their rights" (van Zyl 2005, 31). Though TRP initially functioned as an exclusive social movement organization, founding members aspired to transform it into an "inclusive" social movement organization that would, according to Bernstein (1997, 539), try "to educate and mobilize a constituency or maximize involvement in political campaigns" (see also Zald and Ash 1966). As an inclusive social movement organization, TRP founding members successfully recruited black, biracial, and multiracial sexual minorities from diverse class backgrounds in Windhoek, the capital. They were so successful that several white founding members dropped out of the organization, presumably because of racial tension and divergent class interests.[10]

TRP members believed that the organization had to diversify its membership in terms of race, ethnicity, and class in postapartheid Namibia. If LGBT activists "were going to form a group that only had white members, you were not going to be a voice that people were going to take seriously. You're not going to have any credibility in this country" (TRP staff member, interview, July 11, 2006). The organization held meetings and recruited black, biracial, and multiracial members in Katutura, a black Windhoek township, and Khomasdal, a multiracial

Windhoek township. This resulted in a shift in membership from a dozen white members to several dozen mostly black, biracial, and multiracial members, and membership increased steadily between 1998 and 2002. From 1997 to 2001, a core group of about a dozen white, biracial, and multiracial middle-class volunteers managed TRP.

TRP founding members decided to empower black, biracial, and multiracial members from poor and working-class families, who dominated the organization in number of members, and to encourage them to participate in the organization. To achieve this goal, TRP created a constitution that afforded all members voting power at meetings; ideally, all members would have a voice in determining how the organization would develop. The introduction of such democratic practices reinforced TRP's identity as a promoter of human rights and democracy in Namibia. Members brought new concerns to the organization. Many black, biracial, and multiracial LGBT persons experienced poverty, joblessness, and lack of access to education that compounded their struggles with homophobia in their families, communities, and local social institutions and accentuated their HIV/AIDS vulnerability (Lorway 2007). Members approached TRP staff with these concerns at open monthly meetings, and the organization began to make some basic services, such as a weekly soup kitchen and monthly health clinic, available to members in the late 1990s. Some members with disposable income even "subsidized" the membership fees of "disadvantaged members who [could] not afford to pay" and contributed to a fund that would assist members in times of financial hardship (TRP meeting minutes, September 20, 2001). TRP's office, which opened in 2001, also provided a space for members to socialize safely. Many members began socializing at the small office, and a management committee instituted a rule in 2001 limiting the time for socializing to after 4 p.m. two days a week to prevent social gatherings from interrupting the staff's work (TRP meeting minutes, July 4, 2001).

From 1997 to 2003, TRP held open monthly meetings at which members could voice their concerns or make suggestions about current and future projects. However, beginning in 2001, TRP's open monthly meetings devolved into arguments among members about TRP's tactics. Some members attempted to shift TRP's focus away from a legal rights campaign to social-service provision. In particular, building on members' growing interest in social-service provision, one member who "believed he would eventually become the TRP director" promised to create jobs for TRP members or to give rent money from the organization's budget to members who sided with him, an assurance at which some members scoffed because it revealed how little other members knew about what Northern donors—TRP's main source of funding—would finance (Interview, TRP member, July 11, 2006). Some members also concocted conspiracy theories; disgruntled TRP members accused staff of misappropriating funds and increasing their own salaries. Staff offered to let members examine the organization's finances, but no one took them up on this offer, probably because most members had little experience navigating complex budgets (TRP meeting minutes, April 3, 2002). These episodes contributed to staff's and leaders' decision to draft a code of conduct that outlined how they expected members to behave in the office and at staff and membership meetings. Dealing with these internal conflicts prevented TRP staff from providing services and information to a broader LGBT community for a time because staff had to respond to multiple requests for services and information about how they were running the organization.

Members' support for or opposition to providing social services was largely divided along racial and class lines. Poor, black, biracial, and multiracial members requested that TRP provide basic services, whereas white, middle-class members envisioned the organization's taking on less tangible projects, such as law reform. Many TRP staff and members also cast the provision of social services as an "either-or" choice; either the organization provided social services, or it did not. On the one hand, some members and staff believed that if TRP were to offer social services to members, the effort would overwhelm the organization and prevent it from pursuing legal rights that would lead to social and political recognition of LGBT persons' equality in Namibian society. In addition, they feared that Northern donors would not fund poverty-alleviation programs designed for sexual and gender minorities because other nongovernmental organizations offered such services. On the other hand, some members and staff believed that they owed it to poor, unemployed, and undereducated members to provide social services to them because they had nowhere else to turn, which constituted the redistribution of resources and opportunities that would enable Namibian LGBT persons to improve their everyday material existence. As long as they obtained funds in the name of Namibian LGBT persons, they believed that members should have equal access to them. Members wanted to end the internal fighting before the organization imploded.

Fulfilling poor black, biracial, and multiracial members' basic needs overwhelmed and paralyzed TRP for several years between 2000 and 2003, telescoping core members' plans for law reform. Legal tactics did not make sense to LGBT persons unfamiliar with the Namibian constitution and legal system. Many interviewees cast the concerns of LGBT persons in terms of basic needs like education and jobs, which they interpreted as being far removed from the legal arena. For example, what would LGBT persons do with the repeal of the sodomy law? How would this repeal benefit them directly, tangibly, and immediately? Some TRP staff and members believed that if Namibians could marry persons of the same gender, few poor and working-class black, biracial, and multiracial LGBT persons would marry because marriage held few immediate material benefits; the moral victory of winning the right to marry a person of the same gender or of overturning sodomy laws was too remote for many black, biracial, and multiracial LGBT persons. Several black, biracial, and multiracial members eventually became alienated and defected from TRP because they perceived that the core group was not attuned to their needs. Not being able to assert ownership over TRP or the movement's direction bothered some members. For many members, TRP acted as a social space and haven where they could escape from their personal troubles. Socializing with other LGBT persons sensitized them to the material and emotional needs of other LGBT persons, such as poverty and under- and unemployment. As members sought social services at the organization, they were able to take ownership of TRP. Pursuing legal tactics to the exclusion of engaging in other tactics would likely have alienated TRP members because they lacked the education and expertise needed for such a campaign.

Recognizing and respecting class diversity among members became a sore point for The Rainbow Project. It was easy to run a meeting when twelve middle-class people with similar life experiences, values, and worldviews agreed on a common vision for fighting state leaders' homophobia, but incorporating "250 to 300 voices from diverse backgrounds [became] very difficult" (Interview, TRP member, July 11, 2006). One gay, multiracial member concluded that TRP's original constitution could have worked only if all members had hailed from the middle class: "An organization like ours can't be completely democratic," or else members would run it into the ground with endless basic needs (Interview, TRP member, July 11, 2006). According to this perspective, some members expected the organization to solve their basic problems immediately. While members could voice multiple concerns through the organization's democratic structure, such polyvocality devolved into cacophony as members clogged meetings and decision-making processes with their demands for social services.

Several former and current black, biracial, and multiracial members alleged that TRP's management had been racist in the past. They contended that TRP had hired few black LGBT persons as staff members and failed to include them in important decisions, contrary to founding and core members' claims that the constitution facilitated the incorporation of members of previously underrepresented indigenous groups. One black gay member claimed that because so many black LGBT persons turned out for events, those unfamiliar with or new to TRP might assume that the office staff were all or mostly black, which was not the case (Interview, TRP member, June 30, 2006). The same member contended that staff informed black TRP members about events only when they wanted to show donors how racially diverse the Namibian LGBT movement was and how TRP was doing its part to repair race relations that apartheid policies had damaged (Interview, TRP member, June 30, 2006).

While conflict siphoned TRP staff's and members' attention and contributed to the organization's decision not to pursue a legal rights campaign, founding members asked donors to order and pay for an external review performed by a South African consulting company in 2002 and 2003 because TRP was "being smothered under personal shit" (Interview, TRP member, July 11, 2006). Donors financed an external review that recommended that TRP become a trust, an organizational form in which TRP staff would be accountable only to an executive board and not to dozens of members, and that it abandon social-service provision for members with "bread-and-butter" needs (Interview, TRP member, July 11, 2006). This recommendation is similar to the strategic choice of activists in different countries to "professionalize" social movement organizations, which can reduce internal conflict (Staggenborg 1988). Donors worried that too many service-provision programs like the soup kitchen would bankrupt TRP. As a result of the external review, members voted to transform TRP into a trust that would initiate and execute only programs, such as a law reform project, that would improve the lives and legal situations of LGBT Namibians as a group. If the organization had not shifted its focus from the provision of social services to legal and social advocacy that targeted the state and social institutions, donors would have suspended funding and restarted TRP as a trust after a cooling-off period, forcing the organization into abeyance (Taylor 1989).

TRP deemphasized the pursuit of a legal campaign due to internal disagreements about tactics. Though the organization ultimately resolved these disputes by becoming a trust, TRP had not launched a legal campaign by the middle of 2006. However, in funding proposals that staff created for international donors, TRP staff specified that initiating law reform was a top priority for the organization. Though the organization has not succeeded in persuading white members who left TRP to rejoin, it has managed to retain and recruit black, biracial, and multiracial LGBT Namibians as members. TRP's termination of social-service provision left some members feeling disenchanted with and alienated from the organization because there were fewer opportunities for black, biracial, and multiracial LGBT Namibians to socialize regularly within the organization. TRP has garnered a reputation among Northern donors and African LGBT social movement organizations as an organization that emerged intact from its internal conflicts, and staff members have shared the organization's lessons with small groups of LGBT activists in Kenya, Uganda, and Tanzania.

Conclusion

The Rainbow Project refrained from pushing ahead with a public legal campaign due to external threats from state leaders and internal conflicts among staff and members over what actions the organization should take. State leaders' antigay statements between 1995 and 2005 caused TRP to reconsider whether and how it should launch and run a public legal campaign. TRP staff and members worried that a public legal campaign might anger state and SWAPO leaders, worsen the legal situation of LGBT Namibians, and result in negative sanctions against the organization. The organization strategically transformed itself into a human rights organization as a way to gain civil society support for LGBT rights as human rights; working within the human rights sector siphoned time and attention away from the organization's proposed legal campaign. TRP also faced demands for social services from black, biracial, and multiracial members living in poverty; if it had tried to provide these services, the effort would likely have diverted the organization's resources from a public legal campaign. The organization grappled with state leaders' public homophobia and members' demands for social services in its deferral of legal tactics. The Rainbow Project's indefinite postponement of legal tactics demonstrates that legal tactics may not be easy for LGBT social movement organizations to pursue, especially given state leaders' hostility and members' objection to an organization's tactical choices.

3 Queer Legal Victories

Intersectionality Revisited

Darren Rosenblum

IN MY 1995 article "Queer Intersectionality and the Failure of Lesbian and Gay 'Victories,'" I merged queer and intersectionality theories to critique four lesbian and gay legal "victories."[1] I argued that queer identity intersected with other identity characteristics, yielding queer communities whose diverse needs reflect their various class, race, gender, and sex identifications. This intersectional perspective led me to view these decisions as victories for only a privileged subset of queer communities that, "but for" their gay or lesbian identity, conform to the "American dream" (De Lauretis 1991; Robson 1992).[2] The United States' juridical heterosexism stifled the progressive potential of these cases.

Since that article, the intersectionality of queerness has become accepted wisdom (Eng, Halberstam, and Muñoz 2005). This chapter applies a queer intersectional analysis to more recent queer legal successes, interrogating both their utility and some of the queer critiques that have greeted them. In 2003, the U.S. Supreme Court reversed *Bowers v. Hardwick* (1986) in *Lawrence v. Texas*, finding that state regulation of private sexual conduct violated the U.S. Constitution. A few months after *Lawrence*, the Massachusetts Supreme Judicial Court decided *Goodridge v. Department of Public Health* (2003), in which it found that the restriction of marriage to opposite-sex couples violated Massachusetts' constitution, opening the way for the first legal marriages between two people of the same sex in the United States. About five years later, the California, Connecticut, and Iowa Supreme Courts and the Vermont, Maine, and New Hampshire legislatures followed Massachusetts' lead and established marriage equality.

A queer intersectional analysis remains vital. Time has proven the accuracy of an expansive and fluid understanding of sexuality, both as borders dissipate and as younger individuals battle heterosexism while refusing to be confined to established identity categories. As in the mid-1990s, articulating queer legal needs and assessing whether these cases adequately reflect the breadth of these needs require probing analysis. In that period, the 1989 case, *Braschi v. Stahl Assoc.*, embodied the law's progress and limitations concerning queer issues, which are in part a function of the cultural complexity of queer identity.

Here I apply the queer intersectional yardstick to both *Lawrence* and *Goodridge*, concluding that while the early 1990s "victories" merited questioning, these more recent cases present far more substantive opportunities for queer communities. Although litigation continues to exhibit marginalizing and essentializing propensities that render it an incomplete impetus for queer social change, accounting for these limits does not obligate us to take an exclusively critical posture toward legal developments. Litigation should not define strategy, but in concert with political action, litigation can and does play an important role in advancing queer legal needs.

Part I of this essay introduces some of the theories still relevant to a queer intersectional critique. The 1990's opposition between "queer" and "lesbian and gay" reflected the increasingly legitimized nature of the "lesbian and gay" community. Today, the widespread use of LGBT (lesbian, gay, bisexual, and transgender) encompasses some of the varied identity concerns that prompted the use of "queer." It is also worth noting that any notion of community (in the singular or plural) in a world where borders of all kinds have become a bit more fluid for many is quite complex (Neal 1996; Valdes 1995). This complexity delineates the spectrum of queer identity and forms a queer continuum, a reconceptualization of Adrienne Rich's lesbian continuum. Part II briefly considers *Lawrence, Goodridge*, and other state Supreme Courts cases and the progress and constrictions they represent from various queer perspectives, including those of poor queers, queers of color, sexual subversives, and gender subversives. Part III assesses the implications of this critique for the relationships among queer communities, litigation, and broader goals of social justice.

Queer Theories

Queer identity intersects with sex, race, class, sexual practice, and gender preference. A continuum of queer identity reflects this fluidity of identity elements. Two theoretical contributions, intersectionality from Critical Race Theory ("CRT") and the lesbian continuum from lesbian feminism, yield a queer intersectional perspective.

It is nearly two decades after activists began to reclaim "queer," a word originally used to deride strange behavior or social outcasts. The rehabilitation of the word has been a largely successful endeavor, as queer projects have established themselves at U.S. universities and in tradition-bound disciplines such as international law. Simply put, reclaiming "queer" had two goals: avoiding essentialist implications of "lesbian and gay" and subverting normative presumptions of sexuality. "Queer" as a political category avoids the essentialist meaning presumed by the terms "lesbian and gay" (Boswell 1982, 58–59; Calhoun 1993; Foucault 1978, 43).

Scholars have derided such essentialist constructs as both inaccurate (Halperin 1986, 34; Padgug 1979) and destructive (Halley 1989). "Queer," unlike "lesbian and gay," describes not merely sexual practices but rather a destabilization of heterosexual hegemony (Anonymous Queers 1990).[3] "Queer" as a term suggests "the truly polymorphous nature of our difference" (Harper 1990, 30).

Intersectionality references the bind of multiple identities and its effect on social position and exposure to discrimination. Mainstream feminist understandings of "women" relied on a universalized white identity that rendered women of color invisible (Crenshaw 1989; hooks 1981). Crenshaw describes the bind black women face because of liberation movements: "Black women's Blackness or femaleness sometimes has placed their needs and perspectives at the margin of the feminist and Black liberationist agendas" (Crenshaw 1989). Just as feminist and antiracist agendas fail Black women by centering on femaleness or blackness, lesbian and gay positions may reduce their communities' identifications to same-sex partner choice, sometimes to the exclusion of other diverse identities. "Queer" casts a wide net of intersectionality, as most queer people face additional forms of discrimination based on gender, race, class, or sexual subversiveness. As one Black commentator stated, "[a] lot of times when you're black and gay, you don't know whether the discrimination is due to your blackness or your gayness" (Ronald Price quoted in L. Williams 1993, A1). The multiplicity of antiqueer discrimination moves beyond antilesbian and antigay discrimination.

Although intersectionality retains a certain currency, it is not without its detractors. One of the many critiques, the "infinite regress" argument, holds that that any particular identity can be subdivided into further distinctions, leading to an infinite loop of identities. Intersectionality's potential for infinite regress risks leading to a radical, even existentialist, individualism that vitiates the potential for collective political action (Ehrenreich 2002).

The queer continuum may remedy the infinite regress problem. It builds on Adrienne Rich's formulation of the lesbian continuum, which comprises "the multitude of identities which constitute lesbian existence" (Rich 1993). "Lesbian existence comprises both the breaking of a taboo and the rejection of a compulsory way of life" (Rich 1993). Compulsory heterosexuality, the system that forces women to define themselves in relation to men, dictates women's heterosexuality. The lesbian continuum represents the range of women's resistance to compulsory heterosexuality, while the queer continuum includes a multigendered range of sexual identities that subverts compulsory heterosexuality. In a sense, the long-discarded term "sexual preference" may express sexuality's fluidity more accurately than the widely used term "sexual orientation."

Several parallels between the queer continuum and the lesbian continuum provide a useful comparison. Rich's lesbian continuum includes women who

behave homosocially but do not identify as lesbians. The queer continuum likewise includes a range of people who resist compulsory heterosexuality, including
sexual minority activists and those who do not even identify as a sexual minority
but nonetheless subvert traditional gender and sexual identities. The breadth of
queer existence, like lesbian existence, draws on acts of resistance. Thus, queer
might include men who have sex with men ("MSM") but might loathe the word
"queer" and even "gay." Acts of sexual subversion stand outside what Gayle Rubin
has called the "charmed circle" of socially approved sexual behavior (Rubin 1984)
and constitute a resistance against compulsory heterosexuality.

The queer continuum unites a broad range of disempowered communities. By
including the occasionally subversive and the intersectional, the queer continuum
embraces broad resistance to compulsory heterosexuality. Respecting intersectional
identities fosters the trust necessary for alliances within antisubordination efforts.

Facially, intersectionality and the queer continuum contradict each other:
intersectionality emphasizes differences, whereas the continuum seems to erase
difference. The continuum contains the potential for political unity through the
respect of difference, a fundamental strategy for subordinated communities. It
also prevents the collapsing of different queer communities into a unitary queer
identity.[4] While intersectionality's infinite regress problem may shrink the potential for broad political action, the queer continuum may convert queer intersectionality into social justice coalitions.

Awareness of queer intersectionality reshapes our conception of queer legal
needs. A limited concentration on lesbian and gay legal needs, the extension of
rights to people without regard to sexual orientation, inadequately describes queer
legal needs. If such a narrow focus is taken, intersectional queers will face exclusion
by other forces of subordination in the law, such as classism, sexism, and racism.

To take class as an example, courts subjugate working-class people by pre-
suming that legitimate claims arise from plaintiffs with education, professional
backgrounds, and property. "Covering" poverty may aid working-class plaintiffs
but will not improve their limited access to the courts in the first place (Yoshino
2006). As Marc Galanter (1974) has demonstrated, the legal system and profes-
sion are organized to protect the interests of the powerful. Economic inequality
leaves many queers of color facing this same classism. Sexual and familial norms
differ among social groups, whether those groups coalesce around race, ethnicity,
nationality, and/or language (Rosenblum 2007). Such groups define queerness
differently as a result of their identities (Reid-Pharr 2007). Since manifestations
of homophobia and heterosexism are culturally contingent, remedies that counter white heterosexism fail to address this discrimination. Courts that rely on
traditional sexual and gender norms will fail to understand and, in effect, ignore
sexual and gender subversive litigants and their priorities.

The legal priorities of sexual subversives often differ from those of the privileged "but-for" queers. A "but-for queer" is someone who, "but for" being queer, would be perfect (Robson 1992). Before courts that recognize only discrete categories, "but-for queers," with only one subordinate identity, may constitute the ideal plaintiffs. "But-for" queer litigants permit the courts to focus on antilesbian and antigay discrimination independent from other discrimination. The resulting legal remedies centered in that identity may simultaneously exclude on the basis of class, sex, race, sexual practice, and gender performance. This queer critique of litigation draws on Stuart Scheingold's (2004 [1974]) analysis of what he terms the "myth of rights," that litigation directly links to social change. Rather than establish and advance a particular social priority, activist lawyers search for successful litigation targets. The targets, on the basis of their potential as successful litigants, define the priorities of those lawyers and, therefore, the courts.

One cannot entirely disassociate legal responses from discrimination within queer communities. The maturing of what is now known as the LGBT movement has come with an awareness of discriminatory impulses. Sexism (both against women and against those with nonbinary gender identities), racism, classism, internalized homophobia, and other discriminations that plague heterosexual society also divide queer communities. "Gay and lesbian" litigation, which can further "but-for" queer interests over intersectional queer interests, may deepen such rifts. As intersectional critiques reveal, courts recognize targets of discrimination solely on the basis of their belonging to a specific protected class. Typically, lesbian and gay litigation requires a client who, but for that trait, would not have fallen victim to discrimination. Courts have begun to move beyond this narrow view to consider the sexism and gender stereotyping inherent in much homophobic expression (see Herald, this volume).[5] Even then, courts confronting queer conflicts often feel compelled to dive into either a gender analysis *or* a sexual orientation analysis (*Riccio v. New Haven Board of Education* 2007).

Analyzing the utility of cases for queer movements requires not only an awareness of queer needs, but also a critical posture to serve as a more ambitious yardstick for social change. A queer intersectional perspective may aid the assessment of whether change comes incrementally or radically. Recent court decisions optimize the possibility for assessing queer change.

Queering "Victories"

"Queer Intersectionality" interrogated the meaning of a legal victory for queer communities. In the 1990s, legal groups engaged in lesbian and gay issues justifiably trumpeted successes, particularly in the face of continued judicial homophobia post-*Hardwick*. As other civil rights movements have learned, in part through

Critical Race Theory, legal victories often fail to translate into social change. "Queer Intersectionality" brought this understanding to bear on cases that achieved their goals for the plaintiffs but presented complications for other queer legal goals.

This analysis remains worthwhile, but the legal and cultural landscape has changed vastly since 1995. As legal activists have logged several notable successes, other scholars, both legal and nonlegal, have assessed these victories with a queer critical eye. In contrast to the earlier study, a queer intersectional perspective yields markedly different results when directed at these recent legal victories. Considering the legal needs of this broadly conceived set of queer communities, here I briefly analyze *Lawrence*, *Goodridge*, and other state Supreme Court cases and their respective effects on case law concerning sexuality and relationship recognition.

In 1871, Victoria Woodhull, a feminist from the mid-to-late nineteenth century, aptly expressed the legal aspect of sexual rights: "Yes, I am a Free Lover. I have an inalienable, constitutional, and natural right to love whom I may, to change that love every day if I please, and it is your duty not only to accord [my right], but, as a community to see that I am protected in it" (Woodhull 1872). This statement not only neatly summarizes a queer sexual agenda but serves to measure the success of advances in sexual liberty.

On one end of the queer continuum are individuals and communities that embrace heteronormative (if not heterosexual) relationships and family structures, and on the other end lie sexual subversives. In addition to those queers who do not choose lengthy relationships, monogamy, or marriage for various reasons, there are those queers who explore radical forms of sexuality in what has been called laboratories of sexual experimentation: public sex (parks, backrooms), anonymous sex, group sex, promiscuity, and sadomasochism (Foucault 1989, 225). Many queers do not have or seek to have lengthy relationships; some couple in ways unrecognizable to U.S. courts or view monogamy as a fundamental obstacle to sexual liberation (Crimp 1988, 237–53). Ideally, courts' attitudes toward sexuality would respect these and other divergent and personal choices that exist along the queer continuum.

Lawrence takes a big step toward respecting queer interests. Although the holding does not instruct states to eliminate vice laws that still may be used against sexual minorities, *Lawrence* recognizes a notion of privacy, with sexuality as a core element, as being protected under the U.S. Constitution. The very existence of sodomy laws marked certain people as targets for state regulation (Thomas 1992), even though more than thirty-seven states had repealed or overturned their sodomy laws by the time *Lawrence* reached the Supreme Court, in 2003. *Lawrence* eloquently and forcefully closed the centuries-long story of sodomy laws in the United States, eliminating a key tool for states in the criminalization and oppression of queer communities and identities.

Impressive queer analysis has identified many of *Lawrence*'s challenges. *Lawrence* created strange allies among gay-rights groups and libertarians (Harcout 2004). Although the holding in *Lawrence* focused on autonomy, sexual self-determination, "sexual sovereignty," and a general idea of free choice among individuals (Weinstein and DeMarco 2004), some fear that *Lawrence* may provoke a backlash against gay rights and sexual liberalization (Katyal 2006). More important, some legal commentators fear that *Lawrence*, like *Brown v. Board of Education*, will initially be a "toothless legal formalism" that will be "ill-equipped to provide" justice (Franke 2004). The legal gay rights landscape since *Lawrence* is varied. Although *Lawrence* aligns U.S. jurisprudence with international norms on private consensual sexuality (see Frank et al., this volume), it has not facilitated full queer citizenship in the United States (Hernández-Truyol 2004) and may have unintended consequences, such as fostering polygamy (Emens 2004). Its reliance on privacy doctrine, to the extent we view sex as a public issue, may create a hierarchy of good homosexual sex and bad homosexual sex (Ruskola 2005). One might also argue that *Lawrence* moved sexual minorities into an "interstitial place in constitutional law" as a group that is neither formally recognized, nor formally outlawed (Valdes 2004).

Despite queer critics' concerns about *Lawrence*'s consequences, and despite continued debate over whether liberty or equal protection arguments will serve queer communities better, *Lawrence* takes a step toward fulfilling Victoria Woodhull's dream of sexual freedom, even if some of its language does not reflect queer utopian ideals.

One consequence of *Lawrence*, Justice Scalia warned in his dissent, would be the likely reversal of sex-based restrictions on marriage. As marriage rights begin to include queer couples, many queer theorists continue to criticize marriage rights efforts for shunning subversive sexuality. The effort for marriage equality dates back to the early 1970s, when two state supreme courts rejected challenges (*Singer v. Hara*). In the early 1990s, Hawai'i's Supreme Court took steps toward recognizing marriage equality, only to be negated by a state constitutional amendment. Several years later, Vermont's Supreme Court ruled that barring same-sex couples from marrying was unconstitutional and required the state legislature to provide for same-sex marriage or an analogous institution with all the benefits of marriage. The Vermont legislature responded by enacting civil unions; however, the Defense of Marriage Act prevents the federal system from permitting the portability of these benefits. Other states have since instituted civil unions, but when this volume went to press, Massachusetts, Connecticut, Iowa, Maine, and now Vermont as well remain the only states in which marriage equality exists.

A few years before the Hawai'i Supreme Court's decision in *Baehr v. Lewin*, *Braschi v. Stahl Associates* paved the way for recognition of relationships involving same-sex couples. Reports of the decision gleamed from the *New York Times'* front page. The lead attorney, Bill Rubenstein, stated: "Today's decision is a ground-breaking victory for lesbians and gay men. It marks the most important single step forward in American law towards legal recognition of lesbian and gay relationships" (Gutis 1991).

In *Braschi*, Stahl Associates tried to evict Miguel Braschi, the partner of a deceased tenant, Leslie Blanchard. Braschi sued to inherit the lease as a cohabiting family member, presenting the Court with the issue of whether the noneviction provision should be extended to same-sex couples. The Court of Appeals put forth several indicia for same-sex couples to merit consideration as "family" for rent-control purposes: "exclusivity and longevity of the relationship, the level of emotional and financial commitment, the manner in which the parties have conducted their everyday lives and held themselves out to society, and the reliance placed upon one another for daily family services." The court applied this test to Braschi and Blanchard, found that their relationship was sufficiently family-like and granted Braschi noneviction protection and tenancy inheritance.

Brashi's holding continues to carry great relevance for queer analysis of relationship recognition. Rent-control statutes, which require strict tests to prevent widespread abuse, provided the first, albeit restricted, recognition of lesbian and gay couples' rights. Overtly designed to prevent fraud by "roommates," this strict test enforces a heteronormative relationship structure on queer couples hoping to benefit from rent-control protection. The Court of Appeals test, progressive in moving beyond heterosexual marriage, nonetheless demands relationship traits that queer couples may not seek, such as monogamy, longevity, openness, and financial commitment. *Braschi* provided limited protection for relationships that were simultaneously held to a higher standard. Marriage, in contrast, imposes no such standards on couples. Nearly twenty years after it was decided, *Braschi* remains the only case to recognize lesbian and gay relationships in New York, a disappointing fact after the horribly reasoned *Hernandez v. Robles* decision denying marriage equality.[6]

In *Goodridge v. Department of Public Health*, the Supreme Judicial Court of Massachusetts examined whether the state could legally bar same-sex couples from civil marriage and found that there was no rational basis for denying same-sex couples the right to marry. Because the Massachusetts constitution "affirms the dignity and equality of all individuals" and "forbids the creation of second-class citizens," the court reasoned that Massachusetts's marriage law "violates the basic premises of individual liberty and equality under law protected by the Massachusetts Constitution." The court also noted concrete tangible benefits that flow from civil marriage, including, but not limited to, rights in property, probate, tax, and evidence law. "Marriage also bestows enormous private and social advantages on those who choose to marry . . . [and] is at once a deeply personal commitment to another human being and a highly public celebration of the ideals of mutuality, companionship, intimacy, fidelity, and family."

The Massachusetts Senate responded to *Goodridge* with a civil union bill and made an unusual request for an Advisory Opinion from the court on the bill's constitutionality. The court replied that "[b]ecause the proposed law by its express terms forbids same-sex couples' entry into civil marriage, it continues to relegate same-sex couples to a different status. . . . Group classifications based on unsupportable distinctions, such as that embodied in the proposed bill, are invalid under the Massachusetts Constitution. The history of our nation has demonstrated that separate is seldom, if ever, equal."

The Supreme Judicial Court of Massachusetts's rejection of "separate but equal" marks one of the strongest affirmations of queer couples' rights in the United States. The concept of "separate but equal" was established by the U.S. Supreme Court in 1896 to permit government-sanctioned segregation of the races. Sixty years later (and now more than fifty years ago), in *Brown v. Board of Education*, the U.S. Supreme Court rejected this logic and held that racially segregated schools are unconstitutional. The court's reference to this landmark case links LGBT couples' struggle for equal rights to the core of the civil rights movement. However, this was a connection followed only by the New Jersey Supreme Court, which ultimately accepted civil unions, as Maryland, New York, and Washington rejected marriage discrimination challenges.

Almost five years later, the California, Connecticut, and Iowa Supreme Courts' decisions extended the right to marry. The nation's largest state, California, utilized a strict-scrutiny standard of review to recognize the de jure inequality, entrenched homophobia, and "widespread disparagement that gay individuals historically have faced." The court noted the fundamental interest same-sex couples have in seeing their family receive the "same respect and dignity enjoyed by an opposite-sex couple." California also rejected civil unions as a status for "second-class citizens." The California Supreme Court relied extensively on one of the earliest civil rights cases, the sixty-year-old case *Perez v. Sharp* (1948), in which the California Supreme Court overturned its antimiscegenation law, almost twenty years before the U.S. Supreme Court declared such laws unconstitutional, in *Loving v. Virginia* (1967). Connecticut's decision, which took a similar appraoch to civil unions, became practice without significant controversy. After six months of marriage equality, California's voters narrowly approved Proposition 8, which attempted to deny same-sex couples the right to marry. Although Proposition 8's passage throws *In re Marriage's* effect into doubt, it may not alter the case's landmark status, pending the outcome of the ensuing litigation. In any case, subsequent recognition of marriage rights by the Iowa Supreme Court and the Vermont and Maine legislatures demonstrates that Proposition 8 has not halted the shift toward equality.

In the face of the *Goodridge* and *In re Marriage* decisions, many queer activists continue to question the primacy of marriage and whether it serves queer goals. Despite these changes, queer studies theorists often reject the effort to win the right to marry, citing same-sex marriage as "mimicking" a heterosexual institution, "diluting its traditional patriarchal dynamic," but not "transform[ing] society" (Ettlebrick 1989). More recently, Nancy Polikoff has argued that relationship recognition should be much more nuanced than marriage. This position reflects the long-standing feminist critique of marriage as a patriarchal system of coverture in which wives were the property of their husbands (Dunlap 1991; Eskridge 1993; Polikoff 1993, 2008). Some critics argue that marriage equality positions require an emphasis on the similarity of same-sex relationships to heterosexual marriages, thus preventing a more transformative effort (Polikoff 1993, 2008). Others criticize the marriage effort as a prime example of a litigation-driven strategy that ignores grassroots efforts (Levitsky 2006). More recently, Lisa Duggan has argued that the lesbian and gay political platform for marriage depends on coding liberation as domesticity and privacy (Duggan and Kim 2005; Eng, Halberstam, and Munoz 2005).

Although these critiques point to some real challenges, to a certain extent the arguments essentialize both the queer position and the meaning of marriage, leading to a binary opposition. This presumptive opposition fails to integrate the breadth of queer understandings of social institutions, which can be subverted and transformed from within. These queer critiques of marriage confront several limitations, an understanding of which facilitates a queer recognition of the potential marriage holds for queer people.

First, as a utilitarian matter of meeting individual needs, many people in queer communities may legitimately need to marry. Some may, without respect for the normative implications, need or want to take advantage of the many hundreds of economic and social benefits that accompany marriage (Chambers 2001, Wolfson 1994). Although ideally our state and society would decouple marriage from key social benefits, in the current context, exclusion from marriage economically harms queer relationships, in particular those of poor individuals who may depend on their partner's health or retirement benefits. Without marriage, the efforts of a queer couple to capture, at best, some of marriage's benefits require attorneys and contracts, a process that inherently excludes poor people. Were they permitted to marry, working-class people in queer communities would obtain a wide range of financial and social benefits by virtue of the stealth and ease of a quick civil marriage (Wolfson 2004). Moreover, queer couples' inability to marry deprives their communities of millions of dollars in saved taxes and increased benefits.

Second, the adherence by some in queer communities to anti-assimilationism should not obligate all members of queer communities to follow that principle and abandon their wishes. Simply put, a queer understanding of individual agency should permit those who want lives that include more common and well-established relationship structures to recognize them. Queer arguments that those who seek to marry "mimic" straight people are essentializing those queers and the nature of marriage. Marriage grants a vast array of rights and responsibilities while permitting an equally vast range of acceptable marital behavior, particularly compared with the *Braschi* standard that mandates explicit requirements of longevity, self-presentation as a couple, "exclusivity," and financial interdependence. Heterosexual marriage, by contrast, is not just Ward and June Cleaver; it's also majority of married people who engage in adultery, not to mention the swingers depicted in Ang Lee's *The Ice Storm*, "bridezillas," and the day-long marriages plastered on tabloid covers. In the wake of *Lawrence*'s rejection of state control of private consensual sexual contact, the exercise of sexual liberty calls. Queers may well choose to revel in the instantaneous legitimacy and frivolity that is heterosexual marriage today.

Third, and perhaps most important, marriage equality has the distinctly queer effect of de-gendering marriage. As same-sex and transgender marriages become more common, marriage will be liberated from its historical ties to a Napoleonic Code vision of male property, in which the woman and her belongings are the husband's chattel (Hunter 1991). As Nan Hunter has argued: "What is most unsettling to the status quo about the legalization of lesbian and gay marriage is its potential to expose and denaturalize the historical construction of gender at the heart of marriage." The impact of gay and lesbian marriage "will be to dismantle the legal structure of gender in every marriage" (Hunter 1991, 9). Marriage's gendered nature will dissipate as same-sex and transgender marriages become more common. Removing gender from the calculus of who can marry whom will benefit transgender people, as well. Once accepted into a legal institution considered by many queers to be oppressive, queers might transform the institution itself. Recent studies indicate that same-sex couples evince higher levels of balance and equality between partners. Surely, spreading these egalitarian norms serves the queer goal of making marriage a fairer institution.

Marriage raises different questions for people of color and people of different national origins. The right to marry implicates different technologies and living situations, which, because of economic and social racism and cultural differences, are not often available to many people of color. Gender varies along cultural lines of race, ethnicity, nationality, and/or language (Rosenblum 2007). So does sexuality. Marriage carries different meanings across these lines. For some queers of color or of different religious and cultural backgrounds, marriage carries greater legitimacy than it does for queer whites: many link their relationships' legitimacy to marriage (Dang and Frazer 2005).

In short, domestic-partnership-type recognition structures, whether created by governments or by corporations, require a far higher standard for lesbians and gays than for heterosexuals in marriage. Many have extensive cohabitation requirements that, simply put, do not affect heterosexuals when entering into marriage. Now that marriage equality is imaginable, queers can appreciate its benefits and its costs. They can also savor leaving behind the second-class alternatives that *Braschi* offered. Marriage efforts need not serve as the sole end of social justice efforts; they can and do interact with struggles for state recognition of wider sets of relationships, including those of friendship or other forms of kinship. *Lawrence, Goodridge,* and *In re Marriage Cases* confront serious queer critique and still echo many heterosexist norms. Yet, because they undermine juridical sex binarism and heteronormativity, they merit the moniker "victories" more than prior cases as they undermine juridical sex binarism and heteronormativity.

Pluralist Transformations

As I argued in 1995, litigation should be only one of several vehicles for effecting social change. Litigation's key role in lesbian and gay rights efforts carries risks of essentializing identity. The relationship of law to queer communities should reflect a "plurality of resistances" (Foucault 1978) toward the law: continued litigation and simultaneous political institutional transformation.

Continuing legal strategies presume law's viability for social change despite its exclusions. Progress, in this view, depends on working within the law, and only the law may eradicate discrimination. However, as law reform scholars have noted, individuals and attorneys bring cases for their own reasons without regard to broader political goals, disrupting even the most well-considered legal strategies (Sturm 1993).

Law's centrality in social change faces limits. Queer legal activists draw on broader political agendas and bend the cases to fit those needs. This shift requires closer work between legal advocacy groups and other politically motivated associations working within the same movement. The ideal relationship between cause lawyers and grassroots groups should be complementary (Levitsky 2006, noted in Sarat and Scheingold 2006, 145). Building on her case study of Chicago's LGBT movement, Sandra Levitsky argues that, although legal groups do assist activists, the relationship between the two is often unilateral, rather than reciprocal, and that "many activists in the movement perceive legal advocacy organizations as operating independently from the rest of the movement, imposing their agendas without consultation" (Levitsky 2006, noted in Sarat and Scheingold 2006, 145).

Scheingold advocates the use of political rather than legal strategies to further social change, a process that, depending on the issue and the need, may include litigation as an element (Scheingold 2004 [1974]). Activists often presume that progressive legislation is impossible due to heterosexist entrenchment in legislatures; however, it can serve as a venue for reform. As I have argued elsewhere, lesbian and gay interests would play a larger role in electoral politics if the U.S. electoral system were not so clearly stacked in favor of the two-party system's incumbency. Although legislatures have proven slow to approve lesbian and gay rights measures, political empowerment through increased attention to political representation and voting rights would permit queer communities to achieve legislative change.[7]

Although litigation may exclude, it may also liberate through its distillation of social problems into individual dramas that generate publicity, bargaining leverage, and the mobilization of activists. Litigation can subvert the impact of losses or interact with social movements to invite subsequent, broader applications of limited victories that reach intersectional identities.

Courts' formalist reliance on rigid and discrete identities and their inability to react to fluid and intersectional issues may frustrate queer activists. Taken to its logical end, a litigation-centered strategy may tailor goals to suit conservative courts. One may argue that such efforts forestall more radical change and coopt radical demands to prevent a broader subversion of the current heterosexist order. In this argument, *Braschi*, not to mention *Goodridge* and *In re Marriage*, recognizes some queer relationships so as to avoid more revolutionary queer threats to traditional relationship structures. This reductive cooptation perspective relies on a theory of resistance that dichotomizes law and grassroots political action. Legal tactics, when part of a plurality of resistances, may reflect queer multiplicity and fluidity. Even if on their face they present arguments that courts will adopt, their strategies may nonetheless seek to prevent a broader subversion of the current heterosexist order.

The liberal/radical dichotomy hides more complex interactions of social change that involve strategic and critical engagement with liberal remedies. Social change movement participants may include actors who play both good cop (i.e., lawyers at a negotiation table) and bad cop (street activists and civil disobedience). This array of techniques may even permit reformist conservatives, such as Log Cabin Republicans, to play a role in social change alongside more radical actors. In fact, queer change may arise from the strangest of bedfellows, including some unwilling participants. Although Sex Panic! and other groups spent years trying to draw attention to the lunacy of much sex regulation, it was Larry Craig's arrest that opened up a broad conversation about the legality and fairness of prosecuting public sex.

The plurality of resistances highlights the cost of accommodationist policies. In retrospect, *Braschi*, for example, reflects the allure of inclusion in social structures, which emphasizes "but-for" queer conformist components of the queer continuum and the risk of creating a second-class queer status. Some marriage equality advocates make similar arguments regarding civil union efforts—that seeking a compromise status (civil unions) may in fact institutionalize a subordinate status.

Queer interventions in sexual and relationship regulation carry great transformative potential to alter legal institutions. Nan Hunter has argued that marriage among lesbian and gay people may effectively drain marriage's remnant patriarchy (Hunter 1991). Once accepted within a legal institution (even one considered repressive by many queers), queer lives may act to vitiate marriage's heteronormativity. Although obtaining marriage through courts may require assimilationist rhetoric (Polikoff 2008), marriage will not look the same once emptied of its binary sexual nature. Queer theorists who conceptualize our communities as universally subversive may be disappointed by the rush to join a conservative institution such as marriage. Litigation cannot provide the complete expansion of rights it appears to promise, but it can reform, empower, and raise awareness: queers can work for change and subversion while being aware of the danger of cooptation by the law.

Conclusion

Although queer studies strives to maintain its subversive mantle, examining queer victories fosters a more self-conscious rapport with the law. This relationship reaches beyond the progressive reliance on litigation as the principal vehicle for change (Fiss 1978; J. Greenberg 1974). The language of Massachusetts's Supreme Judicial Court, "separate is rarely, if ever, equal," demonstrates the extent to which lesbian and gay issues have been incorporated into the civil rights paradigm. Queer scholars presume that such cases exclude queer interests. It is an impulse that I myself followed in "Queer Intersectionality," in 1995. Now we must be prepared to accept that this queer critical positionality may err; *Lawrence, Goodridge, In re Marriage,* and *Kerrigan* do open space for significant advancements in queer lives. Recognizing that, in certain contexts, juridical institutions may actually foster queer interests does not betray queer normativity. Diverse tactics, beyond a litigation-driven model, have triumphed: the 2004 civil disobedience of several mayors across the country led to thousands of same-sex marriages, instantly humanizing the debate. The efficacy of such efforts arose from their audacity and even their extralegality. Queer interests advance in myriad ways as the legal landscape of queer lives arises through a multiplicity of resistances and activisms, whether led by national organizations or by queer individuals desiring legal reform or even (unintentionally) by conservatives caught in the trap of their own obsessive sex regulations. Queer legal activists must be aware of their role at once both inside and outside the law: to reform law and eliminate heterosexist legal norms.

4 Intimate Equality

The Lesbian, Gay, Bisexual, and Transgender Movement's Legal Framing of Sodomy Laws in the *Lawrence v. Texas* Case

Nicholas Pedriana

IN 2003, THE U.S. Supreme Court struck down a Texas statute that criminalized homosexual—but not heterosexual—sodomy (*Lawrence v. Texas* 2003). *Lawrence* signaled that the political majority's disapproval of homosexuality, by itself, could no longer justify statutes that legally denied gays and lesbians the full range of intimate human relationships and experiences available to heterosexuals. The decision was hailed as a major victory for the lesbian, gay, bisexual, and transgender (LGBT) movement and has since been used by the movement to further promote gay and lesbian rights throughout American social life.

To be sure, the *Lawrence* case—like all legal disputes—was argued and resolved by legal experts and officials using the vernacular and tools of formal law, including statutory language, constitutional interpretation, and precedent. Yet, the *Lawrence* case represented far more than resolution of a specific legal dispute between two homosexuals and the state of Texas; it was also a political and discursive forum within which the movement symbolically framed its views on homosexual sodomy laws specifically, and homosexual rights more generally. The amicus brief was the discursive vehicle through which LGBT organizations framed Texas's homosexual sodomy law. (An amicus brief is a Supreme Court document in which groups with interests or expertise bearing on the central legal claims in a particular case but no direct legal stake in the case submit a formal argument on behalf of the petitioner or respondent.)

Content analysis of LGBT amicus briefs in the *Lawrence* case serves broader and interrelated scholarly objectives. First, it can help integrate the social movement literature's foundational concept of the collective action "frame" (see, e.g., Benford 1993; Noakes and Johnston 2005; Snow et al. 1986) with a long tradition of sociolegal scholarship focused on "rights discourse." Sociolegal scholars have emphasized that collective actors routinely discuss and socially construct their grievances, identities, and objectives in terms of legal *rights* (see, e.g., E. A. Andersen 2005; Marshall 2003; McCann 1994; Dudas 2005; Scheingold 2004 [1974]).

Second, analysis of LGBT amicus briefs highlights the Supreme Court as a central "discursive field" (Snow 2004; see also Ferree et al. 2002; Steinberg 1999) where political and cultural debates take place and within which collective symbolic meanings are constructed and mobilized. The Supreme Court—for better or worse—has become a central actor in society's most fundamental political and cultural disputes and has been the final arbiter on the most contested and divisive issues that mobilize collective actors of all stripes, including (but not limited to) affirmative action, abortion, criminal procedure, church and state, the death penalty—and homosexuality. And, for precisely this reason, the Supreme Court has become an increasingly influential carrier of collective action discourse through which activists and social movement organizations articulate and diffuse symbolic frames to achieve political and cultural objectives. Only very recently, however, have framing scholars begun to seriously explore legal institutions and courts as key sites of movement discourse and framing (see, e.g., Andersen 2005; Pedriana 2006; Polletta 2000; Saguy 2003). This chapter seeks in part to build upon and further develop this young but steadily growing literature on law and collective action framing.[1]

Finally, exploring the LGBT movement's legal framing strategies in *Lawrence* can shed substantial light on broader developments within the movement itself, including ongoing internal debates over the movement's central identity, objectives, and tactics. As I elaborate, the two distinct but related constitutional arguments available to the movement in the *Lawrence* case—the substantive right to privacy and the right to equal protection—tapped directly into ongoing disputes about the nature of homosexuality as a social category and therefore how—and whether—the discourse of legal rights could promote future movement development and success (e.g., Bernstein 2002, 2003; Seidman 1997).

Master Frames and Rights Discourse

Collective action frames are tightly bundled symbolic packages defined as "action-oriented sets of beliefs and meanings that inspire and legitimate the activities and campaigns of a social movement organization" (Benford and Snow 2000, 614). Frames consciously represent grievances and interpret events in ways designed to appeal to potential supporters and/or recruits. For this reason, frames typically (but not exclusively) borrow their symbolic content from preexisting "cultural stock" (Noakes and Johnston 2005, 8). Collective action frames are assembled from the raw materials of human discourse—language, symbolism, catch phrases, metaphor, rhetoric, narrative, and so on—and are disseminated throughout society by the carriers and disseminators of public discourse, including social movement organizations, the mass media, and the state.

Some collective action frames have broader scope and influence than others. Framing scholars emphasize the importance of "master frames" that strongly resonate with society's most deeply held values and cultural practices (Benford and Snow 2000; Noakes and Johnston 2005; Pedriana 2006; Snow 2004; Snow and Benford 1992). By tapping into these dominant symbolic packages, social movement organizations can enhance their own legitimacy and influence in ways that expand their cultural resources for subsequent recruitment, mobilization, and action.

Rights Discourse

Especially since the 1960s social movement cycle, framing scholars agree that the "legal rights" frame has frequently served as a master frame for a variety of movements, including the black civil rights, the women's, the disabled, the animal rights, and the gay and lesbian movements (Hull 2001; see also Noakes and Johnston 2005; Oliver and Johnston 2005; Pedriana 2006; Skrentny 2002; Valocchi 1996).

Acknowledging the vast symbolic reach of the legal rights frame dovetails with a long tradition in sociolegal scholarship focused on "rights discourse" that emphasizes the cultural and ideological resonance of law and legal rights in American society (see, e.g., Dudas 2005; McCann 1994; Richman 2005; Scheingold 2004 [1974]). Because rights claims "furnish American politics with its most visible symbols of legitimacy" (Scheingold 2004 [1974], 13), they serve as a "sociopolitical trump card" (Richman 2005, 141) and provide a rhetorical and linguistic blueprint "for asserting moral and legal claims" (quoting Westin 1986).

The symbolic influence of rights discourse is informed in part by law's institutional centrality—as both formal-structural rules and cultural norms—in modern democratic societies (see, e.g., Edelman and Suchman 1997; Stryker 1994). The classic works of Weber and Tocqueville and more recent law and society scholarship have consistently stressed the importance of "legality" as a dominant belief system in which social actors "construct and legitimate social relationships . . . in terms of formally articulated rights and obligations enforceable through the state's coercive apparatus" (Pedriana 2006, 1726; see also Edelman 1992; Marshall 2003; McCann 1994; McIntyre 1994).

The upshot is that the legal rights frame is an encompassing symbolic umbrella that in part constitutes the knowledge, language, and meanings through which collective actors shape their discourse and framing strategies. Rights claims and rights discourse connect society's most cherished values and ideals to legal *entitlements*. Social activists often seek to translate their specific identities and objectives into a formal legal relationship among individuals, social groups, and the state (but see Bernstein 2002). In turn, legal recognition of a group's core interests and identities is a powerful legitimating resource for subsequent mobilization and action. "[The] invocation of rights has come to serve both instrumental and ideological goals. . . . The resonance of rights is particularly potent for populations who have been or continue to be deprived of them" (Richman 2005, 142).

Like all master frames, rights frames sit atop a hierarchy of movement-specific frames (see Benford and Snow 2000; Johnston 2005). Because resonant cultural ideals embedded in legal rights exist at a high level of abstraction, they can be used to construct a wide variety of more specific symbolic packages subsumed under the more general legal rights frame. Pedriana and Stryker (1997), for example, found that both supporters *and* opponents of early affirmative action programs framed their positions around the same master legal principle and discourse of equal opportunity for disadvantaged minorities. The authors concluded that "[There] are values eliciting such widespread agreement at the abstract general level 'that virtually all Americans share them' (quoting Yankelovich 1994). It stands to reason that actors would draw on these values to create more specific rhetorical packages to wage political battle" (640).

Thus, freedom and liberty, property and contract, democracy, due process, equal opportunity, and so on are among the most cherished of American values deeply embedded in, and expressed as, fundamental legal and constitutional rights. And precisely because such values exist at high levels of generality, activists can symbolically mobilize and manipulate rights in numerous and diverse ways consistent with a given movement's specific identities and objectives.

For example, the pro-choice movement is consistently framed around a *woman's* right to privacy and personal autonomy. By contrast, the pro-life movement has invoked the *fetus's* right to life (see Oliver and Johnston 2005). Despite being diametrically opposed movements, each nonetheless draws upon a common symbolic framework centered on legal rights. Similarly, both antitax and antipoverty movements invoke economic rights. For the former, however, economic rights means the right to private property against government confiscation (i.e., taxation), while, for the latter, economic rights are often defined as the right to a job, health benefits, and old-age security. Either way, these more specific frames tailored to different social movements draw on a common cultural "tool kit" (Swidler 1986) of society's most resonant cultural principles expressed as codified legal rights. Thus, exploring how a movement constructs specific frame content out of these more abstract legal concepts is one way to gain deeper theoretical understanding of cultural framing processes generally and how master frames influence those processes in particular.

The Supreme Court as a Discursive Field

The discursive field is a central heuristic in the framing literature that refers to the emergent institutional contexts, or "terrain(s) in which meaning contests occur" (Snow 2004, 402, quoting Spillman 1995, 140–41; see also Steinberg 1995, 1999). Although much of the literature focuses disproportionately on the mass media as the primary institutional location for public discourse on contested social and political issues, most scholars acknowledge that the discursive field also encompasses the religious, political, scientific, academic, and social movement arenas (see, e.g., Ferree et al. 2002) Even so, legal institutions generally—including the Supreme Court—is one such discursive context that has not received much systematic attention in the framing/discourse literature.[2] Yet, as noted, Supreme Court cases have become a pinnacle institutional location in which the most visible and divisive political and cultural battles are fought out in modern U.S. society. For many social movements, including the LGBT movement, winning at the Supreme Court is the holy grail of political battle, and the amicus brief is the discursive mechanism through which collective actors make substantive and symbolic appeals to the Court.

Conceptualizing the Supreme Court as a discursive field is especially appropriate for analyzing how rights discourse operates as a master frame. Rights claims are *legal* claims, and the Supreme Court is the final arbiter on the meaning and boundaries of legal and constitutional rights. Moreover, because amicus briefs allow for direct dialogue between social movement organizations and the Court, activists can use such briefs in a specific legal dispute as a vehicle to discuss and represent the movement's broader identities and objectives in highly resonant cultural terms embedded in officially codified rights.[3]

Legal and Historical Background:
Privacy, Equality, and the LGBT Movement

Repeal of sodomy laws had been a movement objective from its origins in the 1960s "both because they are considered the legal cornerstone that justifies discriminatory treatment of lesbians and gay men . . . and because of the cultural message they embody" (Bernstein 2003, p. 354). From the 1960s to the late 1970s, a wave of states began repealing their sodomy laws, even though the LGBT movement was generally unorganized during this period and, for a number of reasons, did not "for the most part . . . target the state on this issue" (360). Much of the early impetus for repeal at the state level came from the legal community itself. The American Law Institute's 1955 Model Penal Code advocated decriminalization of victimless, private sexual behavior, including homosexual sex (Backer 1993; Bernstein 2003).

By the early 1980s, LGBT lawyers and activists had begun to challenge more aggressively sodomy statutes in state and federal court. Organizations such as the Lambda Legal Defense and Education Fund, the National Gay and Lesbian Task Force (NGLTF), and the American Civil Liberties Union(ACLU) successfully challenged sodomy laws in key states, including Pennsylvania and New York (Andersen 2005; Bernstein 2003). Building on these legal victories, the movement looked to build promising cases for a possible Supreme Court challenge in the hope of invalidating all remaining state sodomy laws.

Whatever the venue, legal challenges to sodomy statutes generally rested upon two primary constitutional claims: the right to *privacy* and the right to *equal protection.*

Appreciating the formal legal distinctions between each constitutional claim is crucial for analyzing how the LGBT movement culturally framed Texas's same-sex sodomy law in *Lawrence*. Rights to privacy and equal protection tap into widespread but distinct cultural values. Indeed, both privacy and equal protection are master legal concepts with strong cultural resonance in American society, but for different reasons. Privacy assumes individual freedom and liberty from government snooping, a cornerstone of American political culture, especially when it involves people's homes and bedrooms. Equal protection legally expresses society's ironclad belief in fairness and equal opportunity for individual achievement, regardless of irrelevant—and often immutable—group characteristics. Either way, the fusion of fundamental cultural value and fundamental legal entitlement renders both privacy and equality master legal frames. By tapping into and drumbeating these highly resonant American cultural and legal symbols, the LGBT movement has sought (at least in part) to align itself with two of U.S. society's core principles and values embedded and officially codified in law. The following sections briefly summarize the legal and historical context of sodomy law challenges leading up to *Lawrence*.

The Right to Privacy

In 1965, the Supreme Court recognized an implicit right to privacy located in the substantive component of the Fourteenth Amendment's due process clause. Such privacy rights were envisioned as protecting key decisions in the individual's personal or intimate life from government interference, including the right to use contraception (*Griswold v. Connecticut* 1965; *Eisenstadt v. Baird* 1972), the right of a woman to terminate a pregnancy prior to fetus viability (*Roe v. Wade* 1973; *Planned Parenthood v. Casey* 1992), the right to marry someone of a different race

(*Loving v. Virginia* 1967), and the right to refuse life-saving medical treatment (*Cruzan v. Missouri Dept. of Health* 1990). In their attempts to repeal sodomy statutes, LGBT lawyers consistently argued that this list should include a basic right to sexual privacy between consenting adults.

Movement attorneys took this argument to the Supreme Court in the landmark 1986 case *Bowers v. Hardwick*. The case involved a gay man who challenged Georgia's general prohibition of sodomy (i.e., it prohibited all sodomy, regardless of sexual orientation). *Hardwick* argued that, under the due process clause, all consenting adults, regardless of sexual orientation, had a fundamental right to sexual privacy, which encompassed homosexual behavior. The Supreme Court, however, redefined and narrowed the central legal question in *Bowers* as whether there was a fundamental constitutional right to engage in homosexual sodomy. The Court ruled that the constitutional right to privacy did not include the right to have homosexual sex. The majority further reasoned that society's moral disapproval of homosexuality was a constitutionally permissible reason to prohibit same-sex sexual behavior. *Bowers* was a monumental defeat for the LGBT movement and seemed to close off privacy claims—at least at the Supreme Court—in future sodomy law challenges.[4]

Equal Protection

The equal protection clause targets government *classifications*. If the state chooses to differentiate people on the basis of certain characteristics (e.g., sexual orientation) and then subjects those people to different legal benefits or burdens, it must have a constitutionally legitimate reason for doing so, and the policy must bear a rational relationship to the government's stated objective. Notwithstanding the Supreme Court's privacy ruling in *Bowers*, LGBT organizations have repeatedly challenged the assertion that the political majority's moral disapproval of homosexuality, by itself, is a constitutionally acceptable reason for the state to legally set homosexuals apart from heterosexuals.

This claim was tested ten years after *Bowers*, when the Supreme Court handed down another landmark ruling in a case dealing with homosexuality. *Romer v. Evans* (1996) confronted state action that singled out homosexuals for legal disability and thus triggered an equal protection challenge. The case, however, was not about sodomy. The issue in *Romer* involved a recent amendment to the Colorado constitution that prohibited any political subdivision in the state from enacting legislation protecting homosexuals from discriminatory treatment. The Supreme Court struck down Colorado's amendment, arguing that the state impermissibly singled out one class of people—homosexuals—and subjected them to legal burdens to which no other group in the state was subject. The majority noted that Colorado's justification for the amendment appeared to be nothing more than animus towards all homosexuals and a generalized belief that gays and lesbians as an entire class were immoral. Neither reason passed constitutional muster:

> If the constitutional conception of "equal protection of the laws" means anything, it must at the very least mean that a bare . . . desire to harm a politically unpopular group cannot constitute a *legitimate* governmental interest. (*Romer v. Evans* 1996, 634, quoting *U.S. Department of Agriculture v. Moreno* 1973, 534, emphasis in original)

Bowers and *Romer* thus set the stage for *Lawrence*, a case that involved a state sodomy law that applied only to homosexuals and therefore invoked both privacy and equal protection issues. In his formal petitioner's brief to the Supreme Court (not to be confused with an amicus brief), Lawrence argued that Texas's homosexual conduct law violated both the right to privacy and the right to equal protection. Nonetheless, the evidence suggests that LGBT lawyers and activists generally agreed that, of the two constitutional avenues, the equal protection claim was the more fundamental and promising (see Andersen 2005, 125–34). To a great extent, this was a strategic decision. The privacy route would inevitably run smack into the *Bowers* precedent, which was only seventeen years old, quite young by Supreme Court standards. Many thought it unlikely that the current makeup of a generally conservative court would vote to overturn *Bowers*. By contrast, six justices, including the swing voters Kennedy and O'Connor, voted with the majority in *Romer*, which struck down an antihomosexual law on equal protection grounds. In any event, LGBT activists and lawyers decided to formally include the privacy claim, and, if it failed or the Court refused to reconsider the issue in light of *Bowers*, the equal protection claim would still remain intact.

From a framing and discursive standpoint, however, the movement focused exclusively around equal protection and the equality master frame. Its amicus briefs, representing nearly fifty LGBT organizations, make no mention at all of the case's privacy dimensions, and there is no discussion of *Bowers*. Accordingly, my content analysis of the movement's cultural framing strategies embedded in the briefs likewise revolve around the equality master frame. Here, however, a brief word of interpretive caution is in order.

Private Regulation, Public Consequences: Linking Privacy and Equality

The preceding discussion may give the impression that LGBT activists understood the denial of sexual privacy and the denial of equal protection as inherently distinct issues warranting separate legal and cultural framing strategies. It may even appear that activists saw privacy and equality as competing cultural frames, an argument made somewhat plausible by the movement's exclusive equality emphasis in its amicus briefs. Without speculating as to why the amicus briefs in *Lawrence* make no explicit mention of the case's privacy dimensions, I caution against such an interpretation. The movement's thirty-year effort to repeal sodomy statutes—in and out of court—makes clear that LGBT activists always understood that the denial of homosexual *privacy* had serious *public* consequences for lesbian and gays' social rights and economic opportunities, and thus the right to sexual privacy and the right to equal protection were inextricably linked. In fact, this connection between the private and the public was an ongoing source of internal contention within the movement (e.g., Backer 1993; Bernstein 2003; Halley 1998; Seidman 1997).

Sodomy statute repeal tapped into disagreements within the movement between those who favored incremental legal and political changes for homosexuals as a group on the one hand and those with "ideological opposition to political reformism and a commitment to challenging dominant categories of sexuality" on the other (Bernstein 2003, 361; see also Seidman 1997). Short-term political or legal "victories" culturally reinforced—and legally codified—society's widespread perception that homosexuals are inherently different from everyone else, leading to a movement permanently, but unwisely, ensconced in "identity politics" (see also Bernstein 2002; Halley 1998). The repeal of sodomy laws (whether legislatively or judicially) was seen by some as a Faustian bargain; it encouraged states to decriminalize sodomy on *privacy* grounds while still morally condemning—and prosecuting—homosexual behavior in *public* through police stings and continued enforcement of solicitation laws. For these critics, such "liberal toleration" of private homosexual behavior meant that "sexual nonconformists . . . are tolerated in American society and under American law only if they keep their identities submerged and participate in their own public obliteration" (Backer 1993, 756). Simply put, the privacy strategy could never generate a broader societal acceptance of homosexuality upon which true equality for lesbians, gays, and other sexual nonconformists inherently rested.

But, if some skeptics saw the privacy emphasis—by failing to openly challenge taken-for-granted sexual categories and identities—as a way to reinforce the "heteronormative" order, others saw privacy claims as a vehicle to address the concrete, material, and public consequences of sodomy statutes on lesbians' and gays' unequal social and economic opportunities. States that continued to criminalize homosexual sex—by definition—legally classified all homosexuals as criminal deviants and therefore justified discrimination against gays and lesbians throughout the public domain, including in the workplace, in parental custody disputes, in accessing health care and housing, and so on. If, however, the courts were to require all states to decriminalize private, consensual sodomy, it might be much more difficult for states to legally legitimate overt discrimination against homosexuals in other areas of public life. In this way, the twin goals of privacy and equality became virtually inseparable. Thus, the right to privacy was initially, and would always remain, a dominant theme in attempts to repeal sodomy laws right up to *Lawrence*. Still, the clear public and material consequences that resulted from sodomy laws—and that negatively impacted all homosexuals—increasingly .pushed the LGBT movement to combine equal protection and privacy claims in sodomy law challenges (see Andersen 2005). In so doing, the movement seemed to steadily embrace the construction of sexual orientation as a distinct political and legal identity. In this chapter's concluding sections, I revisit this issue by considering how *Lawrence*'s impact on the private-public relationship (in the context of sodomy statutes) has solidified the LGBT movement's pursuit of a legally recognized sexual orientation identity entitled to equal rights and opportunities in all areas of social life.

Content Analysis of LGBT Amicus Briefs

Three major LGBT organizations, collectively representing nearly fifty separate activist groups, submitted amicus briefs on behalf of Lawrence: the Human Rights Campaign (HRC), the Stonewall Bar Association,[5] and the National Lesbian and Gay Law Association (NLGLA) (see Figure 4.1 for a list of all participating LGBT groups).

Brief of the Human Rights Campaign et al.

Building on Lawrence's core equal protection claim, the HRC's brief (2003) framed the essence of Texas's same-sex sodomy law in terms of legal and social equality:

> Texas' Homosexual Conduct Law violates ... equal protection ... because its solitary purpose is constitutionally illegitimate and irrational: to punish and brand as criminals a class of citizens defined by their emotional and physical attraction to members of the same sex as themselves. ... By singling out [homosexual sodomy] for criminalization ... Texas legally defines the emotional and sexual identity of a substantial segment of our society as criminally deviant, branding the entire class not only as inferior, but as a danger to the community that must be deterred, punished, and excluded. (2–3)

As noted, master frames generally—and legal rights frames specifically—are hierarchical; resonant cultural values (e.g., "equality") embedded in legal rights exist at a high level of abstraction that can encompass and accommodate a variety of subframes closely tailored to a given movement's identities and goals. HRC's comprehensive amicus brief articulated five specific symbolic packages subsumed under the equality master rights frame: (1) history and tradition; (2) animus and discrimination; (3) health and safety; (4) humanity and normality; and (5) societal norms and attitudes.[6] Each symbolic package, in distinct but interrelated ways, clustered around the core principles of equal opportunity and equal treatment under law.

HISTORY AND TRADITION

HRC's first symbolic package considered historical traditions involving state regulation of sexual behavior. It challenged Texas's argument that the state's homosexual sodomy law was rooted in long-standing moral traditions and practices that historically condemned homosexual behavior:

> Texas' law is not a product of general anti-sodomy ecclesiastical traditions—which broadly condemned non-procreative sexual acts in which anyone might engage— but of a uniquely 20th century effort to root out gay people and alienate them from the community. (3)

The brief cited historical evidence and current practices to show that targeting homosexual conduct for criminal sanctions lacked ancient roots in American society; neither was it a common practice "woven from the fabric" of current American society (4). For most of U.S. history, state regulation of sexual conduct made no legal distinctions between homosexuals and heterosexuals, and it was not until the late 1960s that some states explicitly targeted homosexual conduct. The brief noted that the very concept of homosexuality as a recognized category of sexual identity did not exist until the late nineteenth century. While official condemnation of "immoral" sexual practices did indeed have a long pedigree in English and American common law, those laws universally targeted *all* nonprocreative sexual behavior "regardless of whether they were engaged in by same-sex or different-sex couples" (5). Moreover, of the thirteen states that (in 2003) still had sodomy laws on their books, just four targeted same-sex couples. And, finally, Texas itself had no long-standing tradition of prohibiting same-sex conduct; its homosexual sodomy law was not enacted until 1973. Thus, from the standpoint of history, state laws prohibiting deviant or immoral sexual behavior had traditionally made no distinction between homosexuals and heterosexuals. Only recently, and for invidious reasons, did some states set homosexual conduct apart for criminal sanction.

Although it was presented after the history and tradition package, "animus and discrimination" was HRC's most direct and passionate symbolic variation on the equality master frame. To the extent that history and tradition played a role in Texas's homosexual sodomy law, it was a history and tradition of hatred and discrimination toward gays and lesbians. HRC submitted that Texas's same-sex sodomy law was simply an expression of the state's true motives: animosity toward all homosexuals and the desire to deny gays and lesbians the full range of opportunities and life chances available to everyone else. "[Texas's Homosexual Conduct Law] . . . is backed by a tradition . . . of animus, ignorance, and stereotype, and it builds upon that tradition by branding all gay people as criminal deviants, worthy only of contempt and censure rather than basic respect and equal treatment" (1).

HRC's primary concern went far beyond Texas's exceedingly rare prosecutions for violations of its homosexual conduct law.[7] The law's very existence officially branded and stigmatized all homosexuals as criminal deviants in ways that legitimated discrimination against gays and lesbians and subjected them to significant social harms and legal disabilities.

> In states like Texas, to be gay is to be a criminal . . . with or without prosecution, that classification by itself brings severe and far-reaching consequences for gay men lesbians [10] . . . . The criminality of same-sex sodomy in Texas has been invoked by those seeking to close the public library to gay groups, deny permanent residence to gay immigrants, prohibit gay men and lesbians from fostering or adopting children, ban gay and lesbian student groups on college campuses, oppose protection of gay people from discrimination in employment, and deny gay and lesbian Texans protection under proposed hate crime laws. (12)

In short, Texas's law was nothing more than a tool designed to make homosexuals as a group _legally unequal_ to heterosexuals and, accordingly, to promote and justify discrimination against them in all areas of social life.

HEALTH AND SAFETY

HRC's brief emphasized that Texas's law denied gays and lesbians equal access to valued social resources and opportunities involving jobs, housing, education, and parenthood. The official branding of homosexuals through legal stigmatization also had enormous implications for individual gays' and lesbians' psychological health and, indeed, even their physical safety. On the issue of emotional health, the brief summarized:

> One of the most powerful effects of Texas' law, and laws like it, is on the mental and emotional well-being of those in the condemned class. . . . Some gay people

internalize the message that they are inferior, resulting in self-loathing and associated emotional dysfunctions.... Sodomy laws inhibit gay people from "coming out" to friends and family, an act critical to the emotional health of many gay people. (10–11)

To be sure, not all homosexuals suffered psychological harm as a result of Texas's sodomy law. Nonetheless, the brief continued, all gays and lesbians were in greater physical danger because Texas's law "contributes to an atmosphere of hatred and violence that puts gay people, and those perceived to be gay, at risk" (14). The brief cited statistics showing that hate crimes in Texas were more likely to target homosexuals than any other group. Moreover, legal stigma also deterred victims of hate crimes "from reporting those crimes to the police, leading to a lower risk of arrest and still more bias-motivated violence" (15).

Thus, the inequalities homosexuals suffered on account of Texas's sodomy law went beyond social, economic, and political resources. Gays and lesbians were also subject to harms involving their emotional stability, their psychological health, and their very physical safety.

HUMANITY AND NORMALITY

HRC's fourth symbolic package expressed the essential humanity and normality of homosexuals. The brief stressed that gays and lesbians are not a deviant subculture subsisting at the margins of society and thus warranting discriminatory treatment. Homosexuals, rather, are productive, typical people who work in jobs and occupations throughout the labor market and "who live in towns and cities ... who live with long-term domestic partners in committed relationships, who raise children, who serve their country in the military and in the government" (p. 16). The brief cited census data suggesting that same-sex couples resided in more than 99 percent of all U.S. counties (and in 252 of 255 Texas counties). It estimated that "as many as 60 percent of all gay people live as couples, compared to approximately 57 percent for the overall adult population" (18). In addition, studies suggested "approximately 28 percent of lesbians and 14 percent of gay men are raising children in their households ... [children who are] as emotionally well adjusted as children raised in heterosexual households" (18). And, finally, the brief argued that "gays and lesbians serve their country in both civilian and military capacities," noting that openly gay individuals worked in key government posts and were about as likely as heterosexuals to have had some military experience.

Thus, with the exception of being sexually attracted to members of the same sex, homosexuals were essentially no different from heterosexuals. Gays and lesbians held diverse jobs, valued committed relationships, built strong families, and contributed equally to American civil and military life. Texas's attempt to brand them as a monolithic group of social misfits ignored this fundamental reality about the essential humanity and normality of gays and lesbians.

SOCIAL ATTITUDES AND NORMS

HRC's final symbolic package focused on current societal norms and attitudes, which were increasingly tolerant of homosexuals, and the steady expansion of equal opportunities for gays and lesbians throughout American public and private life. Suggesting that "homosexual sodomy laws—not gay people—are the real social and legal deviants," the brief argued that such laws "have become the last gasp of a few recalcitrant jurisdictions, as the larger society has repudiated not only the condemnation [of homosexuals] but also many of its vestiges" (20–21). In the previous twenty years, the number of states with any sodomy laws had plummeted from twenty-four to thirteen, and, as noted, just four continued to single out homosexual sodomy. Expanding equality in employment opportunities was also apparent. In the preceding twenty years, the nation went from having one state that prohibited private employers from discriminating on the basis of sexual orientation to having thirteen such states; twenty-two states banned such discrimination in state employment; and President George W. Bush had let stand a 1998 executive order prohibiting sexual orientation discrimination in executive branch employment. Moreover, in the mid-1980s, no states provided domestic-partner health benefits; by 2003 there were nine states that did so and "at least 129 cities, counties, and quasi-governmental agencies . . . provide domestic partner benefits for their employees" (23). The private sector had become especially responsive on this issue. As of 2002, "more than 30 percent of Fortune 500 and over half of Fortune 50 companies offered domestic-partner health insurance" (26–27).

The role of hate-crimes legislation was also instructive. Between the mid-1980s and the early 2000s, twenty-eight states included sexual orientation in their hate-crime laws; Congress in 1990 required that the federal government gather hate-crime statistics that included crimes against gays and lesbians and instructed the U.S. Sentencing Commission to enhance punishments for crimes "motivated by 'the actual or perceived . . . sexual orientation of any person'" (24, quoting 28 U.S.C. 534).

Laws regulating family relationships were also moving in the direction of greater equality for homosexuals. In 2003, forty-nine of fifty states (Florida was the exception) allowed gays and lesbians to adopt children; half of the states allowed "second-parent adoptions" for gay and lesbian couples jointly raising children; and "a majority of states have now abandoned *per se* rules against gay parents in post-divorce custody disputes" (26).

Each of these changes in American public and private life was, according to the brief, accompanied by a "dramatic shift in social attitudes" (27). Citing various poll data, HRC wrote that majorities (often large majorities) felt that there should be no discrimination against homosexuals in their private sexual practices, in employment opportunities, or in adoption laws, and nearly two-thirds of respondents supported nondiscrimination laws on the basis of sexual orientation.

And, finally, the societal norms and attitudes package pointed out that acceptance and tolerance toward homosexuality could be seen further in two traditionally hostile social institutions; religion and popular entertainment. A growing number of official church doctrines accepted homosexuality and "affirm full and equal civil rights for gay people. Many formally condemn discrimination on the basis of sexual orientation and even call for legal protections against such discrimination" (28). As for popular entertainment, the brief concluded:

> Today ... [television] programs regularly feature gay characters and themes. Popular movies, too, now regularly include accurate and positive depictions of gay characters and relationships—a rarity just a decade ago. And companies no longer fear including gay themes in their "mainstream" advertising. (29)

In sum, the HRC's amicus brief in the *Lawrence* case constructed and mobilized several symbolic frames to challenge Texas's homosexual sodomy law. And, while each package contained distinct symbolic content, all five were clustered around the discourse of "equality," a master legal frame with far-reaching cultural resonance throughout American society. Thus, HRC could argue that history and tradition had not in fact singled out homosexual sodomy for criminal sanctions; that Texas's law represented nothing more than a generalized animus toward all homosexuals that encouraged and legitimated discrimination against gays and lesbians in all areas of social life; that Texas's legal stigmatization of homosexuals subjected gays and lesbians to greater risk of psychological distress and hate-motivated violence; that homosexuals were normal, productive human beings who valued committed relationships and strong families and who contributed extensively to American economic, political, and military life; and, finally, that current societal norms and attitudes showed steady movement toward acceptance of gays and lesbians, as well as increasing support for antidiscrimination laws guaranteeing homosexuals equal treatment under law and equal opportunity throughout society.

Brief of the NLGLA

The National Lesbian and Gay Lawyers Association (2003) wrote the other amicus brief on behalf of the LGBT movement. NLGLA's brief put forth one central argument: that it should be more difficult, not less, for the state to classify people on the basis of sexual orientation. This argument was framed largely in legal-doctrinal terms based on past and current equal protection jurisprudence.

Government classifications on the basis of sexual orientation were currently subject to the most relaxed standard of review, known as "minimum" constitutional scrutiny.[8] And, although NLGLA believed that Texas's law could not survive even that level of review, the brief nonetheless submitted that the Court should constitutionally elevate sexual orientation to a classification requiring a higher level of judicial scrutiny:

> Under this Court's decisions, legislative actions that classify persons on the basis
> of a characteristic warrant heightened scrutiny if they meet two essential criteria:
> 1) the characteristic is unrelated to ability, and 2) the group disfavored by the
> classification has experienced a history of intentional discrimination.... Because
> sexual orientation satisfies these criteria, governmental actions that classify on the
> basis of sexual orientation should be subjected to heightened scrutiny. (4)

On the one hand, unlike HRC's brief, this was partly a technical legal argument and drew predominately on legal sources to challenge Texas's homosexual sodomy law.[9] On the other hand, NLGLA's brief was similar to that of HRC in that it was framed fundamentally around the master legal principle of equality. In articulating its explicit legal argument, NLGLA made explicit reference to four of the five symbolic constructions of equality offered by HRC: normality, history and tradition, animus and discrimination, and health and safety.

NLGLA's brief, citing a list of the Supreme Court equal protection rulings, attempted to put homosexuality on par with other classifications subject to greater judicial scrutiny, including race, gender, national origin, alienage, and illegitimacy. NLGLA wrote that, like these characteristics, homosexuality was unrelated to one's general abilities in life, and thus there was simply no constitutional justification for governments to subject gays and lesbians to legal and social disabilities not imposed on heterosexuals. In making this claim, NLGLA tapped into the "normality" symbolic package discussed earlier:

> The simple fact is that gay men [and] lesbians ... demonstrate the same range
> of abilities as do heterosexual people: some are intellectually gifted, while others
> are not; some are strong while others are not; some are mentally or physically
> disabled, but most are not. The constant factor is that the individual's *sexual
> orientation* is not the determinative element in any of these abilities. (15, emphasis
> in original)

Thus, ability was not the issue. Rather, homosexual classifications were the product of prejudice and discrimination. The brief then elaborated on the animus and discrimination package by claiming a "history of purposeful and invidious discrimination" against homosexuals that "demand[s] heightened vigilance by the courts" (16–17). Mobilizing evidence similar to that found in HRC's brief, NLGLA briefly chronicled widespread societal and governmental discrimination throughout the twentieth century targeted at gays and lesbians. Government-endorsed discrimination likewise restricted gays' and lesbians' ability to "get and keep a job, obtain housing, maintain custody of one's children . . . or—as demonstrated here—be free from arrest" (20).

The brief also mobilized the health and safety symbolic package. It pointed out the psychological harms suffered by homosexuals, especially the pressure to hide their sexual orientation. "This socially imposed pressure to 'pass' is itself a form of discrimination. Constantly keeping secret an important part of one's identity can create shame, increase shame, and undermine physical as well as mental health" (19). NLGLA further implicated antigay sentiment in heightened risk of hate-motivated violence. "Prejudice against gay people continues to take the form of vitriolic hate crimes often marked by unusual viciousness and brutality" (20).

In short, NLGLA's brief was organized around a formal-legal argument that looked primarily to legal sources and to the Supreme Court's own equal protection doctrines. Even so, NLGLA elaborated those legal arguments in large part by mobilizing several of the same symbolic constructions of equality put forth by HRC's brief. Having argued that homosexuals were normal human beings with abilities similar to those of heterosexuals, NLGLA concluded that homosexuals were—historically and currently—the victims of prejudice and discrimination that restricted their life chances throughout society, subjected them to emotional and psychological distress, and threatened gays' and lesbians' physical safety. And this brought NLGLA's brief back full circle to its original constitutional argument:

> The nature and persistence of discrimination against gay men and lesbians distinguish it from other governmental classifications. Indeed, the noteworthy characteristics of antigay discrimination . . . are signposts of invidious discrimination, and are shared by other forms of discrimination accorded heightened scrutiny under the Equal Protection Clause. (22)

The Lawrence Ruling

In a 6-3 opinion written by Justice Kennedy, the Supreme Court struck down Texas's homosexual sodomy law. In a twist of irony, however, the majority's ruling was *not* predicated on the equal protection claim universally promoted by the LGBT movement. Rather, the Court concluded that sexual privacy among consenting adults, including homosexuals, was a fundamental liberty right guaranteed by the substantive component of the Fourteenth Amendment's due process clause.[10] Thus, while the ruling was a tremendous victory for the movement—*Lawrence* also explicitly overturned *Bowers*—the reasoning behind the opinion was arguably not as tightly aligned with the movement's core symbolic representation of the case as an issue of social and legal *equality*. The majority ruling did not speak directly to whether sexual orientation classifications that did *not* involve fundamental privacy rights were also unconstitutional. For example, *Lawrence* gave no definitive answer on whether states could retain sexual orientation classifications in the areas of employment, child custody cases, adoption, access to public resources, and so on.

Even so, the majority opinion's privacy focus revealed a strong undertone of concern for homosexual equality. Consistent with activists' long-standing grievance, the Court's majority explicitly acknowledged that prohibition of *private* sexual behavior had negative *public* consequences for all homosexuals. In fact, several key sections of the opinion were closely aligned with LGBT organizations' own symbolic constructions of the equality master frame, including the history-and-tradition, animus-and-discrimination, and evolving-societal-norms symbolic packages. For example, in its discussion of the history of same-sex sodomy laws, the Court concluded:

> there is no longstanding history in this country of laws directed at homosexual conduct as a distinct matter. Early American sodomy laws were not directed at homosexuals as such but instead sought to prohibit non-procreative sexual activity more generally, whether between men and women or men and men. . . . Far from possessing "ancient roots," . . . American laws targeting same-sex couples did not develop until the last third of the 20th century. (568)

The Court also, like LGBT's amicus briefs, considered how Texas's legal branding of homosexuals legitimated discrimination against gays and lesbians throughout social life:

> When homosexual conduct is made criminal by the law of the State, that declaration in and of itself is an invitation to subject homosexual persons to discrimination both in the public and in the private spheres. . . . The stigma this criminal statute imposes, moreover, is not trivial . . . it remains a criminal offense with all that imports for the dignity of the persons charged. The petitioners will bear on their record the history of their criminal convictions. (575)

And, finally, the Court stated that sodomy laws, whatever their ancient origins or rationales, were steadily passing into the history books of civilized societies, thus indicating an ongoing shift in societal attitudes and norms regarding sodomy and homosexuality. As evidence, the Court first cited trends in the states. Whereas all fifty states in 1960 had sodomy laws, by 2003 that number had dwindled to thirteen, just four of which criminalized homosexual sodomy specifically. And even those states that retained sodomy laws virtually never enforced them against consenting adults in private. Such arguments closely resembled the movement's claim that a growing number of social institutions, both public and private, were steadily moving in the direction of expanded rights and equality for homosexuals.

The Court then took the evolving-norms argument one step further. By 2003, sodomy laws were an outlier not only in the United States but throughout Western civilization. Kennedy noted that Great Britain in 1967 repealed its laws punishing homosexual conduct; the European Court of Human Rights in a 1981 case had also invalidated homosexual conduct laws, a ruling that by 2003 was binding on forty-five countries:

> Other nations . . . have taken action consistent with an affirmation of the protected right of homosexual adults to engage in intimate, consensual conduct. . . . The right the petitioners seek in this case has been accepted as an integral part of human freedom in many other countries. (576–77)

In short, although the *Lawrence* ruling was doctrinally based on the substantive right to privacy, it recognized the close connection between the regulation of homosexuals' private lives and their access to equal opportunities in public life. And it did so with language and reasoning that closely mirrored the LGBT movement's own symbolic constructions of the equality master frame. Of course, whether and to what extent the *Lawrence* ruling will encourage states to revisit and/or repeal other laws that discriminate on the basis of sexual orientation, further expanding gays and lesbians' equal opportunities, remains to be seen. What does seem clear, however, is that this landmark legal ruling has nourished the movement's steady (yet contested) evolution toward an identity-based struggle rooted in legal, political, and cultural recognition of homosexuals as a class of people entitled to the same rights and opportunities guaranteed to the heterosexual majority. I elaborate on this argument in the closing sections of my discussion.

Discussion

This chapter has explored, through content analysis of Supreme Court amicus briefs, how the LGBT movement symbolically framed Texas's homosexual sodomy law in the watershed *Lawrence v. Texas* case. I used this case to illustrate and further develop a law-centered analytic framework on two bedrock concepts in social movement theory: master rights frames and discursive fields.

Mobilizing master frames is a powerful social movement tool because master frames invoke society's most cherished principles and practices. When such frames are also tightly aligned with officially recognized legal rights and entitlements, they can have a powerful legitimating effect on a social movement's grievances and objectives. As I have argued throughout this essay, *equality* is one such master rights frame that has consistently informed and motivated the LGBT movement. And, because Texas's sodomy law singled out homosexuals for criminal sanctions, it presented an opportunity to invoke the equality master frame to represent the movement's broader identity and interests that went well beyond the right to engage in sodomy.

From a symbolic standpoint, however, Texas's homosexual sodomy law did have major consequences for the lives of homosexuals beyond technical criminalization of sexual intimacy. By criminalizing homosexual sodomy, the law went to the very heart of what defines homosexuals as a class: sexual attraction to members of the same sex. In so doing, the state of Texas stigmatized and showed animus toward all homosexuals as immoral, sexual deviants, legitimating discrimination against them throughout social, economic, and political life and further threatening their psychological health and even their physical safety. Moreover, homosexual sodomy laws were rooted neither in American history nor American tradition, and a growing proportion of social attitudes and practices were steadily moving in the direction of greater tolerance for homosexuals in all areas of social life. Each of these claims was expressed as clustered but distinct symbolic packages subsumed under the equality master frame.

All this illuminated a key conceptual feature of master rights frames: they are encompassing and malleable symbolic principles that can accommodate a wide variety of subframes that can be tailored to a social movement's specific identities and aspirations. Now that the LGBT movement has won the legal battle over sodomy laws, scholars have already begun to consider *Lawrence*'s consequences for other discriminatory policies that classify people on the basis of sexual orientation, including the explosive issue of same-sex marriage (see Andersen 2005; Hull 2006). The findings of this chapter suggest that future research should pay close attention to how LGBT activists remobilize and reconstruct the equality master frame in these new legal settings and in light of *Lawrence*.

This chapter also demonstrated that the Supreme Court is an essential discursive field in which master rights frames are constructed and mobilized. The movement's most active and vocal organizations used the amicus brief as the discursive vehicle through which they spoke directly to the Court and framed their broader grievances and objectives around the equality master frame codified in the Fourteenth Amendment's equal protection clause. For both legal and cultural reasons, Supreme Court decisions have a power and resonance that greatly influence how and with what success LGBT activists will frame other homosexual rights issues in and out of court. Indeed, the Supreme Court's ruling in *Lawrence* did not merely settle a specific legal dispute between two homosexuals and the state of Texas; by incorporating much of the LGBT movement's own discourse, language, and narrative on homosexuals' right to equal treatment *under law*, the Court to a significant extent *legitimated*, in formal legal terms, the movement's fundamental cause of homosexual equality throughout social life. It is difficult to imagine a more powerful resource for the movement's future objectives and strategies than a precedent-setting Supreme Court ruling that legally *and* symbolically endorsed its bedrock claim to equal treatment. And the LGBT movement has, and will surely continue, to mobilize *Lawrence's* legal and cultural discourse not only in the courts but in the media, meeting halls, legislative chambers, religious institutions, scientific forums, and so on. For all these reasons, treating the Supreme Court as a central discursive field is a powerful conceptual tool for understanding the strategies, opportunities, and constraints facing the LGBT movement as they mobilize master legal frames both in and out of court.

Some Final Thoughts on Lawrence and the LGBT Movement

Attempting to draw broader conclusions about how *Lawrence* has impacted the LGBT movement and homosexual rights more generally requires significant caution. *Lawrence* is but one (albeit monumental) event in the movement's decades-long struggle to eliminate the stigma that attaches to homosexuality and to end overt discrimination (both governmental and private) against gays and lesbians. The vast majority of that struggle has, and will continue to be, fought outside formal legal settings. And, although it is still unclear whether and to what extent the *Lawrence* decision will translate directly into substantive equality gains in a wide variety of social and economic institutions, I consider some careful speculations about *Lawrence's* implications for the movement more generally.

First, legal victories post-*Bowers*, first in many state courts and, eventually, in the Supreme Court, may partly challenge those skeptics who question the wisdom of using institutionalized political and legal channels to achieve social change. Some would likely claim that "victories" such as *Lawrence* can actually serve as pretexts for the continued stigmatization and marginalization of all sexual nonconformists, thereby reproducing an exclusionary heteronormative cultural order.

For example, Larry Cata Backer's (1993) essay strongly criticized the mobilization of privacy claims against sodomy laws on grounds that official recognition of homosexual privacy rights was a cynical strategy designed to keep homosexuals hidden and isolated from public life. Yet, the LGBT movement's participation and strategies in *Lawrence* seem, at least in part, to challenge such pessimistic views. Both its amicus briefs and the *Lawrence* opinion itself directly acknowledged the negative public consequences that resulted from discrimination against homosexuals in their private sexual lives. It is difficult to see how the Court's ruling about the right to sexual privacy can be interpreted as a ploy to justify animus and discrimination against homosexuals in public life. On the contrary, the movement's amicus briefs argued, and the Court apparently agreed, that repeal of homosexual sodomy laws was one central element in breaking down formal barriers to gays' and lesbians' social and economic opportunities in public life.

Moreover, while "heteronormative" may indeed be an accurate description of current American society, the trends in societal attitudes and norms cited by the movement and repeated by the Court suggested a steadily growing acceptance of homosexuality and homosexual rights among the public at large. One could thus reasonably speculate that the heterosexual majority has begun to find at least some room in public and civic life for gays, lesbians, and other sexual nonconformists.

All this leads to some final thoughts about the LGBT movement and its pursuit of "identity" politics (see Bernstein 2002). Whether sexual orientation should be constructed as a discrete and insular group identity has been a longstanding debate within the movement (e.g., Halley 1998). Activists and scholars have argued that sexual orientation cannot and should not be sorted into distinct groups but rather exists along a continuum of individual sexual identities and preferences. Attempts to institutionalize homosexuality as legal and political classifications can reinforce the notion that gays and lesbians are inherently "different" from the rest of the population (see generally Seidman 1997).

Yet, if the movement's actions in the *Lawrence* case are any indication at all, activists who favor (at least in part) the pursuit of identity politics appear to have the upper hand. The sheer amount of resources expended on the case is revealing. The largest and most influential LGBT organizations were front and center in the case. But, perhaps even more revealing (as evidenced by their arguments in the amicus briefs) was the constant drumbeating of the equal protection dimension of the case. Equal protection claims, by their very nature, assume group classifications and demand that the group at bar be acknowledged and treated the same as everyone else. Such claims cannot be easily made in the absence of a specific political and legal identity. In fact, the extent to which activists pursued a group identity in *Lawrence* can be seen in the NLGLA's amicus brief. Recall that the NLGLA not only pursued an equal protection claim but also explicitly tried to elevate sexual orientation to a legal classification that warranted heightened constitutional scrutiny. One of the key requirements for such a classification is that the group in question have suffered a history of intentional discrimination and disadvantage. Such claims solidify and enhance—rather than downplay—a politics based on group identification.

Of course, none of these final thoughts is meant to be conclusive, nor am I arguing that critics of identity politics are wrong or have somehow become marginalized or irrelevant to these essential debates with the movement. But my analysis of the *Lawrence* case does suggest that the LGBT movement, for better or worse, and to a greater or lesser extent, has become increasingly ensconced in and committed to the pursuit of equality through the processes of identity politics, both in court and throughout social, economic, and cultural life.

FIGURE 4.1
LGBT Organizations Represented in Amicus Briefs

Brief	Participating Organizations
Human Rights Campaign et al.	Human Rights Campaign
	National Gay and Lesbian Task Force
	Parents, Families, and Friends of Lesbians and Gays
	National Center for Lesbian Rights
	Gay and Lesbian Advocates and Defenders
	Gay and Lesbian Alliance Against Defamation
	Pride at Work, AFL-CIO
	People for the American Way
	Anti-Defamation League
	Mexican-American Legal Defense and Educational Fund
	Puerto Rican Legal Defense and Educational Fund
	Society of American Law Teachers
	Soulforce
	Stonewall Law Association of Greater Houston
	Equality Alabama
	Equality Florida
	S.A.V.E.
	Community Center of Idaho
	Your Family, Friends, and Neighbors
	Kansas Unity and Pride Alliance
	Louisiana Electorate of Gays and Lesbians
	Equality Mississippi
	Promo
	North Carolina Gay and Lesbian Attorneys
	Cimarron Foundation of Oklahoma
	South Carolina Gay and Lesbian Pride Movement
	Alliance for Full Acceptance
	Gay and Lesbian Community Center of Utah
	Equality Virginia
	Texas Human Rights Foundation
	Lesbian/Gay Rights Lobby

FIGURE 4.1
(continued)

Brief	Participating Organizations
National Lesbian and Gay Law Association et al.	National Lesbian and Gay Law Association
	Asian American Legal Defense and Educational Fund
	Action Wisconsin
	Bay Area Lawyers for Individual Freedom
	Bay Area Transgender Lawyers' Association
	Gay and Lesbian Lawyers of Philadelphia
	Gay and Lesbian Lawyers Association of South Florida
	Gaylaw
	Lesbian and Gay Law Association of Greater New York
	Lesbian and Gay Lawyers Association of Los Angeles
	Lesbian and Gay Bar Association of Chicago
	Massachusetts Lesbian and Gay Bar Association
	Minnesota Lavender Bar Association
	Northwest Women's Law Center
	Oregon Gay and Lesbian Law Association
	Stonewall Bar Association
	Tom Homann Law Association of San Diego
	Washington Lesbian and Gay Legal Society

5 Deciding Under the Influence?

The "One-Hit Wonders" and Organized-Interest Participation in U.S. Supreme Court Gay Rights Litigation

Courtenay W. Daum

OVER THE PAST few decades, the struggles for and against the advancement of gay rights and interests—equal protection under the law, privacy rights, and same-sex marriage—have been waged in the courts. Landmark decisions by federal and state courts have increased the saliency of gay rights on the public and political agendas and mobilized individuals and organized interests both in favor of and opposed to the advancement of these interests. Interest-group litigation research confirms that interest groups play an instrumental role in identifying legal dilemmas, initiating lawsuits, shaping the legal questions for the courts, and suggesting potential solutions and standards that may influence judicial decisions. In fact, interest groups historically have played a pivotal role in advancing the goals of social movements, such as the civil rights and the women's rights movements, in the courts. Yet, existing research has failed to explore adequately the role that organized interests play in gay rights litigation. As a result, this chapter examines the functions that organized interests perform in facilitating and responding to legal challenges in the courts in the context of gay rights and evaluates whether or not organized interests are able to achieve favorable outcomes at the U.S. Supreme Court.

This analysis focuses on the U.S. Supreme Court because the reach of its authority is unparalleled in the American legal system; it is capable of rendering decisions that impact the laws of all fifty states and the activities of organizations throughout the United States. In contrast, while state courts have been incredibly active in the area of gay rights in recent decades, the reach of their decisions ends at state lines. As a result, the stakes for organized interests whose cases are heard by the U.S. Supreme Court and those whose cases are heard in state courts are different. For example, an organized interest's success or failure at the U.S. Supreme Court may limit additional litigation in the federal and state courts. This chapter focuses attention on the roles that organized interests play as both litigants and amicus curiae in U.S. Supreme Court gay rights litigation.

To date, the Supreme Court has decided five cases involving gay rights and constitutional issues, and its decisions in these cases have not followed a pattern;

three rulings are recognized as detrimental to the advancement of gay rights—*Bowers v. Hardwick* (1986), *Hurley v. Irish-American Gay, Lesbian, and Bisexual Group of Boston* (1995), and *Boy Scouts of America v. Dale* (2000)—and two are deemed favorable to the interests of gays and lesbians—*Romer v. Evans* (1996) and *Lawrence and Garner v. Texas* (2003). The inconsistent nature of Supreme Court decision making in this issue area and the addition of two new Justices in recent years indicate that this area of jurisprudence is still under development.

Interest groups are strategic actors and opportunity maximizers, and the legal uncertainty associated with gay rights litigation at the Supreme Court provides organized interests with unique opportunities to enter the political fray and to define issues in a manner that is advantageous to their interests. In addition, gay rights organizations may be emboldened by the previous successful litigation strategies employed by organized interests such as the NAACP and the ACLU's Women's Rights Project to advance the equal rights of African Americans and women at the U.S. Supreme Court. This chapter examines the mobilization and litigation strategies of liberal and conservative organized interests in Supreme Court gay rights litigation across cases and time and concludes with a discussion of how their involvement affects judicial outcomes. Given the increasing saliency of gay rights at the state and national levels, one would expect that both liberal and conservative organized interests would be active as litigants and amicus curiae at the Supreme Court and that their participation would increase over time as these legal issues gain prominence on the American political agenda. In addition, consistent with the party capability literature, which examines how the resources and litigation experience of litigants affect their chances for success, one would expect those organized interests that are repeat players in Supreme Court gay rights litigation to have more success than those organized interests that are one-hit wonders.

Organized-Interest Litigation Research

While interest groups are only one set of actors among many in the judicial system, they play an integral role in federal litigation and utilize a number of different tools to influence the legal process (Truman 1951). Filing amicus curiae briefs (Caldeira and Wright 1990; Collins 2004; O'Connor and Epstein 1981–82; O'Connor and Epstein 1983) and direct sponsorship of cases are the two most common tools used by interest groups to lobby the courts (O'Connor 1997, 277).

Amicus curiae briefs often play an important role in setting the Supreme Court agenda (Caldeira and Wright 1988; McGuire and Caldeira 1993), and there is a positive relationship between organized interests' amicus curiae participation at the merits stage and legal outcomes (Collins 2004; Kearney and Merrill 2000;

McGuire 1990). In some instances, the Supreme Court may be responsive to the policy objectives of interest groups and incorporate the arguments contained in the groups' amicus curiae briefs into judicial opinions (Ivers and O'Connor 1987).

Interest groups also participate in the legal arena via direct sponsorship of cases. Test cases brought by interest groups make up the majority of important constitutional cases decided by the Supreme Court (O'Connor and Epstein 1984, 72), and there is little doubt that organized-interest litigation has been a powerful tool for pursuing the interests of various social movements throughout recent U.S. history. For example, the NAACP Legal Defense Fund utilized this strategy to great success in its efforts to desegregate schools and to eliminate restrictive housing covenants (Vose 1959), and women's and reproductive rights groups have all participated directly in litigation with varying degrees of success, as well (O'Connor 1980). Interest groups have also participated in First Amendment establishment clause (Sorauf 1976), disability (Olson 1984) and obscenity litigation (Daum 2006a; Kobylka 1987, 1991; McGuire 1990). These participants include conservative-oriented groups that use litigation to advance their goals (Epstein 1985; Koshner 1998).

To increase their likelihood of success in the courts, interest groups may look to each other for cues, support, and even alliances (Gray and Lowery 1996, 184–85; Heinz et al. 1993; Salisbury 1984; Schlozman and Tierney 1986). Groups are likely to coordinate activities and share resources when planning litigation (Epstein 1985), especially when they believe that working with other groups improves the likelihood for success (Hojnacki 1997). There is, however, disagreement about whether or not groups form coalitions and work together to file amicus briefs. According to Caldeira and Wright's (1990, 798) research, groups do not join together to file amicus briefs because they believe that the Justices respond to the number of briefs as opposed to the number of organized interests. In contrast, Olson (1984, 1990) found that groups are willing to form alliances to file amicus briefs when they believe that having a large number of participants may increase the likelihood of success.

Existing research on organized interests suggests that resources influence an organization's ability to participate in litigation, as well as its likelihood of success in the courts. Organized interests with greater resources—money, experience, and expertise—are able to initiate test cases and pursue litigation in the courts (Vose 1957), and these organizations are more likely to see their policy preferences translated into law (Epstein 1985; O'Connor 1980). According to Galanter (1974), those litigants that are repeat players (the "haves") are more likely to meet with success in the courts than the one-shotters (the "have nots") because the former benefit from greater litigation experience and resources. In addition, repeat players "have low stakes in the outcome of any particular case and have the resources to pursue their long term interests," whereas a one-shotter is "a person, business or organizational entity that deals with the legal system infrequently . . . but a one-shotter's interest in winning a particular case is very high" (Grossman, Kritzer, and Macaulay 1999, 803). The party-capability literature substantiates that the "haves" do in fact come out ahead in the courts (Farole 1999; Songer and Sheehan 1992; Songer, Sheehan, and Haire 1999; Wheeler et al. 1987), but there is evidence to suggest that litigants that are repeat players may not meet with greater success than the "have nots" at the U.S. Supreme Court (Sheehan, Mishler, and Songer 1992).

Organized interests with lesser resources may seek to influence case outcomes by sponsoring amicus curiae briefs. While the party-capability literature focuses attention on litigants and not on those parties that file amicus curiae briefs, it is certainly possible that the benefits of repeat-player status may accrue to those organized interests that participate as amicus curiae. Galanter's definitions of one-shotters ("those claimants who have only occasional recourse to the courts") and repeat players (those claimants "who are engaged in many similar litigations over time") and the relative disadvantages and advantages that accrue to each party logically translate to the role that amicus curiae play in litigation, as well (Galanter 1974, 97). Those parties that file multiple amicus curiae briefs in a specific area of litigation benefit from low start-up costs when initiating and writing a brief, the lessons learned from previous interactions with the courts, a breadth of expertise, and established relationships with the other players and judges that impact one's credibility and reputation. In contrast, one-shotter amicus curiae must overcome institutional disadvantages such as high start-up costs and a lack of experience and expertise in a given issue area similar to those confronted by one-shotter litigants.

Current Research on
Organized Interests' Gay Rights Litigation

During the late 1960s and early 1970s, organized interests began to utilize litigation as a mechanism to advance the interests of gays and lesbians. The American Civil Liberties Union (ACLU) was the first organized interest to pursue gay rights litigation, and it was followed soon thereafter by the Lambda Legal Defense and Education Fund (Lambda), the Lesbian Rights Project (now the National Center for Lesbian Rights), and Gay and Lesbian Advocates and Defenders (GLAD) (Andersen 2005).[1] The latter three organizations were founded in the aftermath of the 1969 Stonewall riots, an event that motivated many individuals to participate in the burgeoning gay rights movement, and today they are among the leading gay rights organizations (Andersen 2005, 24; Button, Rienzo, and Wald 1997, 25; Cain 2000, 56; Haider-Markel 1999, 248; Sherrill 1999, 272).

During the 1980s, the ACLU founded the Lesbian and Gay Rights Project and joined forces with Lambda and other allies to host a national strategy meeting to devise a plan to challenge local sodomy laws (Andersen 2005, 40–41; Cain 2000, 69, 170). Gay rights organizations made great efforts to build alliances with a variety of local and national organized interests, including civil rights, women's rights, and religious organizations and churches (Andersen 2005; Button, Rienzo, and Wald 1997).

Existing research on organized interests' participation in the politics of gay rights includes analyses of the emergence of the gay rights movement, as well as the countermobilization of opposing interests and their competing activities at the local and national levels (Button, Rienzo, and Wald 1997; Cain 1993, 2000; Haider-Markel 1999; Rimmerman 2002), as well as the role that these organized interests play in facilitating legal change in the courts (Andersen 2005; Brewer, Kaib, and O'Connor 2000; Cain 1993; Cain 2000; Haider-Markel and Meier 1996; Keen and Goldberg 1998; Pinello 2003; Rimmerman 2002). The research on organized-interest participation in gay rights litigation often focuses on either specific court cases or select organized interests, but there is no cumulative study of their participation in gay rights litigation.

For example, researchers have evaluated the political mobilization and litigation surrounding Colorado's Amendment Two, which culminated in the Supreme Court's *Romer v. Evans* (1996) decision, the only Supreme Court case to date in which a majority of the Justices advanced an equal protection argument in the context of gay rights (Gerstmann 1999; Keen and Goldberg 1998).

In contrast, Pinello (2003) investigated the various factors—organized-interest participation, the individual characteristics of judges, the substance of the legal issues to be addressed—that may impact legal outcomes in state and federal appellate court gay rights cases. He included five gay rights groups in his analysis and concluded that organized-interest participation in gay rights litigation—as counsel or as amicus curiae—increased the likelihood that the courts would issue a pro-gay rights ruling.[2] Similarly, Andersen's (2005) research examined the litigation strategy of a single organized interest across a series of cases in order to illustrate how shifts in the sociolegal structure provided Lambda with opportunities for action.

Current research, however, does not provide a comprehensive picture of organized-interest participation across time. Given the frequency with which the courts are setting policy on LGBT issues, this area of research is ripe for review. This chapter attempts to fill that void by examining the participation of all organized interests active in Supreme Court gay rights litigation. As previously noted, the Supreme Court is a unique venue because of its ability to set policy for the entire nation, rather than a single state. Thus, one would expect a variety of both liberal and conservative organized interests to be vested in gay rights litigation at this venue.

Data and Methods

To examine the participation of organized interests in gay rights litigation and to measure the relationship between organized-interest litigation and the Supreme Court's decisions in gay rights cases, I generated lists of the gay rights cases decided by the Supreme Court and all of the organized interests that participated in these cases. As previously mentioned, I selected five cases to include in this analysis: *Bowers v. Hardwick* (1986), *Hurley v. Irish-American Gay, Lesbian, and Bisexual Group of Boston* (1995), *Romer v. Evans* (1996), *Boy Scouts of America v. Dale* (2000), and *Lawrence and Garner v. Texas* (2003). These cases are included because each was initiated by gay or lesbian individuals who alleged that they were the victims of discrimination because of their sexual orientation, and each resulted in a Supreme Court decision.

The Supreme Court's opinion in each of the five cases was subjected to a content analysis to determine the legal grounds for the decision. Each case was coded to reflect the outcome of the Supreme Court's decision. A case was coded as liberal when the Supreme Court ruled in favor of greater liberties for gays and lesbians and as conservative when the Court ruled in favor of greater restrictions on gays and lesbians. As previously noted, three of the cases resulted in conservative decisions and two in liberal decisions.

The conservative cases include *Bowers v. Hardwick* (1986), in which the Supreme Court ruled that a Georgia sodomy statute was not unconstitutional because the right of privacy did not include legal protections for homosexuals' sexual conduct. In *Hurley v. Irish-American Gay, Lesbian, and Bisexual Group of Boston* (1995) and *Boy Scouts of America v. Dale* (2000), the Supreme Court determined that private organizations may legally exclude gays and lesbians because the former have a First Amendment right to control the content of their speech and the makeup of their membership.

In contrast, in *Romer v. Evans* (1996), the Supreme Court ruled that states and locales may not single out homosexuals and bisexuals in order to deny them the right to seek and receive legal protection from acts of discrimination because this imposes a broad disability on a targeted class of individuals in violation of the equal protection clause. Finally, the Supreme Court ruled in *Lawrence and Garner v. Texas* (2003) that a Texas law prohibiting homosexual sodomy violated the due process clause of the Fourteenth Amendment's liberty guarantees by impeding the rights of adults to engage in consensual homosexual sexual conduct in the privacy of their homes. The Court overturned *Bowers v. Hardwick* (1986) and ruled that states may no longer pass laws prohibiting the private sexual conduct of homosexuals.

The organized interests analyzed include membership and nonmembership organizations, and all are not-for-profit. The membership organizations include both purposive and material associations. Purposive organized interests pursue broadly defined societal goods and reward their members with intangible purposive benefits "that derive from the satisfaction of having contributed to a worthy cause" (Mahood 1990, 12), whereas material organized interests pursue specific goods that provide their members with tangible material benefits (Moe 1980; Olson 1965; Wilson 1995). For example, the Lambda Legal Defense and Education Fund is a purposive group that pursues the rights and interests of the LGBT community, and individuals join because they believe that ending discrimination is a collective societal good that benefits members and nonmembers. In contrast, the Stonewall Bar Association is identified as a material group because, while it seeks to end discrimination against gays and lesbians, it is also a professional membership organization that provides tangible material benefits: lawyers join to network with like-minded peers; enhance career and employment opportunities; and find potential clients. Finally, the nonmembership organizations included in this analysis consist of private institutions and public-interest law firms (Olson 1990; Salisbury 1984).

Organized-interest participation in each Supreme Court case was tabulated and recorded to reflect the type of participation: party to the litigation or amicus curiae. Each organized interest was classified according to its position on the issue of gay rights: liberal if it supported the expansion of gay rights in a given case and conservative if it opposed the extension of legal protections to gays and lesbians.[3] This typology was selected because it enables me to group ideologically similar organized interests together and proves to be more parsimonious than alternative dichotomies. That being said, it may be helpful to examine whether conservative or liberal organized interests are challenging or supporting the status quo in each case. The status quo will refer to the law or practice in place when litigation is initiated, not at the time the appeal is made to the Supreme Court.

In addition, organized interests were identified as repeat players or one-hit wonders. Organized interests that participated in more than one of the five cases—as a party to the litigation or as an amicus curiae—were identified as repeat players, whereas those that participated in only a single case, as either a party to the litigation or an amicus curiae, were identified as one-hit wonders. As previously noted, the party-capability literature primarily examines the behavior and resource disparities of litigants, but this chapter includes amicus curaie in the typology to test the assumption that repeat player litigants and amicus curiae will have more success before the Supreme Court than one-hit wonders.

While Galanter (1974) identifies organizations active in litigation as repeat players and suggests that these groups accrue the benefits associated with repeat-player status, this chapter differentiates among organized interests. Because relatively few gay rights cases have been decided by the Supreme Court, it is possible that organized interests that are repeat players in other areas of litigation may be one-hit wonders in the gay rights cases; these groups may not benefit from the advantages and privileges associated with repeat-player status. In addition, some organized interests may choose to enter the courts in order to participate in one single case; these groups are not able to benefit from the expertise and experience associated with repeat players. A brief review of the organized interests that participated in some of the major state supreme court gay rights cases decided in recent years, such as *Baehr v. Lewin* (Supreme Court of Hawai'i (1993)), *Baehr v. Miike* (Supreme Court of Hawai'i (1999)), *Baker v. Vermont* (Supreme Court of Vermont (1999)), and *Goodridge v. Department of Public Health* (Supreme Judicial Court of Massachusetts (2003)), indicates that the one-hit wonders that participated in gay rights litigation at the U.S. Supreme Court do not appear to have been active in these state court cases, while a number of the repeat players at the U.S. Supreme Court were active in the state courts. Thus, some organized interests are positioned to benefit from repeat-player status, whereas others—those one-hit wonders at the U.S. Supreme Court that are truly one-hit wonders in gay rights litigation broadly defined—are not situated to do so.

Analysis

Do Organized Interests Participate in Supreme Court Gay Rights Litigation?

Between 1986 and 2005, a total of 275 organized interests (198 liberal, 75 conservative, and 2 libertarian) participated in Supreme Court gay rights litigation. Of the 275 organized interests active in gay rights litigation, 200 are one-hit wonders; they participated in a single case at the Supreme Court. The remaining seventy-five organized interests are repeat players and participated in two or more cases before the Supreme Court; fifty-one of these are liberal oriented, twenty-two are conservative oriented, and two are libertarian.

Included in these seventy-five repeat players are thirty organized interests that participated in three or more cases, including twenty-five liberal and five conservative organized interests, as listed in Table 5.1. The high rates of participation among the organized interests identified in Table 5.1 suggest that they have an organizational commitment to enter into and to pursue a particular agenda in gay rights litigation. As a result, it is likely that these organized interests will continue to participate in the future.

The liberal repeat players outnumbered conservative repeat players five to one. This suggests that liberal organized interests are more invested in long-term sustainable participation in gay rights litigation at the Supreme Court than are conservative organized interests. This may reflect the fact that liberal organized interests are more likely to enter into litigation to change the status quo—state laws and court decisions that allowed for differential treatment of and discrimination against gays and lesbians—whereas conservative organized interests are more likely to mobilize in order to preserve the status quo and therefore may be less inclined to participate because the law already favors their interests.

In addition, the liberal repeat players represented a broader array of interests than the conservative repeat players. The former include gay rights groups, civil rights organizations, bar associations, religious organizations, and health organizations, whereas each of the five conservative repeat players is committed to advancing Christian religious and moral principles in the realm of American public policy. This is significant because the legal arguments being advanced by the conservative organized interests were quite homogenous—they were predicated on moral and religious values—in comparison to those being advanced by the liberal repeat players. As a result, the Justices were exposed to a broader array of legal arguments in favor of advancing gay rights (Daum 2006b).

Organized-interest participation in gay rights litigation consists of sponsoring litigation and filing amicus curiae briefs. Six organized interests sponsored litigation, and 274 organized interests participated as amicus curiae in the five cases included in the analysis. The six organized interests that sponsored litigation are the ACLU, the Boy Scouts of America, GLAD, the Irish-American Gay, Lesbian, and Bisexual Group of Boston, Lambda, and the South Boston Allied War Veterans Council. Five of these six organized interests participated as sponsors of litigation and as amicus curiae; the Irish-American Gay, Lesbian, and Bisexual Group of Boston only sponsored litigation. Thus, the number of organized interests sponsoring and directly supporting gay rights litigation was small. This indicates that, with few exceptions, organized interests are not inclined to assume the burdens of facilitating legal challenges in the federal courts in this issue area at this time. On the liberal side, this likely reflects the fact that the ACLU, Lambda, and GLAD have established themselves as leaders in gay rights litigation by seeking out and assuming the costs and burdens of sponsoring cases in the federal courts. On the conservative side, it seems likely that organized interests were not sponsoring litigation because they benefited from the status quo; existing law or the selective enforcement of the law favored their interests. As a result, it is not necessary for a broad array of liberal and conservative organized interests to sponsor

TABLE 5.1
Organized Interests That Participated in Three or More
Gay Rights Cases Before the U.S. Supreme Court

Liberal

American Bar Association	3
American Civil Liberties Union	5
American Friends Service Committee	3
American Jewish Congress	3
American Orthopsychiatric Association	3
American Psychological Association	4
American Public Health Association	3
Anti-Defamation League	4
Bay Area Lawyers for Individual Freedom	4
Gay and Lesbian Advocates and Defenders	4
Gay and Lesbian Lawyers of Philadelphia	4
Human Rights Campaign	3
Lambda Legal Defense and Education Fund	5
Massachusetts Lesbian and Gay Bar Association	4
Mexican American Legal Defense and Educational Fund	4
National Association of Social Workers	3
National Center for Lesbian Rights	3
National Gay and Lesbian Task Force	3
National Lesbian and Gay Law Association	3
NOW Legal Defense and Education Fund	3
People for the American Way	3
Puerto Rican Legal Defense and Education Fund	3
Society of American Law Teachers	3
Unitarian Universalist Association	4
Women's Legal Defense Fund	3

Conservative

American Center for Law and Justice	3
Christian Legal Society (Center for Law and Religious Freedom)	3
Concerned Women for America	4
Family Research Council	4
Focus on the Family	4

litigation in this issue area. Instead, those liberal and conservative organized interests vested in gay rights litigation have opted to submit less costly amicus curiae briefs. This legal strategy allows these groups to signal their interests to the Justices while simultaneously appealing to and cultivating the interests of their members.

Liberal organized interests appear to be more likely to sponsor litigation than conservative groups. Instances of sponsorship among liberal organized interests in Supreme Court gay rights litigation outnumber conservative organized-interest sponsorship seven to two, and the incentive to participate as a sponsor of litigation appears to vary among groups. The ACLU, Lambda, and GLAD entered into litigation on behalf of individuals who believed that they were the victims of illegal discrimination based on sexual orientation. These organized interests model their participation in gay rights litigation on the civil rights movement NAACP model; they proactively enter into litigation in order to advance the civil rights and liberties of gays and lesbians by challenging existing laws and legal enforcement that marginalize or exclude gays and lesbians from the legal protections extended to other members of society. The ACLU sponsored litigation and pursued the advancement of gay rights in *Bowers v. Hardwick* (1986) and *Romer v. Evans* (1996); Lambda did so in *Romer v. Evans* (1996), *Boy Scouts of America v. Dale* (2000), and *Lawrence and Garner v. Texas* (2003); and GLAD sponsored the litigation in *Hurley v. Irish-American Gay, Lesbian, and Bisexual Group of Boston* (1995). The ACLU, Lambda, and GLAD provided legal counsel in each case in which they were involved as sponsors of litigation. In *Boy Scouts of America v. Dale* (2000), Evan Wolfson, a Lambda attorney, served as the Counsel of Record and argued the case before the U.S. Supreme Court, and John Ward, founder of GLAD, was the first openly gay male to argue before the U.S. Supreme Court, in *Hurley v. Irish-American Gay, Lesbian, and Bisexual Group of Boston* (1995) (Gay and Lesbian Advocates and Defenders 2007).

It appears likely that these liberal organized interests will continue to play a predominant role in gay rights litigation because they have an institutional commitment to pursue the interests of gays and lesbians that includes the use of litigation when necessary. As in the civil rights and the women's rights movements, litigation is a powerful tool for the gay rights movement. For example, Lambda is the functional equivalent of the NAACP's Legal Defense and Educational Fund, which sponsors litigation on behalf of individuals who are the victims of racial discrimination. Lambda was founded in 1973 "to seek through the legal process, to insure equal protection of the laws and the protection of civil rights of homosexuals' and in furtherance of that purpose, 'to initiate or join in judicial and administrative proceedings whenever legal rights and interests of significant numbers of homosexuals may be affected'" (Lambda Legal Defense and Education Fund 1985, 1–2).

Similarly, the ACLU's Lesbian and Gay Rights Project is committed to advancing the rights of gays and lesbians through the legislative process and litigation. Both the ACLU and Lambda participated in 100 percent of the Supreme Court's gay rights cases; they filed amicus curiae briefs in each of the cases that they were not directly involved in as sponsors of litigation. Thus, these two groups have an organizational commitment to combat discrimination on the basis of sexual orientation and to advance gay rights that leads them to proactively enter into litigation. As a result, one would expect that these groups will continue to take the lead in sponsoring litigation in the federal courts, including the Supreme Court.

In contrast, the Boy Scouts of America and the South Boston Allied War Veterans Council—the two conservative-oriented groups participating as sponsors of litigation—did not proactively enter into gay rights litigation. Both organized interests were accused of discrimination on the basis of sexual orientation and drawn into litigation. As previously noted, conservative organized interests did not initiate litigation in those cases that wound up before the U.S. Supreme Court because they were interested in maintaining, not challenging, the status quo. The other one-hit wonder, the Irish-American Gay, Lesbian, and Bisexual Group of Boston, is a liberal organized interest that entered into litigation when it sued for admission to the Boston Saint Patrick's Day Parade. Like the Boy Scouts of America and the South Boston Allied War Veterans Council, the Irish-American Gay, Lesbian, and Bisexual Group of Boston is not likely to pursue litigation in the foreseeable future because pursuing political interests through litigation is not an institutional characteristic of such organizations. As a result, it appears that the future sponsors of gay rights litigation will continue to be proactive liberal purposive groups such as the ACLU and Lambda that seek to challenge existing laws and/or the status quo in the interest of advancing the civil rights of gays and lesbians. The function these organized interests perform for the gay rights movement is similar to the roles played by the NAACP's Legal Defense and Educational Fund and the ACLU's Women's Rights Project in previous social movements.

Despite the fact that only 6 organized interests participated as sponsors of litigation, 274 organized interests participated as amicus curiae and sponsored 89 percent of the 131 amicus curiae briefs filed at the Supreme Court in the five gay rights cases. Thus, the primary mode of organized-interest participation before the Supreme Court was the filing of amicus curiae briefs. Table 5.2 illustrates that organized interests sponsored nearly all of the amicus curiae briefs filed in each of the individual cases, as well. While there is no way to be certain that the Justices read or pay attention to the amicus curiae briefs that are submitted, there is no doubt that these briefs send signals to the Justices regarding the saliency of a case and the distribution of support for the parties. As a result, given the dispropor-

TABLE 5.2

Amicus Curiae Filed by Organized Interests in
Gay Rights Cases Before the Supreme Court

	Number	Percentage of Total
Bowers v. Hardwick (1986)	11	85%
Hurley v. Irish-American GLB (1995)	8	100%
Romer v. Evans (1996)	25	86%
Boy Scouts of America v. Dale (2000)	42	89%
Lawrence and Garner v. Texas (2003)	31	91%

tionate amicus participation of organized interests relative to other amicus curiae such as individual states, state legislative and judicial officers, and individuals, it seems likely that organized-interest amicus participation may play a valuable role in Supreme Court decision making. Thus, it is important to understand which groups are participating.

Both liberal and conservative organized interests were active sponsors of amicus curiae briefs, but the number of liberal organized interests (n = 197) substantially exceeded the number of conservative organized interests (n = 75); 72 percent of the organized interest amicus curiae were liberal organized interests, whereas 27 percent were conservative organized interests (and one percent pursued a libertarian agenda). It is clear that liberal organized interests are substantially more likely to participate as amicus curiae in gay rights litigation than are conservative organized interests. This may indicate that there are more liberal than conservative organized interests active on the issue of gay rights. The liberal amicus curiae consist of various gay rights groups, as well as those organized interests that pursue the equitable treatment of gays and lesbians as one part of their larger institutional agendas. Previous research indicates that many of the interests active in the LGBT movement developed at the local level to challenge the enforcement of local sodomy and liquor license laws (Barclay and Fisher 2006; Eskridge 1999; Pinello 2003). Thus, the greater liberal organized interest amicus curiae participation may be an artifact of the geographically and issue-splintered development of the LGBT movement. In contrast, conservative organized interests active in gay rights litigation are not likely to be single-issue antigay rights groups. Instead, they tend to be organizations with broad political, social, and/or moral agendas. Thus, it appears that one of the reasons that liberal amicus curiae may outnumber conservative amicus curiae is simply that there are more liberal organized interests—including an active LGBT movement—than conservative organized interests committed to this issue area.

In addition, the greater participation among liberal organized interests may reflect the fact that liberal organized interests were trying to challenge the status quo and gain recognition for the rights of gays and lesbians at the national level—in three of the five cases, liberal amicus curiae were lobbying the Court to invalidate state action that allowed for the differential treatment of gays and lesbians—whereas conservative amicus curiae were more likely to be defending state laws. As a result, in those cases where liberal organized interests challenge the constitutionality of state laws, conservative organized interests may be less inclined to submit amicus curiae because they recognize the state, as opposed to organized interests, as the primary source for maintaining and defending state law.

Similarly, the twenty-four liberal organized interests that participated as amicus curiae in three or more cases substantially outnumbered the five conservative organized interests that participated as amicus curiae in three or more cases. The twenty-four liberal organized interests included a variety of organizational types—purposive and professional membership, religious organizations, public interest law firms—and they presented a wide range of arguments in favor of extending constitutional rights to gays, lesbians, and bisexuals.

Liberal purposive membership organizations such as the Human Rights Campaign and People for the American Way participated because their organizations' missions include a broad commitment to pursue equality for all as a public good, and their legal arguments reflected this predisposition. Similarly, legal organizations such as GLAD and bar associations such as Bay Area Lawyers for Individual Freedom and the Massachusetts Lesbian and Gay Bar Association argued that it is unconstitutional to exclude gays and lesbians from the equal protection of the laws. Other liberal repeat players included a variety of professional membership organizations such as the American Orthopsychiatric Association, the American Psychological Association, the American Public Health Association, and the National Association of Social Workers, which oppose the criminalization of private consensual adult sexual activity and government attempts to exclude gays and lesbians from legal protections on the basis of their sexual orientation because such classifications may be based on faulty scientific research and evidence and result in harm to the emotional and physical health of gays and lesbians. Finally, religious organizations such as the American Friends Service Committee, the American Jewish Congress, and the Unitarian Universalist Association believe that discrimination against gays and lesbians is inconsistent with the organizations' goals of promoting human dignity and respect, and they argued that it is not the government's job to legislate morality.

In contrast, the five conservative organized interests that participated in three or more cases were less varied—four are purposive membership organizations, and one, the American Center for Law and Justice, is a public interest law firm— and they presented fairly homogenous legal arguments. They opposed the expansion of gay rights and argued that states and/or private organizations may treat gays and lesbians differently in the interest of promoting traditional moral and religious values consistent with state police powers and the First Amendment rights of private organizations (Daum 2006b).

That being said, it is not clear that conservative repeat players are at a disadvantage, considering that the Supreme Court has issued three "conservative" decisions but only two "liberal" decisions in gay rights litigation, but liberal organized interests achieved great success when the Supreme Court rejected the morality-based argument advanced by conservative organized interests in *Lawrence and Garner v. Texas* (2003). As a result, the fact that those conservative organized interests identified as major repeat players repeatedly articulate fairly homogenous legal arguments grounded in a single legal theory may prove to be problematic in future litigation.

Regardless of their various individual motivations for participating, the liberal and conservative amicus curiae identified as repeat players exhibit a long-term commitment to pursuing their respective agendas in gay rights litigation before the Supreme Court. While the diversity of liberal-oriented interests presented the Justices with a broader array of legal arguments promoting gay rights, it is important to note that the total number of amicus briefs filed by liberal and conservative organized interests was comparable. Of the 117 amicus curiae briefs filed by organized interests, liberal organized interests filed 53 and conservative organized interests filed 64. While liberal organized interests accounted for 72 percent of the interests participating as amicus curiae in gay rights litigation, they filed fewer amicus curiae briefs than conservative organized interests. This occurred because conservative organized interests were more likely to work alone than to join with other organized interests when filing amicus curiae briefs, while liberal organized interests were more likely to work with other liberal organized interests in the amicus curiae process than they were to work alone.

It is not clear why conservative organized interests are less likely than liberal organized interests to work together when filing amicus curiae briefs, especially when one considers that the legal arguments advanced by the repeat-player conservative organized interests are very similar from brief to brief. There appear to be two plausible explanations. First, the number of conservative organized interests active in Supreme Court gay rights litigation is much smaller than the number of liberal organized interests, and the former may seek to amplify their interests to the Justices by submitting as many individual briefs as possible. This practice would be consistent with research that has concluded that some groups believe that it is the number of amicus curiae briefs and not the number of amicus curiae that influences Supreme Court decision making (Caldeira and Wright 1990). Second, many of the conservative organized interests participating in these cases are very similar organizations, and they may compete with one another for members, benefactors, and resources. As previously noted, the five major repeat-player conservative organized interests are all committed to advancing Christian religious and moral principles in American public policy, as are a large number of the other conservative organized interests that participate in gay rights litigation. In order to cultivate members and resources, these organized interests may opt to act independently when filing amicus curiae briefs, thereby signaling the valuable, and arguably unique, role that each plays in gay rights litigation.

In contrast, liberal organized interests may be more likely to work together when filing amicus curiae briefs because of the long-standing alliances built by gay rights groups. Throughout the history of the LGBT movement, gay rights organizations have made an effort to cultivate the support of different local, state, and national organizations, including civil rights, women's rights, and religious organizations (Andersen 2005; Button, Rienzo, and Wald 1997). Thus, there is a history of collaboration among gay rights groups and their allies that appears to translate into working together or supporting one another in the amicus curiae process at the Supreme Court.

On the basis of a cumulative analysis of organized interest participation in U.S. Supreme Court gay rights litigation, it is not immediately clear that one ideological position has an advantage over the other. Organized interests are more likely to participate as amicus curiae than as sponsors of litigation, and their participation accounts for nearly all of the amicus activity in these cases. More liberal organized interests participated than did conservative organized interests; this is true for both sponsoring litigation and filing amicus curiae briefs, but conservative organized interests submitted more amicus curiae briefs than did liberal organized interests. These findings reflect the strong presence of the LGBT movement in Supreme Court litigation, a presence that is stronger than that of the more individualistic and less active conservative organized interests. Among liberal organized interests, a select few, notably the ACLU and the gay rights–specific Lambda and GLAD, have assumed a leadership role in initiating and sponsoring litigation on behalf of gay and lesbian individuals that challenges discrimination by states and private organizations in the interest of promoting LGBT civil rights and liberties. They are supported in this process by a variety of gay rights organized interests and their allies, including twenty-four major repeat players, acting as amicus curiae. In contrast, conservative organized interests did not proactively enter into litigation, and the conservative amicus curiae, includ-ing only five major repeat players, were more likely to work alone in their oppo-sition to gay rights. In addition, among major repeat players, liberal organized interests presented the Justices with a greater diversity of legal arguments in favor of advancing gay rights, whereas repeat player conservative organized interests presented fairly homogeneous legal arguments. Thus, the evidence indicates that both liberal and conservative organized interests are active in gay rights litigation, and Supreme Court Justices are exposed to the legal arguments of various organized interests.

Does Organized Interest Participation in Supreme Court Gay Rights Litigation Change Over Time?

One would expect both liberal and conservative organized interest participation—defined as both the number of organized interests and the number of amicus curiae briefs—to increase over time in response to the increasing saliency of gay rights. As the debates about state sodomy laws, public accommodation laws, equal rights, and same-sex marriage move onto political and legal agendas, one would expect organized interests to initiate or increase their participation in Supreme Court litigation, given the Court's broad jurisdiction. In addition, if individual organized interests are increasing their participation over time, there will be more repeat players and one-hit wonders active in Supreme Court gay rights litigation, which may change the balance of interests and influence the Justices' decision making and legal outcomes.

As anticipated, the number of organized interests participating increased from 28 in *Bowers v. Hardwick* (1986) to a high of 133 in *Lawrence and Garner v. Texas* (2003), although the lowest level of participation occurred in *Hurley v. Irish-American Gay, Lesbian, and Bisexual Group of Boston* (1995), in which only twenty-four organized interests participated (see Table 5.3). As a result, the increase in organized interest participation was not consistent from 1986 to 2003, and variation existed in the number of liberal and conservative organized interests participating over time, as well. This indicates that the cases were not coequal in terms of their saliency to liberal and conservative organized interests. For example, liberal organized-interest participation reached an all-time high in *Lawrence and Garner v. Texas* (2003), whereas the number of conservative organized interests peaked in *Boy Scouts of America v. Dale* (2000). Liberal organized interests were heavily vested in defeating the sodomy law at issue in *Lawrence and Garner v. Texas* (2003) because it allowed gays and lesbians to be singled out and subjected to discriminatory treatment at the hands of the state, whereas conservative organized interests were mobilized to participate in *Boy Scouts of America v. Dale* (2000) as a way to protect the rights of private organizations to control their viewpoints and memberships.

In each of the five cases, the number of liberal organized interests participating exceeded the number of conservative interests. Yet, the rate of liberal organized interest participation vis-à-vis that of conservative organized interest participa-

TABLE 5.3
Liberal and Conservative Organized-Interest Participation in
Gay Rights Cases Before the U.S. Supreme Court

	N	Liberal Number (Percent)	Conservative Number (Percent)
Bowers v. Hardwick (1986)	28	25 (89%)	3 (11%)
Hurley v. Irish-American GLB (1995)	24	14 (58%)	10 (42%)
Romer v. Evans (1996)	106	89 (84%)	17 (16%)
Boy Scouts of America v. Dale (2000)	102	55 (54%)	47 (46%)
Lawrence and Garner v. Texas (2003)	133	104 (78%)	29 (22%)

TABLE 5.4
"One-Hit Wonders" Participating in U.S. Supreme Court Gay Rights Litigation

	Total Organized Interests	One-Hit Wonders Number (%)	Liberal One-Hit Wonders Number (%)	Conservative One-Hit Wonders Number (%)
Bowers v. Hardwick (1986)	28	8 (28.5%)	7 (25%)	1 (3.6%)
Hurley v. Irish-American GLB (1995)	24	8 (33.3%)	6 (25%)	2 (8%)
Romer v. Evans (1996)	106	55 (52%)	50 (47%)	5 (5%)
Boy Scouts of America v. Dale (2000)	102	48 (47%)	22 (22%)	26 (25%)
Lawrence and Garner v. Texas (2003)	133	81 (61%)	62 (47%)	19 (14%)

tion varied from case to case. The variation in organized interest participation among cases may largely be attributed to the fact that the majority of organized interests that participate in gay rights litigation are one-hit wonders; organizations motivated to participate in a particular case because they are interested in the outcome and resolution of the specific legal issue.

As Table 5.4 indicates, there is a correlation between the increases and decreases in the number of organized interests participating in a given case over time and the number of one-hit wonders. For example, the total number of organized interests participating in gay rights litigation declined slightly from Romer v. Evans (1996) to Boy Scouts of America v. Dale (2000) as did the number of one-hit wonders.

The increases and decreases in the number of liberal and conservative organized interests across time may largely be attributed to the participation of one-hit wonders, as well. For example, there was a substantial increase in the number of liberal organized interests, from twenty-five in Bowers v. Hardwick (1986) to eighty-nine in Romer v. Evans (1996). Similarly, the number of liberal-oriented one-hit wonders increased from seven in Bowers v. Hardwick (1986), accounting for 25 percent of organized interest participation, to fifty in Romer v. Evans (1996), accounting for almost 50 percent of organized interest participation. The increase in liberal-oriented one-hit wonders in *Romer v. Evans* (1996) reflects the increase in interest among a variety of new players in the outcome of this case. Notably, twenty-two state and local lawyer and bar associations mobilized in opposition to Colorado's Amendment 2 and argued that it violated the Fourteenth Amendment's equal protection clause.[4]

Similarly, the decrease in liberal organized-interest participation and the increase in conservative organized-interest participation in *Boy Scouts of America v. Dale* (2000) may be partially explained by the unique nature of the case and the subsequent participation of one-hit wonders. *Boy Scouts of America v. Dale* (2000) was distinct from the other four cases decided by the Supreme Court because it involved an organization associated with children that was seeking to control access to its membership. As a result, the coalition of groups that participated in this case was quite different from the organized interests that filed amicus curiae briefs in the other cases.

Twenty-six of the forty-seven conservative organized interests that participated in *Boy Scouts of America v. Dale* (2000) were one-hit wonders, and they accounted for 55 percent of conservative organized-interest participation and one-quarter of the total number of organized interests participating in this case. Thus, the increase from seventeen conservative organized interests in *Romer v. Evans* (1996) to forty-seven in *Boy Scouts of America v. Dale* (2000) may largely be attributed to the participation of the one-hit wonders. These organized interests represented a variety of constituencies and included membership organizations and associations representing membership organizations that had an interest in maintaining their right to exclude individuals from their respective organizations,[5] as well as various religious organizations supporting the Boy Scouts' position.[6]

Finally, the substantial increase in liberal organized-interest participation from *Boy Scouts of America v. Dale* (2000) to *Lawrence and Garner v. Texas* (2003) may largely be attributed to the increase in liberal-oriented one-hit wonders in the latter case. Liberal organized interests increased from 55 in *Boy Scouts of America v. Dale* (2000) to 104 in *Lawrence and Garner v. Texas* (2003), and liberal one-hit wonders increased from 22 to 62. In *Lawrence and Garner v. Texas* (2003), liberal one-hit wonders accounted for 60 percent of liberal organized interests and 46 percent of the total number of organized interests. The participation of these one-hit wonders is significant because they accounted for almost half of the organized interests that participated in the case and represented a variety of constituencies, including twenty-eight national, state, and local gay rights organizations and law associations pursuing the equal treatment of gays and lesbians before the law; twenty-one religious organizations interested in promoting the equality of gays and lesbians; six organizations committed to preventing the spread of HIV and AIDS; four libertarian political organizations, including the Cato Institute; and five human rights groups, including Amnesty International and Human Rights Watch.

The participation of the twenty-one religious organizations acting as liberal one-hit wonders in *Lawrence and Garner v. Texas* (2003) is particularly interesting. Twenty of these one-hit wonders joined eight repeat-player organized interests affiliated with religious organizations to file an amicus curiae brief opposing the criminalization of same-sex sexual conduct.[7] The participation of these religious groups indicates that religious organizations are active in promoting gay rights and are not limited to those that advocate a conservative position in gay rights litigation.

The increase in the number of participating one-hit wonders from eight in *Bowers v. Hardwick* (1986) to eighty-one in *Lawrence and Garner v. Texas* (2003) is significant for a number of reasons. These organized interests accounted for less than a third of organized-interest participation in *Bowers v. Hardwick* (1986); yet, by *Lawrence and Garner v. Texas* (2003), they accounted for almost two-thirds of the total number of participating organized interests. Over the years, more organized interests became interested in participating in Supreme Court gay rights litigation as a means of articulating or defending their interests. The fact that these organized interests participated in only one of five cases and that their participation was confined to amicus curiae participation (with the exception of the Irish-American Gay, Lesbian, and Bisexual Group of Boston) indicates that these organized interests are less invested in gay rights litigation than are those organized interests that participated in multiple cases. One-hit wonders selectively enter into gay rights cases that directly implicate their organizational interests. They participate in litigation with a narrow focus on the resolution of a specific legal issue rather than participate in multiple cases in order to pursue a broader agenda on the issue of gay rights as do the repeat players discussed previously. The one-hit wonders illustrate that both the number and the variety of organized interests willing to participate in Supreme Court gay rights litigation have increased, but many of these new players are not likely to become long-term participants.

The one-hit wonders' decisions to participate in gay rights litigation are noteworthy considering the high startup costs associated with writing and filing amicus curiae briefs. These organized interests likely were motivated by a variety of different considerations, including a desire to alert the Justices to widespread opposition or support for certain state laws and court decisions. In addition, one-hit wonders may participate to protect their own organizational interests; the many conservative and religious membership organizations that participated in *Hurley v. Irish-American Gay, Lesbian, and Bisexual Group of Boston* (1995) and

TABLE 5.5
Amicus Curiae Filed by Liberal and Conservative Organized Interests in
Gay Rights Cases Before the U.S. Supreme Court

	N	Liberal Number (%)	Conservative Number (%)
Bowers v. Hardwick (1986)	11	8 (73%)	3 (27%)
Hurley v. Irish-American GLB (1995)	8	2 (25%)	6 (75%)
Romer v. Evans (1996)	25	16 (64%)	9 (36%)
Boy Scouts of America v. Dale (2000)	42	12 (29%)	30 (71%)
Lawrence and Garner v. Texas (2003)	31	15 (48%)	16 (52%)

Boy Scouts of America v. Dale (2000) may have done so in order to defend their right to exclude gays and lesbians or other individuals deemed to be antithetical to their interests from their organizations. Other one-hit wonders may participate in order cultivate and grow their membership by sending strong signals to interest-group constituents, such as the many liberal local and state organizations that filed amicus curiae briefs to articulate their opposition to discriminatory state laws (Barclay and Fisher 2006).

In addition to an increase in the number of organized interests active in gay rights litigation, there was an increase in the number of amicus curiae briefs filed by organized interests, as well. In 1986, organized interests filed eleven amicus curiae briefs in *Bowers v. Hardwick*; eight advocated a liberal position, and three advocated a conservative position. By the time the Supreme Court decided *Lawrence and Garner v. Texas*, in 2003, organized interests filed thirty-one amicus curiae briefs; fifteen advocated a liberal position, and sixteen advocated a conservative position. The number of amicus curiae briefs filed by organized interests peaked in *Boy Scouts of America v. Dale* (2000) before declining, in *Lawrence and Garner v. Texas* (2003). Table 5.5 presents liberal and conservative organized-interest amicus curiae participation in each of the five cases included in the analysis.

Similarly, liberal and conservative organized interests did not consistently increase their amicus curiae participation over time. This finding is contrary to the expectation that the growing saliency of the gay rights debate would lead liberal and conservative organized interests to increase their amicus curiae participation over time. Instead, there was a large increase in the number of conservative organized-interest amicus curiae briefs in *Boy Scouts of America v. Dale* (2000), accounting for 71 percent of the amicus curiae submitted to the Court by organized interests, and a slight decrease in liberal organized-interest participation. This substantial increase in conservative organized-interest amicus curiae activity may be attributed partially to the increase in participation among conservative one-hit wonders in *Boy Scouts of America v. Dale* (2000). Interestingly, however, conservative and liberal organized interests achieved near-parity in *Lawrence and Garner v. Texas* (2003). Even though the number of participating liberal organized interests exceeded the number of participating conservative organized interests, the latter filed one more amicus curiae brief than the former. As previously noted, liberal organized interests are inclined to join together to file amicus curiae briefs, and, as a result, their briefs often have multiple sponsors and participants. In contrast, conservative organized are less inclined to work together when filing amicus briefs, and so they are able to submit more briefs as more conservative organized interests participate in gay rights litigation, despite their smaller numbers relative to liberal organized interests.

While organized interests did not consistently increase their amicus curiae participation over time, the number of amicus curiae briefs submitted to the Court did increase substantially after *Bowers v. Hardwick* (1986) and *Hurley v. Irish-American Gay, Lesbian, and Bisexual Group of Boston* (1995). In addition, the distribution of amicus curiae submitted by conservative organized interests relative to the number submitted by liberal organized interests varied greatly in the first four cases, but in *Lawrence and Garner v. Texas* (2003) there was nearly an equal distribution of amicus briefs, and this may suggest that the balance of interests in gay rights litigation is changing. That being said, whether or not one position has an advantage over the other is difficult to discern.

Does Organized-Interest Participation Influence Supreme Court Outcomes?

Both liberal and conservative organized interests have met with success and failure at the U.S. Supreme Court in gay rights litigation, and it is not clear that the Supreme Court is more responsive to one position than to the other. This is particularly noteworthy considering that the makeup of the Supreme Court was the same for the last four of the gay rights cases considered here. As a result, it is helpful to examine the behavior of liberal and conservative organized interests in each of the cases in order to determine whether there is a connection between organized interest participation and Supreme Court outcomes.

On the basis of the party capability literature and the finding that experienced litigators often have greater success in the courts, one would expect those litigants that are repeat players to have greater success in the courts than those that are one-shotters. Yet, the ACLU, Lambda, and GLAD do not appear to benefit from their repeat-player status. Instead, the South Boston Allied War Veterans Council and the Boy Scouts of America, both conservative one-hit wonders, won their cases at the Supreme Court and defeated the repeat players GLAD and Lambda in *Hurley v. Irish-American Gay, Lesbian, and Bisexual Group of Boston* (1995) and

TABLE 5.6
Liberal and Conservative Organized Interest Participation in
Supreme Court Gay Rights Litigation

	Liberal		Conservative	
	Number of Interests	Amicus Briefs	Number of Interests	Amicus Briefs
Bowers v. Hardwick (1986)	25	8	3*	3*
Hurley v. Irish-American GLB (1995)	14	2	10*	6*
Romer v. Evans (1996)	89*	16*	17	9
Boy Scouts of America v. Dale (2000)	55	12	47*	30*
Lawrence and Garner v. Texas (2003)	104*	15*	29	16

*Indicates the Supreme Court decision favored the position of the organized interests.

Boy Scouts of America v. Dale (2000), respectively. Thus, contrary to expectations, in the context of organized-interest participation in Supreme Court gay rights litigation, repeat-player status does not correlate with greater litigant success. As a result, it may be helpful to look at the total number of organized interests participating in a given case.

Table 5.6 illustrates the number of organized interests and amicus curiae briefs filed by liberal and conservative organized interests in each of the Supreme Court cases under consideration. According to these data, there does not appear to be a correlation between the quantity of organized-interest participation, defined as the number of organized interests favoring a specific outcome and/or the number of amicus curiae briefs filed in a given case, and the direction of Supreme Court decisions.

The number of organized interests and amicus briefs filed by these organized interests coincided with a Supreme Court ruling in line with the interests of the more active participants in only one of the five cases. In Romer v. Evans (1996), the Supreme Court issued a liberal decision in a case where the number of liberal organized interests exceeded the number of conservative interests by seventy-two and the majority of the amicus briefs were filed by liberal interests.

The typology of organized interest participation and Supreme Court outputs shown in Table 5.7 seems to indicate that the relationship between organized interest activity and Supreme Court decision making in gay rights litigation is random.

That being said, organized interests engage in a surge-and-decline pattern that appears to correlate with Supreme Court decision making and outcomes. If one begins by using Bowers v. Hardwick (1986) as a benchmark and compares the number of organized interests that participated in that case with the number of organized interests that participated in Hurley v. Irish-American Gay, Lesbian,

TABLE 5.7
The Relationship Among Supreme Court Decisions and the Numbers of
Amicus Curiae Briefs and Organized Interests in Gay Rights Cases

	Supreme Court Decision Coincides with the Organized Interests Filing More Amicus Curiae Briefs	Supreme Court Decision Coincides with the Organized Interests Filing Less Amicus Curiae Briefs
Supreme Court Decision Reflects the Position of the Larger Number of Organized Interests	Romer v. Evans	Lawrence and Garner v. Texas
Supreme Court Decision Reflects the Position of the Smaller Number of Organized Interests	Boy Scouts of America v. Dale Hurley v. Irish-American Gay, Lesbian and Bisexual Group of Boston	Bowers v. Hardwick

and Bisexual Group of Boston (1995), one finds that there was a small increase in the number of conservative organized interests that participated and a decline in the number of liberal organized interests that participated; the Court issued a conservative decision. Then, in *Romer v. Evans* (1996), there was a substantial surge in the number of liberal organized interests that participated relative to the number in the previous case—fourteen liberal and ten conservative organized interests participated in *Hurley v. Irish-American Gay, Lesbian, and Bisexual Group of Boston* (1995), whereas eighty-nine liberal organized interests participated in *Romer v. Evans* (1996)—and the case resulted in a liberal victory. Then, in *Boy Scouts of America v. Dale* (2000), the number of liberal organized interests declined from eighty-nine to fifty-five, but the number of conservative organized interests surged to forty-seven from seventeen in *Romer v. Evans* (1996); the Supreme Court issued a conservative decision. Finally, the number of conservative organized interests declined from forty-seven in *Boy Scouts of America v. Dale* (2000) to twenty-nine in *Lawrence and Garner v. Texas* (2003). However, the number of liberal organized interests surged from 55 in the former case to 104 in the latter case, and the Supreme Court issued a liberal decision.

This surge-and-decline pattern likely reflects the issues that were at stake in each case and the corresponding organized interest activity. *Bowers v. Hardwick* (1986), *Romer v. Evans* (1996), and *Lawrence and Garner v. Texas* (2003) all dealt with legal challenges to state laws that allowed for the differential treatment of gays and lesbians, whereas *Hurley v. Irish-American Gay, Lesbian, and Bisexual Group of Boston* (1995) and *Boy Scouts of America v. Dale* (2000) dealt with legal challenges to the operations of private organizations. Thus, liberal organized-interest participation surged in the cases that challenged *public* laws that discriminated on the basis of sexual orientation, whereas participation by conservative organized interests surged in cases addressing the membership privileges and First Amendment rights of *private* organizations. Thus, the decline in liberal organized-interest participation in *Hurley v. Irish-American Gay, Lesbian, and Bisexual Group of Boston* (1995) and *Boy Scouts of America v. Dale* (2000) and in conservative participation in *Bowers v. Hardwick* (1986), *Romer v. Evans* (1996), and *Lawrence and Garner v. Texas* (2003) may reflect the distinction between public and private discrimination, which, in turn, impacts the mobilization of different organized interests. Liberal organized interests are more likely to pursue an antidiscrimination civil rights agenda and so are more likely to challenge public laws that are perceived to be discriminatory, whereas conservative groups are more likely to be predisposed to oppose government interference in the business of private organizations, especially religious groups and organizations interested in controlling their membership and viewpoints in order to advance a specific moral agenda.

Thus, there does appear to be a relationship between Supreme Court outcomes and the surge and decline in the number of organized interests advocating a particular position in a specific gay rights case. This correlation suggests that one-hit wonders may play a more pivotal role in gay rights litigation than initially anticipated. As previously mentioned, these organized interests account for a substantial amount of the increase in the number of liberal organized interests in *Romer v. Evans* (1996) and *Lawrence and Garner v. Texas* (2003) and in the number of conservative organized interests in *Boy Scouts of America v. Dale* (2000). The increase in the number of one-hit wonders participating in a given case coincides with surges in liberal and conservative organized-interest activity.

The correlation between the direction of Supreme Court decision making and the surge and decline in the number of organized interests participating in a given case suggests that the Supreme Court may be more responsive to the participation of one-hit wonders than to that of repeat players in certain issue areas. Gay rights litigation is a relatively new area of federal law; in the years since *Bowers v. Hardwick* (1986), the federal courts have acted with trepidation in this area, despite the growing political saliency of these issues throughout the United States and the increase in legal activity in the states. Thus, the Justices may pay close attention to public opinion and political mobilization as exemplified by the one-hit wonders in gay rights cases. This notion runs counter to the conventional wisdom that repeat players have an advantage in the courts (Galanter 1974).

The participation of one-hit wonders may send a valuable message to Supreme Court Justices about the public's predisposition in a given case. Recall that one-hit wonders enter into gay rights litigation to pursue the resolution of a specific legal issue, rather than to advance a broad agenda on gay rights. The fact that these organized interests—the majority of which are membership organizations— are willing to assume the financial and time costs associated with filing amicus curiae briefs in a given case may indicate to the Court that there is momentum one way or the other in a specific case. Thus, while repeat players may benefit from superior resources and expertise, it may be the lack of these resources that is especially valuable to one-hit-wonder participation. The Justices may be attuned to the fact that the one-hit wonders face greater barriers or challenges to participation than repeat players. Thus, the Justices may take note when the former are willing to assume those costs in a given instance because the outcome of the case is so important to them. As a result, additional research on the roles that one-hit wonders play as amicus curiae in Supreme Court litigation and their subsequent influence on judicial decision making may be necessary.

Conclusion

Despite the fact that the relationship between organized-interest participation and Supreme Court outcomes is difficult to discern, it would be inaccurate to conclude that organized-interest participation in Supreme Court gay rights litigation does not matter. A wide variety of organized interests participated in gay rights litigation before the U.S. Supreme Court. These included both repeat players—the standard-bearers committed to pursuing or opposing gay rights and likely to remain active in future cases—and the one-hit wonders—those interests that participated in a single case as a result of their interest in a specific legal issue. The conventional wisdom suggests that repeat players in the judicial arena have an advantage over those individuals and organizations that participate only once because the former have a wealth of experience and expertise and are familiar with the Justices and vice versa. Yet, it appears that the one-hit wonders may play a valuable role in alerting the Justices to their (and possibly the public's) predispositions on specific legal issues in gay rights litigation.

In addition, the organized interests active in gay rights litigation reviewed here represented diverse constituencies and articulated a wide breadth of legal arguments in favor of and opposed to the extension of constitutional protections to gays and lesbians. The number of liberal organized interests substantially exceeded the number of conservative organized interests, reflecting the size of the LGBT movement and its allies, but conservative organized interests were able to amplify their presence in the more recent gay rights cases by opting to work alone or in small groups when filing amicus curiae briefs. Additional research will be necessary to evaluate whether or not conservative organized interests remain confident in their legal strategy and stay the course in light of the additions of Chief Justice Roberts and Associate Justice Alito to the Supreme Court or whether they increase their participation, change their legal arguments, or amalgamate their individual strategies in response to the liberal victory in *Lawrence and Garner v. Texas* (2003).

Finally, the number of organized interests and their amicus curiae briefs have increased substantially since the Supreme Court decided *Bowers v. Hardwick*, in 1986. The fact that organized interests—both conservative and liberal—entered the judicial arena and that new organized interests were motivated to participate in gay rights litigation in each Supreme Court case indicates that organized interests believe that their participation matters.

This is particularly noteworthy because the overwhelming majority of the organized interests included in this analysis are membership groups, and members' interests drive the organizations' missions and thus their participation in litigation. It is clear that the members of both liberal and conservative groups are encouraging or at the very least, supporting their organizations' support for or opposition to gay rights, including their participation in Supreme Court litigation. This appears to be especially true for those purposive groups that are repeat players in gay rights litigation, such as the liberal-oriented ACLU and Lambda and the conservative-oriented Concerned Women for America and Family Research Council. These organized interests participate in gay rights litigation before the U.S. Supreme Court because this issue matters to their members and subsequently contributes to the institutional maintenance of their organizations. Similarly, other types of membership groups, private centers, and public-interest law firms proactively participate in gay rights litigation because their members or leaders believe that their participation or their absence makes a difference at the Supreme Court.

Thus, while it is not clear that organized interest participation influences Supreme Court outcomes, it is clear that organized interests believe it is worth their time and effort to participate. They expend valuable amounts of what is often quite limited financial and staff resources to articulate and, they hope, to advance their interests. Given the unsettled nature of this issue area and the Supreme Court's varied record in gay rights cases, it is likely that organized interests—both liberal and conservative repeat players— will continue to participate and that new interests—including one-hit wonders—will continue to join the fray, as well.

6 Parents and Paperwork

Same-Sex Parents, Birth Certificates, and Emergent Legality

Susan M. Sterett

Birth Certificates and Family Responsibility

The effort to add a second parent's name to a birth certificate has been one site of both individual and collective claims for recognition for queer parenting (Connolly 2002; Dalton 2001).[1] The story of origins that birth certificates tell, cutting off the "back story" of other beginnings (Yngvesson and Coutin 2006), has allowed organizations to litigate claims to equality on behalf of queer families. The National Center for Lesbian Rights (NCLR) and the Lambda Legal Defense and Education Fund in the United States have provided amicus briefs and litigated claims to recognition on birth certificates (see, e.g., *In the matter of infant girl W*, 2006; *In re Bonfield*, 2002; *In re adoption of R.B.F.*,2002). Since birth certificates, like marriage certificates, are issued by states, lawyers can take cases that leverage birth certificate recognition through the full faith and credit clause of the U.S. Constitution. (See e.g., *Davenport et al. v. Little-Bowser et al.*, 2005; *Finstuen v. Edmondson*, 2006, affirmed in part as *Finstuen v. Crutcher*, 2007; for discussion, see Carbone 2006; Ross 1999). The regulation of intimacy through marriage and sodomy laws has been grounds for litigants seeking to claim rights from national legislatures, state appellate courts, and the U.S. Supreme Court (see, e.g., Daum; Frank, Boutcher, and Camp; Fisher; Currier; Rosenblum, all this volume). Parenting has been another ground on which organizations and individuals have claimed intimate responsibility (Richman 2002, 2009). Parenting has included both adults who agree to be parents together so that schools, health insurers, and physicians will recognize them, and the division of responsibility upon separation when divorce law would not apply since parents could not have been married (Andersen, this volume).

In the United States, as of March 2007, eleven states allowed second-parent adoption for same-sex partners or adoption of a child by a parent's partner. Twenty-four states did not. In fifteen states, some lower courts allowed second-parent adoptions (Lambda Legal, "Overview of State Adoption Statutes"). Recognition of an adoption by a lower court in a state that seems not to recognize that adoption creates a peculiar, in-between legal status that social movement scholars do not usually recognize as a gain. That legal recognition may matter for the parents, but it is not visible in the ordinary appellate court documents useful in analyses of litigation as a social movement strategy. Between the late 1990s and the summer of 2007, Colorado was one of the states where a lower court allowed second-parent adoption, without any support from appellate courts. This chapter traces how that happened.

First, I describe the legal strategizing that occurred around how to add the name of a second parent, someone of the same sex as the first parent, to a birth certificate in Colorado. Like the birth certificate cases won in appellate courts by the National Center for Lesbian Rights and the Lambda Legal Defense and Education Fund, a win in a lower court and in the state registrar's office was a victory for individual parents and for a movement. Birth certificates can fall between movement issues and individual concerns, making the local issuance of birth certificates a fruitful place to examine the production of law (Whittier 2002). Because, in Colorado, becoming a legally cognizable second parent depended on *not* making a claim in an appellate court, the case invites reconsideration of victory in appellate court as what counts as "the law," which I address in the second part of the chapter. Third, the changes in the law are not solely the result of movement mobilization. The opportunities available to lawyers and parents have depended on other changes in family law, which parents and their attorneys deployed. Finally, I connect the legal recognition of two legal parents of the same sex on a birth certificate to the movement toward openness about origins and family connections, advocated by adoptee and birth parents' rights groups.

In 1992, Colorado was also the site of one of the more high-profile political fights in the country around equality regardless of sexual orientation, leading to a significant Supreme Court case, *Romer v. Evans*, and movement mobilization. For these reasons, it provides a good case study of emergent legality. I have interviewed almost all of the lawyers in Colorado who have placed two parents of the same sex on birth certificates. Lawyers estimated that perhaps two hundred of these proceedings have been undertaken. I have also interviewed about forty of the parents involved, or just about twenty families. (Some families understand themselves to have more than two parents; for some families I did not interview both parents.) I also rely upon published court cases, as well as some unpublished material that lawyers cited in strategizing for same-sex parents in Colorado. National social-movement litigators did not believe Colorado was a good state in which to bring a test case about adding second names to birth certificates.

Colorado: Tracing a Policy Process

In 1992, the state of Colorado enacted Amendment 2, which prohibited cities from enacting ordinances that would prohibit discrimination on the basis of sexual orientation. The Colorado Legal Initiatives Project organized to challenge the amendment in court, and the effort became a focus of social movement legal work. The U.S. Supreme Court decided that challenge as *Romer v. Evans* on May 20, 1996; in it, the Court held Colorado's Amendment 2 unconstitutional (see, e.g. Andersen 2005; Gerstmann 1999; Keen and Goldberg 1998). Less than a month later, on June 13, the Colorado Court of Appeals decided *In re T.K.J.* The appellate court held that the Colorado stepparent provision in the state adoption statute did not allow adoption by a second parent of the same sex as the first. Judges in Denver had granted second-parent adoptions before 1996; however, the two women in *T.K.J.* had filed for a second-parent adoption in a neighboring county. The judge had denied the petition. Against the recommendation of other lawyers active in the movement for gay and lesbian equality, the lawyer for the women took the case on appeal. They lost, making it no longer possible for any judge in the state to use the adoption statute to grant second-parent adoptions. In Colorado, becoming a legally recognized second parent in a same-sex partnership entirely depended on making a claim that would not be tested in the appellate courts, since no lawyers believed that they could win after *T.K.J.*

Lawyers believe that Amendment 2, *Romer*, and *T.K.J.* are connected. Amendment 2 gave a rough sense of what a majority of the people of Colorado might have been thinking with regard to gay and lesbian rights, though there were many conversations about misrepresentations and an urban/rural split in the vote. A rough sense of the polity did not invite a belief that a claim for legal equality for gays and lesbians could succeed. Although *Romer* countered Amendment 2, it did so through the judiciary, rather than through a change in public opinion. The decision itself disappointed some who were committed to equality on the basis of sexual orientation. Although it struck down Amendment 2, it did so without expanding how courts would evaluate antigay and antilesbian legislation (Gerstmann 1999, 133–39). The Colorado Court of Appeal judges were unlikely to hold that the adoption statute allowed second-parent adoption so soon after *Romer*.

The majority decided that an adult who can adopt under the stepparent exception had to be married to the parent. The women in *T.K.J.* were not married, so they could not adopt each other's child without relinquishing their rights to their own biological children. The mothers gained a concurring opinion by a judge who argued that if adoption is in the best interests of children, then the child should get a second parent, and the state legislature ought to address the problem. Colorado's state legislature did not agree.

A lawyer long active in the gay and lesbian community thought there had to be a solution. She had friends who were the legal parents of one of their children but not of the other because one had been adopted before *T.K.J.* and the other had joined the family afterward. Then two clients who had just moved from Florida and who wanted to put both mothers on their child's Florida birth certificate came through her office door. She explained that she could not get both of them on the birth certificate. They explained that their situation was different from what she expected. Thanks to reproductive technology, one mother was the genetic mother and the other was the gestational mother. The attorney filed a petition in Boulder under the Uniform Parentage Act to get both mothers declared legal mothers.

In response to both changes in family structure and changes in the law, the National Conference on Uniform State Laws drafted the Uniform Parentage Act (UPA) in 1973, after having worked on it for several years. The purpose of that Act was, as a lawyer in Denver explained it in 2005, to provide two loving parents to children. It did not focus on whether the parents were married; indeed, it specifically addressed protecting children regardless of whether they were born in wedlock. Nor did it specify that the parents must be of different sexes; in 1973, unwed fathers and mothers, not same-sex parents, were the concern.

In the case of the two biological mothers, the lawyer argued that both women had a biological connection and that both held themselves out as parents to the child, making them both mothers. She won the court order in Colorado, sent it to Florida (which does not allow gays and lesbians to adopt), and got a birth certificate for the child that had both mothers' names on it. The Florida state registrar said that the state would put the second mother on the back of the birth certificate in a reprotech case, something it seemed the registrar had done before in recognizing court orders from other states. That was fine with the attorney and her clients, and the state issued the birth certificate. Winning recognition in Florida required only that the state registrar recognize a court order from another state, a routine matter, rather than consider whether to recognize lesbian parents. The action might seem to be limited to cases in which reproductive technology created two biological mothers. However, since this case, attorneys have filed petitions in which one mother is biologically related and both are adoptive mothers, though lawyers disagreed about whether the statute could apply in all these cases. The Boulder courts have granted petitions in which both parents were present since the child's arrival in the family, whether through birth or through adoption.

The UPA states that documenting legal parenthood for fathers requires that one have held oneself out as the parent of the child for six months and that there be no contestation of paternity. Later, the UPA says that the terms "mother" and "father" can be used interchangeably. The UPA standard that attorneys use is whether the parents intended to have the child together. If they did, they can both be declared parents. Between 2005 and 2006, actions to add a second name to a birth certificate cost a total of about $1,500 for both parents' lawyers and for the filing of court papers.

UPA actions could stay out of appellate court because few had reason to challenge them. Parents did not have to go to appellate court to get birth certificates recognized. No attorney had ever heard from a client that the birth certificate issued after a court order was not respected by a school or employer or physician.[2] One attorney speculated that a lack of concern might reflect the general respect in the world for the authority of the law. People who might not think same-sex parenting right or moral would nonetheless have before them an official piece of paper from a state office, stating that a child has two mommies. (Every lawyer I talked to refers to these as the two-mommy cases, rather than same-sex parent cases.) Who would challenge that? Who would disbelieve it? Birth certificates stop inquiries into origins, or at least lawyers and parents can hope they will. In Patricia Ewick and Susan Silbey's terms, perhaps those who respect the order are "before the law." People defer to the law's authority, an authority not simply backed by fear but dependent upon the cooperation and deference of those who stand before the law (Ewick and Silbey 1998, 74–75). However, people have every reason to cooperate. Cooperation may be an already existing inclination to accept families of all forms. Furthermore, a birth certificate is just one more piece of paper in the lives of human resource officers, school officials, and staff in pediatricians' offices, hardly central to their jobs. Even were such an official inclined to disbelieve a birth certificate, she would be most likely to challenge it by simply refusing to honor it. Only one parent to whom I spoke explained that her employer's human resources officer had demanded and then not honored the birth certificate. The officer's supervisor told her to honor it.

Without problems in schools or medical offices, only the official ordered to issue the birth certificate, the state registrar, might challenge the lower court's authority. The lawyers advised clients on how to make it difficult for the registrar to challenge such order. In 2000, under the socially conservative governor Bill Owens, a Republican, the state of Colorado did challenge the issuance of orders for birth certificates with the names of two parents of the same sex on them. In reproductive technology cases, which are the most common source of requests for such documents, the court orders under the UPA were issued before the child was born. Lawyers advised parents to file for birth certificates within the time limit allowed for such applications but after the time limit for challenging the court order; by doing so, they would ensure that challenges by the registrar to the orders for the birth certificates would be filed too late. The Colorado Supreme Court dismissed Colorado's challenge (*Colorado Department of Public Health and Environment, State Registrar v. E.C.V. et al.*, #00SA272, September 5, 2000).

If the state registrar couldn't challenge the issuance of birth certificates to two parents of the same sex, who would or could? Lawyers have different interpretations of the rather limited circumstances under which a birth certificate challenge would go up on appeal. What about in a bitter dispute when a couple is splitting up? (See *Wheeler v. Wheeler* [2007], a Georgia case where the court refused to put aside an adoption decree in a relationship dissolution.) One lawyer said that the legal community was "crossing its fingers" that such a case didn't go up on appeal, though not all lawyers agreed that would be a problem. One experienced attorney argued that even if one were to get a homophobic panel on appeal, the birth certificates and the UPA actions supporting them could be challenged only on their own terms; that is, that the birth mother or first adoptive mother had been subjected to coercion or fraud. A more likely alternative as different attorneys learned about how to handle these actions would be for someone to file a petition in a county outside Boulder, be denied, and choose to appeal. Attorneys who practice in this area knew not to do that; one attorney said that the only concern was that someone not part of the network would try it. Semiquiet, semipublic, legal but not fully recognized resolutions allow legal systems both a way to publicly refuse to acknowledge parents and, at the same time, a way to acknowledge them.

In Colorado, the trial judges in Boulder and all the school officials and pediatricians and human resources officers who recognize families as legal families were at the forefront of legal change for queer parents. In at least two cases, Social Security case-level decision makers have recognized same-sex families. One attorney in Colorado worked to gain survivor benefits for a friend's child. She believed that she won at least as much because the decison maker remembered a personal connection to the lawyer. The National Center for Lesbian Rights has also brought successful cases before the Social Security Administration. The plethora of officials the late modern state means that even the federal government has recognized same-sex partners as parents. Social movement theorists have long taught that movements respond to and shape the opportunities available to them. Opportunities for same-sex parents have included policies that are the accretion of policy made for other reasons and the technology that has allowed remaking of family (McCann 1994; Meyer 2002). The proliferation of places that must recognize legal documents in the late modern state means that lawyers and clients can mobilize the law outside the appellate courts when the appellate courts are hostile.

Issues are sometimes left to judges because other institutions can thereby avoid responsibility. The Colorado state legislature had refused to allow second-parent adoptions. It also, however, declined to stop the Boulder judges from allowing second-parent adoptions. When the state legislature tried to do so, in 2003, the bill was stopped in committee after testimony by, as one attorney put it, "mothers with babes in arms." The attorney explained that the practice was on every relevant political actor's radar; they would just as soon not put it on politicians' front burner. As an individual claim, a request to place a second parent on a birth certificate fits well within the limits of ordinary statutory interpretation.

Winning Outside the Appellate Courts

One objection to including placement on a birth certificate, done by lawyers in offices rather than through an appellate court in an analysis of social movements and the law, is that only appellate courts make "real" law. Appellate courts articulate what the formal norms are within a jurisdiction; without a victory in an appellate court, one cannot make a rights claim against officials. The most skeptical work holds that even appellate court victories do not count, because they do not lead to any change on the ground (Rosenberg 2008 [1991]). Skepticism over rights-based politics raises questions about whether the rights have any practical meaning to anyone. Rights as articulated by appellate courts always must be implemented through local power structures; ignoring that and treating rights as self-executing allows one to fall into a trap of the "myth of rights" (Rosenberg 2008 [1991]; Scheingold 2004 [1974]). Local power structures profoundly limit the meanings of rights (Fortun 2001; Rosenberg 2008 [1991]; Silverstein 2007). In the United States, for example, judicial bypass procedures allows local courts to make it difficult for young women to obtain abortions, despite the existence of formally recognized legal rights (Silverstein 2007). The articulation of rights through courts might dampen political organizing, leading activists to pour into litigation resources that might best have been used for efforts to achieve political change through the legislatures and by transforming public opinion (Rosenberg 2008 [1991]). Without attention to follow-through by social movements, rights fail (Epp 1998; McCann 1994, 2004).

People learn the law from places other than appellate courts, and sometimes lawyers and court officials do not learn the appellate law at all (Haltom and McCann 2004; Silverstein 2007). People looking to become legally recognized parents get information from their friends, the news, their lawyers, and Web sites. Although UPA actions are individual rather than collective claims for equality, they depend on a collective movement. Parents learn about how to undertake UPA actions at community workshops, from books written by people active in GLBTQ legal organizations and social movements, from conversations among attorneys (Willoughby 2003; http://www.coloradoglbtbar.org), and from articles on Web sites (Letellier 2001; http://www.nclrights.org/publications/LGBTfamilies.htm; "Second Parent Adoptions: A Snapshot of Current Law"). The proliferation of legal knowledge and the increasing number of places one engages officials in the late modern state requires the decentering of appellate courts as the primary institutions in public law. Knowledge of appellate courts as institutions that state the law available to many via interest organizations' Web sites is still not central to most people's daily lives.

Changes in whom society recognizes as a parent allow us to look again at what it means for a social movement to succeed in law. If a woman pursues a case because she doesn't want to lose her child and the case ends up in appellate court and the judgment recognizes nonbiological parenting as legitimate, does it count as part of a social movement? What if cases accumulate in a way that changes the law? For the people in the case, a primary goal may be one that is a matter of a selective benefit: if I don't pursue this case, I will lose my child. Social movement gains are more commonly framed as a matter of a public good: one pursues a goal because it promotes rule change. Marc Galanter has most famously argued that one-shot players are usually playing not for rule change but to achieve a particular benefit. Many one-shot players are transformed into repeat players, or people who are playing for rule change, by interest organizations and social movements, with their attendant lawyers (Galanter 1974). Without that, we cannot assume that we will see rule change to benefit those who are disadvantaged by the rules (see Daum, this volume).

However, parents and their lawyers can claim their children for their own sake, as well as because it is a fee-paying business and because it pursues social-movement political aims of public recognition (see also Sterett 1998). The practice of gaining legal recognition invites a refocus on legal mobilization and social movements. Building on the work of Gloria Anzaldua, Nancy Whittier has argued for looking at social movements at the borders: "between the individual and the movement, between the movement and the state" (Whittier 2002, 307). Parents who claim legal recognition of themselves as parents may do so in a way that works to their individual benefit and also supports the collective benefits of cultural and political change or at least furthers the goal of greater acceptance of gays and lesbians as parents.

In the United States, leading interest organizations have indeed won significant victories concerning birth certificates in the appellate courts. However, where the appellate law is hostile, parents can sometimes use preexisting changes in the law to gain recognition by local officials. To get a two-parent birth certificate issued for a child requires that the two parents agree that they are the parents of the child and that local legal officials ratify that agreement; ratification does not require an appellate court. Adding a name to a birth certificate can be a parenting strategy as much as a movement strategy, and recognition from local officials can be all parents want. Decisions to grant birth certificates do not remain inert, only a symbolic victory by a distant interest organization, because so many parents see themselves as having reasons to get birth certificates, and the issuance of birth certificates is routine for state registrars' offices. Parents may care more about winning recognition by their children's friends or by an employer's benefits office than about winning in an appellate court. Legal equality emerges in layers (Hull 2006).

Family Law, Birth Certificates, and Unnatural Facts

Transformations in law that allow the placement of two parents of the same sex on a birth certificate long predate the current movement for equality for gay and lesbian families, just as claims to marriage equality are possible in the context of transformations in marriage (see, e.g., Coontz 2005). The names of parents may be placed on a birth certificate outside the framework of appellate law because doing so fits well with changes toward more gender-neutral families charged with private responsibility for members (see also Sullivan 2004). Debates over parenting constitute one part of the legal reasoning in the marriage cases in the states (*Andersen v. King County*, 2006; *Goodridge v. Massachusetts Department of Public Health*, 2003; *Hernandez v. Robles*, 2006; *Morrison v. Sadler*, 2005) and in the constitutional amendments that would define marriage as involving one man and one woman. In Colorado, referenda providing for domestic partnerships and declaring that marriage must involve one man and one woman were on the November 2006 ballot (see, e.g. "Rights, No Marriage," *Rocky Mountain News*, September 19, 2006, 1). Ads for the amendment argued that without a marriage amendment, children would be denied a mother and a father. The domestic-partnership initiative failed, and Coloradans affirmed that marriage was between one man and one woman. Recognizing parents constitutes part of an understanding of rights and responsibilities for queer families. Birth certificates claim state and family recognition through the form of routinely recording natural facts. They are also artifacts of the modern state: without an extensive system of birth registration via certificates and perceptions of benefits tied to birth certificates, the claims could not exist.

Provision of caretaking for children has involved multiple parties for centuries; caretaking has not always rested with biological parents (Berry 1993; Boswell 1988; Carp 1996; Cmiel 1995). The registration of births made production of families through law legally visible, though courts have worked out questions of inheritance and family for many years. In the early twentieth century, birth certificates in the United States created "as if" families for adopted children by issuing new birth certificates that recorded the names of the adoptive parents (Carp 1996,52–54). Birth certificates tell a story of origin, but the story is one that always leaves out alternative beginnings. Over time, those other beginnings have included gamete donation, surrogacy contracts, adoption grounded in international inequality and state policies regulating family, and the termination of parental rights for families in distress in the United States. As part of the legal structure of the state, birth certificates do not declare natural facts but call facts into existence (Yngvesson and Coutin 2006). Putting a second parent of the same sex on a birth certificate provides a current ground for claiming rights for queer families and for relying upon the legal crafting of parenthood. It can evoke a fantasy of a parenthood that is wholly natural, not crafted or enforced through law (Coutin, Maurer, and Yngvesson 2002, 823). When state legislatures discuss queer families as the only unnatural legal family formation, whether in the context of marriage or of birth certificates, they evoke the dream of the unmediated natural, which the law does nothing more than recognize. That dream has had little basis in the multiplicities of caretaking.

In addition to reproductive technology and adoption law, changes in fathers' rights in the United States have facilitated recognition of queer parenting. Unwed fathers' rights cases from the 1970s on were part of a broader movement in constitutional law toward formal gender equality, partially removing gender from family in law (see, e.g., Fineman 1995; Glendon 1997; Jacob 1988; Sullivan 2004). Such cases were also part of the commitment of the welfare state to have fathers pay child support for children whose mothers received Aid to Families with Dependent Children or Temporary Assistance to Needy Families (after 1996). Whatever the state's interest in including fathers, challenges to the termination of fathers' legal rights and to their responsibility for their children have been litigated by families challenging adoptions (Dowd 1996; Shanley 1995; Woodhouse 1993). Reproductive technology has invited the legal system into policing recognition of gamete contribution, gestation, intent, and caretaking as part of parenthood (*Johnson v. Calvert*, 1993; *In re Nicholas H.*, 2002; Hollinger 2004).

State courts have become more likely to recognize custody claims by GLBTQ parents in disputes over children, with a few notable exceptions (Pinello 2003; Richman 2002, 2009). Changed interpretations of parenting, perhaps in part motivated by recognition of gender equality and by public fiscal caution, have been available to lawyers for same-sex parents. Lawyers and parents have said that same-sex parents have been picking up the pieces left by problems within heterosexuality, particularly when adopting children who have been in foster care.

Not only does recognition of a second parent fit with changes in family law; it does not cost states anything and indeed establishes one more person who is legally responsible for a child, minimizing state responsibility. Around the world, courts have proven much more likely to recognize rights that require no redistribution of funds (Hirschl 2004). Like cases involving unwed fathers, birth certificate claims fit with policies that hold families responsible for their children without direct state financial support. It is also consistent with contract as a central format for law in the United States (Friedman 1965; Hurst 1955). In the United States, the Adoption and Safe Families Act of 1988 provided incentives for the states to move children from public care into adoptive homes (Bartholet 1999).

Since then, many cities have recruited gay and lesbian adoptive parents. Many private adoption agencies also work with gay and lesbian couples (Brodzinsky 2003). Advocacy groups for LGBT rights frame gay and lesbian adoption as good for the children who need homes, not as a matter of right for adults (see, e.g., Howard 2006). As the "gayby" boom took hold with the increasing availability of reproductive technology, it was accompanied by an increase in the number of international adoptions from countries that allowed single people to adopt, including China, Vietnam, India, and Guatemala. From the 1990s on, adoption agencies facilitated the transport of thousands of children into the United States. (For statistics, see http://travel.state.gov/family/adoption/stats/stats_451.html.) Though the placing countries did not themselves support same-sex family adoption, gay and lesbian couples could adopt from these countries by working with an adoption agency with a sympathetic social worker who would do a home study, having one person apply for the adoption, then legitimating it with both parents if possible back in the home state. Same-sex adoptive families, like heterosexual or single adoptive families, were inscribed by the state in a climate that sought to hasten adoption of children in public care and to provide a choice for those with access to reproductive technology or international or private domestic adoption. In states that have not allowed gay and lesbian couples to adopt, adoption agencies and public social welfare agencies may be in the odd position of recognizing a couple or a family throughout the adoption process until the final moment when parents' names are placed on a birth certificate. Adoption articulates a narrative of loss, hope, and improvement (Yngvesson and Coutin 2006). To treat same-sex parents as legally not cognizable while also placing children with such couples requires states to act on adoption as incarnating hope and improvement, but not improvement enough for the state to recognize same-sex parents as part of a family.

High-profile disputes over the rights of birth parents and the rights of adoptive parents or contests concerning children within queer families put legal finality on the political table for both parents and lawyers (see, e.g., DeBoer 1994; Dowd 1996; Lambda Legal Defense and Education Fund 1999; Pinello 2003; Richman 2005, 2009; *Thomas S. v. Robin Y.*, 1994; Verhovek 1993). Although lawyers will explain that acting like a parent often gains one the rights and responsibilities of parenthood, that point is hardly reassuring to people who hope to avoid custody disputes and know the horror stories about cases that drag out for years. Lawyers in the United States advise lesbians not to use a known sperm donor in forming their families if they wish to ensure that they will not find themselves later in a custody dispute involving a man. Separating gamete contribution from gestation clarifies how children might have two biological mothers, particularly when the mothers agree, and both are caretaking. Children can also have two cognizable fathers if both are caretaking and one also contributed sperm (Dalton 2000). As one lawyer who represented the legal parent in a custody dispute between lesbian ex-partners explained, bitter custody battles in same-sex couples are no different from bitter divorces. Indeed, the lawyer explained that gay couples have skipped marriage since most states have not granted them the right to marry and have gone straight to divorce (see Andersen, this volume). Court orders require ex-partners to share information about the minutiae of parenting, including children's medical appointments. Some parents wish to avoid a custody dispute among extended family if one parent dies. Birth certificates invite the hope of eliminating any possibility of custody disputes in such cases if the surviving parent is legally fit, since they cut off inquiries into who is really a parent. That caretaking, gamete contribution, intent to parent, and gestation count in winning recognition for parents and that they count differently in different states opens space for multiple ways to legally recognize parents.

The multiplicity in law as it frames technology and defines where children belong is illustrated in Colorado by a custody battle in a contested adoption having nothing to do with queer families. This case set the stage for recognizing same-sex parents based on caretaking. In the case, a child had been placed in an adoptive home; before the adoption was final, the birth mother regretted the placement and asked to have the child returned to her. The putative adoptive parents kept the child, and it took years for the case to wend its way through the courts. The court decided to leave the child where he was and ordered visitation for the birth mother (*In the matter of the custody of C.C.R.S.*, 1995). As a lawyer said, the decision may have been bad for birth parents, but it was useful for queer families. The case counters the high-profile cases that made the news in the 1990s, in which putative adoptive parents had to relinquish a child when they had wrongly dragged out the legal process. The case is an example of the uneasy and sometimes ad hoc resolutions the courts reach in custody battles. Children's advocates believe that children and the legal process operate on very different time lines: one year is very little time in a legal appeal and a very long time for a young child, leading to a sense among some judges that children need to stay in whatever stable home they are in.

Nine years after C.C.R.S., the Colorado Court of Appeals recognized a second parent as a "psychological parent" in the dissolution of a lesbian relationship, although the legal mother denied that her ex-partner was a parent (*In the matter of E.L.M.C.*, 2004). The trial jude, Judge Coughlin, explained that the legal mother and her partner had jointly issued an adoption announcement and the ex-partner had acted as a parent, showing up at medical appointments and being called "mother" by the child. The case was bitter, widely discussed in the local international adoption community, and covered in the local news (e.g., Pankratz

2004; Rodriguez 2004). Both the National Center for Lesbian Rights and the Colorado Legal Initiatives Project presented amicus briefs. One Republican legislator threatened Judge Coughlin with impeachment for his decision, but Judge Coughlin was a widely respected judge who had practiced as a district attorney and in oil and gas law before he became a judge. The legislator gained no support, even from the socially conservative governor (see, e.g., Henley 2004). In many states, courts have recognized both parents' rights in custody disputes, so the unusual adoption case from the 1990s was not the only route into recognizing same-sex parenting in the very flexible law governing the best interest of the child (Richman 2005, 2009).

Recognizing queer parenting through the issuance of two-parent birth certificates requires changes in family law. Those changes represent the best efforts of lawyers and judges to graft a private family model of two married biological parents onto proliferating forms of reproduction and responsibility. Queer activists have intended to disrupt a biological model of family, not match it (see, e.g., Bernstein and Reimann 2001, 5; Weston 1997). Disruption and deployment can work well together.

Powerful Paper and Other Origins

Expecting that recognition of one's self as a parent requires the stamp of authority from official paper is part of the late modern state, in which registration makes people visible to a plethora of officials (on states and legibility see Scott 1998; Agamben 1998). Legality is not dichotomous in a world in which there are extended family members, children's schools, the pediatrician's office, and human resources benefits offices, all of which can recognize one as a parent or not. People come in and out of view as legally cognizable. Birth certificates can seem to make that visibility final and beyond question, but if a birth certificate does not fit with expectations or if one believes one's employer does not usually ask for birth certificates before enrolling in benefits but has done so in a particular case, the paperwork can seem less protective. For most families most of the time, appellate courts are distant and decisions from them an unlikely occurrence. Legal recognition happens for one's self and for one's family in local offices. Law that local officials recognize is all the law most people need, and debates over appellate courts can seem puzzling or pointless.

People can apply official legal understandings of responsibility to themselves. As Susan Coutin has argued, people can reinterpret the law and remake it as it applies to them; officials who are not charged with formal enforcement of law also must interpret it and apply it, sometimes remaking categories as they apply them. Coutin's argument, framed around immigration law, reaches well beyond that area; it is useful in understanding the remaking of family law for same-sex family, in contexts much more informal than appellate courts. Coutin argues:

> The people who carry out immigration law—including not only government officials but also employers, Department of Motor Vehicle clerks, social workers, college admissions officials, and immigrants themselves—must formulate their own interpretations of immigration categories in order to assess others' legal statuses. By acting on these understandings, both the people being defined and the people doing the defining can influence the definitions produced, thus cumulatively creating law, in an informal sense. (Coutin 1998, 903)

When faced with queer families raising children, school officials and pediatricians choose either to recognize someone as a parent or not. So do day care providers, employers' human resource offices, hospitals, and members of one's extended family. Every time one presents oneself as a parent and is accepted as one, all who recognize responsibility redefine the legal and social category of parent. One comes into view in law every time one is not challenged or can document parenthood if asked. The promise of paper blurs distinctions between social movement goals described as cultural or aspirations to social acceptance on one hand and political change or change in state policy on the other (see Bernstein 2002). Unofficial or semiofficial law can feed the aspirations of people, enacting legality to contest the official story (Hull 2006, 200). Making a claim to a human resources officer, with or without a birth certificate, implies an expectation of social, political, and legal recognition of one's family.

Family formation, like immigration law, reveals "the import of having or lacking particular kinds, of papers, [and] the power of legal constructs to own persons" (Yngvesson and Coutin 2006, 187). The ownership of persons by legal constructs can both bring people up against the law and, in other circumstances, promise liberation from more personal forms of oppression (Ewick and Silbey 1998; Williams 1991). Legal categories mismatch the reality they claim to describe; they call it into being. A belief that one is part of a family develops somewhere within and outside the law, in love and caretaking (Connolly 2002). The promise of law for gay and lesbian families in the United States is that legal constructs might describe an origin, one behind which officials cannot inquire. As one lawyer working in family law in Colorado for gay and lesbian families said, it cannot be that clerks want to start asking whether someone listed on a birth certificate is really the father or mother.

Birth certificates also shape the stories one can tell about the future. When one is placed on the birth certificate of a child, one has agreed to be permanently responsible. The state governs those responsibilities; any individual arrangements parents would like to make with each other are only evidence of intent. The state circumscribes responsibilities; what people ask for in asking to be placed on birth certificates is to have the state govern their role as a parent. When one woman went to a lawyer in Colorado to ask to be removed from the birth certificate of the child she'd adopted with her lesbian partner, she received a scolding from the attorney who had done the birth certificate. The attorney explained that the certificate originated from a court order. It could not be rescinded. The claim of parenthood made by same-sex parents today is a claim to freedom from interference not by a unitary state but by unofficial officials with power: pediatricians, hospitals, schools, human resources personnel who can place dependents on an employee's health insurance, or relatives who might contest custody after a parent's death. It is also a claim of freedom to act as a legally responsible party (see also Eng 2003, 5).

The legal facts of birth certificates and caretaking open space for queer families. However, the movement for recognition fits uneasily with a broad move to openness in telling other stories of origins. Children grow up. As adults, many reflect on the stories of their childhood. From the 1970s on, adoptees have argued against the "as if" stories told to them and against the secrecy maintained about records after the Second World War in the United States (Carp 2004; *Daughter From Danang* 2002; Modell 1994). The Evan B. Donaldson Institute, a prominent adoption research and advocacy institute in the United States, issued a report in November 2007 that argued that allowing adult adoptees access to their records, including their original birth certificate, was best for them, for the birth parents, and for adoption practice in general (Freundlich 2007). Birth parents' testimony mourning their loss after the adoption of their children persuaded social workers of the virtues of openness (Modell 2001). Domestic adoptions are increasingly open.

The rights of birth parents are of concern to some adoption advocacy groups, as well, including the Donaldson Institute (Smith 2006). Ethicists argue that children for whom gametes were donated ought to know about that donation, as well (e.g., Ethics Committee of the American Society for Reproductive Medicine 2004). Adoptees'-rights movements have worked on state laws to open adoption records, allowing adoptees access to stories of origins. Searching for birth parents is a business even in intercountry adoptions, which can be the most difficult to trace. The Hague Convention on Intercountry Adoption, for which the United States drafted implementing regulations in 2007, articulates a right to know one's origins. The Convention requires that contracting states maintain information about a child's origins, including identity about birth parents, and provide access to that information when the child reaches adulthood (Hague Convention on Protection of Children and Cooperation in Respect of Intercountry Adoption 1993, Article 30). Many organizations offer trips back to the country in which an adopted child was born (e.g., Our Chinese Daughters Foundation, http://

www.ocdf.org; Yngvesson and Coutin 2006). Memoirs by adoptees expand the stories of family (Brooks 2006; Savage 1999). Birth certificates describe legal origins, so they do not preclude connections between birth and adoptive families. However, on their face, they claim to record a birth, not the legal facts of responsibility, something criticized by many adoptees and their allies (see, e.g., http://www.bastards.org). The victories that come with recognition for queer families can include openness, but open records invite rethinking of birth certificates as a means to allocate legal responsibility.

Conclusion: Multiple Principles in Law

To what extent is an effort to gain recognition as a second parent by an individual application part of a social movement, beyond movement victories in appellate court? Such actions lay the foundation for change through legislation or referendum. In addition, the actions depend on reinterpreting the Uniform Parentage Act, undertaken by lawyers connected by movement networks. Analyzing the opportunities for strategizing created by state structures allows us to see the dynamics of change, even within a difficult political environment. Winning recognition in the Boulder court allowed adults to become legally recognized parents without disturbing a public framework that excluded same-sex parents from recognition in Colorado. The state registrar recognized the court orders when issuing birth certificates, and the Boulder judges recognized the birth certificates when dissolving relationships and ordering custody and child support.

Paper in the late modern state is powerful, yet legal recognition of psychological or de facto parenthood and the infrequency with which people are asked for birth certificates when they live in a metropolitan area call into question the meaning of that paper. For parents, a psychological-parent doctrine is untrustworthy in a world in which paper makes acts official. Furthermore, it comes up only in contested custody cases; it requires a presumption of an adversarial relationship that parents do not like. Parents who worry about what might happen to a child if one parent dies or the parents split up also hope that birth certificates will foreclose that discussion in the future. Birth certificates ratify parents in the daily legal order as parents understand it and their lawyers represent it. In Colorado, parents were not clearly ratified in appellate law, the level that most often counts when public-law scholars consider what the law is. Parents were left between the statuses of fully legally recognized and not that Kathleen Hull describes in her discussion of religious commitment ceremonies for same-sex couples. That in-between status can be useful. Following William Eskridge, Kathleen Hull argues for the virtue of "equality practice" in a context where gaining full legal recognition is unlikely (Hull 2006, 205–10). Granting birth certificates via trial courts while awaiting a collective solution is an equality practice (Eskridge 2002), and it claims public space.

The ironies attached to the use of birth certificates as a ground for family recognition are at least twofold. First, states detached birth certificates from birth in the early twentieth century to create "as if" biological families with two biological parents, just what movements for recognition of queer families have contested. Second, movements for adoptees' and birth parents' rights in the United States have argued against cutting off access to the documents that describe one's origins. Birth certificates describe legal responsibility, but advocates for adoptees and birth parents have argued they should do so in a context of openness concerning other stories of origin.

Finally, appellate law and expectations concerning choice constitute the legal moves that parents, lawyers, and judges make. Law is not an appellate court intervention wholly outside the world it organizes. The appellate law in Colorado was partially hostile to same-sex parents, though the recognition of de facto parents limited the impact of this hostility. Law includes tactical moves, and if one looks only to the appellate courts one excludes much of the strategizing people can do for themselves. By establishing a framework that allows people to become parents, a framework that to parents seems wholly legal and official, parents, lawyers, and the judges who issue orders and the officials who recognize them jointly reinterpret the law in a world of proliferating technologies of family formation.

Coda

In the 2007 legislative session in Colorado, the state legislature enacted House Bill 1330, which allowed a second parent of any sex to be placed on a birth certificate of a child with one parent. Governor Bill Ritter signed it into law ("Governor Signs 26 Bills into Law Today" 2007). The 2006 change in control of the legislature from Republican to Democrat and the election of a Democrat to the governor's house made passage of this law possible. The bill had been repeatedly sponsored by two lesbian activists. As one legislator pointed out, the law recognizing a second parent would create no new gay families and would increase children's claims on adults' resources by providing them with two parents; everyone in the capital who cared was aware of both points. The bill, the legislator argued, had simply been awaiting a partisan shift in the legislature and in the governor's office. The petition became available on the Web on August 23, 2007.

PART II

Activism, Discourse, and Legal Change

7 The Reform of Sodomy Laws From a World Society Perspective

David John Frank, Steven A. Boutcher, and Bayliss Camp

CONVENTIONAL ACCOUNTS OF sodomy-law reforms[1] tend to overstate the role of national factors, including local LGB social movements, and understate the role of global factors in promoting regulatory changes.[2] The tendency is sustained in part by prevailing inclinations to focus analytical attention on particular legal reforms in particular country contexts. In this chapter, we take a different approach. We begin by examining original cross-national data on the criminal regulation of sodomy from 1945 to 2005. The data reveal a global postwar sodomy-law reform wave, under way well before domestic LGB movements gained political standing almost anywhere in the world. Overwhelmingly, these reforms moved in a common liberalizing direction, that is, toward decriminalization, and they occurred in all sorts of countries (e.g., Western and non-Western, developed and lesser developed). We consider this evidence from a world-society perspective—an emerging sociological paradigm that stresses the global cultural and organizational underpinnings of nation-states and other modern entities (Meyer et al. 1997). Our core argument is that encompassing world-level changes—institutionalizing sharply individualized conceptions of society and sex—facilitated the global reform wave and in some countries gave rise to domestic LGB social movements. While these movements clearly played some role in spurring some sodomy-law reforms, the overall evidence suggests the priority of global cultural and organizational changes (cf. Jenness 2004). We conclude by suggesting some general ways a world-society approach can enhance studies of social movements and the law.

Background

Over recent decades, on a global basis, the criminal regulation of sodomy has been the subject of intense debate and scrutiny. During the period, on one hand, there have been celebrated cases of policy liberalization, including the U.S. Supreme Court's 2003 decision to decriminalize sodomy in *Lawrence v. Texas* (Ruskola 2005; Tribe 2004). On the other hand, during the period, there have been prominent cases of heightened regulation, as in a few fundamentalist regimes of the

Middle East (Whitaker 2006). The whole legal domain, it appears, has been in a state of upheaval, with regulatory transformations occurring worldwide.

To understand the upheaval, we begin by presenting original cross-national and longitudinal data on sodomy-law revisions. Most previous work on this topic has been conducted at the case level (e.g., de la Dehesa 2007; Eskridge 1999; Löfström 1998; Weeks 1989), placing some analytical blinders on the literature. We move forward by delineating worldwide changes in the criminalization of sodomy over recent decades, identifying what changes occurred in what countries at what times and then reflecting on the patterns that emerge.[3] This baseline information is essential to developing a general understanding of sodomy-law reforms.

We drew the relevant data from a large study of criminal sex laws in all 196 countries of the world between 1945 and 2005.[4] The raw materials for the study came from penal codes gathered from the libraries of Congress and several universities and various Internet sources. Nation-states are quintessential modern entities, and their central organizational apparatuses—prominently including their criminal laws—tend to be extensively documented and accessible to the public (Boli-Bennett and Meyer 1978; Boyle and Meyer 1998; Go 2003; Meyer et al. 1997).

From each country's penal codes over time, we drew and, where necessary, translated the relevant sodomy laws (assuming there were any) as they appeared and evolved on the books.[5] We then entered the relevant laws verbatim into a master data-file.

While some penal-code data are missing for some countries and most or all penal-code data are missing for others, the resulting dataset is nevertheless unique in its breadth and depth. In Table 7.1, we summarize our data coverage for 125 nation-states—more than half the world's total—including every independent country from Cambodia through Sierra Leone (Cambodia being an arbitrary starting point). For 62 of the 125 nation-states, we have complete data coverage, meaning full records on the country's sodomy laws for at least 50 of the 60 years in question. For another 31 countries, we have substantial coverage, meaning full data for at least 20 of the years between 1945 and 2005. Our coverage is incomplete for the remaining 32 countries.[6] We have, in short, a broad and deep evidentiary base—assembled from the penal codes of many countries over many years—to ground our empirical claims.

To enable systematic comparisons across countries and over time, we coded each sodomy law along two basic dimensions: scope, or the acts and actors covered by the law, and punishment, or the legal sanctions applied to offenders. The two dimensions may change separately or simultaneously.

To illustrate, we show the evolution of Canada's sodomy law between 1945 and 1984 in Table 7.2. The first reform during the period took place along the punishment dimension in 1953, when Article 147 replaced Article 202 and dramatically

TABLE 7.1
Case Coverage for Countries From Cambodia Through Sierra Leone
(n=125 out of total 196 countries)

Complete Coverage (no more than 10 years of missing data)* n=62		Substantial Coverage (more than 20 years of data) n=31	Incomplete Coverage (from 0 to 20 years of data) n=32
Cameroon	Japan	China	Cambodia
Canada	Kenya	Cote d'Ivoire	Cape Verde
Cen.Af. Republic	Korea, South	Czechoslovakia	Chad
Chile	Lebanon	Denmark	Comoros
Colombia	Liechtenstein	El Salvador	Congo
Costa Rica	Luxembourg	Ethiopia	Djibouti
Croatia	Madagascar	Gabon	Dominica
Cuba	Malawi	Gambia	Georgia
Cyprus	Malaysia	Ghana	Grenada
Czech Republic	Mali	Greece	Guinea
Dom. Republic	Malta	Hungary	Guinea-Bissau
Ecuador	Mexico	Iran	Indonesia
Egypt	Micronesia	Iraq	Jordan
Equatorial Guinea	Morocco	Israel	Kiribati
Eritrea	New Zealand	Kazakhstan	Kuwait
Estonia	Niger	Korea, North	Kyrgyzstan
Fiji Islands	Nigeria	Laos	Lesotho
Finland	Pakistan	Latvia	Lithuania
France	Pap. New Guin.	Liberia	Maldives
Germany	Paraguay	Libya	Mauritius
Germany, East	Peru	Macedonia	Moldova
Germany, West	Philippines	Mauritania	Monaco
Guatemala	Poland	Mongolia	Mozambique
Guyana	Portugal	Namibia	Nauru
Haiti	Romania	Netherlands	Nepal
Honduras	St. Lucia	Nicaragua	Oman
Iceland	Samoa (Western)	Norway	Palau
India	Saudi Arabia	Panama	Qatar
Ireland	Senegal	Russia	Saint Kitts
Italy	Seychelles	Rwanda	Saint Vincent
Jamaica	Sierra Leone	Serbia & Montenegro	San Marino
			Sao Tome

* For the former Soviet Republics and other countries that achieved independence between 1989 and 1993, complete coverage is defined as data for at least twelve years, and substantial coverage means data for at least six years.

decreased the crime's maximum penalty from life to 14 years in prison. The second revision took place along the scope dimension in 1970, when Articles 155 and 158 replaced 147, decriminalizing sodomy committed in private between consenting adults over the age of 21.[7] We coded each law in the dataset along these lines.

In Table 7.3, we summarize the sodomy-law reforms that occurred in all 125 countries in question. Between 1945 and 2005, we count a total of 72 regulatory amendments in 50 different nation-states.[8] Among these, only 8 took place along the punishment dimension, of which 7 decreased criminal penalties for sodomy. All 64 remaining reforms brought about changes to the scope dimension of the

TABLE 7.2
The Reform of Canada's Sodomy Laws 1945–1984

1945–52, CRIMINAL CODE, OFFENCES AGAINST MORALITY

Article 202: Every one is guilty of an indictable offence and liable to imprisonment for life who commits buggery, either with a human being or with any other living creature.

1953–69, CRIMINAL CODE, SEXUAL OFFENCES

Article 147: Every one who commits buggery or bestiality is guilty of an indictable offense and is liable to imprisonment for 14 years.

1970–84, CRIMINAL CODE, SEXUAL OFFENCES

Article 155: Every one who commits buggery or bestiality is guilty of an indictable offense and is liable to imprisonment for 14 years.

Article 158: (1) Articles 155 and 157 do not apply to any act committed in private between (a) a husband and his wife, or (b) any two persons, each of whom is 21 years or more of age, both of whom consent to the commission of the act. (2) For the purposes of subsection (1), (a) an act shall be deemed not to have been committed in private if it is committed in a public place, or if more than two persons take part or are present; and (b) a person shall be deemed not to consent to the commission of an act (i) if the consent is extorted by force, threats or fear of bodily harm or is obtained by false and fraudulent misrepresentations as to the nature and quality of the act, or (ii) if that person is, and the other party to the commission of the act knows or has good reason to believe that the person is feeble-minded, insane, or an idiot or imbecile.

law, and fully 57 of them—the overriding majority—involved scope *contractions*, either removing blanket prohibitions against sodomy or lowering homosexual ages of consent (33 and 24 of the changes, respectively). Often, the two forms of scope contraction happened sequentially. For example, Costa Rica deregulated sodomy for persons over 17 in 1970 and then reduced the homosexual age of consent from 17 to 15 in 1999.

Only the remaining 7 reforms entailed scope expansions in sodomy laws, and they tended to occur much earlier in the period than contractions (with median dates of 1973 for scope expansions and 1992 for scope contractions). Five of these extended or imposed blanket prohibitions on same-sex sex, while the two others increased homosexual ages of consent. Altogether, the changes were many and sweeping.

At the outset, then, the data in Table 7.3 confirm our initial impressions. They also provide the empirical backdrop for our discussion. Between 1945 and 2005, the sodomy laws of a great many countries underwent dramatic revision.

The Commonality of Legal Reforms

Beyond simply accumulating in number, sodomy-law reforms exhibited great substantive commonality over the postwar period. It could have been otherwise, of course. Even a great many legal changes could have taken the form of

TABLE 7.3

Sodomy-Law Reforms Across 125 Countries
(Cambodia through Sierra Leone), 1945–2005

I. Altering the law by decreasing or increasing punishments for same-sex sex:

		Decreasing	Increasing
Czechoslovakia	1950	5 years maximum to 1	
Canada	1953	life maximum to 14 years	
New Zealand	1961	life maximum to 7 years	
Romania	1969	10 years maximum to 5	
Samoa	1969	14 years maximum to 7	
Liberia	1976	5 years maximum to 1	
Malaysia	1976	life maximum to 20 years	
Pakistan	1980		0 years minimum to 2

II. Altering the scope of the law by lifting or imposing blanket prohibitions on same-sex sex:

		Lifting	Imposing
Portugal	1945	decriminalization (persons >16)	
Czechoslovakia	1961	decriminalization (persons >18)	
Hungary	1961	decriminalization (persons >20)	
Mongolia	1961	decriminalization (men >16)	
Germany, East	1968	decriminalization (men >18)	
Germany, West	1969	decriminalization (men >21)	
Canada	1970	decriminalization (men >21)	
Costa Rica	1970	decriminalization (persons >17)	
Finland	1971	decriminalization (persons >18)	
Cameroon	1972		criminalization (for persons >18)
Norway	1972	decriminalization (men >16)	
Libya	1973		criminalization (extended to private acts)
Malta	1973	decriminalization (men >17)	
Colombia	1980	decriminalization (persons >14)	
Iran	1982		criminalization (extended to women)
Panama	1982	decriminalization (men >12)	
Mauritania	1984		criminalization (for men >21)
New Zealand	1986	decriminalization (men >16)	
Israel	1988	decriminalization (men >18)	
Liechtenstein	1989	decriminalization (men >18, women >14)	

TABLE 7.3
(continued)

II. Altering the scope of the law by lifting or imposing blanket prohibitions on same-sex sex:

		Lifting	Imposing
Laos	1990	decriminalization (persons >14)	
Estonia	1992	decriminalization (men >16)	
Latvia	1992	decriminalization (men >18)	
Ireland	1993	decriminalization (men >17)	
Lithuania	1993	decriminalization (men >16)	
Russia	1993	decriminalization (men >16)	
Serbia & Mont	1994	decriminalization (men >18)	
Moldova	1995	decriminalization (men >16)	
Macedonia	1996	decriminalization (men >16)	
Romania	1996	decriminalization (persons >18)	
Ecuador	1997	decriminalization (persons >12)	
Chile	1998	decriminalization (men >18)	
Cyprus	1998	decriminalization (men >18)	
Kazakhstan	1998	decriminalization (men >16)	
Kyrgyzstan	1998	decriminalization (men >16)	
Malawi	2000		criminalization (extended to women)
Georgia	2000	decriminalization (men >16)	
Cape Verde	2004	decriminalization (men >14)	

III. Altering the scope of the law by lowering or raising the homosexual age of consent:

		Lowering	Raising
Cameroon	1967	age of consent (21 to 18)	
Gabon	1969		age of consent (15 to 21)
Luxembourg	1971		age of consent (14 to 18)
Netherlands	1971	age of consent (21 to 16)	
Germany, West	1973	age of consent (21 to 18)	
Denmark	1976	age of consent (18 to 15)	
France	1978	age of consent (21 to 18)	
Hungary	1978	age of consent (20 to 18)	
France	1982	age of consent (18 to 15)	
Canada	1985	age of consent (21 to 18)	
Germany, East	1989	age of consent (18 to 14)	
Czechoslovakia	1990	age of consent (18 to 15)	
Iceland	1992	age of consent (18 to 14)	

TABLE 7.3
(continued)

III. Altering the scope of the law by lowering or raising the homosexual age of consent:

		Lowering	Raising
Luxembourg	1992	age of consent (18 to 16)	
Germany	1994	age of consent (18 to 16)	
Croatia	1998	age of consent (18 to 14)	
Latvia	1998	age of consent (18 to 16)	
Costa Rica	1999	age of consent (17 to 15)	
Finland	1999	age of consent (18 to 16)	
Israel	2000	age of consent (18 to 16)	
Liechtenstein	2000	age of consent (18 to 16, men)	
Estonia	2001	age of consent (16 to 14)	
Romania	2001	age of consent (18 to 14)	
Hungary	2002	age of consent (18 to 14)	
Moldova	2002	age of consent (18 to 14)	
Lithuania	2004	age of consent (16 to 14)	

regulatory churning, representing random, contradictory, or orthogonal reforms, wrought in bounded country contexts. This is not the result observed. On the contrary, the reforms documented in Table 7.3 are strikingly patterned, almost uniformly moving in a common, liberalizing direction.

In particular, more than 90 percent of the amendments adopted between 1945 and 2005 limited, reduced, or lifted criminal sanctions against sodomy (cf. Frank and McEneaney 1999). Decriminalization was a seldom-broken rule. The clarity of the pattern is exceptional.

A first subwave of reform began when Portugal decriminalized sodomy (for the second time in its history; see discussion later in this chapter) in 1945. Czechoslovakia, Hungary, and Mongolia followed suit in 1961, all withdrawing their comprehensive bans on same-sex sex. They, in turn, were tracked by 29 other countries. The decriminalization reform wave continued to the end of the period, most recently altering Cape Verde's laws in 2004. Of course, over time, there were fewer and fewer sodomy prohibitions left to repeal.

Late in the 1960s, a second and related subwave of reform emerged (first in Cameroon, in 1967), which ultimately reduced homosexual ages of consent in 24 countries, often to a level on par with that for heterosexuals.[9] A few countries reduced the homosexual age of consent more than once during the period (e.g., France in 1978 and 1982). While these changes were less dramatic than decriminalization, they, too, involved the contraction of sodomy laws.

In 64 of 72 cases, in short, sodomy laws disappeared or retreated during the post–World War II period, with reforms decriminalizing sodomy, reducing homosexual ages of consent, or lessening punishments. The common thrust of the changes was very strong.

Exceptions to the liberalizing trend were accordingly rare (numbering only 8), and they occurred relatively early in the timeframe (with only one appearing after 1984). In most cases, exceptions were associated with regime change. Take, for example, the reforms adopted in Gabon in 1969 and in neighboring Cameroon in 1972. Both countries once formed parts of French Equatorial Africa, and both achieved independence in 1960. Their contrarian reforms—expanding criminal regulations of sodomy—represented efforts by local politicians to "localize" penal codes inherited from colonial overlords, thereby flexing the muscles of sovereignty. In several countries, over recent decades, political leaders have sought to advance their political aims by depicting sodomy (and sexual license generally) as decadent and bourgeois, foisted upon natives by Western colonialists (de la Dehesa 2007; Murray and Roscoe 1998). By bucking the global trend and strengthening sanctions against sodomy, Gabonian and Cameroonian officials signaled their resolve to reclaim their countries, standing apart from the West and the world.

Similarly, Pakistan increased the punishments for sodomy (and reformed several other sex laws) after a military takeover, and Iran expanded its sodomy regulation after the Islamic Revolution, rendering sex between women as punishable with 100 lashes (extending the existing British colonial-era ban on sex between men). In both cases, reforms sharply increased religious influences on the law and served to distance the countries' new leaders from past regimes more open to the West and the world (Rahami 2005).

It was precisely because of the prevailing global trend toward liberalization that such exceptions carried such heavy symbolic weight and could be leveraged by political leaders. We emphasize again that they were few in number.

Clearly, in aggregate, the sodomy-law reforms detailed in Table 7.3 and summarized in Figure 7.1 embody a potent global "social movement," in the literal senses of those words. They show a decisive shift in the criminal regulation of sex during the post–World War II period, legalizing sodomy between consenting adults on a very widespread basis.

The Diversity of Affected Countries

Beyond a common liberalizing logic, the reforms documented in Table 7.3 exhibit a second and equally striking pattern. They occurred in all sorts of countries. Changes in sodomy laws, that is, transpired with little sensitivity to nation-state-

FIGURE 7.1

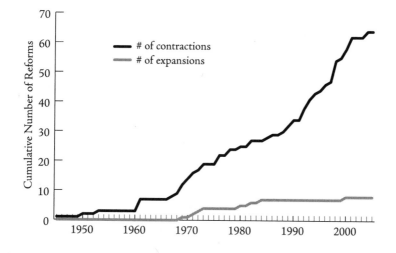

level characteristics. For instance, a poor Catholic country in Europe (Portugal) spearheaded the decriminalization reform wave in 1945, and it was followed by four communist countries (three in Europe, one in Asia), two Western Protestant countries, and a small Catholic democracy in Central America. Later in the same decade, the West African nation of Cameroon initiated the age-of-consent reform wave, and it was followed by four Western European countries and communist Hungary. Overall, between 1945 and 2005, we see liberalizing reforms in both rich and poor countries (e.g., Canada and Cape Verde); in Protestant as well as Muslim countries (e.g., Denmark and Kyrgyzstan); and in democratic and communist countries (e.g., West and East Germany). Also, we notice regional diversity, with Latin America (e.g., Ecuador), Western Europe (Iceland), Eastern Europe (Estonia), Central Asia (Kazakhstan), the Middle East (Israel), and sub-Saharan Africa (Liberia) all represented. Obviously, sodomy laws evolved very generally in the post–World War II period, reconstituting sex regulations in diverse countries all over the world.

Notwithstanding this striking heterogeneity, European nation-states (East and West) still appear to be overrepresented among the reformers in Table 7.3. A thorough analysis of this possibility lies beyond the scope of this chapter, but we wish to note at least one important reason it might be true. Europeans might be overrepresented among the reformers because they might have been disproportionately likely to have sodomy laws on the books from the outset. Countries with no such laws, after all, were unlikely to revise them. The importance of this factor is demonstrated in Table 7.4, which lists European and non-European countries without sodomy laws in the period 1945–2005. We observe that many

TABLE 7.4

*Countries (Cambodia Through Sierra Leone) With
No Sodomy Laws to Reform, 1945–2005*

European (n = 8)	
Denmark (decriminalized 1930)	Netherlands (decriminalized 1811)
France (decriminalized 1791)	Poland (decriminalized 1932)
Italy (decriminalized 1792 and 1889)	San Marino (decriminalized 1864)
Luxembourg (decriminalized 1792)	Monaco (decriminalized 1793)

Non-European (n = 31)	
Cambodia (colonized by France)	Iceland (colonized by Denmark)
Central African Republic (colonized by France)	Indonesia (colonized by Netherlands)
Chad (colonized by France)	Iraq (colonized by Great Britain)
China	Japan
Congo (colonized by France)	Jordan (colonized by Great Britain)
Dem. Rep. of Congo (colonized by Belgium)	North Korea (colonized by Japan)
Cuba (colonized by Spain)	South Korea (colonized by Japan)
Dominican Republic (colonized by Spain)	Madagascar (colonized by France)
Egypt (colonized by Great Britain)	Mali (colonized by France)
El Salvador (colonized by Spain)	Mexico (colonized by Spain)
Equatorial Guinea (colonized by Spain)	Micronesia (colonized by U.S.)
Eritrea (colonized by Great Britain)	Niger (colonized by France)
Gabon (colonized by France)	Paraguay (colonized by Spain)
Guatemala (colonized by Spain)	Peru (colonized by Spain)
Haiti (colonized by France)	Philippines (colonized by Spain)
Honduras (colonized by Spain)	

non-European countries, particularly those colonized by France or Spain, did not have sodomy laws during the period (we discuss this later). Obviously, thus, they never experienced reforms.

The important point is that the liberalization of sodomy laws took place in a highly diverse set of nation-states during the postwar period. The process seemingly transcended striking differences across a variety of domestic factors.

Existing Explanations of Reform

Most current analyses of sodomy-law (and other) reforms are pitched at the nation-state level of analysis and thus prioritize country-level explanatory variables (see, e.g., Haider-Markel 1998; Kitschelt 1986; Skocpol 1985; McCammon 1998). To explain the adoption of reforms, for instance, scholars invoke configurations of domestic political institutions (e.g., political parties), fissures between local populations (between religious groups, say), national economic structures (such as emerging service sectors), and so on. Many social movement perspectives on sodomy-law revisions follow along these lines.

Such explanations are useful and often persuasive in particular country contexts, but, with regard to the data in Table 7.3, they face significant hurdles. The first concerns the deep commonality of reforms. According to nation-state-centered logics, one should find a highly differentiated collection of legal revisions, tailored to domestic needs and national interests. Instead, however, the observed reforms almost uniformly represent liberalization, decreasing punishments, lifting blanket prohibitions, or lowering homosexual ages of consent. The commonality of reforms appears even in the details of statutory change. For instance, after 1989, every country that revised its age of consent lowered it to 14, 15, or 16. The variability is obviously low. In short, the sodomy-law reforms documented in Table 7.3 appear to follow a common global logic, contrary to expectations derived from state-centric perspectives.

The second problem for state-centric explanations concerns the diversity of reforming nation-states. If country-level characteristics were in fact track switches in policy adoption, then we should observe clear differentiation between reformers and nonreformers and also between various kinds of countries pursuing different pathways to reform. Instead, however, the data show that a wide variety of countries participated in a shared liberalizing movement.

On these grounds, it seems clear that standard nation-state-level arguments are ill equipped to explain cross-national and longitudinal patterns of sodomy-law reform. The problems beset all sorts of state-centric accounts, including those that center domestic LGB social movements.[10] Of course, many sodomy laws restrict not only homo- but also heterosexual behaviors. Nevertheless, LGB social movement organizations have mobilized clearly against them (Adam et al. 1999; Altman 2001; Bernstein 2005; Weeks 1996).

A stripped-down social movements explanation of sodomy-law reforms asserts that postwar policy amendments should have been most likely to occur when and where grassroots LGB mobilization was the strongest. Obviously, however, liberalizing reforms began well before politically viable LGB movements developed anywhere in the world, and they occurred in many countries where domestic LGB social movements even now barely exist. Consider, for example, the first dozen cases of decriminalization in Table 7.3: Portugal in 1945; Czechoslovakia, Hungary, and Mongolia in 1961; East Germany in 1968; West Germany in 1969; Canada and Costa Rica in 1970; Finland in 1971; Norway in 1972; Malta in 1973; and Colombia in 1980. It is difficult to imagine local, bottom-up, LGB mobilization in any of these cases exercising decisive sway over legislative processes (cf. Frank et al. 2007).

On the flip side, in countries where LGB social movements first gathered steam in the postwar era, sodomy-law reforms were not especially prevalent.

Writing around 1975, Robert Roth, a gay-rights pioneer and founder of the *International List of Gay Organizations and Publications*, placed the English-speaking and Western Germanic countries at the forefront of mobilization: "The Rhine and the British Isles are, so far, the centers of the Gay movement . . . along with the East and West coasts of the United States and Canada" (Robert Roth Papers).[11] Most pre-1975 sodomy-law reforms, however, occurred outside the English-speaking and Western Germanic worlds (e.g., in Portugal, Czechoslovakia, Hungary, Mongolia), while the United States—the country with the largest and strongest LGB movement during the period—did not conclusively decriminalize sodomy until 2003, in *Lawrence v. Texas*.

On reflection, it is perhaps obvious that grassroots LGB social movements offered neither necessary nor sufficient catalysts for sodomy-law reforms in the post–World War II era. After all, in most countries, before the late 1980s, embryonic LGB organizations consisted largely of loosely tied networks of friends, often operating underground to avoid harassment from hostile governments. While a few burgeoning groups functioned more openly, publishing newsletters and holding rallies, for instance, few of these had the strength to muster genuine political mobilization.

Take, for example, the Gay Freedom Movement in Jamaica (founded around 1974), which published the *Jamaica Gaily News*. While the organization clearly sought the repeal of Jamaica's repressive sodomy law—which endures to this day—it was nevertheless poorly positioned to promote (much less demand) legislative action. As one Jamaican activist wrote in 1978: "Our greatest obstacle . . . is the rampant homophobia in the society in general. The majority of our population is poor, black, and illiterate, while being at the same time fundamentalist. There are numerous myths and fallacies about homosexuality which we [must] dispel" (Robert Roth Papers).

The correspondent went on to highlight the priority of community building over politics: "[W]e are attempting to encourage a vibrant social scene for ourselves, developing a sense of belonging and of community. Our stance tends not to be activist or militant since few individuals will ever come out. Thus we lack a strong leadership team, cohesion and commitment" (Robert Roth Papers).

In the 1970s, then, the limited resources available to Jamaica's Gay Freedom Movement were channeled toward more prosaic goals than sodomy-law reform. Legal amendments remained a distant aspiration.

Likewise, in Mexico, the country's first LGB consciousness-raising group emerged in 1971, and the first public demonstration took place in 1978. But overall mobilization remained weak through the late 1990s, when social movement organizations finally rose to the challenge of legislative activism (de la Dehesa 2007, 28–32).

Indeed, in many countries, the only material residue of the LGB movement between 1945 and 2005 appeared in the forms of bars, clubs, and homes where individuals could socialize (Cain 2000). This was true in the United States through the mid-twentieth century (D'Emilio 1983; Kennedy and Davis 1993). These venues green-housed evolving social movements, offering safe havens for politically ambitious LGB organizations. Even these "safe havens," however, were imperiled by regular police raids (e.g., Eskridge 1999; Fleischmann and Hardman 2004). Thus in 1978, a gay activist from South Africa wrote: "The gay clubs are like mushrooms here in the city [of Johannesburg]. . . . One moment they are in existence and the next you hear that they have been closed down. This makes for a very unstable sort of life for gay people" (Robert Roth Papers).

Into the 1980s, with few exceptions, nascent social movement organizations around the world remained small, weak, and poorly funded. They seldom enjoyed the political leverage needed to demand sodomy-law amendments.

The point here is not to diminish the importance of grassroots LGB movements, the goals of which extend well beyond sodomy-law reform (Bernstein 2003). Rather, we align ourselves with those who articulate conditions under which social movements are more and less likely to catalyze regulatory revisions (Amenta et al. 1994; Guigni et al. 1999; McVeigh, Welch, and Bjarnason 2003). In a few, mostly Western democracies over the past two decades, a movements-based causal imagery makes good sense (Bernstein 2003; Kane 2007). But the simple argument that grassroots LGB social movements provided the key impetus for worldwide legal reforms in the postwar era is not well supported by the data. Too many changes transpired without obvious local LGB support.

With so many countries liberalizing their sodomy laws in such a short period of time (and with so few countries doing otherwise), virtually all state-centric accounts of reform in the postwar period face the same difficulties as domestic movements-based accounts. It seems that a world-level explanation is in order.

A World-Society Perspective

Thus, we propose a global understanding of sodomy-law reforms. In doing so, we build on the foundations of sociological neoinstitutionalism, which questions the assumed naturalness of "actors" (such as nation-states and social movement organizations) and calls attention to evolving world-cultural models of actors and their capacities, needs, and interests (Jepperson 2002; Meyer et al. 1997). Insofar as such models are built into the assumption structures of world society and embedded in transnational cultural scripts and organizational rules, we refer to them as *global institutions*, which appear as empirical "facts" (often of a scientific variety), natural "laws" (e.g., those that underlie human rights), and universal "standards" (typically purveyed by professionals; see Brunsson and Jacobsson 2002).

Penal codes themselves are globally institutionalized, that is, they are taken-for-granted features of modern nation-states (Boyle and Meyer 1998; Meyer et al. 1997). Indeed, only a tiny handful of countries in the world operate without one, and the huge majority of codes take highly standardized forms, having evolved in the bosom of colonialism (Benton 2001). For instance, according to the Malawi Law Commission (2000, 8), the criminal laws of that country were "drafted [in the U.K.] in the last century . . . first introduced in India in the mid 1800's . . . later applied to other colonies . . .[and then] enacted in Malawi in 1929." Almost 80 years later, Malawi's original penal code remains largely unchanged, and it little reflects the particular values, beliefs, and interests of Malawian society. Given global origins such as these, it makes sense that penal codes have strong substantive similarities across national borders.

One indicator of the scripted character of criminal laws is the fact that most former British colonies had sodomy laws on the books at the start of our study period, in 1945, whereas most former French and Spanish colonies did not (the Roman Catholic Church notwithstanding) (see Table 7.4). A century and a half earlier, before the French Revolution, the punishment for sodomy in France, as in Britain, was death by burning at the stake (Tatchell 1992). In 1791, however, buoyed by Enlightenment ideals of individuality, rationality, privacy, and secularism, the French National Assembly abolished the country's old sodomy prohibition, on the ground that "Liberty consists in the freedom to do everything which injures no one else" (Declaration of the Rights of Man 1789). To an unprecedented extent, the Declaration entitled French citizens to do as they pleased, so long as they harmed no one else in the process. Sodomy, conducted in private between consenting adults, was decriminalized accordingly.[12]

The significance of this development in France was multiplied many times over by the Napoleonic Wars (1803–15), through which versions of the French Penal Code spread to Italy, the Netherlands, Belgium, Spain, and Portugal, and then by colonial expansion, which diffused the same code on a worldwide basis. To all of the exposed countries, regardless of native conditions, these processes carried a penal-code template lacking any sodomy prohibition.[13]

For inverse reasons, many countries, especially those touched by the British Empire, entered the post–World War II era with sodomy laws intact. The legitimacy thereof, however, declined rapidly after 1945 with shifts in the global-institutional environment.

Spurred by the Nazi genocide and the Allied victory, global blueprints of "society" became sharply individualized in the wake of World War II. For instance, the individual's choices in the voting booth (institutionalized in democracy), in the marketplace (capitalism), and in everyday life (mass education) all took on increasing importance worldwide. Individualized human rights and women's rights proliferated, taking form, for example, in international treaties, such as the 1948 Universal Declaration of Human Rights, and in international nongovernmental associations, such as Amnesty International, founded in 1961 (Suarez and Ramirez 2007; Tsutsui and Wotipka 2004). In the changing rules of world society, the individual increasingly occupied a position as society's root building block, its ultimate motivator and beneficiary, free from the constraints of family, nation, and religion.[14]

This leads to our central proposition—that the broad individualization of "society" in the global-institutional environment gave rise to new understandings of sex in the postwar period, resetting the boundaries around legitimate sexual activities and recasting the foundations of criminal regulation. In the collectivized context prevalent earlier in the modern period, sex was seen as the ultimate means of maintaining the collective order (Bernstein 2003; Foucault 1978). Under the old rules, "Sexual activity of any kind . . . was sin. The only exception was sexual relations for purposes of procreation of humankind. This was permitted only to married persons. Sex not for purposes of procreation was 'unnatural' and therefore sinful (whether performed intra- or extra-maritally)" (Burchell and Milton 1994, 561).

Of course, these rules applied not only to sodomy (Frank 2008), but they emphatically included sodomy: "[B]ecause it denies the procreation of the species, [sodomy] has been long condemned as being contrary to the order of nature and thus in violation of fundamental societal norms and moral attitudes" (Burchell and Milton 1994, 570).

Under the old regime, even consensual sodomy, that between adults in private, was conceived to be highly problematic, intermingling the wrong kinds of body parts with no hope of procreation. Penal regulations accordingly forbade the transgression, upholding collective boundaries and the supremacy of procreative sexuality.

By contrast, in the individualized global context ascendant after World War II (foreshadowed by the French Revolution), the locus of sex increasingly shifted from corporate entities (the family, the nation, the Church) to autonomous human persons. Individualization gave rise to expressive and pleasure-oriented definitions of sex (legitimating, for example, the rapid and global postwar spread of contraception), and, increasingly, criminal regulations eschewed questions of collective order and public morality and aimed instead to restrict those sexual activities that threatened individual sovereignty. Procreation ceased to be the legitimating goal of sexual activity, replaced by the rule of individual consent. Under the emerging rules of world society, dramatically institutionalized in human rights, consensual sodomy lost its cultural sting. Even where the activity continued to be regarded as morally repugnant (as in many contexts; see Widmer, Treas, and Newcomb 1998), the legitimacy of *criminal* sanctions faded. Sodomy increasingly came to be regarded as a matter of individual taste or choice (Frank and McEneaney 1999; Frank and Meyer 2002).

In sum, we argue that a fundamental reconstitution of world society in the post–World War II era—from a collective to an individual basis—spurred a world-level reconception of sex and thus a recalibration of sodomy regulations in nation-states globally. As the collective foundations of "unnatural" sex laws eroded after 1945 and the individual foundations of "nonconsensual" laws grew in kind, the global supports for sodomy regulations collapsed, and liberalizing reforms multiplied worldwide.

Mechanisms of Change

The preceding discussion raises an immediate question. By what mechanisms did the individualization of the global-institutional environment translate into domestic criminal-law reforms? How did the former spur the latter? There were many mechanisms, of course, and they often worked in concert. Nevertheless, under the labels *coercion, acculturation,* and *persuasion,* we can distinguish three interrelated types (Goodman and Jinks forthcoming; cf. DiMaggio and Powell 1983).

Coercive mechanisms promoted sodomy-law reforms during the period via the explicit demands of powerful or authoritative entities, compelling particular countries to bring their criminal laws into conformity with global standards. For example, as a condition of membership in the European Union, Romania was induced to lift its prohibition on same-sex sex in 1996. While nothing required Romania to seek membership in the E.U., its pursuit of that goal nevertheless obligated the country to adopt E.U. human-rights principles, including gay-rights protections (Stychin 2003).[15] In cases such as these, the mechanisms of change linking global to local were direct and explicit.

Mechanisms of acculturation operated more diffusely, on cognitive and normative bases, with countries approving sodomy-law reforms in pursuit of higher-order goals only loosely tied to LGB rights (see Strang and Meyer 1993). For example, when U.S. states began adopting the American Law Institute's Model Penal Code of 1955, decriminalizing sodomy in the process, they typically did so without any compelling commitment to LGB rights.[16] D'Emilio (1997) describes the U.S. process thus: "In the 1960s, 1970s, and early 1980s, virtually all [sodomy-law] repeals came through a rewriting of a state's entire penal code. In other words, sodomy law reform was hidden beneath an avalanche of changes in the criminal law and was not the focus of public controversy." Throughout the 1950s, U.S. legal experts promoted the Model Penal Code as an efficient means of modern and secular state administration, and states acted on their general professional advice. LGB issues per se were low on the agenda (Kane 2007). In reform processes such as these, the catalysts for sodomy-law reform were buried deep within larger commitments to globally legitimated conceptions of the modern nation-state and citizen (de la Dehesa 2007).

Finally, mechanisms of persuasion linked changes in the global environment to domestic sodomy-law reforms via policymakers' immediate instrumental goals, such as satisfying the demands of social movement constituencies. Sometimes, such demands emanated from grassroots LGB associations, as stressed in conventional accounts of statutory change. For example, before Ireland overturned its ban on homosexual activity, in 1993, local activists waged a campaign for homosexual law reform for more than 20 years. At other times, social movement demands emanated from "above"—that is, from transnational activist networks and international social movement organizations (Keck and Sikkink 1998; Ramirez 1987; Smith et al. 1997; Tarrow 1998). For instance, the world's foremost international nongovernmental LGB organization, the International Lesbian and Gay Association (ILGA), began actively promoting gay and lesbian rights in countries around the world upon its founding, in 1978.[17] Increasingly, over recent decades, the global LGB movement has aligned itself with global human-rights groups, such as Amnesty International and Human Rights Watch, and these in turn have endorsed sodomy-law reform. Mechanisms of persuasion operated when countries actively assessed the benefits of sodomy-law amendments and reoriented their criminal laws accordingly (Goodman and Jinks forthcoming).

All three of these mechanisms could, and sometimes did, represent lateral diffusion—spreading a policy innovation from one country to another. Often, however, they represented top-down diffusion, carrying newly individualized notions of sexuality from the cultural and organizational structure of world society to nation-states around the world.

Of course, in many cases of sodomy-law reform in the period 1945–2005, mechanisms of coercion, acculturation, and persuasion overlapped, blended together, and mutually supported one another. For example, behind the coercive mechanisms of the European Union, which compelled sodomy-law reforms as a condition of membership, there were persuasive mechanisms from local and transnational LGB and human-rights movements, lobbying the E.U. and the Council of Europe to prioritize the issue. Modern individualism had many messengers during the period, and, in this sense, country-level sodomy-law reforms were often highly overdetermined.

Limitations and Contributions

This chapter considers the relationship of domestic LGB social movements to sodomy-law reforms from a world-society perspective. Our main point is not that social movements were never associated with legal reforms during the post–World War II period. Clearly, in some cases they were. Rather, our point is that domestic LGB movements were neither essential nor universal precursors to reform and that, when they were involved, they derived their authority and legitimacy from a changing global-institutional environment. Furthermore, we emphasize that the key social movements involved were often (a) global rather than local, (b) nonspecific to LGB issues, and (c) catalyzed *by* as much as catalysts *for* sodomy-law reforms. Thus, with regard to sodomy laws, the world-level "social movement" that reconstituted modern nation-states and penal codes around individualized citizens has been at least as important to reforms as domestic LGB movements (de la Dehesa 2007; Meyer et al. 1997). Grassroots LGB movements sprang from within these larger movements.[18] Thus, we argue that a reorientation of standard social movements imageries away from local, goal-oriented, and unilinear thinking is necessary to explain worldwide sodomy-law reforms that took place between 1945 and 2005.

Like any study, this one has limitations. One of these is its focus on formally codified written laws. It is well known that official policies are sometimes poorly enforced and that in particular settings the loose coupling of policy and practice is glaring. Compared to changes on the ground, formal policy reforms are more likely to be symbolic and ceremonial—that is, to "reflect the myths of their institutional environments instead of the demands of their work activities" (Meyer and Rowan 1977, 341). Practice is more deeply bound to immediate action contexts, within which local social movements may exert more decisive pressures. Grassroots LGB mobilization and other domestic factors, in other words, may be more relevant to everyday practices than to official policies. This is a question for future research.

We believe our focus on formal laws is nevertheless justified by the facts that, even in the presence of extreme loose coupling, laws on the books (1) maintain enforcement threats and social control, (2) inform policy debates (as in the discussion of gays in the U.S. military), and (3) contribute cognitive and normative materials to the general social (as versus criminal) regulation of sex (Bernstein 2003; Posner 1994). Furthermore, at least one recent study shows a strong positive association between official sex-law reforms and their implementation on the ground (Frank, Hardinge, and Wosick-Correa 2009). Thus are formal sex laws important objects of investigation.

A second limitation of our study is that it downplays cross-national variations in the timing of reforms (cf. Kane 2007). From a global viewpoint, a difference of 15 or 20 years may seem small, so that, for example, the decriminalization of sodomy in Colombia in 1980 and neighboring Ecuador in 1997 blend together in a single wave. From an individual's perspective, however, the same difference may be life changing. Domestic LGB movements may play pivotal roles in advancing or delaying particular statutory reforms by 5, 10, or even 20 years.

Notwithstanding these limitations, our study makes several contributions to the understanding of social movements and legal reforms. First, it calls attention to empirical phenomena that are currently underinvestigated—that is, the global dimensions of legislative reforms. Through a wide-angle lens, it seems obvious that neither national criminal laws nor domestic social movement organizations arise independently of broader world social forces, and these have been under-recognized in the literature. Second, our world-society view helps explain two aspects of the reform process that stymie most country-level explanations: the commonality of legal reforms and the diversity of reformers. Third, our perspective counterbalances explanations that overlook the global-institutional underpinnings of actors, including local social movement organizations, and their stated interests. While we live in a world in which interested actors make all kinds of differences, which "actors" with which "interests" make which kinds of "differences" are heavily scripted matters, presented in a global theater of democracy (Frank, Longhofer, and Schofer 2007; Jepperson 2002).

In short, we argue that, over recent decades, the global institutions that underpin world society grew increasingly individualized, elevating personal consent and pleasure to the forefront of sexual concerns. This shift redefined the meaning and purpose of "sex" in global culture and organization, and thus it spurred transformations in sodomy regulations in countries worldwide. Clearly, social movements were involved in the process, but their roots were more global, more distant from immediate LGB concerns, and more interdependent with particular legal reforms than many existing explanations have led us to expect.

8 Like Sexual Orientation? Like Gender?

Transgender Inclusion in Nondiscrimination Ordinances

Amy L. Stone

BETWEEN 1990 AND 2000, local public officials across the country added explicit transgender protections to twenty-six nondiscrimination ordinances (Currah and Minter 2005).[1] These transgender protections often involved redefining gender or subsuming gender identity within the definition of sexual orientation in the language of these antidiscrimination ordinances.[2] This inclusion of transgender protections came at the behest of local lesbian, gay, bisexual, and heterosexual ally (LGBH) or transgender activists and was supported by local policy elites such as city council members. This chapter examines how political actors—both the policy elites that author the ordinances and the activists who support them—comprehend transgendered individuals as a new minority group that needs legal protection. Through an examination of nondiscrimination ordinances in two Michigan cities in the late 1990s, our research concludes that political actors in both cities had strong moral perceptions of the need for transgender protections. However, political actors in both cities had a weak definitional perception of what transgender is, leading to differences in how transgender protections were included in local ordinances and the effectiveness of these protections.

Supporting the enactment of local nondiscrimination ordinances has been a long-standing strategy of the American LGBT movement since the first unsuccessful ordinance attempt in 1970 by New York City activists (Button, Rienzo, and Wald 1997). Transgendered people represent an addition to a growing list of categories traditionally included in local antidiscrimination ordinances, ordinances often created to provide local protections in areas where state and national civil rights are insufficient.[3] Gay rights activists have worked within these constraints to pass local ordinances; these constraints include frequent challenges to passed nondiscrimination ordinances by referendum, often leading to the defeat of the ordinance by voters (Donovan and Bowler 1998; Gamble 1997; Haider-Markel, Querze, and Lindaman 2007). Civil rights legislation has been critiqued by scholars as weak, symbolic, and based on reified identity categories that offer rights only to "immutable" categories rather than to behaviors (Post 2001). Despite these critiques, these local ordinances (and, increasingly, statewide legislation) are an alternative to a juridical system that can be ambivalent and unpredictable with regard to giving rights to transgendered individuals (Eskridge and Hunter 2004; Kirkland 2003) and to a national legislature hesitant to pass transgender-inclusive legislation, as demonstrated by the current version of the Employment Nondiscrimination Act (ENDA), which does not include transgender protections.[4]

Despite the importance of this increase in transgender protections, little empirical work has been done on how these ordinances are created, more specifically how political actors comprehend transgendered individuals as a new minority group that needs protection within the law.[5] John Skrentny's (2002, 2006) recent work on the minority rights revolution of 1965–75 charts the gradual expansion of civil rights legislation from protections for African Americans to its inclusion of the disabled and women. Skrentny argues that existing accounts of this legislative revolution ignore the way policy elites craft both moral and definitional perceptions of minority categories and that these perceptions have more explanatory power in the understanding of civil rights legislation than the activities of social movements.

Our research applies Skrentny's theories to both local politics and less well known minority categories, generating new theoretical understandings of how local political elites may understand minority categories through processes different from those accepted by their national counterparts. This analysis reintroduces the social movement activist into the analysis of how elites create these moral and definitional perceptions. By examining the role of the social movement activist more carefully, this chapter reveals the lack of clear distinction between social movements and the state in local politics, evidenced by the close connections and occasional lack of distinction between social movement activists and local policy elites.

This chapter interrogates how local political actors create and enact social perceptions about the importance of transgender protections. These political actors develop their own moral and definitional perceptions of transgender inclusion and make either "like sexual orientation" or "like gender" analogies, with consequences for the language of transgender protections. These perceptions are part of a larger construction of transgender as a new minority, one that is inextricably linked to the LGBT movement. In this chapter I compare two Michigan cities—Ypsilanti and Ferndale—where public officials passed transgender-inclusive nondiscrimination ordinances in the late 1990s. In both of these cases, lesbian, gay, bisexual, and heterosexual ally (LGBH) activists were critical in communicating the necessity for transgender protections. Both LGBH activists and local public officials rarely had definitional perceptions of transgender issues but were swayed by moral concerns about discrimination.

Social Meanings and Social Movements

Skrentny's (2002, 2006) study of the creation of civil rights legislation focuses on the "minority rights revolution," the period from 1965 to 1975 during which national policy elites developed definitions of what constitutes a minority group, which minority groups should receive federal protection, and what this federal protection should entail (i.e., nondiscrimination protections, affirmative action). Instead of examining the role of social movements in advocating for civil rights legislation, Skrentny instead emphasizes the social perceptions that policy elites use to understand minority rights, social perceptions that may have little to do with direct advocacy by social movements. These social perceptions inform policy elites' decisions about which minority groups deserve legal recognition (i.e., those based on race or gender) and which ones do not (i.e., those based on ethnicity or sexual orientation).

These policy elites developed both definitional and moral perceptions that they then applied to understanding which minority groups deserve recognition. Definitional perceptions are elites' understandings of the fundamental characteristics of a minority group. For example, policy elites already have understandings about how immutable or unchangeable identities like race and gender are. Moral perceptions are elites' understanding of the deservingness and level of discrimination experienced by the group. Policy elites in Skrentny's account established moral perceptions by making comparisons between new potential minority groups and race; if new minority groups were "like race" definitionally and morally, they were more likely to receive legal recognition.

Skrentny's account removes the role of social movement framing from his analysis and describes these social perceptions instead as unintentional or subconscious, based on long-standing perceptions about race, gender, and ethnicity. However, my research suggests that policy elites rely upon social movement activists for information and education about transgender issues. This reliance may be related to the difference between well-known marginal identities (i.e., African Americans, women, the disabled) and lesser known identities (i.e., intersexed, transgendered, people with AIDS), most of which have become visible only in the past twenty years. In the case of transgender issues, policy elites may not have existing social perceptions of who is transgendered and whether or not transgender issues constitute a legitimate minority group deserving of protection.

There are considerable differences between the social movement spillover effects (Meyer and Whittier 1994) of movements organized around well-known marginal identities (i.e., the civil rights and the feminist movements) and advocacy for a group that is marginalized within an already marginal community, a position that Cathy Cohen (1999) refers to as secondary marginalization. This marginalization may increase the necessity of making analogies to other social identities in order to get legislative protections in local ordinances. The secondary marginalization of transgender issues within the larger LGBT movement also means that inclusion of transgender protections in nondiscrimination ordinances often requires the explicit support of lesbian, gay, bisexual, and heterosexual ally (LGBH) activists (Stone 2006); indeed, as this research demonstrates, sometimes LGBH activists are solely responsible for the education of policy elites about transgender issues.

LGBH activists develop their own definitional and moral perceptions of transgender issues, perceptions that are affected by an ambivalent history of transgender inclusion in the LGBT movement. Although transgender and transsexual issues were gaining media visibility in the mid-1990s (Gamson 1998; Meyerowitz 2002), even within the LGBT movement there was considerable confusion about the nature of transgender identity and issues (Minter 2006; Weiss 2003), complicated by tension within the transgender community itself about what it means to be transgendered (Broad 2002). Some LGBH activists in the mid-1990s were unaware of what "transgender" means, why it is included in the movement, and what separate issues transgendered individuals may have (Weiss 2003). The ambivalence within the LGBT movement toward transgender inclusion was contextualized within a larger ambivalence about the "politics of difference" within the movement (Seidman 1993), as LGBT activists reconciled the inclusion of groups such as leathermen and bisexuals in a movement that was becoming increasingly professional and institutionalized (Armstrong 2002). Transgender inclusion was further complicated by a movement history of ambivalence toward gender variance, particularly in the inclusion of butches, drag queens, and transsexuals (Gamson 1997; Marotta 1981; Meyerowitz 2002; Rubin 2003). Within this context, LGBH activists developed an understanding of transgender issues; unlike Skrentny's policy elites, activists rarely made "like race" analogies but rather defined transgender issues as either "like sexual orientation" or "like gender."

Because of the marginal nature of transgender inclusion, it was necessary for LGBH activists to communicate these "like sexual orientation" or "like gender" understandings to local policy elites. This communication was facilitated by the close connections between local activists and policy elites, connections that may include being neighbors or working on campaigns together. Skrentny does build on existing work on social movement insiders within state and federal politics (Santoro and McGuire 1997); however, there are many striking differences between his study of national politics and this study of local politics. The majority of existing social movement literature is based on the premise that social movements exist outside and in opposition to the state (Amenta and Young

1999). However, this assumption disintegrates when one examines local politics. In local politics, social movement activists may become policy elites, policy elites become social movement activists, and state-organized committees become social movement organizations. Nondiscrimination ordinances are often written by gay or lesbian city council members; heterosexual ally human relations commission members become actively involved in LGBT organizations, defending the ordinance when it is challenged by a referendum. This analysis contributes to social movement theory on the relationship between social movements and the state, suggesting that in local politics the division between a social movement and the state can be an artificial one.

The dense social network between policy elites and social movement activists allows for an easier flow of communication about transgender inclusion. However, policy elites also develop weak definitional perceptions of transgender issues due to selective communication and messaging from social movement activists. LGBH activists' struggle to understand transgender issues becomes intensified as they attempt to communicate a well-articulated message about transgender inclusion to policy elites.

Michigan Transgender Inclusion

This chapter is part of a larger historical comparative study of transgender-inclusive nondiscrimination ordinances in Michigan cities between 1992 and 2002. Michigan is an excellent case for the study of disputed municipal nondiscrimination ordinances, as many ordinances were proposed or passed in the 1990s. Michigan is second only to Oregon in the number of ordinances contested in referendums or initiatives between 1992 and 2002. This time period was also critical for transgender inclusion in the LGBT movement, as transgender inclusion became a visible and contested issue within the movement. Nationally, between 1990 and 2000, twenty-three cities and one state passed transgender-inclusive legislation (Currah and Minter 2005).

In this chapter, I compare Ypsilanti and Ferndale, two Michigan cities that considered and adopted transgender protections as part of a broader nondiscrimination ordinance. These cases were selected because of the similarity in their ordinances and towns, as well as in the composition of their city councils and in the demographics of their LGBT community. What was significant in both cases was the presence of a primarily lesbian, gay, bisexual, and heterosexual ally organization making a conscious decision to advocate for the inclusion of transgender protections in the two ordinances, as these examples best illustrate how LGBH individuals and public officials understand transgender issues without their being articulated by transgendered individuals.

Both cases were investigated using a combination of extensive archival research and semistructured qualitative interviews. In Ypsilanti and Ferndale, I conducted fifty-five interviews with public officials, LGBH activists, coalition members, opposition leaders, and transgendered community members. Interview respondents were selected with theoretical sampling in an attempt to include leaders, committee members, volunteers, and disgruntled former members of social movement organizations alike. In addition, I used group meeting minutes, ordinance rough drafts, newspaper articles, e-mails, and other archival materials to triangulate my findings. All data were coded and analyzed using grounded theory.

Ypsilanti is a small city of 22,000 residents that boasts its own university, Eastern Michigan University. The most significant political cleavages in Ypsilanti are based on race and class, centering on the town/gown division and stark residential segregation. Ypsilanti influences and is influenced by nearby Ann Arbor, particularly in the existence of an Ann Arbor/Ypsilanti LGBT community. There is a growing transgender and transsexual community in both Ann Arbor and Ypsilanti that is tied to both the Gender Comprehensive Services center at the University of Michigan and the two university communities. After a public anti-gay incident in 1997, the Ypsilanti City Council adopted a broad nondiscrimination ordinance that included transgender protections, an ordinance that was later upheld during a referendum. In Ypsilanti, LGBH activists advocated transgender inclusion as subsumed within sexual orientation.

Ferndale is a predominately white Oakland County suburb of Detroit with a population of 22,000 residents. Ferndale has a long history as a white, working-class ethnic suburb, a history that was disrupted by the growth of Ferndale into the "gay suburb" of Detroit in the 1990s. The movement of LGBT individuals into Ferndale included the relocation of LGBT services and organizations. There is a growing transgender and transsexual presence in Ferndale as a result of the increased lesbian, gay and bisexual presence in the area. After a failed attempt at a voter initiative in 1991, Ferndale City Council members created an ad hoc committee of citizens to author a broad nondiscrimination ordinance, which included a transgender-inclusive definition of gender. The City Council passed the ordinance as written by the committee, but it was overturned by referendum.

Ypsilanti: Transgender as Sexual Orientation

In Ypsilanti, transgender inclusion was framed by social movement activists and policy elites as a sexual orientation issue, the addition of one more group to the LGB movement, without consideration of separate gender-related issues that may exist for transgendered individuals. The consideration of transgender issues as "like sexual orientation" was common for this time period; between 1990 and

1999, almost a third of all transgender-inclusive ordinances used sexual-orientation language to include transgender protections (Transgender Law and Policy Institute and National Gay and Lesbian Task Force 2007).[6] This perception of transgender as a sexual-orientation issue led to unintended discriminatory consequences in the language of the Ypsilanti nondiscrimination ordinance.

In February 1997, an LGBT organization at Eastern Michigan University took its raffle tickets for an antihate rally to a local printing shop, Standard Printing, where the print shop owners refused to print the tickets for religious and moral reasons. As a result of this incident, the Ypsilanti City Council deliberated the necessity of a local nondiscrimination ordinance that would include sexual orientation. Local LGBH activists formed a group, Ypsilanti Campaign for Equality (YCFE),[7] to defend the ordinance from Citizens Opposing Special Treatment (COST), a local group that threatened to torpedo the ordinance. In December 1997, the Ypsilanti City Council passed a broad nondiscrimination ordinance that included protections for sexual orientation. The ordinance was authored by a subcommittee of three City Council members, along with a ghostwriter, a lesbian attorney. YCFE members encouraged both the subcommittee and the lesbian ghostwriter to add transgender protections to the ordinance.

YCFE was an organization composed almost entirely of white, middle-class lesbian, gay, bisexual, and heterosexual ally (LGBH) activists from either Ypsilanti or nearby Ann Arbor. Many YCFE activists worked at the nearby universities as staff or faculty and became involved because of the dispute with Standard Printing. There were no known out transgendered activists involved in the decision-making body of YCFE, although some transgendered volunteers were tangentially involved in the organization. However, within YCFE, there was a small contingent of people of color, queer activists, and older social-justice-oriented activists who had been involved in gay liberation; these activists operated as transgender allies within the organization as they placed transgender inclusion on the agenda of YCFE and facilitated its articulation to public officials.

YCFE members had varying attitudes about the inclusion of transgendered people in the LGBT movement. In Ypsilanti, most activists had a moral perception of transgendered individuals as a group that was discriminated against, but they were unclear about the definition of transgender. YCFE activists described their willingness to include transgender issues within the movement, but they had only a limited sense of what separate issues transgendered individuals might have (i.e., bathroom access, different types of work discrimination) vis-à-vis lesbians or gay men.

Many activists described the necessity of transgender inclusion as rooted in the way transgendered individuals are discriminated against, and they drew parallels between their experiences as LGBH individuals and transgendered individuals. One Ypsilanti activist noted that "For a trans person to be out takes a whole lot of courage. They take the backwash of everything. They do. Being gay or whatever, I've had a lot of things said to me because I'm gay. But I would venture to say that any trans person has had a hundred times that."

In YCFE, most LGBH activists could comprehend transgender issues only when they understood transgender as "like sexual orientation." Most YCFE activists, particularly lesbians within the group, supported transgender causes that substantially intersected with lesbian and gay issues; as long as transgender issues were "like sexual orientation" issues, they were supportive of transgender inclusion. However, most YCFE activists were not supportive of transgender issues that "distracted" the movement from its focus on issues that affect lesbians and gay men. For example, several lesbians in this group criticized the involvement of a transgendered woman in a statewide campaign for gay marriage, suggesting that she insisted on transgender-inclusive policies when they believed that gay marriage was not a transgender issue. This transgendered activist wanted a group position statement on the status of transgender marriage, as courts often dissolve transgender marriages because of the legal ambiguity of transgender sex or gender. These lesbian YCFE activists were critical of the fact that the transgendered activist had distracted the gay marriage organization from its political message. Some of this criticism was rooted in political tensions about the role of referenda and initiative campaigns in the LGBT movement, but it was also connected to the larger ambivalence about transgender inclusion.

Almost all advocacy for transgender inclusion in the Ypsilanti ordinance was undertaken by three or four YCFE activists who identified as transgender allies.[8] These LGBH activists both placed transgender inclusion on the YCFE group agenda and communicated the necessity of transgender protections to public officials. One of these queer activists described the persuasive power of "one-on-one conversations with people at meetings and stuff like that. . . . I knew it was worth it, and I knew that I was having an impact. And they were thinking about stuff and nobody was malicious or anything like that."

After transgender inclusion had been discussed and placed on the agenda, YCFE activists began communicating their concerns about transgender inclusion in the ordinance to the City Council and particularly to the subcommittee writing the ordinance. These communications were not necessarily formal or calculated by the organization, partly because of the close connections between City Council and YCFE members. However, many transgender-supportive allies were concerned about making sure that transgender protections were included. YCFE activists were closely connected to City Council members, because of their participation in campaigning and their involvement in local commissions, a connection that had consequences described by the gay YCFE member below:

Unlike other places, we didn't have to start from scratch with City Council, saying "these are gay people" or anything like that. We were already integrated and
involved in campaigns. It was not a big leap to understand the issue. I think it was
harder for the other side to demonize us that way. They'd say "these people are
evil," and City Council would scratch their head and say "that's odd." There was a
history of integration.

All City Council members mentioned both this community involvement and
their own personal connections with gay men and lesbians as motivating their
support for the nondiscrimination ordinance. In addition, one member of the
City Council, Pam Cuthbert, was a closeted lesbian who later came out publicly
during the time of the ordinance passage. Most City Council members interviewed mentioned their lack of substantial perceptions about transgender issues,
beyond their understanding of gender deviance, such as butches and drag queens,
in the LGBT community; many of them described the process of writing the
ordinance as an educational process in that regard.

Most of this communication was focused on two sources: the subcommittee
formed to draft an ordinance in the summer of 1997 and the lesbian ghostwriter
of the ordinance. One of the subcommittee members, the lesbian Councilwoman
Pam Cuthbert, enlisted the help of this ghostwriter attorney, who then created
the first draft of the ordinance, including the transgender protections. This attorney described the inclusion of transgender protections as a result of both "talking
with the people who were involved in wanting to get the ordinance and looking at many other ordinances throughout the country." This attorney felt that it
was part of her duty as a lesbian to ensure the inclusion of transgender protections, but she described it as a learning process for her, as well, as she knew little
about transgender issues. Early drafts of the ordinance included the term "transgendered" under the definition of sexual orientation, which was later changed to
"gender identity." In the end, sexual orientation was defined as "heterosexuality,
male or female homosexuality, bisexuality or gender identity" and it was decided
to bury transgender protections in the definition of sexual orientation. Although
the other two members of the subcommittee were aware of transgender protections, communication between YCFE members and both Cuthbert and the
ghostwriter were critical in getting transgender protections included in the ordinance.

Other subcommittee members described the importance of input from local
transgender-supportive gay and lesbian activists in their decision to include
transgender protections. One subcommittee member noted that, through conversation with "activists specifically for transgendered people," he developed "this
notion in incorporating gender identity or transgender was something that had
real value to include in the ordinance, and it was just a matter of working with

the attorney as to, well, where do you put it in?" However, subcommittee members had limited knowledge of transgender issues, even with this education; they all described their understanding as an extension of their relationships with gay men and lesbians, as something related to sexual orientation and not as something that needed additional or special considerations.

An unintended consequence of framing transgender issues as "like sexual orientation" was that transgender-specific issues were ignored in the ordinance. For example, the subcommittee authored a clause excluding bathrooms from coverage by the ordinance, even though bathroom use is a common site of discrimination for transgendered individuals. This clause was copied from a model ordinance used by the committee without reflection on its consequences for transgendered individuals. Although the subcommittee members had strong moral perceptions that transgendered individuals were an important new minority group that needed to be protected, they had limited definitional perceptions about what it actually meant to be transgendered.

Because of these YCFE members' communication with subcommittee members, other City Council members also had basic knowledge about the need for transgender protections. One City Council member was educated about transgender issues by subcommittee members. She noted:

> I think what happened was, we had a subcommittee who was working on the text of what the new ordinance would look like and when they ran the first draft by me I remember saying, "Why do you need that in there? Transgender? Doesn't this cover it just to say sexual orientation?" And the folks who were involved in drafting the ordinance . . . felt like that language really needed to be in there. "Well, okay, if that's what you think, then fine."

This public official, along with many others, had problems differentiating between sexual orientation and gender identity, seeing transgendered people as just another type of gay person, without separate needs or issues. For many City Council members, this was the first time they had encountered transgender issues, and they were educated at hearings and through testimony by transgendered people at City Council meetings. Ultimately, the City Council presented this version of the ordinance to the public, and it passed unanimously, in December 1997.

In Ypsilanti, YCFE activists' limited definitional perceptions of transgender issues were communicated to the policy elites responsible for writing the Ypsilanti ordinance. Although the policy elites became easily convinced of the necessity of transgender inclusion in the ordinance, their lack of understanding of transgender issues had consequences for the strength of transgender protections within the ordinance. For transgendered individuals in Ypsilanti, these protections may have seemed more symbolic than statutory. In addition, when the Ypsilanti ordinance was used as a template for including sexual orientation and gender identity in a nondiscrimination ordinance, the Ypsilanti language and bathroom exclusion were used in additional Michigan ordinances.

Ferndale: Transgender as Gender

In Ferndale as in Ypsilanti, the creation of a transgender-inclusive ordinance emerged from the growth of LGBT political power. However, in Ferndale, many activists and policy elites viewed transgender as a gender issue, rather than as an issue that needed to be subsumed under sexual orientation. This definition of transgender as gender, sex, or gender identity accounts for almost 60 percent of transgender-inclusive ordinances passed between 1990 and 1999, and more than 80 percent of the ordinances passed between 2000 and 2007 (Transgender Law and Policy Institute and National Gay and Lesbian Task Force 2007). Ferndale activists' attempts to achieve inclusivity by using the category of gender ultimately made the transgender-inclusive nature of the ordinance invisible to transgendered individuals. However, it did provide protections for a variety of gender-variant behaviors.

In 1991, voters in Ferndale defeated a gay rights initiative by an overwhelming majority, in a divisive political battle. Since then, the LGBT community in Ferndale has grown into a political voting bloc, a metamorphosis aided by the work of the openly gay activist and politician Craig Covey and of Ferndale Friends and Neighbors (FANS), a homeowners association for gays and lesbians. In Ferndale, the 1999 human rights ordinance was written by a group of local citizens and business people who made up the Ferndale Blue Ribbon Ad Hoc Committee, a committee that was formed in accordance with a campaign promise by then-Mayor Chuck Goedert. In Ferndale, the ordinance was a result of the growth of gay political power in the face of considerable opposition and was initiated as a result of pressure on local politicians.

In response to campaign promises and a series of publicly visible hate crimes, Goedert and Councilwoman Gerry Kulick formed the Blue Ribbon Ad Hoc Committee (hereafter the Committee) in December 1998 to study and create a local human rights ordinance. Membership in the committee was open to any community members who wanted to join, and all committee meetings were open to the public. Many committee members suggested that the formation of a citizen's committee to write the human rights ordinance was motivated by a desire to take the political heat off the mayor and to add legitimacy to the ordinance.

The composition of the Blue Ribbon Committee was a mix of gay and lesbian community members, heterosexual allies, and heterosexual community members with little experience with gay politics. There were also two members of the committee who were strongly opposed to the ordinance; they joined the committee initially but dropped out within the first few months. Most committee members were committed from the beginning to a human rights ordinance that would include sexual orientation; indeed, many heterosexual allies and gay community members became involved specifically to guarantee that sexual orientation was included. The Blue Ribbon Committee was a social movement organization in formation, composed of local activists who would later create an organization to protect the ordinance when it went before the voters in a referendum.

Three transgender-supportive LGBH Committee members initiated the inclusion of transgender protections in their early drafts of the Ferndale human rights ordinance. In contrast to the YCFE activists, these activists described the importance of transgender protections in terms of gender, not sexual orientation. The most supportive gay committee member described his support for inclusion this way: "just because I knew people who actually practiced cross-dressing or were active transvestites. Or were in the process of gender reassignment." As a consequence of this personal acquaintance, he did his own research on the process of gender reassignment surgery. Another supportive committee member, an older white lesbian, discussed transgender issues in terms of gender rather than sexual orientation when she described her experiences with butch "diesel" dykes in the bars in the 1980s:

> INTERVIEWEE: People who were absolutely sure that God or whatever had played this hard, hard joke on them, that something was wrong. Because nobody knew a lot. Was it something at birth? Was it something wrong at gestation? They absolutely knew they were not women.
>
> AUTHOR: Were these women who would have been called butch?
>
> INTERVIEWEE: Or diesel dykes. They just didn't identify as women at all. Where else could they go? Where else could they go? Often hung out together. Often took lesbian lovers.

This lesbian group member described her understanding of these butch women as rooted in her understanding of their gender identity, the ways they were at odds with their own sex. She clearly described a place for these butch women within the lesbian community at that time, but she contrasted their experience with the "lesbian lovers" that they took.

Other committee members who knew little to nothing about transgender issues at the beginning of the committee meetings were educated by these transgender-supportive committee members. One heterosexual ally with little knowledge of LGBT issues before her committee involvement described the understanding she developed of the intersection between gender identity and sexual orientation as follows:

Even if a straight person walked into a restaurant and was perceived to be gay. It may be a man perceived to be more effeminate or a woman with a short haircut. They can be rejected because of that, so it doesn't matter if you're really truly gay or straight but about how you can be perceived. And we thought that was important too. And transgenders are more involved in physical surgeries and whatnot, but you also got the ones that do just cross dress. If you want to be perceived as a woman that's just fine with me. And that's what we felt.

This heterosexual ally suggests that the foundation of discrimination against gay men and lesbians is often gender presentation.

Beyond their understanding of gender discrimination, most committee members stressed moralistic reasons for including transgender protections, namely their desire to be inclusive of groups that are marginalized in society regardless of whether they understand those groups. One or two committee members suggested that the inclusion of diverse discriminatory categories was a way to deflect public concerns about a gay rights ordinance. However, most committee members described the drive to include transgender issues as motivated by a desire to be inclusive. One lesbian committee member described the discussions as not that sophisticated: "we just knew we had to include people that kind of, the new wave of people that no one was sure about." One heterosexual member suggests that ultimately the politics of inclusion and open-mindedness prevailed over actual comprehension of the importance of transgender inclusion.

Ultimately, transgender protections were included in the first draft of the ordinance under the category "gender," which was defined as "the real or perceived physical characteristics that identify an individual as male or female." An early consideration of "gender identity" was quickly changed to "gender" (or, alternatively, "sex") (Blue Ribbon Committee 1999). One of these subcommittee members described his influence in writing this definition.

We felt that it was probably more not just more politically correct, but more—I guess from a language perspective—"gender" was a better term to use. We also felt that "gender" would be inclusive of, we hoped, the words, "transsexual, transvestite . . ." without having to put in every single potential category. You know? Transgender, transvestite, male, female. . . . Whatever, whatever.

This committee member made several critical decisions about the wording of the ordinance language and the inclusion of transgender protections, and he described it entirely in terms of gender.

The moral necessity for transgender protections was communicated to the mayor and to the City Council as the committee submitted the final draft of the ordinance for a vote. During the writing of the ordinance, there was a developed understanding that the gender category would include transgendered individuals. For example, the city attorney wrote a memo early in the drafting process that questioned what the reference to "perceived" physical characteristics within the definition of gender would include (Christ 1999). However, most communication came during meetings between a subcommittee of the committee and members of the City Council at which a final draft of the ordinance was developed. Committee members used the legitimacy of the group to support transgender inclusion. One activist recalled that "I know we had the discussion to change it from sex to gender. And we did that, I pretty much think we did that before the mayor. And we said that we preferred that. And we all voted for it."

Public officials' understanding of transgender inclusion emphasized primarily its moral benefits, with little understanding of transgender issues beyond their relationship to members' gay and lesbian constituencies. One committee member remembered a City Council meeting distinctly:

> And when it came to Council and somebody that night, when they were voting on it, they were getting questions "why did you use gender and not sex?" [Mayor] Goedert specifically said we wanted to make sure we included gender identification and that's a better word. He was great, he made a point of it on the record.

City Council members involved in the ordinance even now retain an understanding of the ordinance as being transgender inclusive and knew that the category of gender was intended to cover transgendered individuals. Public officials described transgender inclusion in the ordinance as a concern of their gay constituency but also as a general gender issue. Most of the supportive public officials emphasized that they considered transgender inclusion an important issue both because of the work of the committee and because of their communications with a local gay politician.

The use of gender terminology—namely terms like "gender identity," "expression," and "orientation"—is the increasingly accepted standard among transgender activists. However, in the late 1990s, the vagueness of the gender definition led many Ferndale transgendered individuals to feel excluded from the ordinance. Some transgendered activists believed that they had been ignored by the local lesbian and gay community, because the language of the ordinance did not use familiar terms such as "gender identity" or "expression."

In Ferndale, committee members, many of whom later became leaders of an organization that worked unsuccessfully to defend the ordinance at the ballot box, had strong moral beliefs about not only transgender issues but also "like gender" definitional perceptions. These understandings were communicated easily to City Council members, who viewed transgendered people as an extension of their LGBT constituency. Ultimately, the vagueness of the ordinance had consequences for the local transgender community; it left many transgendered individuals feeling excluded from the ordinance; several years after the ordinance was passed, transgendered activists lobbied for a transgender-inclusive nondiscrimination ordinance. The invisibility of transgender inclusion in this case had consequences for the local LGBT community, including a disregard for the work of transgender allies who wrote the ordinance and a sense of exclusion among the transgendered community.

Conclusion

Most of the political actors described in this research knew little about the definition or specifics of transgender issues, yet in both cases they passed ordinances that contained transgender protections. Both public officials and LGBH activists supported the inclusion of transgender protections out of a moralistic perception that transgendered individuals were discriminated against in society and that protecting their rights was an important aspect of the ordinance. Surprisingly, these political actors rarely raised questions about immutability or the expansiveness of the definition of "transgender." In Ypsilanti, these perceptions focused on the way transgender was "like sexual orientation," leading inevitably to the subsuming of gender identity within the definition of sexual orientation in the ordinance. In Ferndale, both activists and public officials thought of transgender as "like gender," although public officials' conceptions were particularly vague.

These different social perceptions of transgender issues had consequences for the inclusion of transgender protections. Although from a legal viewpoint transgender protections were included in both ordinances, the Ypsilanti protections were limited by restrictions on their applicability to bathroom usage, a major location of transgender discrimination. The perception of transgender as "like sexual orientation" without the recognition of separate transgender issues such as bathroom access led to this problem. In Ferndale, "transgender" was subsumed into the larger category of "gender," creating an invisibility problem and a sense that transgender issues were not addressed by the ordinance.

This research elaborates on Skrentny's account of how policy elites develop understandings of minority groups by examining the creation of minority protections with less well known minority groups on the local level. The consequences of these two additional elements included policy elites' dependence on social movement activists to communicate moral and definitional perceptions. In contrast to their understanding of minority categories such as race, policy elites did not have well-developed definitional perceptions of what it meant to be transgendered. This communication between social movement activists and policy elites focused on moralistic perceptions and the justification of transgender protections within the nondiscrimination ordinance.

In addition, the local nature of these ordinance politics led to blurry boundaries between social movement activists and local policy elites. In the case of

Ferndale, a state-created committee included the social movement activists who created and defended the ordinance. These close connections between social movement activists and the state offer a sharp contrast to existing social movement theories about the relationship between social movements and the state.

This research is just the beginning of the study of transgender-inclusive nondiscrimination ordinances. My study could be improved by including a larger number of cases, particularly the inclusion of a case with active out transgendered activists involved in group decision making. This dynamic might change the communications between activists and public officials or permit education to have a more significant impact that would outweigh preexisting beliefs. However, it is significant that, without either intervention by transgendered activists or full comprehension of transgender issues, LGBH activists and public officials in relatively contentious political environments decided to include transgender protections in their local ordinance. In future research, it would be beneficial to examine the perceptions of policy elites at the state level, as transgender protections are increasingly included in or added to statewide nondiscrimination or civil rights bills.

9 Pushing the Envelope

Dillon's Rule and Local Domestic-Partnership Ordinances

Charles W. Gossett

A MAJOR PART of the struggle for gay and lesbian rights in the United States has centered on efforts to have the relationships between same-sex couples recognized by society and treated in a manner comparable, if not identical, to the way in which relationships between opposite-sex couples are treated. One aspect of this struggle sought legal recognition of the relationships by local, state, and national governments. As early as 1971, American gay and lesbian couples were filing legal actions seeking to force state recognition of their de facto marriages, albeit without success (Dupuis 2002; Rubenstein 1993, chapter 5). Rather than simply resigning themselves to the lack of recognition of their relationships, gay and lesbian activists developed a new approach in the 1980s. This new approach consisted primarily of asking local government and private-sector employers to allow same-sex couples and, in some cases, unmarried opposite-sex couples to have access to the same employee benefits that they provided to employees who were married. To at least some extent, these demands carried a sense of urgency resulting from the AIDS crisis, which was ravaging the gay male community. As young men became sick, were unable to work, and thus lost any employee health benefits they had, their partners faced the need to provide for medical care from their own resources, all the while watching their married co-workers simply enroll for family coverage in order to cover a spouse. This obvious unequal treatment of employees in the face of tragedy helped activists persuade some employers, public and private, to develop a mechanism to provide equal benefits to their employees who were in coupled partnerships not recognized by the state (Gossett 1994).

Since 1984, more than 150 cities, counties, and school districts have adopted some form of domestic-partnership benefits for employees who are in committed partnerships but who, for one reason or another, are not legally married (Human Rights Campaign Foundation 2006, 11).[1] In doing so, local governments had to make a series of political decisions about whether they wanted to offer the benefits, whether they could afford them, how they would structure the benefits, and, perhaps most fundamental, whether they had the legal authority to design and implement such a program. Adoption of these programs frequently came after a long and contentious political struggle characterized by charges that the proposals were immoral and violated fundamental religious principles (Bailey 1999; Button, Rienzo, and Wald 1997; DeLeon 1999; Gibson 1999; Haider-Markel, Joslyn, and Kniss 2000; Kass and Ryan 1997; Meier 1994; Riggle and Tadlock 1999; Sharp 1999, 3–4). Bernstein (2001, 439)has suggested that the adoption of domestic-partnership programs by local governments indicates that advocates were successful in "circumventing the challenge to heteronormativity that underlies disapproval of homosexuality." Still, a number of local governments that have considered such programs have failed to approve them (Borowski 1999). Even when domestic-partnership programs have been adopted, however, losing parties have often continued to oppose the programs by challenging them in court. Such challenges have had mixed success. This chapter examines the reasons why some challenges have failed and others have succeeded by looking at both the state legal environments in which the particular local government operates and the legal arguments and strategies employed by those who challenged and by those who defended the laws.

Legal Principles

The idea that local governments are "creatures" of their states is a principle well known to political scientists and lawyers, though this notion often comes as a surprise to citizens (Berman 1995a; Syed 1966; Yeoman 1997; Zimmerman 1995). Whether a "municipal corporation" chartered by the state or a county established with or without a charter, all local governments ultimately exercise their authority (and even continue to exist) at the pleasure of their state legislatures, as occasional state takeovers of municipal governments demonstrate (Berman 1995b). There is an ongoing debate among scholars as to whether or not local governments are anything more than powerless pawns of the state government and whether they can be independent political actors capable of implementing innovative policy changes (Briffault 1990a, 1990b; Frug 1980, 1999; Goldsmith 1995; Gurr and King 1987; Krane and Rigos, 2000).

In the late 1800s, Judge John F. Dillon ruled that local governments had only the powers expressly delegated to them by the state legislature, the powers reasonably inferred from those expressly delegated, and the powers essential to keeping the municipality functioning. While there is still room for dispute over what may or may not be allowed in a particular city, the burden of proof essentially rests on the local government to demonstrate that it does have the authority to undertake any action being challenged. In the latter part of the nineteenth century, the "home rule" movement developed as a counterapproach to state supervision of local governments. Essentially reversing the premises on which Dillon's Rule rested, home rule was based on the idea that municipal governments could have broad and unspecified authority to act with respect to local affairs unless some action were specifically prohibited (Readler 1998, 786). Again, there was lots of room for disagreement. The local government's task when challenged was to show that there was nothing in state law that prevented it from acting in the manner it had chosen. Home rule, when enshrined in the state constitution, sometimes also allows local governments to challenge the state's actions when they impact on what are seen as constitutionally protected rights of municipalities and/or counties. And, in a few states, local laws may at times take precedence over state laws so long as the issue at hand is deemed to be a local affair (Cole 1991; Gillette 1997; Marks and Cooper 1988).

While one might expect that challenges to local government actions would most often be initiated by a state that thinks a local government has gone "too far," the principle of local subordination to the state is most often enforced by private individuals challenging a local government action. Persons who are (or who believe they are) adversely affected by a local government decision, often the same people who fought against the policy adoption in the first place, move the dispute from the local legislative arena in which they lost to a different playing field where they may have a better chance of prevailing. To many citizens, this is one of the best features of American democracy; to others, it is the reason that some issues never seem to be settled once and for all (Nice and Fredericksen 1995, 33–35; Schattschneider, 1960). But, when it came to recognizing domestic partnerships, the change in venue brought with it a change in the language and strategies of the parties. The arguments over whether or not domestic-partnership programs were a matter of "equal treatment" (advocates for domestic partnerships) or a sign of moral decay (opponents) gave way to an argument over a number of relatively obscure provisions of the relevant state's municipal code.

Though challengers to local-government domestic-partnership-benefit ordinances raised a number of grounds for invalidating the local action, courts have tended to focus their analysis on the issue of whether or not there was authority for the government to act in the manner it chose. The basic issue is whether or not the action taken was *ultra vires*, or "beyond the powers" of the particular local government in question. In states where the judicial logic of Dillon's Rule is applicable, judges looked for a specific grant of authority from the state legislature to the local government for the action taken. In states where cities and counties have some measure of home rule, the courts' analyses tended to view this question from two perspectives: (1) does the action taken result in an impermissible *conflict* with a superseding state law; or (2) is the action taken in a field of activity that the state has, in some manner, reserved to itself, thereby preempting the local action? Rarely are the answers clear cut; there is always room for judicial interpretation (Andersen 1980; Clark 1985).

With respect to the issue of "conflict," two principal types of conflict may be argued. The local law either permits something that state law prohibits or the local government prohibits something that the state government allows. For the the issue of conflict to arise, the state law in question must neither authorize local deviation from the standard set by the state nor allow local government ordinances to supersede state laws on "purely local" matters.

Although language is sometimes loosely used to suggest that when a conflict exists between state law and a local ordinance, the former preempts the latter, there is a distinction that can be made that will assist in understanding the cases in this study. As used here, "preemption" does not necessarily mean that there is a conflict between the two laws; in fact, the local and state laws may be nearly identical (Readler 1998). In preemption cases, the argument is made that *only* the state may make laws on this particular subject. There are commonly four different ways in which preemption is established: (1) the state law specifically declares that only the state can legislate on the particular subject; (2) the legislative history behind the law indicates that the lawmakers intended that only the state should have authority to legislate on the particular subject; (3) state laws that govern the particular subject are either so comprehensive or so numerous that there is "obviously" an intent to limit legislation in this field to the state; or (4) the nature of the particular subject matter is such that statewide uniformity is required and exclusive state authority to legislate is the only reasonable way to handle the issue (Weigel 1997).

Arguments involving preemption tend to be much more complex than those involving conflict. First of all, there is often disagreement among the disputing parties as to what the "subject" is and which state laws are relevant to an investigation of possible preemption. Second, unlike the U.S. Congress, which has available extensive documentation of legislative deliberations and intent, most state legislatures do not have such documentation. Third, there is no standard agreement on just how "comprehensive" laws must be to be deemed to preempt local action. Finally, whether or not statewide uniformity on an issue is required is rarely agreed upon, with the existence of a legal challenge as evidence of such disagreement. Again, the domestic-partnership cases examined here frequently raise one or more of these preemption arguments.

Earlier work has examined the role that Dillon's Rule—the legal principle that a local government's authority is limited to specific grants of power from the state government—played during political debates when local governments attempted to adopt ordinances prohibiting discrimination on the basis of sexual orientation (Gossett 1999). That work found that Dillon's Rule is, in effect, a malleable tool that can be used in a variety of political contexts to support and oppose local government activities in uncharted policy domains. Michael Wood (2003) has also commented on the "propriety" of local governments adopting employment nondiscrimination acts based on sexual orientation. This chapter seeks to extend that earlier work by looking at what happens when a local government's authority to act in a new policy field is challenged in court as having violated the principles set forth in Dillon's Rule.

Scope of the Study

Eighteen cities, four counties, and two school districts in twenty different states have been identified where the local governments were challenged in state courts on the issue of whether they had the authority to provide their employees with domestic-partnership benefits.[2] In all but one case, the cases against the city were filed by opponents of the domestic-partnership program that was adopted; in the Kalamazoo, Michigan, case, supporters of domestic-partnership benefit programs filed suit after the city ended its existing domestic-partnership benefits following an opinion by the state attorney general that the city had no authority to offer the benefits after the adoption of a state constitutional amendment prohibiting same-sex marriages. Cases in nineteen states that have final court decisions form the core of this analysis. The case in New Orleans, Louisiana, was returned to the trial court after the state supreme court found that the plaintiffs did have standing to bring the suit; a retrial of the case in a state district court resulted in dismissal in favor of the city and that case is on appeal (365Gay.com 2008; Alliance Defense Fund 2008). A case in Albany, New York, was dismissed for failure to establish standing on the part of the plaintiff and was never appealed. The Ann Arbor, Michigan, School District case has been dismissed by the state supreme court on technical issues concerning standing and the filing procedure. And cases in two cities, Gainesville, Florida, and Cambridge, Massachusetts, were each tried shortly after their respective states' highest courts ruled on similar cases from other jurisdictions; the decision in each case was consistent with the high court's ruling on the similar case, and neither was appealed. Table 9.1 includes all the cases that either set a precedent in their state or are currently active in the courts.

Local governments that offer or have tried to offer domestic-partnership ("DP") benefit programs for their employees are not distributed randomly across the country (see Table 9.2). In addition to the four states where the DP benefits program was overturned by the courts, fourteen states contain no local jurisdictions that currently offer domestic-partnership benefits. Of the remaining thirty-two states where at least one jurisdiction has successfully adopted a DP benefits program, lawsuits challenging the authority of the local government to adopt them were filed in sixteen of them.

TABLE 9.1
Cases Involving Challenges to Local Domestic Partnership Benefit Programs
(Status as of March 9, 2009)

Status	City	Case (Date Of Last Decision)
Domestic Partnership Program Overturned —Final	Atlanta, GA	*McKinney et al. v. City of Atlanta* (March 14, 1995; GA Supreme Ct.—overturned in 1997)*
	Minneapolis, MN	*Lilly v. City of Minneapolis* (March 29, 1995; MN Supreme Ct. denied review)
	Boston, MA	*Connors et al. v. City of Boston* (July 8, 1999; MA Supreme Ct.)
	Arlington County, VA	*Arlington County et al. v. White et al.* (April 21, 2000; VA Supreme Ct.)
	Kalamazoo, MI	*National Pride at Work v. Granholm and City of Kalamazoo* (May 7, 2008; MI Supreme Ct.)
Domestic Partnership Program Upheld— Final	Atlanta, GA	*City of Atlanta v. Morgan* (November 3, 1997; GA Supreme Ct.)
	Pima County, AZ	*LaWall v. Pima County* (July 14, 1998; AZ Ct. of Ap., not appealed)
	Santa Barbara, CA	*Jacks v. City of Santa Barbara* (Santa Barbara County Superior Ct., January 13, 1999; not appealed)
	Denver, CO	*Schaefer and Tader v. City and County of Denver* (April 12, 1999; CO Supreme Ct. denied review)
	Chicago, IL	*Crawford et al. v. City of Chicago* (October 6, 1999; IL Supreme Ct., denied review)
	New York, NY	*Slattery et al. v. City of New York* (February 29, 2000; NY Ct. of Ap. denied review)
	Chapel Hill and Carrboro, NC	*Godley et al. v. Town of Chapel Hill and Town of Carrboro* (May 16, 2000; Superior Ct., Orange Co., not appealed)
	Broward County, FL	*Lowe v. Broward County* (April 4, 2001; Florida Supreme Ct. denied review)
	Madison, WI (School District)	*Pritchard et al. v. Madion Metropolitan School District* (May 8, 2001; Wisconsin Supreme Ct., denied review)
	Vancouver, WA	*Heinsma v. City of Vancouver* (August 23, 2001; WA Supreme Ct.)
	Montgomery County, MD	*Tyma et al. v. Montgomery County* (June 14, 2002; MD Supreme Ct.)
	Portland, ME	*Pulsifer et al. v. City of Portland* (April 28, 2004; Superior Ct., Cumberland Co., not appealed)
	Philadelphia, PA	*Devlin et al. v. City of Philadelphia* (Dec. 6, 2004; PA Supreme Ct.)
	Salt Lake City, UT	*In the Matter of Utah State Retirement Board's Duties and Salt Lake City Ordinance No. 4 of 2006* (May 11, 2006; 3rd District Ct., not appealed)
	Kansas City, MO	*Buckner v. City of Kansas City, Missouri* (November 9, 2007; Circuit Court of Jackson County, not appealed)
Domestic Partnership Program— Pending	New Orleans, LA	*Ralph et al. v. City of New Orleans* (May 5, 2006; LA Supreme Ct.)— granted plaintiffs standing to pursue the case; no trial date yet

*Date is that of the last available opinion or the denial of a review by a higher court, whichever is most recent.

What is important to recognize is that a successful legal challenge against one city in a state is often enough to effectively close down similar programs in other cities in that state. This happened in Massachusetts, where the cities of Brookline and Northampton voluntarily terminated their programs after Boston lost its appeal to the state supreme court and the city of Cambridge was unable to defend its DP program at trial (Weber and Sweet 2000). Likewise, a successful defense of a domestic-partnership program often sets a precedent that "protects" domestic-partnership programs in other jurisdictions within the same state. This occurred in the case of Gainesville, Florida, which was decided after the state supreme court declined to review a decision in a similar case that was favorable to Broward County (Washington 2000). Of course, much of the work of attorneys is aimed at "distinguishing" cases from each other—what may be authorized for city governments is not authorized for county governments; a program that reimburses employees for expenses for domestic partners is different from a program that enrolls and subsidizes domestic partners in a manner similar to spouses; what cities with home rule charters may do cities without such charters cannot. However, it is significant to note that, of the twenty states included in this study, only two had a case challenging the local government's authority in this area after an initial court ruling on the subject. This is likely to change in the future because campaigns have been successfully concluded or are planned in some of the states discussed here to amend state constitutions to prevent the recognition of same-sex marriages, so opponents of domestic-partnership programs may seek to relitigate cases under the constitutional amendment.

For those cases included in the study, judicial decisions in the case were obtained from the Lexis database whenever possible. Copies of briefs were sometimes available from the parties in the case, usually the city or county attorney's office or, in several cases, the offices of the Lambda Legal Defense and Education Fund (LLDEF), which represented intervening parties in several of the suits. Copies of judges' orders were also obtained for cases where the final decision occurred at a judicial level that does not publish decisions through electronic databases. A "case list" appears in Appendix A as a supplement to the other reference citations.

The Cases

In his book *Judges and the Cities*, Gordon Clark (1985, 86) makes the point that "the politics and legalities of social discourse [through making public policy] are very much related" while, at the same time, "law is more than politics transposed[; t]he political texture of an original dispute need not enter into the legal picture." Other scholars have noted that the system of American government

TABLE 9.2
Status of Local Government Authority to Offer Domestic-Partnership Benefit Programs (as of June 30, 2008)

States Where Courts Ruled DP Benefit Programs as not *Ultra Vires*	States Where *Ultra Vires* Cases Are Pending	States Where No *Ultra Vires* Lawsuits Have Been Filed	States Where Courts Ruled DP Benefit Programs Are *Ultra Vires*	States Where No Local DP Benefit Programs Are Offered
Arizona	Louisiana	*Alaska*	**Massachusetts**	Alabama
California		**Connecticut**	Michigan	Arkansas
Colorado		Delaware	Minnesota	Kansas
Florida		**Hawai'i**	Virginia	Kentucky*
Georgia		Idaho		Mississippi
Illinois		*Iowa*		Nebraska
Maine		Indiana		Nevada
Maryland		*Montana*		North Dakota
Missouri		**New Hampshire**		Oklahoma
New York		**New Jersey**		South Carolina
North Carolina		New Mexico		South Dakota
Pennsylvania		Ohio		Tennessee
Utah†		**Oregon**		West Virginia
Washington		*Rhode Island*		Wyoming
Wisconsin		Texas		
		Vermont		

States in italics provide domestic-partnership benefits to state-government employees.

States in boldface have been identified as legally recognizing the relationships of same-sex couples in some form, ranging from marriage (MA) to relatively limited recognition programs (Maine and Hawai'i) (National Gay and Lesbian Task Force 2007).

*Lexington, Kentucky, had adopted local government DP benefit programs, but the program was repealed by the local governing body (Evans 2003).

†Utah's law was written so that it allowed designation of an "adult designee" rather than a "domestic partner"; it was this definition that was seen as not being *ultra vires* by conflicting with the state constitution's provision defining marriage.

provides numerous forums in which governmental actions can be challenged, both with respect to the different parts of each governmental level—legislative, executive, or judicial branches or by direct democracy (e.g., referenda)—or at different levels of government—local, state, or national (Nice and Frederickson 1995; Haider-Markel and Meier 1996; Schattschneider 1960). In the cases under review here, with the exception of the Michigan case, opponents of domestic-partnership benefits policies who have lost in the local legislative arena moved the conflict to the state judicial level (and, occasionally, simultaneously, the state legislative levels) in an effort to have their policy preferences prevail. For the most part, these legal challenges were argued by attorneys affiliated with or financed by conservative public interest law organizations, most notably the American Center for Law and Justice (ACLJ), the Alliance Defense Fund (ADF), and the Northstar Legal Center (NSLC). City, county, and school district attorneys served as the defense lawyers, although occasionally outside counsel was hired to act on their behalf. Gay rights public-interest law organizations, principally the Lambda Legal Defense and Education Fund (LLDEF) and the American Civil Liberties Union (ACLU), often participated in the cases either by intervening on behalf of employees who could benefit from the DP program or by organizing *amici curiae* briefs on behalf of the local government (see Table 9.3). Although, as noted by Clark, the emotional character of the political debate may get lost in a legal debate over relatively abstract legal principles, the public presentation of the cases in news reports and on Web sites sponsored by advocacy groups kept the focus on issues with high salience for the public.

The cases in which final decisions have been reached were initiated between December 1993 (Minneapolis, Minnesota) and May 2008 (Kalamazoo, Michigan). Each case was filed in the relevant state court and appealed within state court systems; none were filed in or appealed to a federal court. In Georgia, there were two cases; the second case reviewed a rewritten version of the law following a defeat for the city in the first case. In all but two of the cases (Pima County, Arizona, and Salt Lake City, Utah), the person or persons challenging the ordinance based their standing to file the suit on the fact that they were taxpayers and were supported, directly or indirectly, by conservative legal public interest groups; in Arizona, the case was filed by the county attorney under

TABLE 9.3
Legal Histories of DP Cases.

States Where Ultra Vires Lawsuits Have Been Filed	Date Filed	Plaintiff Interest Groups	Defendant Interest Groups	Trial Court Action on Local Gov't DP Benefits Program	Appellate Court Action on Local Gov't DP Benefits Program	High Court Action on Local Gov't DP Benefits Program
Arizona	1997, July 2		LLDEF	**Upheld**	Not Appealed	
California	1998, April 24	ACLJ		**Upheld**	Not Appealed	
Colorado	1996, December 11	RMFLF		Upheld	**Upheld** (3-0)	Review Denied
Florida	1999, February 8	NSLC	LLDEF	Upheld	**Upheld** (3-0)	Review Denied
Georgia (McKinney)	1993, August 12	SELF	ACLU	Overturned		**Overturned** (3-4)

TABLE 9.3
(continued)

States Where Ultra Vires Lawsuits Have Been Filed	Date Filed	Plaintiff Interest Groups	Defendant Interest Groups	Trial Court Action on Local Gov't DP Benefits Program	Appellate Court Action on Local Gov't DP Benefits Program	High Court Action on Local Gov't DP Benefits Program
Georgia (Morgan)	1996, September 10	SELF	LLDEF	Overturned		**Upheld** (6-1)
Illinois	1997, May 7	ADF	LLDEF	Upheld	**Upheld** (3-0)	Review Denied
Louisiana	2003, June 27	ADF	LLDEF	Upheld	Pending	
Maine	2003, August 12	ACLJ		**Upheld**	Not Appealed	
Maryland	2000, May	ACLJ	ACLU, LLDEF	Upheld		**Upheld** (7-0)
Massachusetts	1998, November 10	ACLJ	GLAD	Overturned		**Overturned** (0-6)
Michigan*	2004, April	ACLU		Upheld	Overturned (3-0)	**Overturned*** (5-2)
Minnesota	1993, December 20	NSLC		Overturned	**Overturned** (1-2)	Review Denied
Missouri	2004, August 25	ADF		**Upheld**	Not Appealed	
New York	1998, July 22	ACLJ		Upheld	**Upheld** (5-0)	Review Denied
North Carolina	1999, June 7	ADF, NCFIR		**Upheld**	Not Appealed	
Pennsylvania	1998, August 15	UFC	CLGCR, ACLU	Upheld	Overturned (0-7)	**Upheld** (6-0; 1 abstain)
Utah	2006, May 11	ADF	ACLU	**Upheld**	Not Appealed	
Virginia	1998, March 10	NSLC		Overturned		**Overturned** (0-7)
Washington	1999, February 24	NSLC	ACLU, LLDEF	Upheld		**Upheld** (8-1)
Wisconsin	1998, July 9	ADF		Upheld	**Upheld** (3-0)	Review Denied

Bold lettering indicates the final written decision in the case addressing substantive issues.

* In Michigan, the role of plaintiff and defendant are reversed, with DP supporters challenging a decision to stop a benefits program; nevertheless, "overturned" is used to make clear that the decision prohibited local governments from offering DP programs.

Abbreviations: <u>Plaintiffs</u>: ACLJ —American Center for Law and Justice; ADF—Alliance Defense Fund; NCFIR—North Carolina Foundation for Individual Rights; NSLC—Northstar Legal Center; RMFLF—Rocky Mountain Family Legal Foundation; SELF—Southeast Legal Foundation; UFC—Urban Family Council; <u>Defendants</u>: ACLU—American Civil Liberties Union; CLGCR—Center for Lesbian and Gay Civil Rights; GLAD—Gay and Lesbian Advocates and Defenders; LLDEF—Lambda Legal Defense and Education Fund.

a statute authorizing her to prevent illegal spending by the county commissioners, and in Utah the case was filed by the state Public Employees Health Program, which wanted judicial clarification on whether it could allow Salt Lake City to offer the benefits to its employees without violating the state constitution's prohibition on same-sex marriages. Nine of the remaining local government cases (Atlanta, Georgia; Chapel Hill and Carrboro, North Carolina; Denver, Colorado; Minneapolis, Minnesota; Philadelphia, Pennsylvania; Portland, Maine; Salt Lake City, Utah; and Arlington County, Virginia; and the Madison, Wisconsin, school district) were the first jurisdictions in their states to adopt such an ordinance. In the Michigan case, roles were essentially reversed, with the suit being filed by employees who had lost domestic-partnership benefits when the city of Kalamazoo stopped offering them after passage of a state constitutional amendment redefining marriage (on the instruction of the state attorney general); the plaintiffs received assistance from the ACLU in their action against several state officials and the city.

Arguments in Domestic-Partnership Cases

Although expressed in a variety of ways, the legal arguments raised by plaintiffs ultimately rest on a claim that the local government exceeded its state-granted authority when it adopted an ordinance or program providing health benefits to domestic partners of employees and the children of those domestic partners. Most, but not all, challenge the act on several different grounds, though the arguments fall into two broad categories: (1) the local government is improperly attempting to establish a marital relationship called "domestic partnership," and/or (2) the state has already established the limits specifying to whom local governments may provide health benefits, and domestic partners are not included.

Marriage Arguments

PLAINTIFFS. Clearly, the arguments that local governments cannot create a new "marital status" carry the most emotional weight. As noted earlier, many of the plaintiffs are the same persons who opposed adoption of domestic-partnership programs in the first place. News reports of the council meetings where domestic-partnership ordinances were discussed or adopted are filled with quotes that focus on the moral and religious grounds on which opponents sought their defeat. Abstract questions of the spheres of authority of state government and local government concerning employee benefits are generally, though not completely, absent. Ironically, one can well imagine that the opponents of domestic-partnership programs would become strong advocates of local authority if the local government were seeking to adopt a policy more to their liking, for example, allowing landlords to discriminate against domestic partners in rental housing.

The legal arguments about marriage take several forms, but the generic language of any dispute involving the extent of local authority is well utilized. Some plaintiffs argued that the field of marital relations is wholly occupied by state laws, that there is no room for local regulation, and that marriage is neither a matter of "local concern" nor a "municipal affair." And, if marital relations are solely the state's responsibility, then so are nonmarital relationships. Others argued that there must be uniform state regulation in this subject area, because the confusion would be too hard to handle. Plaintiff's attorneys in *Jacks v. Santa Barbara* argued that people who register as domestic partners in one jurisdiction would be disadvantaged because they might travel to another jurisdiction (within the state) that did not recognize the relationship or that did not provide the benefits they expected on the basis of their experience with the jurisdiction in which they first registered. Citation of state laws that indicate that only the state can define marriage, establish laws governing marital rights, and determine grounds and procedures for divorcing is also not unusual as parties try to establish the state's supremacy over local government action when it comes to regulating interpersonal relationships.

Others charge that conflicts exist with other state laws in the portions of complaints based on what is seen as the local government's attempt to create a new marital status. First, they argue that domestic-partnership programs that include opposite sex partners are, in effect, reestablishing common-law marriages that have been outlawed. Second, in some cases heard prior to the U.S. Supreme Court decision in *Lawrence v. Texas* (2003), opponents argued that recognizing domestic partners condoned or encouraged violation of various state laws against certain sexual acts, such as fornication and sodomy.

In recent years, a number of states have passed their own versions of the federal Defense of Marriage Act, stating that marriage is permitted only when the partners are of opposite sexes. Some, like the law in Florida, go further and specify that neither the state nor local governments may give legal recognition to "relationships between persons of the same sex which are treated as marriages." Domestic-partnership benefit programs, in the plaintiff's eyes, are clearly in conflict with these laws. Even more recently, several states have passed state constitutional amendments defining marriage as between a man and a woman and prohibiting the state from offering the benefits of marriage to other types of couples or families. In the cases where the city sought to defend its domestic-partnership program, only Utah had such an amendment in place at the time of the lawsuit, but the specific benefits program set up by Salt Lake City received court approval despite the second clause of the amendment, which stated, "No other domestic union, however denominated, may be recognized as a marriage or given the same or substantially equivalent legal effect."

A final set of arguments states that the domestic-partnership act violates the state's public policy favoring marriage. In some states, there is specific language in one or more laws saying that the state laws should be interpreted as favoring or encouraging marriage. In other cases, the state's position is implied by a variety of benefits that are provided to married couples and not to unmarried couples (e.g., protection of rights in a divorce but not in a "palimony" suit).

LOCAL GOVERNMENTS. Local-government defendants, of course, responded to each of these arguments, but the responses in this case are relatively uniform: domestic partnerships are not marriages, common law or otherwise, and thus the arguments of the plaintiffs were irrelevant. Some defendant municipalities demonstrated how differently married couples are treated with respect to other benefit programs and by the state, hoping to show that domestic partnerships are clearly a relationship inferior to marriage, which also supports an argument that the state's public policy preferring marriage remains intact. Others pointed out the differences in requirements for becoming married and ending a marriage and those for entering and leaving a domestic partnership. Thus, city attorneys, on behalf of the city's elected officials, encouraged the courts to join them in "discursively mark[ing] lesbian and gay unions as less than heterosexual marriages" (Bernstein 2001, 436).

Local governments also defended themselves against charges of conflict with criminal statutes in much the same way, claiming that they are not relevant to the issue of domestic partnership. When a plaintiff charged violations of fornication and sodomy laws, defendants pointed out that nothing in the domestic-partnership eligibility criteria requires partners to violate the state's criminal laws, though some gay rights advocates find this argument a bit disingenuous (Feldblum 1999). In cases where state law prohibited cohabitation, the argument was a bit trickier, since the eligibility requirements for domestic partnerships in most jurisdictions require a joint residency; by registering, the partners are basically holding themselves out as a couple (Gossett 1994). In response, local governments generally argued that those laws are neither enforced nor enforceable today, even if they might remain on the books. Furthermore, cohabitation laws would apply only to opposite-sex domestic partners, since there are no laws prohibiting two persons of the same sex from sharing accommodations.

Thus, with respect to arguments about whether or not state marriage laws preempt local laws recognizing domestic partnerships, there is a classic disagreement about defining the problem, with plaintiffs claiming that domestic partnerships are "sham marriages" and defendants claiming that they have nothing at all to do with marriage. Neither side challenged the heteronormative premises of the other; they simply debated about how those premises apply in the case of domestic-partnership benefits. The courts were asked to resolve this dispute.

Employee Benefit Arguments

PLAINTIFFS. The second broad set of arguments against the adoption of domestic-partnership benefit programs by municipalities or counties involves claims that state laws limit the local governments' options in the area of employee benefits. The critical question is whether the local government can itself define the term "dependent" for its own employee benefit programs or whether the state has defined that term in a way that supersedes (and prohibits) any local government effort to cover domestic partnerships for health-benefit purposes. The argument over this particular point tends to be very technical and to lack the emotional punch of arguments involving marriage.

In all of the states where domestic-partnership ordinances have been challenged, the authority of a local government to provide employee benefits to its employees and their dependents derives from a state law. This may not be the case in other states (Weigel 1998). One key difference among the states where local governments provide benefits under the authority of state law is that some laws use the general term "dependent," while others specify "spouse and dependent children" as eligible for benefit coverage. Some states go even further and define what is meant by "dependent children." In the latter cases, as in Minnesota, the plaintiffs simply pointed out the inconsistency between the definition in state law and the class of people eligible for the local program. In the former cases, which include most of the states under discussion, the plaintiff attempted to make the argument that, even though there is no definition of "dependent" in the benefits law, there are many other laws where the term "dependent" is defined, and in most states, until recently, none of those definitions included "domestic partners." Thus, it is unreasonable for the local government to expand the definition to include such a category, since it is not used anywhere else in state law. Most of the other laws cited for purposes of comparison limit the definition of dependent to a spouse, children, and a person who receives more than 50 percent of his or her financial support from the employee.

In a few of the cases, the argument was made that the issue of local-government employee benefits either is treated by the state as or should be treated by the state as an issue of statewide concern. Here the argument is that uniformity is required to prevent unequal treatment of employees by different jurisdictions within the state. Such uniformity is sometimes deemed desirable to prevent "bidding wars" among local governments for qualified employees.

LOCAL GOVERNMENTS. Local-government defendants countered these arguments in a number of ways. In cases where the law is specific in identifying eligible dependents, the argument was made that the state law should be treated as a floor, not a ceiling. This means that, while local governments must offer benefits for the categories of spouse and dependent children, the fact that the law does not specifically prohibit offering benefits to others should be interpreted as allowing the domestic-partner benefits to be offered if the city or county or school district so chooses.

In cases where the term "dependent" is not defined at all, local governments made the argument that they must develop a local definition of the term or else there is no way they can implement the law, and, again, since domestic partners are not specifically excluded, it is their option whether or not to include that category. This argument was sometimes supplemented by claims that the purpose of the state law is to ensure that local governments can be competitive employers and that, in many of these places, private employers are offering domestic-partnership benefit coverage and in order to remain competitive, so must the local government. In some other cases, local governments are able to identify state laws and court decisions that define "dependent" broadly to include persons who receive some financial support, though not necessarily half of their financial needs. Probate laws are sometimes cited to support this position. If a variety of definitions exist in state law, the local governments argued, there should be no presumption that the most restrictive one should be applied to the law governing employee benefits. In fact, it is claimed, the state's interest in seeing that its citizens are well cared for should lead it to adopt the most expansive definition available. One defendant argued that expanding the number of persons covered increased the purchasing power of the city and could result in lower costs for everyone, thus following state mandates to ensure efficient use of local tax dollars.

Arguments that local government employee benefits are a matter of statewide concern were often countered by reiterations of the argument that local governments operate in different competitive markets for employees and must develop different employment packages to attract a competent workforce. Also, salaries are not uniform across local governments within a state, so it is unclear why such uniformity should be required in the area of health benefits. In most states, over the years, many differences among local-government benefit programs have developed and been allowed to exist, largely because no has ever raised the question of uniformity in a lawsuit until now; therefore, went the argument, insisting on uniformity now is not appropriate.

Thus, with respect to arguments about whether or not state laws preempt local-government attempts to define "dependents" as including domestic partners, the issue is one of local autonomy and authority to innovate under state law. Unlike the marriage arguments, where local governments concede that they have no authority to engage in regulation of marriage, when it comes to defining eligibility for employee benefits that are paid for primarily with local tax dollars, they directly challenge the effort to limit their freedom to act.

Judicial Responses to the Arguments

Judges in nineteen states have issued final rulings on these disputes, accepting and rejecting some of the arguments described in the preceding section. Grouping the decisions by judicial outcome facilitates an understanding of how judges have seen these cases. A summary can be found in Table 9.4. Of these, in all but *City of Atlanta v. Morgan* and *Devlin v. Philadelphia*, the decision of the lower court was sustained, which suggests some consistency in understanding of the powers of local governments by the state's judicial branch, as can be seen in Table 9.4.[3]

DOMESTIC PARTNERSHIPS OVERTURNED. Four final decisions (Minneapolis, Atlanta [*McKinney*], Boston, Arlington County, and Kalamazoo) required local governments to abandon their domestic-partnership benefit programs. In both Minneapolis and Boston, the judges found that the state law specifically defined the term "dependent" in a way that did not include domestic partners. In these states, the law not only referred to "spouse and dependent children" but included provisions for older children who may be full-time students or mentally or physically incapable of caring for themselves. In these cases, the judges said that the state had shown a specific interest in regulating this matter either because, at the request of local governments, the definition had been amended (Minnesota) or because there was an expressed legislative intent to keep cities from competing with each other, with counties, or with the state by offering greater benefits to their employees (Massachusetts).

Judges pointed out, in both of these cases, that the municipalities had implicitly acknowledged that employee benefits were a matter of state regulation. In the Minneapolis case, the court cited a phrase in the City Council resolution authorizing supplemental payments for domestic partners' health benefit costs that says the city will "seek an affirmative inclusion of the term 'domestic partners' in state legislation on health care benefits," which seems to concede the state's authority in this area. Boston officials had previously gone to the state legislature for authority to adopt a domestic-partnership ordinance, and only after the governor vetoed the legislation authorizing the city to provide the benefits did the mayor issue an executive order establishing them. In neither case, though both cities were their state's largest municipalities and both possessed "home rule" authority, did the courts find that they could avoid preemption by the state law. The Boston

TABLE 9.4

Judicial Assessment of Arguments Used by Plaintiffs in Challenges to Local Government Domestic Partnership Benefit Programs

States Where Ultra Vires Lawsuits Have Been Filed	Status of DP Benefits	Arguments Accepted/Denied by Courts Making Final Decision					
		Marriage Law Preempts	Contrary to Public Policy	State Benefits Law Preempts	Definition of Family/ Dependent Conflicts	Benefits a Statewide Matter of Concern	Home Rule Exceeded or Dillon's Rule Violated
Arizona (98)	Upheld**				Denied		Denied
California (99)	Upheld**	Denied	Denied	Denied			Denied
Colorado (99)	Upheld	Denied		Denied	Denied		Denied
Florida (01)	Upheld	Denied		Denied	Denied		Denied
Georgia (95)	Overturned				Accepted		Accepted
Georgia (97)	Upheld				Denied		Denied
Illinois (99)	Upheld	Denied	Denied	Denied		Denied	Denied
Louisiana (04)	Pending						
Maryland (02)	Upheld	Denied	Denied			Denied	Denied
Maine (04)	Upheld	Denied					Denied
Massachusetts (99)	Overturned	Denied		Accepted	Accepted	Accepted	Accepted
Michigan (06)	Overturned	Accepted					
Minnesota (95)	Overturned	Ignored*		Accepted	Accepted	Accepted	Accepted
Missouri (04)	Upheld	Ignored*			Denied		Denied
New York (00)	Upheld	Denied		Denied	Denied		Denied
North Carolina (00)	Upheld**	Denied	Denied	Denied			Denied
Pennsylvania (04)	Upheld	Denied	Denied			Denied	Denied
Utah (06)	Upheld	Denied	Denied	Denied	Denied		
Virginia (00)	Overturned	Ignored*					Accepted
Washington (01)	Upheld	Denied	Denied	Denied	Denied		Denied
Wisconsin (01)	Upheld		Ignored*	Denied	Denied		Denied

* In the Minneapolis, Minnesota, case, the dissenting opinion makes it apparent that this issue was raised by the plaintiff, and the dissent says it is without foundation; the majority opinion, however, never directly addresses this issue (Minnesota Court of Appeals 527 N.W.2d 107; 1995 Minn. App.). In the Kansas City, Missouri, case, the decision summarizes the arguments as "Essentially, Plaintiffs claim that the City . . . exceeded its constitutional home rule authority to enact [a registry] and its administrative regulations . . . because the enactment is in conflict with existing state law relating to the definitions of 'dependent.'" The judge concluded that there was no conflict, hence no case. (Declaratory Judgment, see Appendix A for full citation) The plaintiff's brief (also cited in Appendix A) suggests that they raised the marriage argument to no avail. In the Arlington County, Virginia, case, the majority opinion, in a footnote, said, "Accordingly, we need not address the Taxpayers' argument that the County has attempted to legislate in the field of domestic relations"; the dissenting opinion was based on the fact that the majority opinion did not address the plaintiff's claims that the domestic partnership benefits ordinance illegally created same-sex marriages (a field preempted by state laws), though the dissenters concurred in the result (Virginia Supreme Court, 2000 Va. LEXIS 71). In the Madison School District case, the judges explicitly chose not to deal with the policy questions raised by the plaintiffs (Wisconsin Court of Appeals, Dist. Four, 2001 Wisc. App. LEXIS 141).

decision, however, did leave open the possibility that the city might have another option for funding domestic-partnership benefits—the very method of supplemental payments to some employees that was overturned in the Minneapolis case, in fact. The court states: "We express no view on whether the mayor could authorize the city to pay for nongroup health insurance benefits for registered domestic partners of city employees" (*Connors v. Boston* 19).

In the *McKinney* case, in Atlanta, three laws were being challenged. The sexual-orientation nondiscrimination ordinance and the domestic-partnership registry were found to be acceptable exercises of local government authority. The effort to provide health benefits to domestic partners was not allowed because of the way the city attempted to achieve this. With an eye toward avoiding a conflict with state marriage laws, the ordinance stated that "The City of Atlanta recognizes domestic partners as a family relationship and not a marital relation" and that benefits shall be available for a domestic partner "as for a spouse to the extent that the extension of such benefits does not conflict with existing laws of the State of Georgia." In this case, the court found that the critical issue was the city's effort to define domestic partners as a "family relationship." The law authorizing municipalities to offer benefits did not define dependents, but the court noted that other laws did, and none of these definitions included domestic partners. However, the critical sentence in the decision, as shall become clear in *Morgan*, states, "We conclude that the city exceeded its power to provide benefits to employees and their dependents by recognizing domestic partners as 'a family relationship' and providing employee benefits to them 'in a comparable manner . . . as for a spouse'"(*City of Atlanta v. McKinney* 10). This language posed too much of a challenge to the privileged place of heterosexual marriage and the nuclear family in both the law and society at large for the court to ignore it.

The decision in the Arlington County case turned on the question of whether or not the benefits program was "a reasonable method of implementing its implied authority" under state benefit statutes, and the courts found that it was not (*Arlington County et al. v. White et al.* 10). Two arguments were particularly persuasive to the court. One was that the Attorney General's opinion, requested by a state legislator before Arlington County acted, had said that local governments did not have authority, under Dillon's Rule, to include domestic partners

---

**In the Carrboro and Chapel Hill, Pima County, and Santa Barbara cases, only brief summary judgment findings were issued, although the standing of the plaintiffs had been established. Thus, the author inferred the denials recorded here on the basis of language in the court order and the issues raised in the briefs of the plaintiffs and defendants (North Carolina, Orange County, Superior Court Division, File No. 99 CVS 844, Judge Orlando F. Hudson, Jr., May 16, 2000; Arizona, Pima County, Superior Court, Case No. C-320550, Judge Allen G. Minker, March 13, 1998; California, Santa Barbara County, Superior Court, Case No. 224122, Judge Thomas P. Anderle, January 13, 1999).

in health benefit plans. Second, the county's definition of the term "domestic partner" focused on "financial interdependence" and not "financial dependence." "Interdependence" suggested a violation of the image, if not of the fact, of a traditional marital arrangement in which one partner (the wife) was usually financially dependent on the other partner (the husband).

One fact critical to note is that *none* of the majority opinions turns on the issue of whether or not the local governments were inappropriately interfering with the definition of marriage or marital relationships. The Boston, Atlanta (*McKinney*), and Arlington County decisions include statements that the court does not see any conflict between state marriage laws and the creation of domestic partnerships, while the Minneapolis decision is silent on the question. In both the Atlanta (*McKinney*) and the Arlington County cases, a frustrated high court justice criticized the majority in a concurring opinion for ignoring what the dissenting judges saw as an obvious conflict between the local domestic-partnership ordinances and state laws governing marital and family relationships.

The newest and probably most critical change in these decisions comes in the Kalamazoo case. As noted, this is the only case in which the city was a defendant because it had *stopped* providing domestic-partnership benefits. This case began only after a successful initiative campaign to amend the state constitution to include a restrictive definition of marriage. The key section of the amendment stated that "the union of one man and one woman in marriage shall be the only agreement recognized as a marriage or similar union for any purpose." In the end, and unlike the courts in any of the other states, the state supreme court found that domestic partnerships were indeed a "similar union" (to marriage) (*National Pride at Work v. Governor* 2008, 12) and that entering a domestic-partnership program for same-sex couples constituted an "agreement" (22) that had a "purpose" (23) that neither cities nor the state could legally "recognize" (21). This decision is likely to become precedential for courts in other states where constitutional amendments go beyond simply defining marriage as between a man and a woman and include language that references other relationship statuses and, specifically or generally, bars them from receiving equal treatment with marriage.

DOMESTIC PARTNERSHIPS SUSTAINED. In four cases, Atlanta (*Morgan*), Montgomery County, Philadelphia, and Vancouver, the state high court sustained the authority of local governments to provide health benefits for domestic partners of municipal employees. In five cases—Broward County, Chicago, Denver, the Madison (WI) School District, and New York City—the high court refused to review lower-court decisions upholding the DP benefit programs. Challenges to ordinances in Carrboro and Chapel Hill, Pima County, Portland, Salt Lake City, and Santa Barbara were not appealed from trial court decisions favorable to the local governments. The courts in these cases supported their decisions in a number of ways.

The charge that the DP benefits program conflicted with state laws on marriage or public policies favoring marriage was raised in all but two of these cases (it was not raised in Atlanta [*Morgan*] or Pima County). In all but one of the remaining cases, the court rejected this argument; in the Madison School District case, the judges said "it is not the role of this court to weigh the social and political policy implications" of the decision to offer a DP benefits program (*Pritchard v. Madison Metropolitan School District* 17). In dismissing the marriage arguments, many of the cases pointed out the differences between the legal status and legal rights of married partners and those of domestic partners. In particular, the court in the New York City case (*Slattery v. City of New York* 6–14) enumerated many of these differences and concluded that, "as compared to marital relationships, domestic partnerships are marked by their lack of formalization, lack of legal protections, and by the significantly fewer rights that are extended to the domestic partners" (*Slattery v. City of New York* 14). The New York court then cited the Colorado court in finding that domestic partners "qualif[y] as a separate and distinct group of people who are not eligible to contract a state sanctioned marriage to receive health and dental insurance benefits from the City" (*Slattery v. City of New York* 14–15). The Pennsylvania court characterized Philadelphia's "life partner" as "yet another 'unmarried status'" along with single, divorced, and widowed (*Devlin* 21).

The public-policy argument puts forth the idea that the state favors marriage because it gives many rights and privileges to married couples that are not provided to unmarried couples. Domestic-partnership benefit programs, it is argued, discourage people from getting married by allowing them to enjoy some of the same benefits that married people receive. This argument is most powerful when the program includes opposite-sex as well as same-sex partners, since the former do have an option to marry. But, as they have with arguments that these programs directly conflict with marriage laws, these courts have found that the limited nature of domestic-partnership benefit programs is insufficiently broad to endanger the state's public policy favoring marriage. Again, this reaffirms the subordinate social and inferior legal status of gay and lesbian relationships, even if they mimic in form a traditional marital relationship.

After disposing of the marriage arguments, the courts turned to the arguments concerning employee benefit programs. In each of these cases, including the cases where the program was overturned, the courts found that the local governments had the authority to provide health benefits to employees, their spouses, and their dependents. The question, however, concerned whether or not the state law allowed each jurisdiction to innovate in its definition of the term "dependent" so that it could include domestic partners of employees. Depending on the specific law in a particular state, the argument presented by the plaintiffs took one (or more) of three different forms: (1) state law on employee benefits specifically preempts the local jurisdictions from coming up with their own categories for benefits eligibility; (2) the term "dependent" used by the local jurisdiction conflicts with the term's definition in state law; and/or (3) the issue of local government employee benefits is a matter of statewide concern, and local governments cannot be allowed to go their own way.

In each state there was at least one state law that authorized local governments to offer health benefits to employees and their spouses and dependents. These laws came in varying degrees of specificity, but none of them explicitly authorized inclusion of domestic partners as dependents. When the courts upheld the domestic-partnership program against these arguments, they tended to find that the state law did not preclude local governments from expanding the definition of dependent if they so chose. In some cases, such as the one in Chicago, the court noted that unlike the situation in Minneapolis where the legislature could preempt the city's authority by implication, in Illinois any preemption had to be explicit, and the legislature had not forbidden cities from adopting domestic-partnership benefit programs (*Crawford* 24).

Similar arguments arose over whether or not there was a conflict between the state law's definition of "dependents" and that of the local government. In the Atlanta (*Morgan*) decision, the court found that "the City followed our holding in *McKinney* and carefully avoided the constitutional flaw in its previous benefits ordinance by eliminating . . . [in the] definition of 'dependent' any language recognizing any new family relationship similar to marriage" (*City of Atlanta v. Morgan* 5). This time, the Georgia Supreme Court turned to dictionary definitions of "dependent" as well as definitions found in other state laws and found that the way the city defines domestic partner as "one who relies on another for support" (*Morgan* 5) regardless of the specific amount of that support meets the "ordinary meaning" of the term. Other states, including Washington and Colorado, also used the dictionary for assistance in finding that the "ordinary" meaning of "dependent" did not exclude the definition of domestic partner as developed by the local government.

With respect to the argument that local-government employee benefits were a matter of statewide concern, an issue important in the Boston and Minneapolis cases, the judges consistently found that, to the contrary, employee-benefits policy was a classic matter of local concern in these states. Judges often emphasized the economic argument that the local government had an obligation to run an efficient and effective operation, and, if they determined that offering domestic-partnership benefits enabled them to attract the best employees, they could choose to do so. There might be political disagreement with this decision, but such a disagreement needed to be resolved politically, not by the courts.

In general, decisions upholding local domestic-partnership laws emphasized the importance of local autonomy and the need to construe local authority "liberally." Courts concluded that they should restrict local actions only when there was a clear intent on the part of the state to define the parameters of local-government employee-benefit programs in general. Otherwise, courts found that providing employee benefits is clearly a local matter.

Discussion

The cases in which domestic-partnership benefit programs were overturned involved states with either very specific authorizing statutes (Minnesota and Massachusetts) or strong and long-standing adherence to Dillon's Rule (Virginia). In each case, the local government indicated some doubt about its authority prior to or concurrent with taking action to adopt domestic-partnership benefits. Only the *McKinney* case, in Atlanta, turned on judges' choosing to read a possibly ambiguous law in a way that limited the city's discretion to act, though, even in that case, the court found in favor of the city on two important related programs—the nondiscrimination ordinance and the domestic partner registry—and laid the groundwork for the city to amend its law in a manner that would allow them to rule in its favor in *City of Atlanta v. Morgan*.

In all of the remaining cases, the courts found that local governments had the authority to act in this highly controversial area. Judges sided with local governments in finding that domestic partnerships were not attempts to create a new type of marital status. Likewise, judges found that, in the absence of clear state-level instructions on how to define "dependents" for employee-benefit purposes, local governments had a great deal of leeway in defining that term for themselves. However, it must be noted that, with one possible exception, that of Salt Lake City, the domestic-partnership plans did not challenge the traditional concept of a household as consisting of two adults and minor dependents.

Evidence discussed here suggests that courts are willing to give cities room to experiment with issues that contain elements of "morality politics." As Clark (1985, 108) noted, there is a tendency for political issues to lose their "texture" once they are transformed into legal arguments. That certainly seems to be the case with issues of "morality." Highly contentious political debates became transformed into technical arguments over precedent and the application of legal principles. For the most part, judges downplayed the arguments concerning domestic partnership's threats to traditional marriage and focused on the issue of defining dependents for employee-benefit purposes.

The Future

However, as noted earlier, even if an issue has been "lost" at one level or in one part of government, in the United States one (or a group) can always seek other venues for achieving policy goals. In this case, we can see examples where "losing" sides have sought other ways of getting their preferred policy positions adopted. For example, in Massachusetts, the legal battle evolved from one over domestic-partnership ordinances to a successful effort to permit same-sex marriages (*Goodridge v. Department of Public Health* 2003). The city of Minneapolis has adopted an ordinance requiring that city contractors provide domestic-partnership benefits to their employees even though the city government is not allowed to provide benefits to its own employees (Bayse 2004). Several states, such as California and New Jersey, have adopted state-wide recognition of domestic partnerships or civil unions and sometimes require that local governments provide domestic-partnership benefits. In Alaska, the state supreme court found that local governments that provided benefits for spouses but did not provide domestic-partnership benefits to employees were in violation of the state constitution (*ACLU v. State of Alaska and Municipality of Anchorage* 2005). Following a court loss, however, some opponents of domestic-partnership benefits have promoted the adoption of state constitutional amendments that may be effective in overturning the earlier judicial decisions favorable to domestic-partnership programs. The New Orleans case is still pending, and the terms of its state constitutional amendment seem particularly onerous,[4] although this did not stop a lower-court judge from ruling in the city's favor (365Gay.com 2008). Likewise, the decision in the Kansas City case restricted itself to the question of how "dependents" were defined, completely sidestepping the question of "marriage," despite a constitutional amendment that says that "No relationship, other than a marriage, shall be recognized by the state as entitling the parties to the rights or incidents of marriage" (Kansas Constitution, Article 15, Section 16(2)).

In September 2005, Mayor Rocky Anderson issued an executive order establishing domestic-partnership benefits for unmarried opposite-sex and same-sex couples that work for the Salt Lake City government. He was immediately challenged on three fronts: suit was filed against the mayor with the assistance of the Alliance Defense Fund; a majority of the City Council moved to supersede the mayor's order by adopting a program that would allow unmarried employees to name any "adult designee" as a dependent for purposes of employee health benefits; and the state Public Employees Health Program (PEHP) requested an opinion from the state district court as to whether or not the executive order was legal. After the City Council passed the "adult designee" ordinance, in January 2006, the mayor vetoed it, but the veto was overridden by the Council. The mayor cited concerns that the Council was dodging the issue of sexual-orientation equal rights, that the Council's plan would be more costly than his, and that the Council plan was unfair to married employees since they did not have the option of "designating" anyone other than their spouse (Thomson 2006). In May, after shifting its focus from the mayor's executive order to the Council's ordinance, the district court hearing the PEHB request ruled that there was no conflict between the "adult designee" program and the state's constitutional amendment prohibiting same-sex marriages. The Utah court pointed out that "No spouse of an employee . . . can require an employer to provide health insurance on account of his or her married status, unless such dependent coverage is already provided by the employer as a matter of contractual or other similar legal obligation" (*In the Matter of the Utah State Retirement Board* 4). Including "adult designees" as dependents for health-benefit purposes is merely an expansion of a contractual relationship, not a legal relationship. In February 2006, a state legislator succeeded in getting the Utah House of Representatives to pass a bill prohibiting local governments from spending funds for health benefits for any dependents other than spouses and children of employees, but the bill was amended in the Utah Senate specifically to allow such funding, and the amendment and the bill were defeated when reconsidered by the House.

Salt Lake City was not the first jurisdiction to define domestic partners so broadly that one did not have to be a "partner" in the sense of being in an intimate relationship with the employee to qualify for benefits. Washington, D.C., in 1990, had adopted a similar approach allowing employees to include any other cohabiting adult, even a family member, as part of a strategy to convince the U.S. Congress, which has veto power over its local legislation, that it was merely expanding who was eligible for health benefits (Gossett 1994). But Salt Lake City's ordinance came into being in the context of the push for state constitutional amendments limiting marriage rights, and it is already having an impact. City officials in Kalamazoo, Michigan (as well as officials at several state universities that had domestic-partnership benefit programs in place before the amendment passed) have begun exploring the "adult designee" approach used by Salt Lake City.

> Kalamazoo, though, thinks it has found a solution. Late last month, the city's commission voted to skirt the constitutional limitation—by altering the wording. . . . Instead of "domestic partners," the new "other qualified adult" program provides medical and dental insurance to a person close to the employee—and who meets a list of seven criteria, including having lived together for at least a year "with the intent to do so indefinitely." (Huffstutter 2007)

Oddly, the same article quotes a spokesman for the state attorney general as saying that the official concern was that the original format of the domestic-partnership program recognized gay couples in committed relationships, which made it seem that the state was saying that such a relationship was similar to a marriage. Because the proposed "other qualified adult" program doesn't require such a commitment, it is not inconsistent with the constitutional amendment (Huffstutter 2007). Whether or not advocacy groups will support that interpretation remains to be seen.

Finally, it must be noted, as it was at the beginning of this chapter, that the American political system is structured so that a political loss in one arena doesn't necessarily end a dispute but rather sends the advocates of the losing side in search of another forum to achieve their objectives. Thus, domestic-partnership advocates in Minneapolis not only have been seeking a change in state law that would allow cities to offer domestic partnerships but also have succeeded in having the city adopt a law that requires companies doing business with the city to provide their employees with domestic-partnership benefits (Bayse 2004). In Massachusetts, advocates of partnership rights for lesbian and gay male couples mounted a successful court challenge to the state's refusal to recognized same-sex marriages and then successfully lobbied the legislature to prevent a citizens' referendum on a constitutional amendment to overturn the judicial decision and prohibit same-sex marriages (Phillips and Estes 2007). In Virginia, on the other hand, in an effort to cement their victory in court, opponents of domestic partnerships succeeded in amending the state constitution to prohibit recognition of any partnership between two people other than a marriage between one man and one woman (Stallsmith 2006).

After a long string of courtroom victories in which courts largely deferred to the prerogatives of local governments in managing their own personnel systems, it appears the tide may be turning with respect to the use of courts as a way of defending domestic-partnership benefit programs. Having benefited from court rulings that generally interpreted existing laws in a way that favored cities that wanted to establish such programs, opponents have begun to use the legislative track (including the citizen initiative process where available) to rewrite the laws to leave less room for interpretation by the courts. Certainly, that is what seems to have happened in the Kalamazoo case, although lower-court judges in Utah, Louisiana, and Missouri were not persuaded that recent constitutional language prevented such programs. One should count on further efforts in this direction from those opposed to domestic-partnership benefits.

From another perspective, however, it must be acknowledged that the entire national debate has moved quickly beyond simply the issue of domestic-partnership benefits; several states are now wrestling with the question of legalizing same-sex marriages. This issue, most would acknowledge, is an issue that must be decided at the state level, although the mayor of San Francisco did unsuccessfully try to make it an issue of local authority, as well (Gordon 2004). The public no longer perceives the issue simply as "recognition of domestic partnerships" versus "nonrecognition"; rather, it is beginning to view accepting domestic partnership as a compromise position between recognizing same-sex marriages and not recognizing same sex relationships at all (Lewis and Gossett 2008). This suggests that advocates of domestic-partnership programs may want to take advantage of this environment to push local and state governments to adopt these policies. It may be true that the advocates will see this as a step toward eventual recognition of same-sex marriages, while others may see it as a means for putting off such advances, but that is how public policies are often made—with each side seeing a different beneficial effect from the compromise policy position.

The other lesson that one can take from this study is that local governments continue to have an important role in advancing (or retarding) social justice. Among political scientists, it is a commonplace that the states are the "laboratories of democracy," as Justice Brandeis once put it, but perhaps it needs to be recognized that the same can be said of local governments. Many advances in equal rights for lesbian, gay, and bisexual citizens began with local government action, and that trend is continuing as the need for equal protection of the law for transgendered citizens is becoming more apparent to progressive political leaders. Local governments often have a lot of room for maneuvering within what might appear to be a constricted legal system, although it takes courage to step forward and willingness to spend resources to defend actions that opponents will challenge in courts. State courts appear, for the most part, to want to support local governments whenever they can, even to the point sometimes of providing legal guidance on how to "fix" problems that can't otherwise be finessed (e.g., the advice the Georgia Supreme Court gave the city of Atlanta in the *McKinney* case). The climate that is then created by dozens or hundreds of local governments having put a practice into place with neither financial ruin nor moral degradation resulting from the action helps create the climate for larger victories in the years to come.

Appendix A: Court Cases

This section is organized alphabetically by the city or county involved in the case.

ALBANY, NY
James H.K. Bruner and Gretchen Bruner v. City of Albany, Common Council, Mayor Gerald Jennings. 1996. Decision and Order, Index #3444-96, Supreme Court, Albany County. October 18, 1996.

ANN ARBOR, MI

Teri Rohde et al. v. Ann Arbor Public Schools et al. 2005. 265 Mich. App. 702; 698 N.W.2d 402; 2005 Mich. App. LEXIS 910.

Teri Rohde et al. v. Ann Arbor Public Schools et al. 2007. 2007 Mich. LEXIS 1630.

ARLINGTON COUNTY, VA

Andrew White et al. v. Arlington County et al. 1999. Final Order, Chancery No. 98-144, March 22, 1999, Judge Benjamin N. A. Kendrick.

Arlington County et al. v. White et al. 2000. Va. LEXIS 71.

ATLANTA, GA

City of Atlanta v. McKinney. 1995. 265 Ga. 161; 454 S.E.2d 517.

City of Atlanta v. Morgan. 1997. 268 Ga. 586; 492 S.E.2d 193.

BOSTON, MA

Connors et al. vs. City of Boston. 1999. 1999 Mass. LEXIS 482.

BROWARD COUNTY, FL

Lawrence Lowe v. Broward County. 1999. Final Judgment, April 30, 1999; Case No. 99-2775 (09), Judge Robert L. Andrews.

Lowe v. Broward County. 2000. 2000 Fla. App. LEXIS 11893, September 20.

Lowe v. Broward County. 2001. 2001 Fla. LEXIS 819, April 4, 2001 (petition for review denied).

CAMBRIDGE, MA

Catavalo v. City of Cambridge. 2000. "Findings of Fact, Conclusions of Law and Order for Judgment," Middlesex Superior Court, Civil Action No. 00-1319, October 30, 2000, Judge James McHugh.

CHAPEL HILL AND CARRBORO, NC

Godley et al. vs. Town of Carrboro and Town of Chapel Hill. 2000. Order, File No. 99-CVS 844, May 16, 2000, Judge Orlando F. Hudson, Jr.

CHICAGO, IL

Crawford et al. v. City of Chicago et al. 1999. 1999 Ill. Appl. LEXIS 211, March 31.

Crawford et al. v. City of Chicago et al. 1999. 185 Ill. 2d 621; 720 N.E.2d 1090; 1999 Ill. LEXIS 1083; 242, Ill. Dec. 135, October 6, 1999 (petition for leave to appeal denied).

DENVER, CO

Schaefer and Tader v. City and County of Denver. 1998. 973 P.2d 717; 1998 Colo. App. LEXIS 255.

Schaefer and Tader v. City and County of Denver. 1999 Colo. LEXIS 361, April 12, 1999 (petition for leave to appeal denied).

GAINESVILLE, FL

Martin v. City of Gainesville. 2000. "Order Granting Motion to Dismiss," 8th Judicial Circuit Court, Case No. 2000 CA 1814, November 12, 2000, Judge Stan R. Morris.

Martin v. City of Gainesville. 2001. 2001 Fla. App. LEXIS 16945.

KALAMAZOO, MI

National Pride at Work et al. v. Granholm and City of Kalamazoo. 2005. Opinion and Order, Case No. 05-368-CZ, Circuit Court for the County of Ingham, State of Michigan, Judge Joyce Draganchuk, downloaded on 8/25/07 from http://www.aclumich.org/pdf/briefs/dplawsuit-decision.pdf.

National Pride at Work et al. v. Granholm and City of Kalamazoo. 2007. 2007 Mich. App. LEXIS 240.

National Pride at Work et al. v. Granholm and City of Kalamazoo. 2008. 748 N.W.2d 524; 2008 Mich. LEXIS 915.

KANSAS CITY, MO

Buckner v. City of Kansas City. 2004. Complaint filed in Circuit Court, Jackson County, Missouri, downloaded on 8/25/07 from http://www.alliancedefensefund.org/userdocs/Bucknerv-KansasCityComplaint.pdf.

Buckner v. City of Kansas City. 2007. Declaratory Judgment and Order Granting Summary Judgment in Favor of Defendant City of Kansas City, Missouri. Division 14, Circuit Court of Jackson County, Missouri, Judge John M. Torrance, November 13.

MADISON, WI

Pritchard et al. v. Madison Metropolitan School District. 2001. 2001 Wisc. App. LEXIS 141, February 8.

Pritchard et al. v. Madison Metropolitan School District. 2001. 2001 WI 88; 246 Wis. 2d 166; 630 N.W.2d 220; 2001 Wisc. LEXIS 505, May 8, 2001 (petition for review denied).

MINNEAPOLIS, MN

Anglin v. City of Minneapolis. 1992. Findings of Fact, Conclusions of Law, and Order for Judgment, Minneapolis Commission on Civil Rights, File No. 88180-EM-12, November 17.

Lilly v. City of Minneapolis. 1995. 527 N.W.2d 107; 1995 Minn. App.

Lilly v. City of Minneapolis. 1995. 1995 Minn. LEXIS 264, March 29, 1995 (denial of review).

MONTGOMERY COUNTY, MD

Steve Tyma et al. v. Montgomery County Council et al. 2000. Order, Civil No. 211250, October 30, 2000.

Steve Tyma et al. v. Montgomery County. 2002. 2002 Md. LEXIS 345, June 14.

NEW ORLEANS, LA

Ralph et al. v. City of New Orleans. 2006. 928 So.2d 537; 2006 La. LEXIS 1431.

NEW YORK CITY, NY

Eileen F. Slattery et al. v. City of New York et al., 179 Misc. 2d 740; 686 N.Y.S.2d 683; 1999 N.Y. Misc. LEXIS 35, February 8, 1999.

Eileen F. Slattery et al. v. City of New York et al. 1999. 1999 N.Y. App. Div. LEXIS 11158, November 4, 1999.

Eileen F. Slattery et al. v. City of New York et al. 2000. 2000 N.Y. LEXIS 231, February 29, 2000 (appeal dismissed).

PHILADELPHIA, PA

Devlin et al. v. City of Philadelphia. 2000. 48 Pa. D. and C.4th 86; 2000 Pa. D. and C. LEXIS 150, October 5, 2000.

Devlin et al. v. City of Philadelphia. 2002. 2002 Pa. Commw. LEXIS 683, August 29, 2002.

Devlin et al. v. City of Philadelphia. 2004. 2004 Pa. LEXIS 3059.

PIMA COUNTY, AZ

La Wall v. Pima County. 1998. Arizona Superior Court, Pima County, Case No. C-320550, Minute Entry, March 13.

PORTLAND, ME

Pulsifer et al. v. City of Portland (ME). 2004. Superior Court, Cumberland County, No. CV-03-448, April 27, 2004.

SALT LAKE CITY, UT

In the Matter of the Utah State Retirement Board's Trustee Duties and Salt Lake City Ordinance No. 4 of 2006. 2006. Utah Third District Court, Salt Lake County, Civil No. 050916879, May 11, downloaded on 8/18/06 from http://www.acluutah.org/normanruling.pdf.

SANTA BARBARA, CA

Order on City's Demurrer to First Amended Complaint, Motion for judgment on the Pleadings and Requests for Judicial Notice, January 13, 1999; Case No. 223122, Judge Thomas P. Anderle.

VANCOUVER, WA

Roni Heinsma vs. City of Vancouver. 2000. Court's Decision, No. 99-2-00772 1, June 26, 2000, Judge John F. Nichols.

Heinsma v. City of Vancouver. 2001. 2001 Wash. LEXIS 549, August 23.

10 Explaining the Differences

Transgender Theories and Court Practice

Marybeth Herald

THE CATEGORIES OF male and female have long been viewed as representing two separate and complementary sexes. Persons identifying as transgender, however, do not fit neatly into this binary model.[1] But the yin-and-yang symmetry of the classification system, engraved in our collective unconscious, has a primal appeal that resists challenge, no matter the evidence. The terms "male" and "female" actually represent a blend of factors that may not yield to easy labeling but rather present a more complex picture (Greenberg 1999; Greenberg and Herald 2005).

When the comfortable binary simplicity is threatened, how do we reconcile the conflict? Several courts have taken on the challenge as transgendered persons seek recognition of their gender identity, an identity in conflict with the sex label assigned to them at birth. When transgender persons wish to marry, for example, courts must grapple with an ill-fitting binary classification system—how to classify someone who does not identify with the sex assigned at birth? Moreover, they must cope with a system that rigidly enforces heterosexual norms and requires the parties to a marriage to adhere to an assigned role in the sexual relationship. In employment discrimination cases, courts must also decide how to classify transgender persons to determine whether the bias is actionable as gender discrimination. This chapter discusses some emerging and divergent trends in Europe, Australia, New Zealand, and the United States and suggests some common themes as courts confront these issues.

What we learn from this sampling of cases is that courts initially resist data that counter long-standing categorical assumptions. Presenting new scientific evidence is not itself sufficient when asking courts to reconsider long-accepted categorical rules. Rather, the most successful challenges use new information to prod courts to accept, sometimes slowly, that the issue is more complex than originally thought. Once the courts reach this stage, reframing the debate to incorporate other angles from which to view the problem is effective in sidestepping the categorical traps.

The winning theories leave the binary sex structure and heterosexual marriage undisturbed, however. The court cases reflect changing cultural norms; they do not significantly alter those norms (Rosenberg 1991 [2008]). In the transgender cases, for example, courts are more comfortable with arguments about sex stereotyping and human rights. These theories allow the court to bypass the difficult problem of defining the terms "male" and "female." In practice, urging these side avenues is a more effective strategy than a headlong assault against categories long cemented in our minds. When considering the evidence contradicting the exclusivity of two sexes, for example, courts are more likely to decide to ignore the evidence, or, if they acknowledge it, to adopt a new legal theory that can coexist with a binary sex structure or a heterosexual perspective so as to minimize the change to the social status quo.

Considering these cases may enlighten us as to what courts are actually doing, rather than what they claim to be doing in the area of transgender rights. These cases suggest the trajectory of future doctrinal developments will be one that painstakingly adapts existing structures rather than constructs a new model.

International Progress

The Changing Cases

Europe has taken a lead role in restructuring its laws to accommodate transgender persons. Several recent court decisions and legislative developments in Europe have allowed transgendered persons to marry in their self-identified sex roles. This development reflects a great leap forward from the 1970s, when Great Britain set the rule it would follow for twenty years: you are your birth sex.

Initially confronted with medical science's revolutionary ability to reconfigure a person's anatomy through surgery, the courts took the position that the original birth certificate trumped, despite any current visual evidence to the contrary (Corbett v. Corbett 1970). In Corbett, the English court considered a challenge to the validity of a marriage between a postoperative male-to-female transgender person and a male. The transgendered wife had male chromosomes (XY) and, at birth, genitals (a penis) and male gonads (testicles). The chromosomes remained unchanged at the time of trial, but the genitals and gonads had been altered. Nevertheless, the court voided the marriage as an illegal same-sex marriage. The court decided that the sex assigned at birth was unchangeable, no matter the current state of a person's genitalia or self-identity (Corbett v. Corbett 1970, 104). The result was the marriage was deemed one between two males and thus invalid.

But why focus on birth when subsequent history rendered that event a questionable marker? The answer is that it provides a convenient tool to avoid defining male and female. The court's discussion of chromosomes, gonads, and genitalia purports to defer to science, but selectively. Its conclusion that plaintiff possessed only "the pastiche of femininity" (Corbett v. Corbett 1970, 104) captures the gut instinct that underlies the result. The court's filtering of the science was also on display when it questioned whether "natural heterosexual intercourse" (necessary for the marriage relationship) (*Corbett v. Corbett* 1970, 104) could occur within the parties' relationship. According to the court, a male-to-female postoperative transgender person could not perform the "essential role of a woman in a hetero-sexual marriage" (*Corbett v. Corbett* 1970, 104), although the court did not define this essential role that defines a female. The court was left unsatisfied with the transgender person's sexual performance because the court deemed the surgical alteration of the vagina insufficient (*Corbett v. Corbett* 1970, 83, 107). The court's discomfort with the situation led to a categorical rule that no one need apply in the future; sex had been decided at birth.

The *Corbett* case illustrates that it is not necessarily a lack of information that leads to problematic decision making—the court did discuss biological factors—but it is our inability to process it without bias that contributes to the problem. As medical science boldly facilitated change, the law's first response was to feign ignorance that any change could occur and indeed to label the transgender per-son's claim for recognition as a female "bizarre" (*Corbett v. Corbett* 1970, 83, 107).

Courts favor the status quo (deciding cases on a precedential system) as an occupational rule, but precedent often allows multiple interpretations, such as that the marriage in *Corbett* was between a male and female. Yet, when choosing which path to follow, the human need to favor our current coordinates anchors us and keeps us from drifting far from our original spot. Here, despite the medi-cal evidence that the person's sex was altered, the court declared that the birth certificate could not be impeached by any later developments, providing a carica-ture-like example of the status quo bias (Kahneman, Knetsch, and Thaler 1991, 199–203; Korobkin 1998, 625–30).

The court in *Corbett* was unwilling to stray from the immutability of the binary sex structure. That structure is tough to breach. The division of people into male and female is one of the prime categorizations that we learn from birth, making it an especially potent one. Moreover, transgender issues go beyond pushes for gender neutrality, that is, the belief that males and females should not be auto-matically associated with certain behaviors and the rejection of stereotypes such as the idea that boys don't cry and girls do. Rather, a transgender challenge is an assault on the principal classification itself and a threat to a very refined and entrenched organizational structure.

In the transgender cases, we are confronting the deeply embedded and basic script that the sexes consist of two mutually exclusive and immutable catego-ries—male and female. An associated script is that male and female are the only pairing appropriate in a marriage. The *Corbett* court stuck to these scripts despite receiving dissonant information, which is quite normal. When long-held beliefs are questioned, such as the belief in two distinct sexes, our cognitive processes tend to go into deep denial mode, repelling the onslaught of new information through illusions that help us reaffirm our views in the face of contrary evidence (Guthrie et al. 2001; Kahneman 1982; Plous 1993). The court's pronouncement of the infallibility of the original birth certificate reflected its discomfort with the details of the postbirth events and the difficulty of fitting them together with entrenched beliefs about sex and marriage.

Corbett's ostrich-like approach proved popular and established the sex assigned at birth as the status quo for a generation of courts. In Canada and Singapore, judges cited Corbett, denying any legal effect to medical alterations of sex (C.(L.) v. C.(C.) 1992 (Can.); Lim Ying v. Hiok Kian Ming Eric 1991 (Sing.)). On numerous occasions, the European Court of Human Rights (ECHR) rejected challenges under the European Convention on Human Rights (European Convention), finding no rights violation when a country refused to allow postoperative transgender persons to marry in their self-identified gender role (Rees v. United Kingdom 1987; Cossey v. United Kingdom 1991; Sheffield and Horsham v. United Kingdom 1999).

Two jurisdictions—New Jersey and New Zealand—appeared to buck this trend (M.T. v. J.T. 1976; Attorney-General v. Otahuhu Family Court 1991). The New Jersey decision, M.T. v. J.T., considered the situation of a postoperative male-to-female transgender person married to a male. Although the court rejected the Corbett rule of birth sex as determinative, the court in M.T. also focused on the adequacy of M.T.'s reconstructed body "for traditional penile/vaginal intercourse" (M.T. v. J.T. 1976, 206). In some respects, the Corbett and M.T. courts used the same criteria—the capacity of the reconstructed vagina to support penetration by the penis. One saw it as inadequate (the Corbett court characterized the reconstructed vagina as an "artificial cavity"), and the other adequate (the M.T. court noted that the reconstructed vagina had a "good cosmetic appearance and was the same as a normal female vagina after a hysterectomy") (M.T. v. J.T. 1976, 206). In both cases, the common concern was whether the transgender person's sexual machinery looked and could operate like that of a traditional female in performing heterosexual intercourse, that is, as a vessel for male pleasure. Whether a vagina is the source of female sexual pleasure is an entirely different question with a different answer (see Herald 2004), but the traditional male viewpoint of penetration for pleasure seemed to be the concern of the court. For this purpose, sexual reassignment surgery was a necessary but not sufficient component of recognition necessary for the transgender person to fit comfortably within the existing binary structure.

In the New Zealand case, Attorney-General v. Otahuhu Family Court, while the court found that "in order to be capable of marriage two persons must present themselves as having what appears to be the genitals of a man and a woman," they did not "have to prove that each can function sexually" or "that penetrative sexual intercourse is possible" (*Attorney-General v. Otahuhu Family Court* 1991, 612). The step forward in *Otahuhu* was that, as long as the two persons presented as being of the two sexes and one of each sex was represented in the marriage, appearances were served and no further information was required. *Otahuhu* thus moved away from making private details the subject of public court scrutiny.

The *M.T.* and *Otahuhu* courts acknowledged an ability to cross over from one sex to the other, but the accompanying physical characteristics needed to be in place. In effect, the courts reconciled the binary sex and heterosexual marriage scripts to fit a somewhat divergent pattern. One could cross over and become a member of the opposite sex, but one could not disturb the binary sex or heterosexual marriage scripts. Andrew Sharpe (2007, 65) argues that the *Otahuhu* court's decision reflects less an adherence to a heterosexual script and more a "homophobic anxiety." Thus, he frames the requirements of surgery as driven by an aversion to same-sex coupling rather than a wish to promote opposite-sex coupling.

Corbett, however, remained the standard legal view, and a tidal shift in thinking did not occur until more than thirty years later. A key ECHR opinion, *Goodwin v. United Kingdom*, held that Great Britain's refusal to recognize a transgendered person in his or her postoperative sex violated the Charter of Fundamental Rights of the European Union (*Goodwin v. United Kingdom* 2002). The decision acknowledged the accessibility and recognition of sex reassignment surgery in the medical community. Adopting a more open and compassionate stance than previous decisions, the ruling seemed more receptive to new information and theories and the justices more sympathetic to the plight of the transgender persons. But the cases that came between *Corbett* and *Goodwin* reveal the incremental nature of the assimilation of new information and the need to maintain the binary sex structure and the traditional view of marriage as a union between male and female.

The Change in Reasoning: More Information and a New Frame

Presented with the predicament of postoperative transgender persons who were forced to assume identities incompatible with their self-identified sex, the ECHR initially deferred to legislative bodies. But, perhaps in part because the ECHR recognized the overwhelming importance of sex classifications to everyday life, the court became impatient with the legislative refusal to fix what the court increasingly recognized was a problem with using the original birth certificate to categorize transgender persons as male or female.

The Intervening Cases—
Beginning to Understand That a Problem Exists

The cases decided between *Corbett* and *Goodwin* reflected a gradual awakening and an attempt to resolve the gap between law and reality. In *Rees v. United Kingdom*, decided in 1986, a postoperative female-to-male transgender person alleged a violation of the European Convention on Human Rights (European Convention) because he could not change the sex on his birth certificate under the law, a certificate he was required to produce (*Rees v. United Kingdom* 1986, 63, 65). The ECHR was unwilling to force a judicial modification of the system but rather gave a wide berth to the governments because "the law appears in a transitional stage" and changes would require "detailed legislation" (*Rees v. United Kingdom* 1986, 67). It was enough for the court that transgender persons could change their first and last names as well as signal their preferred sex by their use of Mr., Mrs., Ms., or Miss.

Four years later, in 1990, a postoperative male-to-female transgender person challenged her inability to change her birth certificate as a violation of European Convention in *Cossey v. United Kingdom*. The lack of a new birth certificate prevented Cossey from marrying a male because of the opposite-sex requirement for marriage. Following *Rees*, the ECHR did not find enough developments to change the result, but the vote of 10-8 was closer than the 12-3 vote in *Rees*. The ECHR now expressed its discomfort with the situation, noting that "[i]t is conscious of the problems facing transgenders and the distress they suffer. Since the Convention always has to be interpreted and applied in the light of current circumstances, it is important that the need for appropriate legal measures in this area should be kept under review" (*Cossey v. United Kingdom* 1990, 641).

In 1998, the ECHR again rejected a challenge by male-to-female transgender persons who alleged violations of the Charter of Fundamental Rights because the United Kingdom did not recognize them as women after gender reassignment surgery. In *Sheffield and Horsham v. United Kingdom*, the ECHR deferred to the United Kingdom, but by an even closer vote (11-9) and with even more impatience, reflecting its concern with the uncertain status that transgender persons occupied even if it could not articulate a legal theory: "Even if there have been no significant scientific developments since the date of the *Cossey* judgment . . . it is nevertheless the case that there is an increased social acceptance of transgenderism and an increased recognition of the problems which post-operative transgender persons encounter" (*Sheffield and Horsham v. United Kingdom* 1998, 193).

These cases gave the court time to assimilate new information. The relatively rare appearance of transgender issues gave decision makers little exposure to information, and the tendency for transgender persons to prefer privacy rather than public misunderstanding compounded the difficulties. As transgender pe. brought more cases and as information became more readily available, the trans formation in understanding began. As the ECHR came to understand that transgenderism was a complex issue, its willingness to give the issue closer examination increased. Presenting the individual problems in more vivid detail seemed to capture the court's attention (Plous 1993). The court's emotional response evolved from one of indifference to one of empathy with the problems caused by the law's failure to recognize a change in gender identity after surgical reassignment.

Goodwin: A New Frame for the Problem

When the *Goodwin* case presented itself, in 2002, the ECHR had a more sophisticated understanding of the problem and a more sympathetic ear. Rather than trying to figure out whether to label someone as male or female and to buck the binary system, the court focused on a different angle to the problem: the right of an individual to enjoy life as part of society. This frame covered a much bigger picture than the *Corbett* court, which was concerned with the details of the parties' private sex lives.

The way a question is framed by and for the courts may affect the outcome of a case because we are vulnerable to how our choices are described. Studies confirm that people will view the same problem differently depending on how it is stated. For example, people are more likely to undergo a risky medical procedure if they are told that "90 percent [of people who undergo this procedure] are alive in five years" than if they are told that "10 percent [of people] are dead after five years." In the first example, one's brain connects to the risk of death, not a positive frame when one is deciding whether to undergo a medical procedure. In the second example, one's brain connects to the idea of survival, which is far more appealing. The first choice is cast as a gain, and the second is cast as a loss, which makes all the difference in preferences (Lau and Schlesinger 2005; Sunstein 2004). The frame affects the answer because it provides the mental structure that our brain uses to connect to other ideas. Once the brain has the frame highlighted, it is hard for our mind to rid itself of the image; it infects our thinking about the whole issue. The lesson is that we may manipulate preferences by the way we frame the question we ask because we can appeal to underlying biases.

The difference in frames between *Corbett* and *Goodwin* is dramatic. In *Corbett*, the question was whether a postoperative male-to-female transgender person was female. This very specific question triggers male-female associations that are deeply engrained. In *Goodwin*, the question was whether an individual had a right to enjoy life as a part of society. The beauty is in its breadth and the difficulty of denial. As the *Goodwin* court explained, the government did not have r denial of the right and, indeed, "may reasonably be expected to ... inconvenience to enable individuals to live in dignity and worth with the sexual identity chosen by them at great personal cost"

in court also shifted the frame from *Corbett*'s very searching inquiry male anatomy to sheltering private details from public regulation. to what the court referred to as a "serious interference with private life" (*Goodwin*, 450), the ECHR focused on general themes of human dignity, human freedom, and personal autonomy. The ECHR discussed a right to a private identity:

> The very essence of the Convention is respect for human dignity and human freedom. . . . [W]here the notion of personal autonomy is an important principle underlying the interpretation of its guarantees, protection is given to the personal sphere of each individual, including the right to establish details of their identity as individual human beings. (*Goodwin* 451)

The themes are broad, with a relatively narrow application in the individual case. In other words, the court discusses a universal theme of human rights and then applies it to the specific case of transgender persons. The use of "human" diverts attention from the categories of male and female and allowed the ECHR to avoid confronting those categories and their definitions. The ECHR acknowledged that science had not provided definitive answers about transgenderism (*Goodwin* 450). The focus on protecting the "personal sphere" shields the details of the genitalia from examination, rejecting the approach of the *Corbett* court, but also avoiding spelling out the definitional details of male and female.

Through the cases leading up to *Goodwin*, the ECHR developed the desire to assist transgender persons and to remove some legal roadblocks in their path. A human rights approach provided the framework that allowed the court to accomplish that result. But avoiding the definitional details did not make them disappear, and society's attachment to the male-female paradigm continued unabated.

New Rulings but the Same Scripts

Goodwin did not dispose of the binary sex paradigm. The case was made easier because it involved a postoperative transgender person. The court could reject the argument that individuals would capriciously embark on the risky and difficult path to surgical alteration of their sex in order to jump the fence to enjoy the other sex's greener grass. Requiring surgical intervention ensures that a true crossover from one sex to the other occurs and allows the court to adhere to the binary paradigm. One may cross over to the other category, but one must make a choice between the two.

A similar emphasis on fitting into the binary sex structure was apparent in the Australian case of *In re Kevin* (*Attorney Gen. v. Kevin* 2003). The Australian court rejected the *Corbett* decision and its own precedent based on the recent scientific evidence on gender identity formation and concluded that "a woman or a female, as those terms are generally understood in Australia today, includes a post-operative transsexual person" (*Attorney Gen. v. Kevin* 2003, 32). The female-to-male transgender person in *In Re Kevin* had undergone only partial reassignment surgery—a mastectomy and a total hysterectomy—and still had a vagina. Nevertheless, the court noted: "[W]hatever might be the position with pre-operative transsexuals, the irreversible surgery that completes the sex-reassignment process provides a convenient and workable line for the law to draw. No significant difficulties are posed by including post-operative transsexuals in their reassigned sex" (*Attorney Gen. v. Kevin* 2003).

Although there is a movement toward acceptance of transgender persons in the case, acceptance as a male even without a penis, and acceptance of marriage without reproduction as its focus, it is movement that clings to and reinforces the binary sex paradigm. The Australian court placed emphasis on evidence that Kevin had always been perceived to be male through the testimony of thirty-nine witnesses. It is the ability of Kevin to act stereotypically male that gives him the freedom to cross over from one sex to the other. Any drift away from stereotypical male behavior might have proven fatal to the claim.

The two sexes are also a constant in the Gender Recognition Act, passed by the British parliament in 2004, which allows transgender persons to marry in their self-identified status, without undergoing surgery (Gender Recognition Act 2004). The Act allows adults to apply for a "gender recognition certificate" on the basis of "(a) living in the other gender, or (b) having changed gender under the law of a country or territory outside the United Kingdom." Although a majority of countries in Europe now permit a postoperative transgender person to marry in that person's self-identified sex, the dropping of the requirement of surgery, which limited remedies to transgender persons, was a step forward. Unfortunately, a "biological understanding of sex persists as an important subtext" and "is inextricably tied up with the homophobia of the law" (Sharpe 2007, 59).

Within the act, the imprint of the binary sex structure is visible. For example, if there is no surgical reassignment to one of the two sexes, the applicant for a certificate under the act must demonstrate gender dysphoria. The requirement that one must acknowledge mental illness pays homage to the binary sex model and fits nicely with the existing status quo. There is a need not to change the underlying model but to acknowledge medical exceptions to the general rule that may be based on failure to conform to stereotypes of male or female behavior. It is the individual, not the system, that is the problem. Moreover, transgender persons are anchored in a mental illness model that perpetuates the notion that they are psychologically disturbed (Sharpe 2007, 38).

A general pledge of new allegiance is required as well, in the form of requirements that the applicant live in the alternate gender for two years and that the applicant declare "inten[t] to continue to live in the acquired gender until death" (Gender Recognition Act). Living in the gender means conformance to gender stereotypes—generalizations that impede rather than help us move forward into gender neutrality (Levit 1998), reinforcing the "his" and "her" varieties that characterize everything from job preferences to emotional descriptions (Burgess and Borgida 1999). It is counterintuitive to require adherence to unhelpful and downright destructive gender stereotypes (Williams 2003). But the value lies in reinforcing the basic two-sex structure.

Moreover, the act reinforces heterosexuality as the norm for marriage. If one is already married, one must get a divorce in order to receive certification under the act to avoid the specter of a same-sex marriage (Civil Partnership Act 2004). The legislation is unique in its encouragement of the dissolution of happy families in service of the social ideal of heterosexual marriage. Moreover, the act adds as grounds for annulment of marriage that one party did not know the gender history of the second party (Gender Recognition Act 2004, Paragraph 42). Although ostensibly accommodating transgender persons, the legislation displays a preference for marriage as an exclusive heterosexual institution as opposed to marriage as an enduring commitment. These legislative and court developments opened up new rights for transgender persons but without straying far from the deeply embedded binary sex script and heterosexual marriage requirements. The developments rely in part on reframing the issues within broader themes of human rights and privacy that allow the cases to fit within well accepted scripts.

Developments in the United States

The recognition of the broad umbrella of human rights protection in Europe has not been replicated in the United States. Marriage cases in the United States involving transgender persons are stalled while the courts try to fit transgender persons into ill-defined and narrow concepts of male and female and cope with the binary sex and heterosexual marriage scripts. It is ironic that, in some cases, despite stated policies against same-sex marriages, some courts are so wedded to their binary notions of male and female that they are led to the anomalous result of coercing same-sex marriages.

A broader theory, however, has driven employment discrimination claims of transgender persons, resulting in some successful claims under Title VII. The higher success rate makes sense. Marriage cases require the courts to simultaneously deal with defining male, female, and marriage. Add in the primacy of heterosexual sex, and one has a complicated juggling act. Employment discrimination claims are simpler. Courts are able to handle bias claims by framing the discrimination more broadly in terms of general gender stereotyping, similar to the broad framing of human rights claims in Europe.

The Stagnant Marriage Cases

During the past decade, some lower courts in the United States have followed the European trend toward recognizing post-operative marriage of transgender persons, but those courts have been reversed on appeal. Appellate courts continue in the vein of the earlier English decision of *Corbett v. Corbett*, which held that one is—despite any surgical alteration or other evidence to the contrary—the sex one was stamped at birth. The binary sex and the heterosexual marriage structures command court allegiance. In the marriage cases, the courts start with the heterosexual marriage requirement of one male and one female and work backwards. When the cases are framed by that requirement, the courts feel bound to ensure, by a variety of creative methods, that heterosexual norms are not breached. Because the starting definition of male and female has never been established in statutes requiring marriages to be between one male and one female, courts must make it up, conscious of the need to maintain the heterosexual status quo as the basis of marriage but unsure of how to do it. The courts struggle to determine when one has moved across the spectrum far enough to be classified as male or female. Some courts define male and female by reproductive capacity, others by capacity for intersexual intercourse, and still others by traditional male and female appearance.

RETREATING TO THE SEX ASSIGNED AT BIRTH AND
OTHER COGNITIVE DISTORTIONS

The courts in the United States, like the courts in Europe, confront a picture of conflicting regulations that place transgender persons in a legal quagmire. For example, when J'Noel Gardiner was born, she was identified as a male on her Wisconsin birth certificate (*Gardiner I*, 2001). After undergoing surgical and hormonal treatment, J'Noel applied to have the sex on her birth certificate amended to indicate that she is a female. By virtue of this amendment, if J'Noel had married a man in Wisconsin, Wisconsin would have treated them as a heterosexual couple, and as long as J'Noel and her husband never left the state of Wisconsin, they could be confident that they would be treated as all other heterosexual couples were treated. If, however, they decided to move to a different state, they could not be certain that another state would recognize that J'Noel was a female, as indicated on her amended birth certificate. If a sister state refused to acknowledge that J'Noel was a female, J'Noel would be considered a male, and her marriage to her husband might be considered an illegal same-sex union.

In fact, it was so considered. The Supreme Court of Kansas, the Court of Appeals of Florida, the Court of Appeals of Texas, and the Court of Appeals of Ohio have all ruled that, for purposes of marriage, transgender persons remain forever the sex that was assigned to them at birth (*Gardiner II* 2004; *Kantaras II* 2004; *Littleton v. Prange* 1999; *In re Marriage License for Nash* 2003). The courts' struggle to justify this result in their decisions is evident as they cope with imprecise definitions of male and female. The courts in Kansas, Florida, and Ohio found that the plain meaning of the terms "male" and "female" could be found in the dictionary. The Kansas Supreme Court quoted Webster's dictionary and determined that "'[m]ale' is defined as 'designating or of the sex that fertilizes the ovum and begets offspring: opposed to *female*.' 'Female' is defined as 'designating or of the sex that produces ova and bears offspring: opposed to *male*'" (*Gardiner II* 2004, 135). In other words, these courts have implied that those who cannot fertilize and beget are not true men and those who cannot produce ova and bear offspring are not true women, a result that may be shocking to the millions of people who are contained in these categories. Obviously, there are many persons who consider themselves male or female who are not capable of reproducing, and couples are not required to show fertility potential to marry generally. The court's definition is not even superficially convincing. The court did not want to confront the fact that the simple binary categories of male/female may not always fit. Rather, the court adopted *Corbett's* formalistic answer: it is so because the birth certificate says it is (Robson 2006, 302).

The practical effect for postoperative transgender persons stuck with the label of their sex assigned at birth is that the marriage partners that remain legally available to them are persons of the same sex (Frye and Meiselman 2001). The courts reach an anomalous result, forcing same-sex marriages when they are committed to a heterosexual norm. The actual result illustrates their difficulty in reconciling the various competing scripts and their willingness to engage in cognitive distortions such as ignoring surgical alterations. In *Gardiner*, the Kansas Supreme Court seemed to go even further by implying that the Kansas statute precluded marriage for transgender persons: "The plain ordinary meaning of 'persons of the opposite sex' contemplates a biological man and a biological woman and not persons who are experiencing gender dysphoria" (*Gardiner II* 2004, 135). Ruthann Robson argues that the *Gardiner II* court prevents transgender persons from marrying because "they would have no 'opposite sex'" (Robson 2006, 303, 304).

Whether caused by a devotion to heterosexuality, aversion to homosexuality, or simply an inability to cope with complexity, the courts, as in *Corbett*, retreat to the simpler time of birth as the marker. At that point, any discordant signs are hidden from plain view and silent. For example, a Florida appellate court ruled that a postoperative transgender person was not authorized under Florida law to marry in his or her reassigned sex. The appellate court in *Kantaras v. Kantaras* claimed that the "common meaning of male and female, as those terms are used statutorily . . . refer to immutable traits determined at birth" (*Kantaras v. Kantaras* 2004, 161). The court held that a female-to-male transgender person who had undergone sex reassignment surgery remained the sex assigned at birth, despite common-sense indications that sex reassignment surgery had altered the seemingly immutable through irreversible medical surgery.

The Florida case arose when Michael Kantaras petitioned for a divorce after his surgery. His spouse countered that the sex reassignment rendered the marriage void. Custody of two children was a major issue. Although Michael had undergone extensive surgery and lived as a male, he did not undergo a phalloplasty but did have an enlarged clitoris, which he considered his penis. After extensive review of the expert testimony, which focused on Michael's appearance, his lifestyle as a male, and the functionality of his sex organs as a male, the trial court concluded that "Michael Kantaras accomplished all that medical science required to succeed in the transition from female to male" (*Kantaras v. Kantaras* 2004, 161).

But the appellate court started with its primal fear and worked backwards. It honed in immediately on Florida's laws prohibiting same-sex marriage. If Michael was determined to be a male, those laws would be irrelevant because the same-sex-marriage issue would not arise. The Florida appellate opinion is striking in its failure to discuss the expert evidence parsed and considered by the trial court in reaching its conclusion. Unwilling to even consider the issue, the court rationalized its result by listing the cases from other jurisdictions that it agreed with and distinguishing the conflicting precedent with the very brief rebuttal "[w] e disagree." Ohio courts have taken a similar approach (*In re Marriage License for Nash* 2003; *In re Ladrach* 1987).

Many of the recent decisions in which courts have refused to allow transgender persons to legally adopt their postoperative sex were also grounded in a finding that the courts did not have the power to determine the test for legal sex in the face of legislative inaction (*Gardiner II* 2004, 136; *Kantaras II* 2004, 161; *In re Nash* 2003; *Littleton* 1999, 230). Although the legislative histories in these jurisdictions indicate that the legislatures had not considered or discussed the issue of sex determination for transgender persons, these courts decided that legislative silence is equivalent to legislative disapproval. In contrast, the ECHR, while deferring to legislative bodies in the early cases, expressed disproval of the failure to act to correct an injustice. The ECHR ultimately forced the hand of both the legislative and the judicial bodies of member nations when they failed to act.

At the same time, other courts reconcile the competing scripts in ways that privilege the heterosexual norm and produce different cognitive distortions. For example, in *In Re Marriage of Simmons*, the court recognized the surgical changes but required a complete crossover to avoid the specter of same-sex marriage. Although the transgender person had some surgical procedures, there were several remaining to complete the transition. The court found this failure to totally cross over dispositive because although the petitioner did not have a uterus, fallopian tubes, and ovaries, "petitioner still possesses all of his female genitalia" (*In Re Marriage of Simmons* 2005, 309). The appellate court approved the trial court's dissolution of the petitioner's marriage because "same-sex marriage was invalid under Illinois law" (*In Re Marriage of Simmons* 2005, 309).

The *Simmons* court knew the consequences of the sex determination for the marriage determination. The close interplay illustrates how difficult it is to unwind the same-sex marriage issue from the definition of male or female. Similarly, in *In re Heilig*, the court was willing to endorse a change in birth certificate as long as the petitioner provided sufficient medical evidence that "he has completed a permanent and irreversible change from male to female" (*In re Heilig* 2003, 87).

Other traditional appearance guidelines are also employed. The court must be satisfied that one looks the part of male or female. For example, in *Anonymous v. Anonymous*, a 1971 New York court decision, the court invalidated a marriage between a male and a male-to-female transgender person, stating that "mere removal of the male organs would not, in and of itself, change a person into a true female" (*Anonymous v. Anonymous* 1971, 500). New Jersey did not follow the trend, instead acknowledging a transgender person's postoperative sex—as long as it conformed to female anatomy (*M.T. v. J.T.* 1976). Although noting that external genitalia—in the vast majority of cases—could serve as the determining factor in identifying a person's sex at birth, the New Jersey court was also willing to acknowledge that the matter was far more complex after surgical alteration. When the individual had undergone surgery to alter his or her genitalia, the New Jersey court decided that both postoperative anatomy and gender identity were important because "[s]exual capacity . . . requires the coalescence of both the physical ability and the psychological and emotional orientation to engage in sexual intercourse as either a male or a female" (*M.T. v. J.T.* 1976, 209). But, as noted earlier, functioning as a male or female was narrowly focused on the ability to use one's genitalia "for traditional penile/vaginal intercourse" (*M.T. v. J.T.* 1976, 209). This focus on the need to choose a sex and to conform to the prevailing sexual performance norms allows the court in *M.T.* to adhere to the script while seeming to make exceptions for medical science. Never mind that even those on the far end of the female spectrum might not find "traditional penile/vaginal intercourse" very satisfying (Waldman and Herald 2005). Finally, the attention directed to the sexual aspects of marriage overshadows the more important social and economic facets of marriage, including property and inheritance rights and pension, health, and social security benefits. Even prisoners are given the right to marry, although there is no ability to consummate any sexual relationship between the parties (*Turner v. Safley*, 1987; Robson 2006, 304–05). That marriage is a relationship that encompasses more than sexual coupling is recognized in society generally, but ignored in these decisions.

The Changing Employment Discrimination Cases

In cases from the early 1970s, courts uniformly held that discrimination against transgender persons was not covered under Title VII. The courts consistently rejected claims brought on behalf of transgender persons, finding that discrimination against transgender persons was not discrimination "because of . . . sex" under Title VII (*Ulane v. Eastern Airlines* 1984; *Sommers v. Budget Marketing* 1982; *Holloway v. Arthur Anderson and Co.* 1977).

During the past few years, transgender persons have used a sex-stereotyping theory to convince courts that discrimination against them was sex discrimination. In *Price Waterhouse v. Hopkins*, a woman based a Title VII claim on the allegation that she was discriminated against because she was too "macho" (*Price Waterhouse v. Hopkins* 1989, 235).

The Supreme Court found such sex stereotyping actionable as discrimination based on sex. Not only should employers not discriminate against a woman because she is a woman, but neither should they discriminate when they think a woman is acting too much like a man.

Using this theory, transgender persons bringing claims after *Price Waterhouse* alleged that they were being discriminated against because of sex stereotyping— that is, because their behavior did not conform to sex stereotypes. In one Sixth Circuit case, for example, a male transgender person working as a firefighter and diagnosed with gender identity disorder claimed that he was discriminated against because he did not behave in a sufficiently masculine manner. The court emphasized that discrimination against "a transsexual [who] fails to act and/or identify with his or her gender—is no different from the discrimination directed against Ann Hopkins in *Price Waterhouse*, who, in sex-stereotypical terms, did not act like a woman" (*Smith v. City of Salem*, 2004, 235). This outcome contrasts with those in earlier cases that rejected Title VII protection for transgender persons because they were not within the statute's protected classes (*Dobre v. Nat'l R.R. Passenger Corp.* 1993; *James v. Ranch Mart Hardware*, 1995).

What the courts have done in this case is to reframe the question as one involving sex stereotypes. After several decades of litigation and social change, the problem of sex stereotyping is more easily understood. As the Supreme Court stated almost nonchalantly in *Price Waterhouse*: "[W]e are beyond the day when an employer could evaluate employees by assuming or insisting that they matched the stereotype associated with their group" (*Price Waterhouse v. Hopkins* 1989, 251). Instead of asking whether discrimination occurred against a transgender person, the question is framed as whether the discrimination occurred because of the person's failure to conform to a gender ideal. This framing eliminates the need to delve deeply into the science of gender identity, although it reinforces the binary sex categories through a pleading requirement that forces one to detail how the forced conformity to the stereotypes of one of the sexes occurred.

The claim still depends on the binary categories as a frame of reference. Thus, a plaintiff must allege that he or she is being discriminated against because of a failure to act as much like a male or a female as the boss thinks the person should. But the value of this framing is that the focus is on the limits of constraining a person's behavior through these categories. Although the Supreme Court may not have intended the broader theoretical use when it crafted the *Price Waterhouse* opinion, the sex-stereotyping formulation reflected a deeper understanding of the ingrained nature of gender discrimination in our society, and, from that deeper understanding, discrimination against transgender persons could be more easily explained and understood by the courts without disturbing the binary system. In the *Smith* case, for example, the firefighter alleged that he was discriminated against because he was not masculine enough, just as Ann Hopkins in *Price Waterhouse* was not feminine enough. Plaintiff's transgender status is, at most, a side issue. By hiding this issue, this theory offers some relief for transgender persons.

The Differences in Reasoning

In summary, courts have limited transgender persons to marriages based on the sex assigned at birth and refused to recognize the complexities of sexual identity. What is the reason for the difference in treatment in employment discrimination and marriage? One explanation is that the employment discrimination cases involve only one categorical imperative—the binary sex paradigm. They were helped by the broader principles of sex stereotyping and gender nonconformity developed in *Price Waterhouse*, principles that could be applied in a way to the context of employment discrimination involving transgender persons without treading on the binary sex concept. In the marriage cases, the courts need to deal with how to overcome the binary sex and heterosexual marriage concepts. When marriage is introduced, the concept of heterosexuality overwhelms the consideration of the science. The facts assimilate to the worldview rather than change the worldview. The idea of a person whose birth certificate assigns him to one sex marrying a person of the same sex causes the courts to blind themselves to the science presented.

The institution of marriage is a concept laden with social, biblical, and emotional baggage. Humans tend to be biased in favor of the ideas that they already possess and to engage in a variety of behaviors to avoid changing them, even to the point of irrationality (Baron 2000). If we are to take account of the new science, we need to override the highly developed mental magic tricks that help us maintain our original beliefs in the face of new data. We need to deal with the smoke and mirrors by creating new frameworks. To present those new frameworks to the court and achieve victories will not change cultural norms, but it will remove legal barriers that reinforce cultural norms.

Conclusion

The transgender cases illustrate how we are anchored to labeling humans as unambiguously male and female, losing the ability to recognize the complexity of sex and gender. The broad theories of human rights and gender nonconformity provide specific protection for transgender persons. These theories allowed the courts to bypass defining the terms "male" and "female." With regard to marriage, the cases are complex because they require courts to overcome both the binary definitions of male and female and their own bias in favor of heterosexuality. In the employment discrimination cases, the courts need only understand and accept the theory of gender stereotyping, a theory that has been developed and applied in other areas of employment discrimination. There is no need to tinker with heterosexuality to apply that theory to transgender plaintiffs.

The marriage cases have more bias to overcome, however. The data alone will not change minds. Courts have shown embedded fears of same-sex marriage in dealing with transgender couples, even if their relationships may be heterosexual. Thus, a transgender person's ability to marry becomes intertwined with the fate of same-sex marriage. Broader frames used to challenge these limitations benefit transgender persons, as well. For example, advocates litigating in the time between *Corbett* and *Goodwin* before the European Court of Human Rights successfully emphasized the destructive impact of foreclosing participation of transgender persons in society by denying them recognition in their self-identified sex. Similarly, the Massachusetts Supreme Court's ruling that the state may not deny same-sex couples the right to marry emphasized the centrality of marriage to economic, social, and emotional attachments and argued that the denial of access to that legal benefit is compounded by the reinforcement of the illegitimacy of relationships outside that circle (*Goodridge v. Department of Public Health* 2003). Limiting marriage—the current gold standard for state-recognized relationships—to heterosexual couples closes off access and opportunities for others to participate fully in society. A broader framework offers the opportunity to understand marriage in a context much larger and more realistic than the current focus on the nature of the sexual relationship. Stepping back and putting marriage in the larger context is one way to clarify the complexity and minimize the focus on heterosexuality, a viewpoint that would remove the barrier to a transgendered person's ability to marry.

PART III

Legal Symbols

Constraints and Possibilities

11 It Takes (at Least) Two to Tango

Fighting With Words in the Conflict Over Same-Sex Marriage

Shauna Fisher

> If it takes two to tango it takes at least two to "contend." That is, contentious politics always involves the mobilization of at least two groups of actors. We should be equally concerned with the processes and settings within which both sets of actors mobilize and especially interested in the unfolding patterns of interaction between the various parties to contention.
>
> —McAdam 1999, xiv

IMMEDIATELY FOLLOWING THE California Supreme Court's ruling in favor of same-sex marriage, on May 15, 2008, the Family Research Council issued a press release with the following statement: "The California Supreme Court has taken a jackhammer to the democratic process, and the right of the people to affect change in public policy."[1] On the same day, the Lambda Legal Defense and Education Fund issued a press release applauding the decision. "We're tremendously gratified that the Court today has fulfilled its traditional duty," said Jennifer Pizer, senior counsel for Lambda Legal.[2]

Two weeks before Massachusetts began issuing marriage licenses to same-sex couples, in 2004, Tony Perkins, president of the Family Research Council, was quoted as saying, "If the court's shotgun wedding takes place on that day, the rest of America will see that they had better speak up now. . . . This takes it from a Massachusetts problem to an American problem."[3] Two years later, following a Supreme Court ruling in New Jersey, David Beckel, a lawyer for Lambda Legal, reflected on the marriages that had been taking place in Massachusetts for more than two years: "The sky didn't fall. People see that some families are helped and nobody else's families are hurt."[4]

In the first set of arguments, the focus is on the democratic process and the appropriate role of courts and judges. The Family Research Council suggests that, in supporting same-sex marriage, the California Supreme Court has behaved antidemocratically, while Lambda Legal argues that the court is simply fulfilling its proper role in a democratic society. In the second set of arguments, Tony Perkins and David Beckel disagree about the extent to which issuing same-sex couples marriage licenses is a problem or is harmful to members of American society. These and similar arguments are interesting precisely because they are not specifically about the details of same-sex-marriage policy or policymaking. Instead, they represent moments in the same-sex-marriage debate when discourse was shifted to issues like democracy and social order.

Why would a group pursuing or opposing a particular policy that is important to them shift away from direct discussion of that issue? The way social movement groups talk about, or frame, an issue is an important technique for drawing attention to perceived injustices and shaping public agendas. Whether a proponent of same-sex marriage talks about the issue as one of discrimination and equal rights or as one that illustrates the proper role of courts in a democracy matters. As a result, the processes that shape social movement agendas are important to understand. A cause broadly defined by the pursuit of equality and the empowerment of a traditionally marginalized social group can target a number of different possible laws and practices (Shamir and Chinski 1998). Furthermore, any specific policy issue can be framed and defined in a variety of ways (Jones and Baumgartner 2005; Stone 1989). Research that studies social movement framing tends to focus on identifying frames at a particular point in time or on the endogenous processes and internal dynamics that result in group agendas and strategic framing (Meyer and Staggenborg 1996).

Provoked by the assertion of legal rights that challenge the status quo, opposition groups often mobilize in response to progressive rights claims. Competing for the same agenda space and public attention within a policy sphere, these groups also engage in strategic framing and issue definition. Too often, studies of social movement group discourse tend to focus either on the mobilization of progressive rights claims by (or on behalf of) marginalized groups *or* on the backlash and countermobilization. This chapter shifts away from movement-centric analysis to examine movement-countermovement interactions, with particular focus on interactive framing dynamics and how they shape social movement issue agendas.

In this chapter, I use the case of mobilization and countermobilization around the issue of same-sex marriage to highlight the dynamic, interactive character of social movement issue framing and definition. Specifically, I focus on the conflict that has developed over same-sex marriage. The growing visibility of gay, lesbian, bisexual, and transgendered (LGBT) individuals has resulted in a number of legal and political struggles that have generated opposition. However, no other decision has generated so contentious a cultural dispute as has the decision by LGBT organizations to pursue equal marriage rights. Almost immediately following the first favorable state court ruling on the issue of same-sex marriage, conservative groups and legislators began mobilizing in opposition. In the debate over a controversial policy issue, competition for control over the agenda space or issue definitions is particularly intense. The debate over same-sex marriage, therefore, provides a fruitful case with which to examine the interaction of the framing efforts of both sides.

Information in Politics and Fighting With Ideas

This chapter builds on the insights of scholars interested in the role of information and ideas in politics and policymaking. Ideas, knowledge, and meaning matter because they shape our understandings of reality. Central to much of this work is the recognition that information is uncertain, ambiguous, and multidimensional (Jones and Baumgartner 2005). In the context of policymaking, each interpretation of policy relevant information implies something different about the particular situation, the nature of the problem, the possible solutions, and/ or the possible groups that may be targeted and affected (Baumgartner and Jones 1993; Chong and Druckman 2007; Schneider and Ingram 1993; Stone 1989).

Scholars interested in social movements have examined the interpretative processes involved in collective mobilization. As Doug McAdam notes, such sensemaking processes are particularly important in the context of social movements because they "require participants to reject institutionalized routines and taken for granted assumptions about the world and to fashion new world views and lines of interaction" (1999, xxi). In other words, central to the development and evolution of movements is the shift and transformation of intersubjective perceptions about the world (Felstiner, Abel, and Sarat 1980–81; McAdam 1999; McCann 1994).

Social movement scholarship frequently uses the concept of framing to examine these intersubjective perceptions of information. Following Snow and Benford, a "frame" is defined as "an interpretive schemata that simplifies and condenses the 'world out there' by selectively punctuating and encoding objects, situations, events, experiences, and sequences of actions within one's present or past environment" (1992, 137; see also Chong and Druckman 2007; Kinder 1998). Frames select out and give weight or salience to particular issues and attributes in an effort to make sense of the wealth of information contained within the social and political world. Interpretive frames define problems, diagnose causes, make moral judgments, and suggest possible remedies (Entman 1993; Gamson 1992).[5] Collective action frames in particular are intended to inspire action and mobilization. Framing is the process through which social movement actors engage in this "signifying" behavior (Snow and Benford 1992). However, this behavior may not be consistent across the multiple actors and groups involved in a movement, as some may have different ideas of how best to frame the issue in question (Hull 2001; Javors and Reimann 2001).

Social movement actors must draw from existing ideological and cultural meanings in their sense-making activities. Ideology and culture act as both resources and constraints, providing the tools from which new meanings are constructed, as well as limiting the possible and probable meanings from which actors might draw (Ewick 2004, 85; see also Benford and Snow 2000; McCann 1994; Tarrow 1992, 189). In addition to ideological constraints, human beings suffer a number of cognitive limitations (Baumgartner and Jones 1993). Selective attention is the most important cognitive constraint that shapes politics and policymaking. Individuals can pay attention to only a limited number of things at a time; organizations and institutions suffer from these cognitive constraints, writ large (Jones 1994, 2001). Limited attention at an aggregate level implies a finite agenda space. Agenda setting—the process through which attention to issues is allocated and those issues are defined—therefore, is a hotly contested process.

Because of the nature of information, the limited nature of attention, and the limited space of the public agenda, it matters how policy issues are understood and constructed by different parties. Issue framing influences not only agenda access but also the issue dimensions that become the boundaries of choice and the evaluation of the problem. Shifts in the issue dimensions understood to be important regarding a policy issue have the potential to produce changes in public opinion (Chong and Druckman 2007). This generates opportunities for the strategic manipulation of ideas and information. Frames can be created and used by political actors in order to manipulate issue characteristics. Individuals and groups compete for the predominance and subsequent maintenance of social constructions which they perceive as strategically beneficial to them or, conversely, as harmful to the opposition (Haltom and McCann 2004; Stone 1989).

It Takes At Least Two to Contend

On the basis of prior research on the backlash in response to Native American treaty rights claims (Dudas 2003) and same-sex-marriage rights claims (Dugan 2005; Gerstmann 1999; Goldberg-Hiller 2002), we can expect the counter-mobilization to progressive rights claims to have a number of characteristics. First, opposition groups in these studies adopted and mobilized a language of "special" rights. In doing so, anticivil rights groups coopted the language of equal rights and interpreted rights claims by these marginalized groups as excessive and exclusive and as undermining an historical commitment to equality. Labeling certain rights claims as "special" rights delegitimizes them and sets them up in opposition to legitimate equal rights claims. By appealing to universal claims of abstract equality, such groups construct any apparently particular claims to civil rights as harmful to American political culture.

Second, parallel to arguments made in literature on legal mobilization and legal consciousness (Engel and Munger 2003; Ewick and Silbey 1998; McCann 1994; Silverstein 1996), the discourse used by opponents in the politics of backlash (re)shapes (and is shaped by) the constructions of the individual and group identities and interests of the majority. Third, the discourse of special rights transforms what are originally conflicts of interests and status into conflicts over American values. In an effort to avoid having to defend privilege, opponents justify resisting contemporary civil rights claims with appeals to sovereignty, popular control, security, equal opportunity, individual merit, the past, and traditional morality (Dudas 2003; Engel 1984; Goldberg-Hiller 2002). Furthermore, these are understood to be endangered by minority-rights mobilization. Finally, the discourse mobilized by opposition groups reverses majority and minority positions in the conflict. In the politics of backlash, special-rights talk highlights the opposition's sense of injury and attributes blame to marginalized populations (Dudas 2003). The opponents to civil rights claims come to understand themselves as the victimized, injured group needing protection and defending.

How might a group respond to the framing efforts of differently situated, or opposing, groups? Theoretically, they can do nothing and continue to advance their own issue frames and definitions. The social movement group can address the frame, attempting to deny or refute the issue definition advanced by the opposition, appropriating and reinterpreting the frame to suit their own ends, or responding with a counterframe. This interaction has been referred to as a "framing contest" (Benford and Snow 2000, 626). Finally, the group can shift its focus to a different dimension of the policy issue in debate in an effort to shift the public's attention to a different attribute of the issue (preferably one that would both appeal to the public and make it more difficult for the opposition to respond).

The struggle over meaning is at the center of social movement scholarship interested in framing and interpretive processes (Benford and Snow 2000). This motivates a focus on "narrative constructions motivated by an instrumental purpose or goal" (Haltom and McCann 2004, 271). With some exceptions (Dugan 2005; Ellingson 1995; Steinberg 1999), studies of this sort continue to remain fairly movement-centric, focusing on one or the other component of the struggle, highlighting the discourse mobilized in pursuit of progressive rights claims, or analyzing the ideas and meanings mobilized in the backlash (Dudas 2003; Goldberg-Hiller 2002; McCann 1994; Silverstein 1996). For scholars interested in the ongoing development of movements, the interaction and relationship between these discourses is important (Meyer and Staggenborg 1996). After all, it is the influence of the responses of other groups to a movement that in some ways separates the continuing evolution of the movement and its agenda from the early movement-building stages (McAdam 1999, 146).

Data and Methodology

In this chapter, I use newspaper coverage of the same-sex-marriage debate to analyze group framing of a controversial policy issue. News media are an important resource for social movement groups to use as they advance their favored understandings of an issue. My sample of newspaper articles was obtained using the Lexis-Nexis Academic Universe key word search. I selected two prominent pro-same-sex-marriage groups and two prominent anti-same-sex-marriage groups to include in the Lexis-Nexis search. The Lambda Legal Defense and Education Fund (Lambda) and Gay and Lesbian Advocates and Defenders (GLAD) were the two pro-same-sex-marriage groups I included in my search terms. Formed in 1973 and 1978, respectively, they are leading organizations in the national pursuit of equal rights for gay, lesbian, bisexual, transgender, and HIV-positive individuals. Lambda has been at the forefront of the issue of same-sex marriage since the establishment, in 1994, of the Marriage Project, headed by Lambda staff attorney Evan Wolfson (see Andersen 2005). GLAD has been involved since the filing of *Baker v. Nelson* in Vermont, in 1997.

The two opposition groups I included in my search terms were the American Family Association (AFA) and the Traditional Values Coalition (TVC). The AFA is a leading national conservative organization that was founded in 1977. The organization's broad goals include the furtherance of traditional family values and morality, with a focus on the influence of the media on society.[6] Founded in 1980, the TVC has become the nation's largest church lobby for most Christian denominations. Both groups have rather broad agendas but have devoted a substantial portion of their resources to, and drawn national attention because of, their opposition to same-sex marriage.[7]

My sampling strategy was constructed this way for two reasons. First, I am interested in group agendas and issue frames advanced by groups, not general coverage or media framing of an issue. If a frame or argument was not contained in a direct quote from a group representative, in a paraphrased quote or statement ("She said that . . .", "They said that . . .") or attributed to a group's published materials (Web site, pamphlet, case brief), it did not get recorded. Including the groups in my search ensured that a greater portion of my sample of articles would include mention of at least one group involved in the same-sex-marriage debate, thereby reducing the likelihood of irrelevant articles. Including the groups was also a way to refine my search in order to obtain a manageable sample. This type of Lexis-Nexis search has been used before for the purposes of obtaining data regarding the framing and argumentation associated with particular policy issues (Haltom and McCann 2004, Smith 2000).

The Lexis-Nexis search yielded a total of 193 unique, relevant domestic articles that contained at least one argument attributed to a specific group regarding

TABLE II.I
Sample of Groups Recorded as Having at Least One Argument
Attributed to Them with Regard to Same-Sex Marriage

Pro-same-sex marriage	Anti-same-sex marriage
Lambda Legal	American Family Association
Gay and Lesbian Advocates and Defenders	Traditional Values Coalition
Human Rights Campaign	Focus on the Family
Basic Rights Oregon	American Center for Law and Justice
Equality California	Concerned Women for America
Freedom to Marry Coalition	Christian Coalition
National Gay and Lesbian Task Force	Family Research Council
Ohioans for Growth and Equality	Ohio Campaign to Protect Marriage
Michigan Equality	Massachusetts Family Institute
Religious Coalition for the Freedom to Marry	Alliance for Traditional Marriage
Nebraska Advocates for Justice and Equality	Nebraska Coalition for the Protection of Marriage
Marriage Project	Defense of Marriage Coalition
American Civil Liberties Union	Alliance Defense Fund
Log Cabin Republicans	Campaign for Children and Families

same-sex marriage from November 5, 1989 (the date of the first hit) to November 30, 2007.[8] Appropriately, the period under study begins in the year that Lambda went public with the marriage debate that was taking place among its leadership and covers the time during which the most significant events took place at both the state and the national levels with regard to same-sex marriage.[9] Within this group, the number of articles per paper ranges from a single article in the *Buffalo News*, *Chicago Sun-Times*, *Christian Science Monitor*, *Hartford Courant*, and *San-Diego Union-Tribune* to 44 articles in the *San Francisco Chronicle*. The number of articles per year ranges from no articles in 1990, 1992, and 1994 to 63 articles in 2004.

I coded this sample of articles for argument frames regarding or related to same-sex marriage *attributed to specific groups*. I coded frames attributed to *any* specific group involved in the same-sex-marriage debate. These included the Human Rights Campaign, the National Gay and Lesbian Task Force, Focus on the Family, and Concerned Women for America, for example. The four groups—Lambda, GLAD, AFA, and TVC—were included in order to refine my search, not because I am interested particularly in the framing activities of these four national social movement organizations. I also recorded whether or not the group to which the argument was attributed was considered *for* or *against* same-sex marriage. For a list of groups recorded as pro- and anti- same-sex marriage, see Table 11.1. I am interested in how groups on either "side" define and frame the issue of same-sex marriage and how/whether those

TABLE II.2
Argument Frame Codebook and Counts

Frame	Description	Count	Pro	Anti
hetero-family	It's important to protect traditional heterosexual family structure	32	2	30
family	Gay and lesbian couples have stable families that love each other	11	11	0
children	Heterosexual marriage is in the best interest of children/same-sex couples have children that need protecting	37	9	28
love	Marriage is about love and personal freedom and choice	14	13	1
discrimination	It is wrong to discriminate/fairness	52	44	8
benefits	Gay and lesbian couples need economic and legal benefits/legal equality	77	74	3
rights	Marriage is a civil rights issue/should not be compared to the civil rights movement/basic rights/equal rights	59	44	15
special rights	Same-sex marriage is not about equal rights but is about special rights	12	0	12
portability	Marriage is a portable institution/don't force states to recognize/ state's right to recognize or ban same-sex marriage	23	9	14
legal	Frame questions legality/constitutionality of same-sex marriage and same-sex marriage laws and bans	35	24	11
threat	Same-sex marriage is no threat to heterosexual marriage and society	33	33	0
diversion	Same-sex marriage is a divisive wedge issue/campaign to prohibit diverts attention from more important issues	41	40	1
status	Marriage gives equal social status to same-sex couples/ alternatives to marriage relegate couples to second-class status	35	35	0
morality	Same-sex marriage is immoral/against God's will and religious values/ no church would be forced to recognize same-sex marriage	51	6	45
culture	Same-sex marriage threatens traditional American values and culture	15	2	13
slippery slope	Slippery slope/same-sex marriage will cause disorder, lead to other bad things	25	0	25
public	The public is opposed to same-sex marriage/public opinion is changing in regards to same-sex marriage/ democratic representation	90	14	76
judges	Same-sex marriage is the work of activist judges/ judges are doing their job by protecting minority rights	33	9	24
institution	Must protect the institution of marriage/marriage is the foundation of society/redefinition of marriage	85	1	84
nature	Same-sex relationships are unnatural/harmful	35	2	33
market	Denial of marriage rights would hurt market, businesses, states	3	3	0
	Totals	798	375	423

definitions and frames change over time, both independently and in response to the opposition's framing.

Arguments regarding same-sex marriage were coded into one of 21 separate argument frames. One of the main concerns when content coding is whether or not the possible coding categories are exhaustive and mutually exclusive (Babbie 2001). However, my list of arguments was finalized only after coding all of the articles, as I occasionally encountered an argument frame that I did not originally anticipate.[10] This allowed me to capture more of the discussion regarding same-sex marriage than I would have been able to do had I not allowed the development of new frames while reading the articles and also helped to ensure the categories are exhaustive (Stenger 2005). I used quasi-sentences as my unit of observation in order to reduce the concern that categories of frames were being collapsed or merged, a concern that would have been more prominent if I had chosen to code entire paragraphs or whole documents. An individual article could have an essentially unlimited number of frames, but only one argument frame was recorded for any single sentence. If more than one argument frame was used in a single sentence, the dominant frame of that sentence was recorded. This was determined on the basis of two factors: the proportion of the sentence devoted to each frame and which frame was mentioned first. While these 21 different arguments could be collapsed into fewer more general frames for purposes different from my own, I use "argument frame" to refer to these more specific arguments made in the same-sex-marriage debate (Stenger 2005).

I coded a total of 798 statements framing or defining same-sex marriage. The number of arguments per article ranged from 1 to 22. Of the total arguments coded, 375 were attributed to groups in favor of same-sex marriage and 423 were attributed to groups opposed to same-sex marriage. The list of argument frames can be found in Table 11.2.

The Same-Sex-Marriage Debate

The distribution of total argument frames over the time period is consistent with the events that have unfolded related to same-sex marriage since the early 1990s. Public policy literature has long acknowledged the potential agenda-setting effects that events can have (Baumgartner and Jones 1993; Birkland 1997; Kingdon 1995). Birkland has defined a focusing event as an event "that is sudden; relatively uncommon; can be reasonably defined as harmful or revealing the possibility of potentially greater future harms; has harms that are concentrated in a particular geographical area or community of interest; and that is known to policy makers and the public simultaneously" (1998, 54). Such events are often dramatic and draw greater elite and mass attention to an issue. The public typically learns about

FIGURE II.I
Distribution Counts of Frame Arguments Across
Sampled Time Period, 1989–2007

such events through the mass media, where "news imperatives make sudden, novel, and injurious events particularly attractive to news coverage" (Birkland 1997, 30; Kingdon 1995). The events frequently discussed in this literature are things like natural disasters and major accidents (e.g., hurricanes, oil spills) that generate some visible physical damage. However, events like judicial decisions, acts of civil disobedience, and the introduction of legislation may also be or seem sudden, dramatic, or novel and may be perceived as harmful to a particular community or communities. They are also similarly amenable to news coverage.

Figure II.I shows the distribution of the 375 argument frames attributed to pro-same-sex-marriage groups and the 423 argument frames attributed to anti-same-sex-marriage groups. During most years, the number of argument frames attributed to pro- and to anti-same-sex-marriage groups is approximately equal. While the sample contained articles dating back to 1989, the majority of my sample, and the resulting coded argument frames, are from 1996 or later.

It is not surprising that the first major peak in Figure II.I occurs in 1996. Concerned about the implications of a decision in favor of same-sex marriage, Senator Don Nickles introduced the Defense of Marriage Act (DOMA) in May 1996, while the trial court decision in *Baehr v. Lewin* (1993 74 Haw. 530) was pending.[11] After the bill received overwhelming support in Congress, President Clinton signed it (28 USCS 1738C) into law on September 21, 1996, in the midst of his campaign for reelection. Meanwhile, legislation mirroring DOMA was introduced in a majority of state legislatures and passed in 14 states in 1996 alone. On December 3, 1996, the Hawai'ian trial court decided in favor of the same-sex couples, agreeing with the Supreme Court's decision that prohibiting same-sex marriage was unconstitutional and arguing that the state of Hawai'i had failed to demonstrate a "compelling state interest" to justify such sex-based discrimination.[12]

The second major peak in Figure 11.1, spanning 2003, 2004, and 2005, covers a period during which there was an abundance of activity related to same-sex marriage at the local, state, and national levels. At the national level, efforts to pass a Federal Marriage Amendment defining marriage as between only opposite-sex couples intensified and gained increasing attention. In 2003, the U.S. Supreme Court handed down its decision in *Lawrence v. Texas*, overturning the remaining state sodomy laws as unconstitutional. Justice Scalia lamented the decision, expressing in his dissent his fear that it removed the final legal barrier to same-sex marriage, a sentiment echoed by conservative groups and politicians shortly after (123 S. Ct. 2472).

At the state level, the Massachusetts Supreme Judicial Court ruled in favor of same-sex marriage on November 18, 2003 (*Goodridge v. Department of Public Health* 2003, 440 Mass. 309), and on May 17, 2004, marriage licenses were legally given to same-sex couples for the first time in the United States. On February 10, one week after the advisory opinion in *Goodridge* (2004 SJC-09163), San Francisco mayor Gavin Newsom ordered city officials to begin issuing marriage licenses (Lahey and Alderson 2004, 65). City officials in a number of cities followed his lead and issued marriage licenses to same-sex couples shortly thereafter. The actions of these city officials set off a wave of litigation regarding same-sex marriage. That year, voters in Missouri and Louisiana approved amendments to their state constitutions during their primary elections.[13] Voters in another 11 states approved constitutional amendments during the general election later that year.[14] Immediately following the election, some blamed same-sex marriages in Massachusetts, Gavin Newsom's actions in California, and the subsequent ballot measures for drawing conservatives voting for "moral values" to the polls, costing John Kerry, the Democratic presidential nominee, the election.[15]

The tail of the last major peak shows a decline in salience for the issue of same-sex marriage as the events following *Goodridge* moved further into the past. Marriage proponents suffered a handful of setbacks during this period. The Washington state Supreme Court ruled against same-sex marriage in July 2006 (*Anderson v. King County*). Later that year, the New Jersey Supreme Court ruled that same-sex couples must be granted all the benefits and responsibilities of marriage but allowed the state legislature to choose between marriage and civil unions (*Lewis v. Harris*).[16] Several court cases were pending during these two years, as well. Oral arguments were heard in the Connecticut case *Kerrigan v. Commissioner of Public*

Health in May 2007. Case briefs were also filed in 2007 by proponents of same-sex marriage in California (*In re Marriage Cases*). Such activities are likely to mobilize less attention from both proponents and opponents of the issue.

The framing peaks seen in Figure 11.1 around these events are a result of the interaction of two forces. First, the institutional constraints of the media necessarily influence the data I collected. The space available in newspapers (as well as the number of journalists available to write articles) is limited, requiring papers to make decisions about which issues to pay attention to. Events like historical court cases focus attention on policy issues; naturally, if the issue is particularly contested or controversial, newspapers will be motivated to cover it (Patterson 1993). Second, such events also encourage social movement groups to engage in instrumental activity, particularly strategic framing. Strategic framing activities result in not only fluctuations in the number of frames but also variations in their content. This is especially true when groups perceive that they're verging on success (Chong 1991). The next section of this chapter examines the types of argument frames used by groups involved in the same-sex-marriage debate.

Framing in the Same-Sex-Marriage Debate

Statements that frame same-sex marriage using the language of rights are predominantly advanced by pro-same-sex-marriage groups. If we compare Figure 11.2 with Figure 11.1, we find that rights-related frames were among those most consistently adopted by pro-same-sex-marriage groups. Such frames were advanced by groups pursuing same-sex marriage in all but 2 of the 15 years (1989 and 2002) during which there were any coded frames in my sample.

The backlash opposing progressive civil rights claims is in many ways itself a form of rights mobilization (Dudas 2003; Goldberg-Hiller 2002). Seventy-one statements in the sample used the language of rights to frame the issue of same-sex marriage. Twelve of these statements, advanced by opposition groups, referred to same-sex marriage as an excessive, unnecessary "special right." The remaining statements used an equal rights or civil rights frame to talk about same-sex marriage. Not surprisingly, the majority of these were attributed to pro-same-sex-marriage groups. While conceptually distinct enough to require its own code, framing the issue in terms of discrimination is closely related to making an argument about equal rights. The majority of these frames, 44, were advanced by pro-same-sex-marriage groups, but 8 statements using a discrimination frame were advanced by opposition groups. Figure 11.2 displays the distribution of these frames over time.

Along with framing same-sex marriage as a basic right and an equal rights issue, pro-same-sex-marriage activists have made connections to the civil rights movement and the struggle to overcome miscegenation laws that banned interracial marriages.

FIGURE II.2
Distribution of Statements Using Rights or Rights-related Argument Frames

The graph combines the discrimination, rights, and special rights frames

For example, following the Senate's approval of DOMA, the head of the Massachusetts Gay and Lesbian Political Caucus expressed his disappointment: "I kept thinking how prejudice and homophobia won today in Congress. . . . I just wish the senators knew their history—up until a few decades ago interracial marriage was illegal."[17]

Opposition groups have responded by denying the analogy to the civil rights movement. Allowing interracial marriages to take place, opposition activists argue, "didn't redefine the institution of marriage. . . . This is not about equal rights. It's not about civil rights. It's about people living in sin and trying to be justified by a society that says it's wrong."[18] In particular, they criticize any comparisons between race and sexuality. "You don't base a constitutional protection upon the sex partners that somebody may choose," said attorney Benjamin Bull of the Alliance Defense Fund, following the same-sex weddings that took place in San Francisco. "We fought a Civil War in which hundreds of thousands of Americans died to end race discrimination, to end slavery . . . gays as a class . . . have incredible freedom and rights. They have the same rights that I or any other heterosexual has. They can even get married. They just cannot marry a same-gender person."[19] Rights-related framing by pro-same-sex-marriage activists has motivated opposition groups to coopt the language of rights and to respond with counterframes and arguments.

There are a number of instances, however, where framing by anti-same-sex-marriage groups has motivated pro-same-sex-marriage groups to respond with

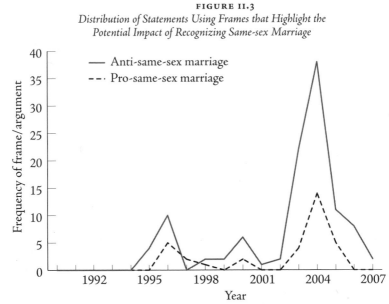

FIGURE II.3

*Distribution of Statements Using Frames that Highlight the
Potential Impact of Recognizing Same-sex Marriage*

The graph combines the threat, slippery slope, and institution frames

counterframes. The most obvious evidence for the influence of opposition framing on pro-same-sex-marriage group framing is in the presence of the *threat*
frame advanced by pro-same-sex-marriage groups. In the sample, pro-same-sex-
marriage groups made 33 statements defining same-sex marriage as posing no
threat to society or to heterosexual marriage. We would not expect to encounter
such arguments if not for the opposition's efforts to frame same-sex marriage as
a threat to the foundation of society and as a change that would result in social
chaos and disorder. The distribution of these argument frames over the time
period is illustrated in Figure 11.3.

Opposition groups most frequently framed same-sex marriage in terms of its
potential impacts on the institution of marriage, making 84 statements defining the issue in these terms (*institution*).[20] The first of these appeared in 1995
and came from Robert Knight, director of the Family Research Council. His
statement begins with a counterargument to the use of a discrimination frame
by LGBT groups. "The law doesn't discriminate against homosexuals," he said.
"It merely says that each sex must be represented in marriage. Same-sex couples
do not qualify. It might be called a partnership, but if it's called marriage, it's a
counterfeit version. And counterfeit versions drive out the real thing."[21] Following
the Supreme Court decision in *Lawrence v. Texas*, in 2003, that overturned the
1986 decision in *Bowers v. Hardwick*, conservatives cited Justice Scalia's dissent to
support their fears that the ruling would result in same-sex marriage. Ken Con-

nor, president of the Family Research Council, expressed these fears: "This case will be ammunition for a full-scale assault on the institution of marriage by the homosexual lobby. . . . What this decision will be used to do is to try to deconstruct marriage, as Justice Scalia recognized in his dissent, and to empty the word of any meaning."[22]

Opposition groups made 25 more general statements framing same-sex marriage as a "gateway" or slippery slope to disorder and other social ills (*slippery slope*). Opposition groups have argued that if the institution of marriage is expanded to include couples of the same sex, then there will be nothing to stop people seeking legalization of other, less desirable, relationship arrangements. "Why not three men? Three women? A man and a boy?" Robert Knight has asked.[23] "We don't want it left up to states. Otherwise you'll have bedlam in this country. You'll have cases hanging out of your nostrils," Sheldon said.[24]

While such frames are obviously dominated by anti-same-sex-marriage groups, pro–same-sex-marriage groups made 33 statements recorded in the sample in which they denied such alleged harmful impacts (*threat*). The first of these occurs in 1996, a year after the first of the impact-related frames was advanced by an anti-same-sex-marriage group. In response to the opposition's use of phrases like "homosexual extremist," Evan Wolfson of Lambda Legal and Freedom to Marry asked, "They're [same-sex couples] so extreme, they want to get married. My God. Who are they threatening? What is the harm here?"[25] Similar statements were frequently attributed to Evan Wolfson. Two weeks before marriage licenses were issued to same-sex couples in Massachusetts, he was quoted as saying, "When the dust settles, we'll see that no one is hurt, families are helped, gays did not use up all the marriage licenses, and there's enough marriage to share."[26] He was not alone, of course. "The minute you pose the question to somebody, 'How will this hurt you?,' they never have an answer," Matt Foreman, head of the National Gay and Lesbian Task Force, said in an article published the day before same-sex-marriage licenses were issued in Massachusetts. "As this discussion has gone on and people have seen these images of regular people thrilled to be married, it has dispelled the myth and a lot of the fear around same-sex marriage."[27] Arguably, pro-same-sex-marriage groups would not have to frame the issue as unharmful if not for the opposition's efforts to frame same-sex marriage as harmful and dangerous.

Closely related to those issue frames in Figure 11.3 are those that define the issue of same-sex marriage in terms of family values and children. The distribution of these argument frames is illustrated in Figure 11.4. Again, these frames are dominated by anti-same-sex-marriage groups, with 30 statements (*hetero-family*) arguing that the traditional heterosexual family structure needs protecting and 28 related statements (*children*) arguing that such a structure is in the best inter-

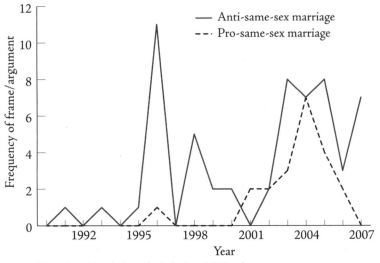

FIGURE II.4

Distribution of Statements Using Family and Children Related Frames

The graph combines the hetero-family, family, and children frames

est of children.[28] Only 9 statements attributed to pro-same-sex-marriage groups frame the issue in terms of the children of same-sex couples (children), and 11 statements frame the issue in terms of gay and lesbian families (*family*). This imbalance was particularly evident during the first part of the time period. Through 2000, there were only two statements (one each of *children* and *family*) associated with family and children attributed to pro-same-sex-marriage groups. Beginning in 2001, while such frames were still favored by opposition groups, the use of related frames by pro-same-sex-marriage groups became visibly more frequent.

The distribution of these frames over time suggests that opposition groups adopted family- and child-related frames prior to the serious use of similar frames by pro-same-sex-marriage groups. The highest peak, in 1996, reflects the fact that the relationships among marriage, family, and children were key issues in the debates surrounding DOMA, as well as in the same-sex-marriage case in Hawai'i. Central to the state's defense in *Baehr v. Miike* was that it had an interest in protecting heterosexual marriage for the sake of the well-being of children. A key component of the court's decision involved discussion of the medical and psychological studies and evidence presented by both sides. Following the ruling, Robert Knight referenced "the mountain of evidence that kids do best with a mother and father present."[29] According to Glenn Stanton, policy analyst for Focus on the Family, "The different-gendered unit is a self-contained unit. . . . It has everything a child needs."[30] Some opposition groups go further, suggesting that exposure to same-sex couples and parents will confuse children. A pastor from a church in Fresno, California, that is opposed to same-sex marriage argued, "The kids are the ones who are left trying to figure out what's life all about. They're saying, 'Now my dad is wearing a dress and getting his facial hair burned off, trying to get that figured out so he can do whatever he's going to do, and I'm supposed to figure out what's normal in my life.' And there's nothing normal about it."[31]

Speaking in support of the introduction of the Defense of Marriage Act, Gary Bauer, president of the Family Research Council, argued, "Without defending our nation against the current threat of a redefinition of marriage, the traditional family unit will never be the same."[32] Arguments about the traditional family and development of children are obviously closely related. A statement from Len Deo, president of the New Jersey Family Policy Council, following the filing of a lawsuit in New Jersey, captures this: "Marriage between a man and a woman has stood the test of time for thousands of years. . . . It creates the best environment for raising children and traditionally carries the benefits that help create a stable family."[33]

In response to opposition efforts to frame the issue as one about family and children, pro-same-sex-marriage groups and same-sex couples began to point to their own children and families. "We share the aspirations of any couple who wants to marry and have a family," said one of the women represented by GLAD in the lawsuit filed in Massachusetts. "I wish the governor could come to our house and see how we get ready to go to work and school in the mornings or how we get our daughter to her karate lessons. . . . She would see a family that's very much like hers, in almost every way."[34] One of the couples represented by Lambda in the lawsuit filed in New Jersey expressed similar sentiments. "We're good citizens, we pay our taxes and one of us always waits for the kids to get off the school bus. . . . In many ways we embody the ideal of American family values, so why can't we have the same rights to raise our family as everyone else?"[35] This is not to suggest that groups pursuing same-sex marriage would have refrained from framing the issue in terms of same-sex couples' families and children if the opposition had not used such frames. Family, children, and the institution of marriage have long been closely related issues. However, the fact that pro-same-sex-marriage groups adopted family- and children-related frames later than did opposition groups suggests that the former may have increased its use of such frames in order to respond to the efforts of the latter.

The issue of same-sex marriage has generated debates over not only traditional family values but American values associated with democracy (Hull 2001). Associated with the relationship between majority and minority populations and the role of various policymaking branches, such frames are heavily favored by the

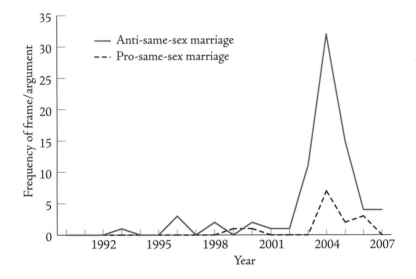

FIGURE 11.5
Distribution of Mentions of the Public Frame Across Time

countermobilizing forces. The second most numerous frame used by anti-same-sex-marriage groups is the *public* frame. Opposition groups made 76 statements that framed same-sex marriage as an issue to which the majority of the public was largely opposed, while pro-same-sex-marriage groups made 14 statements related to public opinion and attitudes toward the issue. The distribution of this frame over time is illustrated in Figure 11.5. The peak in 2004 is a reflection of the battles over constitutional amendments that took place at that time in 13 states. The justifications advanced by amendment supporters in many states for having the public vote on the issue were framed in terms of democratic beliefs about majority rule. Soon after, lawsuits were filed in several states over the language of the voter-approved amendments. Those conflicts are reflected in the second highest peak, that in 2005.

Closely related to the *public* frame is the *judges* frame. The distribution of this frame over time is shown in Figure 11.6. Opposition groups made 24 statements framing the issue as one imposed on the public by activist judges. While not accounted for in this chapter, the "activist judges" claim has been particularly popular with elites and politicians. In response, there were 9 statements attributed to groups in favor of same-sex marriage that defended the activities of courts on the issue. The *judges* frame is an example of a frame generated in response to an important event. Opposition groups exploited the opportunity presented by the Hawai'ian trial court ruling in favor of same-sex marriage to raise the issue

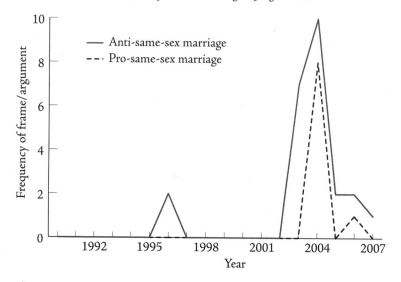

FIGURE 11.6

Distribution of Statements Using the Judges Frame

of the proper role of courts and judges in a democracy. The first peak in Figure 11.6 reflects the discussion following the decision in Hawai'i in 1996. The peaks in 2003 and 2004 reflect the discussion leading up to and following the Massachusetts Supreme Judicial Court decision in *Goodridge* in 2003 and the resulting issuance of marriage licenses to same-sex couples in 2004.

The *public* and *judges* frame categories, as they are used by opposition groups, transform the debate about equal marriage rights into one about respecting the roles of democratic institutions and their responsibilities in relation to democratic majorities or publics. Often, they are used together. "Unelected judges have usurped the power of the Legislature in the case of marriage. . . . Let the people vote on the definition of marriage," said Ronald A. Crews, spokesman for the Coalition for Marriage, at a rally intended to pressure the Massachusetts legislature to approve a constitutional amendment banning same-sex marriage.[36] Opposition groups have accused judges who have made positive rulings on the issue of same-sex marriage of overstepping their powers, imposing their will on the public, and being "activist." Following the decision in *Baehr v. Miike* in 1996, groups opposed to same-sex marriage accused Judge Chang (the Hawai'ian trial court judge who issued the ruling) of engaging in "judicial tyranny."[37] Similar accusations continue to be made about the judges on Massachusetts Supreme Judicial Court who decided *Goodridge*. "In today's judicial climate, no law is safe," said Don Wildmon, chairman of the American Family Association. "You've

always got judges in Massachusetts or somewhere who think they are above the law."[38]

In 2004, Lambda Legal initiated an advertising campaign in several states in an effort to counter the opposition groups' arguments about "activist judges." "Our major goal is to reshape the public discussion, so that people know judges are doing the right thing," said Kevin Cathcart, executive director of Lambda Legal, with regard to the campaign.[39] According to an article from the *Houston Chronicle* (Texas was one of the several states targeted, in part to counter the backlash that resulted from the Supreme Court's ruling in *Lawrence v. Texas* the previous year), the campaign hoped "to spread the message that the judiciary has a critical role to play in the government, which was divided into three branches so they could check and balance each other."[40] "They [anti-same-sex-marriage groups] are dressing up their bigotry with arguments about democracy, and they pretend that the courts should not have made this [*Goodridge v. Department of Public Health*] decision, but they would not have objected to the court making the decision if the court had decided their way," said Arline Isaacson, executive committee member of MassEquality. "It is fundamentally un-American for the tyranny of the majority to determine the rights of any minority. That's what this country was raised on. You don't have popularity contests about who is equal under the law."[41]

The *judges* frame is a fairly clear example of the influence of opposition framing efforts on the framing activities of pro-same-sex-marriage groups for two reasons. Groups in favor of same-sex marriage did not begin to defend courts and judges until 2004, after anti-same-sex-marriage groups began popularizing the "activist judges" argument. The meanings associated with the frame further suggest this influence. Pro-same-sex-marriage groups responded by referring to courts as protectors of minority rights that are simply fulfilling their proper role by recognizing equal marriage rights. LGBT rights organizations probably would not have decided to advance such an argument without conservatives' attacks on courts.

Interactive Framing Dynamics

Using content analysis of newspaper articles on same-sex marriage, this chapter illustrates that the framing agendas of competing social movement groups are interrelated. The framing efforts of competing groups interact to generate the evolving debates about policy issues. The framing patterns highlighted in this chapter show that groups supportive of and opposed to same-sex marriage have responded to the issue frames advanced by the other side. There are several instances where a particular argument frame is dominated by one side of the conflict, but a few cases exist where the argument frame is attributed to groups on the other side. Thus, differently situated groups engaged in framing contests

FIGURE 11.7

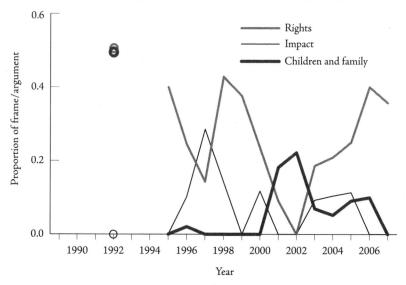

The Proportion of All Argument Frames Advanced by Pro Same-sex Marriage Groups
Represented by the Rights/Discrimination and Children/Family Categories

respond to one another. These responses are important, particularly if they cause groups to shift their focus from other favored argument frames. Another way to examine interactive framing dynamics is to look at the patterns in the proportions of argument frames used by groups over time.

In some years, pro-same-sex-marriage groups' responses to particular frames pushed other potentially favored frames out of their side of the debate. Examining the framing patterns in Figures 11.3, 11.4, 11.5, and 11.6 suggests that the groups mobilized in opposition to same-sex marriage have set a substantial portion of the same-sex-marriage agenda. The aspects of the same-sex-marriage debate that highlight family and children, the potential impacts of recognizing same-sex marriage, and the relationship between institutions and the public in a democracy have largely been raised by groups opposed to same-sex marriage. For example, pro-same-sex-marriage groups advanced more threat/impact frames in 1997 than rights and discrimination frames (the third and fourth most frequent frames attributed to pro-same-sex-marriage groups) combined. In 2001 and 2002, pro-same-sex-marriage groups advanced a greater proportion of children- and family-related frames than rights and discrimination frames. This is illustrated in Figure 11.7. Between 2003 and 2006, the proportion of rights/discrimination frames put forth by pro-same-sex-marriage groups was lower than it was before 2000.

FIGURE II.8

Measure of Dispersion Across Frames

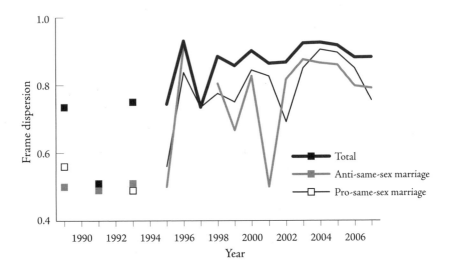

Measure of dispersion (1-Herfindahl) across all frames, across frames attributed to pro same-sex marriage groups, and across frames attributed to anti same-sex marriage groups, 1989-2007. The absence of a point for a year indicates no frame for that year. Note that the left axis does not begin at 0; rather, since none of the calculated values fall below 0.4, the axis is truncated in order to better show the variation in the measure.

Another result of pro-same-sex-marriage groups' responding to the frames used by opposition groups is an increase in the variety of frames present in the debate at any time. If frames are not abandoned when new ones are adopted, then the debate becomes spread out across increasingly greater numbers of arguments. Calculation of a measure of dispersion of frames across the time period suggests that this is true for the same-sex-marriage debate. These dispersion measures are shown in Figure II.8.[42] Values close to zero indicate that the same-sex-marriage debate is concentrated on one or a few frames. Values close to one indicate the debate is dispersed across many frames.[43]

The measure for all of the frames is consistently high across years, particularly beginning in and after 1996. The highest dispersion value for all of the frames is for 1996, where 19 of the 21 coded argument frames were present in the same-sex-marriage debate. The next highest dispersion value for all of the frames was found for 2004, when all of the 21 argument frames were represented in my sample. The highest dispersion value for frames attributed to anti-same-sex-marriage groups was also for 1996, when 13 of the coded argument frames were advanced by groups opposed to same-sex marriage. The value for frames attributed to pro-same-sex-marriage groups was high for 1996, but the highest value occurred for 2004, when

16 of the argument frames were advanced by groups in favor of same-sex marriage. The effect of adopting frames in response to opposition groups, such as the *impact* and *childfam* frames, is to make the arguments of pro-same-sex-marriage groups less focused over time.

The heightened framing activity surrounding important events is largely responsible for the peaks and increases in the measure of dispersion over the period seen in Figure 11.8. In many ways, 1996 marked the introduction of the issue of same-sex marriage into the national agenda, particularly with the introduction and passage of the Defense of Marriage Act. In response to this, differently situated groups in relation to the issue wanted to take the opportunity during these earlier stages of conflict to pursue and test a wide variety of issue frames with the public. It was an especially critical year for the opposition, as the passage of DOMA legitimized its goals and further mobilized conservative and religious groups. With the exception of 1997, we find consistently high values for the measure of dispersion after 1996, suggesting that no single frame category dominated the same-sex-marriage debate after this year. The approval of same-sex marriage in Massachusetts made 2004 an especially important year for groups pursuing same-sex-marriage rights. Of course, 2003 and 2004 were also important years for the opposition, as the activities in Massachusetts, San Francisco, and other places confirmed the opposition's fears that same-sex marriage would become a reality.

Conclusion

This chapter examines the influence of countermobilization on the evolution of social movement agendas, with particular emphasis on social movement issue framing. Framing is a complex social process that takes place among dynamic social groups. However, research that studies social movement framing tends to focus on identifying frames at a particular point in time or on the endogenous processes and internal dynamics that result in group agendas and strategic framing. For example, several works have been written on the complex internal dynamics—the interactions among lawyers, group leaders, members, and funding sources—and their interactions with broader political and social changes in the evolution of the NAACP and other group agendas in the civil rights movement (Andersen 2005; Goluboff 2003; Tushnet 1987). Too little attention has been paid to countermobilization, despite acknowledgment that the mobilization of opposition groups clearly changes the broader political and social context and climate (McAdam 1999; McAdam, Tarrow, and Tilly 2001; Meyer and Staggenborg 1996).

Attention to issue framing by competing groups is important because argumentation is at the heart of policymaking. Framing matters because it affects "the attitudes and behaviors of [its] audiences" (Chong and Druckman 2007, 109). Baumgartner and Leech note that "groups are most influential when they can be effective in promoting a particular issue definition." Such activity is "dedicated in large part to directing limited attention to particular pieces of information or particular aspects of an issue. These efforts at agenda setting, issue definition, and framing do more to determine winners and losers in politics than any arm-twisting before the final roll-call vote" (Baumgartner and Leech 1998, 178). In a policy conflict, groups' issue definitions do not win or lose on their own merits but do so relative to the other alternatives.

A result of many of the frames advanced by anti-same-sex-marriage groups is that direct discussion of the original policy issue in question is actually avoided. The discourse advanced by opposition groups has tended to shift the debate to broader, more abstract issues like democracy, social order, culture, and religion/morality or God's will. Some of the most commonly used frames by anti-same-sex-marriage groups are *public, morality,* and *slippery slope.* Furthermore, using these frames, opposition groups have controlled a substantial portion of the same-sex-marriage debate. The continued reluctance of portions of society to accept the idea of same-sex marriage is evidence of the success of the democracy and morality frames relative to rights-and benefits-related frames. If LGBT groups have difficulty controlling the debate with their preferred frames and the actual issue of same-sex marriage fails to get discussed, that has important implications for group strategies as they continue to pursue same-sex-marriage rights.

12 Do Civil Rights Have a Face?

Reading the Iconography of Special Rights

Jonathan Goldberg-Hiller

THIS CHAPTER EXPLORES the aesthetics of an emergent move-
ment in the United States that has most recently politicized, opposed, and limited
same-sex marriage. Organized by conservative religious groups and Republican
politicians, its call for law reform has become increasingly popularized through
new political themes designed to modulate the value of rights and the place of law
in efforts to roll back or prevent advances in gay rights. Seen broadly, the effort to
reign in the courts seeks to rearrange the very scheme of government in favor of
one with fewer legal restrictions on majority power, and it builds and motivates
its majorities in its voiced outrage over excessive rights. This movement's reflexive
and sovereign logic linking marriage rights to democratic authority—and social
movement activists to a broader electorate—is my focus. I suggest that this link-
age has a significant aesthetic dimension evident in its public campaigns that has
given civil rights a new face.

Aesthetics underscores the ways in which legal and political norms are assimilated and performed by activists as a commitment to a new ideal of justice embedded in a fundamental common sense. Exposing more than a tactical and rhetorical politics, aesthetics situates the scholar's gaze beyond the collective dynamics
of, or the resource bases for, social movement development. Aesthetics concerns
itself with the forms of life in which this popular sovereignty is invested and the
broad cultural contexts surrounding movement efforts to create and control these
worlds of meaning. Aesthetics involves the "images, tropes, perceptions, and sensibilities that help shape the creation, apprehension, and even identity of human
endeavors, including . . . law" (Schlag 2002, 1050), or what the political theorist
Jacques Rancière has called "the distribution of the sensible."

> Aesthetics . . . is a delimitation of spaces and times, of the visible and the invisible,
> of speech and noise, that simultaneously determines the place and the stakes of
> politics as a form of experience. Politics revolves around what is seen and what can
> be said about it, around who has the ability to see and the talent to speak, around
> the properties of spaces and the possibilities of time. (Rancière 2004b, 13)

Aesthetics can be understood in this sense to have always been a part of the
legal imagination, for what makes law legitimate to many is the patterning of

time, space, speech, and silence that makes law look enduring and just. Despite law's naturalization through these frameworks, divergent constellations or aesthetic regimes have often been caught up in larger political projects, resuscitating the importance of aesthetics for new forms of popular sovereignty.

Aesthetics is significant for social movements but not only as a tactic for political change. The aesthetic realm "is not political owing to the messages and feelings that it conveys on the state of social and political issues. Nor is it political owing to the way it represents social structures, conflicts or identities. It is political by virtue of the very distance that it takes with respect to those functions" (Rancière 2004a), a distance that allows new political schemas and competing arrangements of democratic sovereignty to become cognizable. The contemporary politics of distancing associated with the anti-same-sex-marriage movement, I argue in this chapter, increasingly relies upon an iconography to authorize what can be said and seen and known, and it is around the icon that it discovers its limit. It is an aesthetic of rights that has hovered in the very recent past on the borders between life and death, citizenship and private life, the married family and Terri Schiavo.

In what follows, I discuss and then further illustrate the relationship between the mobilization of popular sovereignty and aesthetics. My illustrations are mostly drawn from advertisements and public discourse involved in the campaigns around federal and statewide amendments against same-sex marriage in 2004 and are selected here for their representation of dominant themes that emerge from my national research. I add a discussion of the political struggles to end the state court jurisdiction over the case of Terri Schiavo in 2005 in order to explore where such aesthetics begin to fail in their efforts to create a sovereign form of life. I find the reason for this failure in the particular iconography of marriage that has been propounded in the same-sex-marriage campaigns, and I use this to speculate on the weakness of progressive attempts to use the same register of appeal. Finally, I draw some lessons for contemporary social movement struggles.

Sovereignty and Aesthetics

The implicit values of equality and nondiscrimination against which lesbian and gay identities and demands are assessed have displaced medicalized pathologies and dogmatic moralism, opening up the very possibility of rights claims (Fortin 1995). Parallel to these discursive developments, a growing social acceptance of many of the political demands of gays and lesbians has emerged. Strong public support for employment antidiscrimination protection is regularly voiced in opinion polls (Avery et al. 2007). Employers frequently grant benefits for same-sex partners, and unions increasingly bargain for these advances (Hunt 1999; Santora

2001). Cultural acknowledgment of gays and lesbians has become commonplace (Seidman 2002). With this background, sexual minorities' access to civil rights, recently ensured by many courts, would seem to be embedded in common sense.

Despite this growing liberalization—indeed, in its very enunciation—the public discourse of antidiscrimination frequently declares the limits to the acceptable. For nearly every voice supporting the propriety of nondiscrimination in employment, there is another raised against same-sex marriage,[1] and referenda on other civil rights issues remain common, volatile, and limiting (Gamble 1997; Haider-Markel, Querze, and Lindaman 2007; Wolfe 1998, 77 ff.). Public opposition to a broader rights agenda is articulated within this ambivalent sentiment. Although discrimination is opposed and the democratic values of antidiscrimination extolled, some rights demands are seen as a hyperextension of the law and a challenge to its authority. In popular substitutions for the authority of case law, public majorities have attempted to reconstitute legality, constitutionalize it through amendment, and reimagine the nature of public/private relations (Goldberg-Hiller 2002).

This new foundation for a democratic sovereignty materializes rights while it loosely sutures a plural culture into a more common set of norms. The idea that rights are material—for example, that one couple's access to marriage necessarily affects another—reacts against a more progressive tradition of pluralism in which civil and human rights are understood to be immaterial and flexible; the protection of cultural difference for one group does not unduly impinge on the democratic rights enjoyed by others (Goldberg-Hiller and Milner 2003; Patton 1997, 7 ff.). Distinguishing one group from another—that is, changing the dynamic register from one of equality, in which rights mark and sustain a generality and sameness, to one of inequality, in which only one subset of a group contains both a difference and a sovereign representativeness that marks and contains the social whole—illustrates precisely what Rancière has called the function of *police*. *Police* is an aesthetic problem, for it uses what is visible or invisible to establish both a share of what is in common and a piece of what is shared out. *Police* corresponds to a given form of life and the social and governmental attempts to make it exclusive; it is, in Rancière's (1999, 29) terms,

> an order of bodies that defines the allocation of ways of doing, ways of being, and ways of saying, and sees that those bodies are assigned by name to a particular place and task; it is an order of the visible and the sayable that sees that a particular activity is visible and another is not, that this speech is understood as discourse and another as noise.

Latent within the *police* order is *politics*, according to Rancière: the possibility of making visible and euphonious what has previously been hidden or derided as noise in an effort to assert a new form of life definitional of community. *Politics* "defines the common of the community . . . as divided, as based on a wrong that escapes the arithmetic of exchange and reparation" (1999, 12). Common to the aesthetics of *politics* are images that can disclose both exclusion and inclusion, a visibility that can reveal what has been left out and mobilize a group under a novel interpretation of equality. The now iconic African American civil rights movement and its theory, propounded by Dr. Martin Luther King, did just this, proving that it was necessary to show the majority the very humanity of those it continued to oppress. Analogies built on the example of the civil rights movement or the ideals of racial antidiscrimination that it enshrined in contemporary civil rights law are one important way that this political sensibility is carried forward (Richards 1998, 1999; Sunstein 1993; West 2003, 116).

The challenge to social order made by quarantining civil rights law, as conservatives have tried to do in the case of same-sex marriage, leaves a complex field of contestation. While *police* is "essentially the law" for Rancière (1999, 29), we must not take this literally; where law is understood to be the dominant order of representation, here representation must take place without law, or at least be oriented in opposition to the judges and jurisprudence that have imagined same-sex marriage specifically, and gay rights more generally, as compatible with a jurisprudence of antidiscrimination, that is, as a form of equality. This doesn't entirely eliminate the need to engage with the law itself: the analogies to interracial marriage by which rights to same-sex marriage have been accepted[2] and the movement of gays and lesbians for acknowledgment of their rights that have been analogized to those of the African American civil rights movement have had to be displaced or defused, often through the aesthetics of political campaigns.

Popular Sovereignty and the Aesthetics of Life

The new common sense—the form of life—that is aesthetically maneuvered by anti-same-sex-marriage activists to replace legal analogies and the authority of judges to extend their meanings invites religious authority, "traditionalism" of various kinds, and other social languages to step into the breach, sometimes in the guise of law. This invitation serves to link the sovereign community to the biopolitical[3] realms of life that religion and tradition most often shepherd. As Douzinas and Nead (1999, 66) suggest,

> The [sovereign] war of images involves . . . three vital anthropological tasks. The first is concerned with the internalization of absolute otherness and the domestication of death. The second organizes the field of representation, defining what passes as true or natural, with the obvious normative connotations of those designations. The third, more detailed, flexible, and historically changing, is about

positive evaluations of certain images within the dominant regime of representation that are ascribed a culturally specific normative superiority against other, competing ones.

The problems of subjectivity, epistemology, and hierarchy involved in these tasks and their mutual concerns for life, death, and nature are played out in contemporary civil rights struggles. Efforts of those seeking to extend civil rights protections in the case of same-sex marriage (*political* claims, in Rancière's terminology) have relied as much on legal ideas of equality as they have visualized the suffering of humanity that can be redeemed by law.

The conservative countermand to these images of universal vulnerability in efforts to reassert hierarchy and status plays the biopolitical and the juridical against each other in different ways. Rather than attempt to close the gaps between life and law in the name of lessening suffering as do civil rights supporters, the expanded rift between law and life enforced by the conservative restriction of courts has become both externalized and silenced. It is externalized where the gaps appearing between authentic community and courts are naturalized as the deserved lot of those, such as "homosexuals," who suffer on the outside of social boundaries or where the realm stripped of the protection of the law is imagined as the essential purview of the new sovereign. Giorgio Agamben's recent work illustrates this process. Rather than understand law as an ally against individual suffering, Agamben has argued that the biopolitical realm of necessity inhabits the voids where law once used to be, reaffirming but limiting the nature of law. Sovereign power, in his recent scholarship, is increasingly organized around a control over life; "modern democracy . . . is constantly trying to transform its own bare life into a way of life," in order to make life "sacred" (Agamben 1998, 9; Passavant 2007). It does this through legality, by paradoxically authorizing an exception over legal rules, an exception that marks the sovereign power. Agamben (2005) suggests that the war on terror and, specifically, the Guantanamo prisoners, who lack a clear legal subjectivity, epitomize this sovereign effect (see also Butler 2004), an analogy (although at a different scale) to the extralegal status of those sexual minorities that are denied the right to sue for equal protection in the courts.

Nonetheless, the form of life imagined in both progressive and conservative arguments differs significantly. The threat of individual suffering articulated by equal rights activists is counterpoised against the threat to species-life emerging in the sovereign language of conservatives. The conservative variation on the idea that "society must be defended" raises biological and evolutionary considerations to political standing (Foucault 2003, 60–62). These concerns, while externalized, are also partially hidden and silenced. For example, Foucault (2003) has argued that this biopolitical discourse is subsumed under issues of race. The war on terror also has its own forms of silence. Images of violence, death, sexual torture, and imprisonment are policed from the media, circulating wildly within the military at the "front" but erupting into the public with calamitous consequence, as the Abu Ghraib photos have made clear. In the case of dead soldiers brought back from Iraq, images are absent altogether.

The aesthetic of image and absence around which this sovereignty operates has its genealogy in what Kantorowicz (1957) called the King's two bodies, one corporeal, finite, and cyclically replaceable and the other institutional and enduring. While the sovereign body of the king could have a specific representation, the institution endured in more iconic forms such as the crown and the flag. Democratic sovereignty today maintains this tension between the sovereign body-subject and the enduring Body Politic. Progressives cling to the image of the suffering body to justify their demand for civil rights, while conservatives, seeking a new form of sovereignty in which rights are no longer automatically extended to those claiming need, reference the biopolitical realm that haunts and promotes the iconography of civil rights.

Iconography and the New Sovereign Body

The *iconomy* (Douzinas and Nead 1999, 9) that represents popular sovereignty takes several forms. In an echo of earlier struggles for social control of a common law, representations are sometimes *iconophobic*, unifying through an expressive lack of contextual imagery. Iconophobia expresses "the fear of images, displaced into judicial hermeneutics, . . . the fear of plural meanings and interpretations, of diverse, local, and informal jurisdictions, of different logics and particular reasons" (ibid., 8): a pluralism that threatens the congealing boundaries of a new sovereign community. Figure 12.1 represents one contemporary image that tries to do something similar with marriage. Marriage is metonymically represented by two rings, one with an embedded gem to indicate a gendered difference. Rings stand for the ceremonial aspect of a relationship. While gay couples may ritually wear rings, the implication of this advertisement is that the ceremonial and symbolic aspects of marriage supply the reason to rethink the law, to constitutionalize the supremacy of only one interpretation of marriage, to *police* it. This iconophobic image is given authority in the ad through its biopolitical value. "No other cultural institution provides for the health, safety, and well-being of children than a married mom and dad," the text reads, in part, suggesting that these abstract commitments to health, safety, and happiness justify such an extraordinary political intervention.

The aesthetics of *police* other times draws explicitly on images of bodies in an effort to repel countervailing meanings. These *iconophilic* representations are

America protects marriage because marriage protects our future.

No other cultural institution provides for the health, safety and well being of children than a married mom and dad. Call your Congressional Representatives today to say you support the Federal Marriage Amendment. **202-224-3121**

Support the Federal Marriage Amendment

Marriage: One Man One Woman

For more information and to sign a petition supporting the Federal Marriage Amendment, visit www.NoGayMarriage.com

Figure 12.1. Source: Family Research Council.

deeply worried about the possibility of confusion between original and copy, and every iconoclastic diatribe uses the most vivid imagery to combat the evil of images. The law loves and fears images, it both prohibits them and organizes its own operation in a spectacular and visual manner. (Douzinas and Nead 1999, 8)

Figure 12.2 depicts two sets of iconophilic images that put a face to the new sensibility of civil rights. Representations of families are most frequently white, but certainly of the same race, in order to dispel any analogies to the antimiscegenation decisions that have underpinned the jurisprudence upholding same-sex marriage. The families portrayed in Figure 12.2 snuggle closely, illustrating marriage and family as a single organic entity. There is no space between the individuals that could symbolize or reveal the interpersonal nature of the relationship, an arrangement repelling the imagination of alternative permutations. Lacking internal boundaries, the family is presented as whole, self-contained and inwardly secure; these are not individuals but instead primal generative units around which healthy communities must rally.

The iconomy of image and absence relies upon the representational genre of kitsch. Murray Edelman (1995, 29) understands kitsch as "art that sentimentalizes everyday experiences, or that appeals to beliefs and emotions encouraging vanity, prejudices, or unjustified fears and dubious successes." According to Edel-

Traditional Marriage & Family.

Figure 12.2. Sources: *Salt Lake City Tribune* October 31, 2004, p. A9.

man, kitsch evokes fears, hatreds, enthusiasms, nostalgias, and victories, all of which can mobilize. But, he adds, kitsch mobilizes in a peculiar way: by playing on hopes and fears, it asks mostly a passive response. "It does not postulate an observer with an active mind, with the imagination and creativity to grasp a work's potentialities" (ibid., 33). Eric Méchoulan (2004, 6) anchors this reading of kitsch to Rancière's framework: "the question of knowledge is a question of *police*, the problem of thought is a matter of *politics*."

Unmodified, the law is a dangerous intrusion for those trying to police the image of the family. Law, for all its formalism, can trouble a *police* aesthetic because it does require and compel thought, even abstract thought. For example, law can require that justification be made for heterosexual privilege and hierarchy as occurred in Hawai'i in 1996 (see Goldberg-Hiller 2002). That year, the state's various arguments for granting marriage licenses only to opposite-sex couples were rejected on all counts by a trial court. In continued efforts to replace this legal compulsion for the justification of privilege with a popular sovereign effectively able to reclaim hierarchy, law's authority must be neutralized through aesthetic processes that I call *domestication, inversion,* and *suspicion,* which I illustrate in the sections that follow. Nonetheless, while the practice of popular sovereignty is motivated by antagonism to judges, to the civil rights law that they have developed and enforced, and to the legal subjects who claim protection against majorities, law—appropriately modified and disciplined—is also useful to this movement to reclaim the boundaries of the new *distribution of the sensible.* Law is returned within the new sovereign spaces through novel forms of knowledge and the reconstitution of status. These aesthetic practices depend upon images and rhetoric from biopolitical themes that Foucault, Agamben, Butler, and others have demonstrated to be increasingly caught up in the imagination of modern sovereignty.

Domestication

Civil rights law has long developed through analogy in order to build a basis for inclusion and "equality." Since 1998, ads urging rejection of statewide amendments against same-sex marriage have often used graphic reference to the African American civil rights movement as a trope to express the kinds of discrimination at stake. For example, an Ohio advertisement in 2004 urging repeal of a provision of Cincinnati's charter that prevented antidiscrimination protection on the basis of sexual orientation quoted Coretta Scott King as saying, "When any group experiences injustice, it undermines the quality of justice in our society at large. It hurts us all."[4] The justification for including sexual orientation into a legal framework of antidiscrimination is nowhere explained in the ad. This abstraction of "injustice" invites others to interpret and universalize the meaning of equality, giving space to the political claims of new civil rights subjects. These subjects' political invisibility is thereby made visible in ways akin to the civil rights movement led by Ms. King's late husband.

Those who refuse to support gay rights or the equality arguments made on their behalf try to disrupt this analogy, suggesting not only that the civil rights movement is abstractly distinguishable but that blacks themselves do not support the analogy (see Patton 1995). An ad purchased by conservative antigay rights activists in the same Cincinnati struggle said, in part,

> Fred Shuttlesworth [depicted marching with Martin Luther King] understands the mistake of legislating special rights for anyone. The truth he speaks hasn't always been welcome. But it's always been right. And the truth for Cincinnati is that special rights demanded by homosexual activists here will elevate one group of Cincinnatians over another, *based solely on sexual preference.*

The ad copy suggests, further, that this truth can be established through Shuttlesworth's bodily suffering.

In the struggle for equal rights, Fred Shuttlesworth marched with Martin Luther King, Jr. For that, he was set upon by dogs, and his body kicked, punched, and beaten bloody. To silence his voice, his home and family were bombed, twice. But it never changed the truth he spoke.

This suffering is depicted as a central feature that distinguishes the truth spoken by authentic civil rights subjects from the false claims of gay rights supporters who have not successfully exploited similar images of suffering and have offered no iconic leaders from their own social movements. By implication, sexual minorities are unfairly holding onto images owned by others, rendering them unrepresentable and invisible.

As an aesthetic system, domestication polices universal access to dominant civil rights analogies by authenticating some struggles and denigrating others. When suffering is written onto the bodies of iconic civil rights activists, its interrogation is impeded and the appropriation of its political meanings by other activists deflected. In this way, law is resisted both as something intruding into a sovereign community and as something always already present, as unquestioned as common sense.

Inversion

The images of activists from the civil rights movement that abound in antigay rights advertisements authenticate real victims and, by making them historical and iconic, allow the majority to identify safely with them. As the copy in Figure 12.3 makes clear, special rights rhetoric helps to create this identification. Neal Milner and I (2003) have argued that special rights language is useful for delegitimating some rights claims and the institutions, resources, identities, authorities, and other meanings that undergird them, while calling upon another set of institutions, resources, identities, authorities, and meanings that are upheld as contrasting supports for "equal rights." The tension between special rights and equal rights, glimpsed in graphic simplicity in this ad, invokes a set of power dynamics with broad political and social consequences. These dynamics derogate some social movements or their demands as unfit for inclusion or assimilation while substantiating that an "equal rights" space—citizenship more generally—is not in question.

Accusations that activists seek special rights in these advertisements creates an inversion that aesthetically polices social relations. The idea that political majorities are vulnerable, that they are the actual and authentic victims of a gay rights agenda, envisions the rights-harassed majority as the true minority, reversing the rights-based notion of injury and the duty of protection. This meme is often invoked in the counterclaims to the argument that opposition to gay rights is a sign of homophobia. Gays who accuse others of homophobia are, through

BIRMINGHAM, ALABAMA APRIL 12, 1963

REV. FRED SHUTTLESWORTH — REV. RALPH ABERNATHY — REV. DR. MARTIN LUTHER KING, JR.

"I know quite a few things about fighting discrimination. Cincinnati, Issue 3 is NOT about discrimination. If it was, I'd support it. But Issue 3 is about special rights, not equal rights. I've fought my whole life for equal rights — not special rights — so I'm voting NO on Issue 3."

– Reverend Fred Shuttlesworth, Cincinnatian

Figure 12.3. Source: *Cincinnati Enquirer*, October 28, 2004

the lens of inversion, seen as the real bigots because of the way they denigrate naturally aversive reactions; stigmatized for their intolerance, they are as undeserving of civil rights as if they had barred the school door in historical fights against integration.

This is illustrated in a letter to the editor published on behalf of the anti-same-sex-marriage amendment campaign in Georgia.

> *Bigot label fitting for Tucker, Too*
>
> The ease with which Cynthia Tucker is ready to label some people as bigots exposes the bigotry in her own thinking.

She would have us believe that homosexuality is "determined by a complex interplay of factors . . . (*sic*) and is determined so early in a child's formation that it cannot be considered a choice.

Let us assume that this is correct. Why then should any heterosexual's complex feelings, reactions and responses to homosexuality be judged by a different standard?

Why is the behavior on the one hand a choice and on the other hand bigotry? I would argue that the only reason is Tucker's blind devotion to her own beliefs—and isn't that the very definition of bigotry?

Robert Curry, Stone Mountain.[5]

This letter writer explicitly ties bigotry to the biopolitical through a reference to its psychopathology, affirming a genealogy of social control. Homosexuals were policed through the 1970s under the rubric of public health that permitted a policy of containment. The medicalization of public policy returned in later decades with the association of gays and AIDS in an effort to demonstrate the bodily excess that endangered society. The emergent claim of homophobia (a term coined in the year of the Stonewall uprising) turns this biological argument back on rights opponents, claiming that it is *their* primal fears that beset sexual minorities that assert their basic equality. That rights opponents now grab back the argument of an intrinsic bigotry through claims that gays misconstrue the majority's innate squeamishness rhetorically gives force to their overarching claims that conflicts played out in the political and legal arenas are best understood as reflections of biological difference not amenable to judgments and unavailable to legal solutions.

This biopolitical theme might leave an equal rights frame intact, because it depicts the minority's claim for rights as essentially indistinct from majority demands and because innate difference appears to bolster the analogy between racial antidiscrimination and issues of sexual citizenship. This potentially *political* aesthetic supporting progressive civil rights analogies is nonetheless defeated by aspersions that any claimed commonality is something both disingenuous and excessive. One sign of this excess is the idea, never far away from special rights accusations, that gays and lesbians are wealthy and thus distinguishable from true civil rights subjects such as African Americans, whose poverty demonstrates their authentic desert and justifies political action by noble cultural defenders.

The identification of the majority with authentic victims can also be used to indirectly return the criminal law to relevance for policing sexual minorities, a utility vacated by the Supreme Court's decriminalization of sodomy in *Lawrence v. Texas* (2003). That decision inhibited the notion of gays' virtual criminality as a justification for denying antidiscrimination protection. In the 2004 Cincinnati struggle, one campaign advertisement promoting an amendment against gay rights protections asked the reader to inhabit the subject position of a victimized girl. "If Cincinnati city council has their way, someone committing a crime against a six year-old girl could receive LESS punishment than for THE SAME CRIME against a homosexual adult," suggests the copy. Against the appeal of a vulnerable girl, gays are made to seem unfit subjects for criminal protection: this would be nothing more than special rights. The concern over children's fate tends, on the other hand, to recriminalize gays by resonating with older but common arguments that gays are dangerous to children's security, a threat magnified by misappropriated rights claims.

The embattled identity of otherwise secure majorities gains its sovereign strength within registers of what Lauren Berlant (1999, 53) has called "national sentimentality, a rhetoric of promise that a nation can be built across fields of social difference through channels of affective identification and empathy." This sentimentality, invested in the body of a young girl, leverages what Thomas Frank (2004, 257) labels "the glamour of authenticity, combined with the narcissism of victimhood," a sense of vulnerable security challenged by a rights culture imagined as foreign and aggressive. The narcissism of victimhood produces a keen sense that rights culture should not be flushed entirely, as rights talk provides one of the most familiar languages of victimized self-recognition. But these rights are linked to notions of bodily security, more appropriate for the protection of the criminal law than for antidiscrimination doctrine.

General cultural stereotypes—perceptions reinforced by a racist criminal and prison system—that African Americans are the real criminal population also tend to ensnare gay rights activists when race is made relevant within conservative advertisements. The entanglement of race and sex has a unique biopolitical genealogy. Somerville (2000) has shown how the heightened state surveillance associated with race after *Plessy v. Ferguson* (1896)—the case that accepted separate treatment as an expression of constitutional equality—helped to define the homosexual/heterosexual binary, eventually culminating in sodomy statutes directed at gays. At the same time, some homoerotic activities were made culturally "normal" by racial coding: same-sex behavior between blacks and whites was not necessarily coded as homosexual, whereas interracial heterosexual desire was always a form of perversion. Over the twentieth century, this construct of deviance eventually faded and reversed (consider, for example, that the defendants in *Lawrence* were of mixed race). Somerville points out that these cultural dynamics can explain why race is no longer easily coded black/white but sexuality seems to be increasingly binary. "The denaturalization of one identity category is often achieved through a renaturalization of another category. Current contestations over race, gender, and sexuality enact a productive search for new language and models of subjectivity" (ibid., 175).

Conservative attempts to reassert a proper analogy for race have frequently operated through the idiom of pain in an effort to renaturalize the racial body, recuperate it from its own criminal associations, and distinguish it from the claims of gay rights advocates. As illustration, consider Shuttlesworth's comments presented earlier or this congressional testimony on behalf of a federal amendment against same-sex marriage.

> As an African-American, I know something about discrimination. The institution of slavery was about the oppression of an entire people. The institution of segregation was about discrimination. The institution of Jim Crow laws, including laws against interracial marriage, was about discrimination. . . . It boggles my mind that people would compare the traditional institution of marriage to slavery. . . . The family and the traditional institution of marriage are fundamental to progress and hope for a better tomorrow for the African-American community. . . . Traditional marriage—as well as our democratic system of government—is now under attack. Without traditional marriage, it is hard to see how our community will be able to thrive. . . . It's not just that they want to silence us—they also want to write our values out of the Constitution as well.[6]

Race is deployed here as a legitimate sign of authentic suffering, and the perceived attack on the family is represented as a further marginalization of the African American community if not, more literally, a slow social genocide. Pitting the legitimacy of racial victimization against gay and lesbian discrimination—in the same way that the victimization of children is pitted against antigay violence—works to shape the public space as finite and zero-sum, an intimation that the machinery of government is unable to simultaneously ameliorate the suffering experienced by both types of victims.

Suspicion

The isolation and denigration of legal authorities provide another opportunity to resist civil rights in antimarriage advertisements. For example, one ad promoted by the Family Research Council headlines, "The courts failed us. Legislators too. It's time the people voted." Suspicion of judges, legislators, and their aims can be marshaled into a call to the people for protective redress, but aesthetically this popular expression lacks the democratic sign of Rancière's notion of *politics*. Eric Méchoulan (2004, 5) has argued that the traditional democratic claim for Rancière is poetic in a way that suspicious exhortation is not. Civil rights analogy, for example, depends upon a lyrical trust in language.

> The man of democracy is a man of speech; he is a poetic being, and since he trusts language, he is confident in language as a structure of appearance for designating objects, events, perceptible beings in the world, and at the same time for implying

a distance between the sounds of words and the reality they describe or interpret. This trust in the operations of speech does not lead to an illusion of closeness or identity between words and things. Just the opposite. Poeticallness, like democracy, is the experience of distance, the evaluation of the right distance between beings or between words and things. . . . In democracy or poetry, man acts *as if* his speech can be heard and understood: equality means above all an equality of intelligences.

There is some attempt among opponents of gay civil rights to assert an equality of intelligences, especially in the claim that sufficiently robust benefits of citizenship are in place without the addition of new rights for sexual minorities. But, most often there is a refusal to accept the distance between words and things. This suspicion often focuses on the deceptive formality of the law, justification for intervening in the civil rights analogies that seem to promise same-sex marriage.

For example, some advertisements depict civil rights law as inhumanly complex in contrast to state or federal amendments that are able to collapse words and things. One Salt Lake City newspaper ad[7] fills its boundaries with eye-daunting paragraphs of fine print, with the language of the statewide amendment in a larger and bolder font standing out as a legible, contrasting simplification. The copy says, "If you are a bit confused by the war of words over Utah's marriage amendment . . . maybe you have wondered whether the only way to reach the right conclusion is to go to law school." By implication, supporters of civil rights are revealed to be obfuscating, legally inclined intellectuals unable to articulate a commonsense thought. Advertisements in this model call for a revision of ways of knowing the family, one less dependent on the experiences made falsely relevant by legal education.

Domestication, inversion, and suspicion are tropes that deflect and distance the authority of civil rights law from political contests over same-sex marriage. This distancing is an aesthetic practice, an effort to open new conceptual and political spaces and to govern them. For conservative social movements attempting to gain control of this gap, social hierarchy is redeployed on the authoritative basis of electoral mobilization in the name of common sense. Their preferred *distribution of the sensible* takes a *police* form, configuring a set of social hierarchies intended to limit access by sexual rights activists. As Rancière reminds us, any aesthetic distancing remains vulnerable to *political* reconfiguration that exploits images and silences in an effort to upset hierarchies and to build a basis for inclusion. What has solidified conservative efforts to re-create American sovereignty is, I show in what follows, a peculiar epistemology of common sense whose political limits are ironically constrained less by progressive *politics* than by its own aesthetic logic.

Knowledge, Biopolitics, and Governance

When civil rights law is depicted as complicated and threatening by conservative campaign advertisements, popular sovereignty is shown to depend on a new epistemology based on what Berlant (1997, 58) has called "a hard-wired truth, a core of common sense." "Common sense" reinforces a rational and meaningful national order, and judicial meddling with sexual rights can be opposed on the tautological basis that "marriage . . . is what it is";[8] "the definition of marriage seems to . . . the vast majority of the American people, as a matter of common sense and social reality."[9] This self-evident production of truth also reinforces the ahistorical idea that civilized marriage has always been as it is now. One advertisement in support of the statewide marriage amendment in Utah argued that the language of the amendment ("Marriage consists only of the legal union between a man and a woman") is not a matter of rights; instead, "it's just right," a slogan for common sense. A letter writer to the *Portland Oregonian* makes a similar tautological argument in that state's campaign: "Gays and lesbians should not be afforded the same rights as a married couple. Why? Because it isn't the same."[10]

The concepts of sameness and of distinctiveness are animated in logos used by pro-amendment forces that represent heterosexual marriage with the visual semaphore of interlocking bathroom signs, such as in Figure 12.4. Washrooms are one of the last exceptions to the jurisprudence of equal gender rights in the United States, a fact that provides a handy reminder of base, natural differences brought appropriately together through the proper application of the law. These images reinforce Berlant's ironic observation that "where regulating sexuality is concerned the law has a special sentimental relation to banality" (1997, 59). The idea that common sense (materialized in the tautologies and these logos) should trump legal sense helps to overcome the idea—otherwise anathema to conservatives—that government intrusion will result from amendments designed to regulate sexuality. When family is what government is about, the contradiction vanishes. As the state senator who sponsored Georgia's amendment argued:

> Without a doubt, we must limit the role of government in the lives of Georgia's residents and maintain our freedoms at all costs. The commitment to the maintenance of individual rights, however, should have nothing to do with the redefinition of something as basic and sacred as marriage defined by one man and one woman.[11]

The notion that marriage is sacred, that it lives in some space beyond the case law, constituted by common sense and protected by electoral majorities, acclaims the biopolitical realm as a function of good government. This biopolitical dimen-

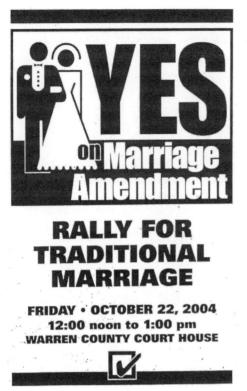

YES on **Marriage Amendment**

RALLY FOR TRADITIONAL MARRIAGE

FRIDAY • OCTOBER 22, 2004
12:00 noon to 1:00 pm
WARREN COUNTY COURT HOUSE

Figure 12.4. Source: *Park City Daily News* (Bowling Green, KY), October 21, 2004, P. 5C.

sion is a commitment to life in the absence of law. Since the legalization of abortion, conservative social movement politics has often projected itself onto the fetus, an icon abstracted from history, race, sexuality, knowledge, money, or war, yet useful as a figure able to metonymically capture the sentimental politics of the injured adult and the utopian promise of a reimagined citizenship (Berlant 1997; Edelman 2004). More recently, the anti-same-sex-marriage campaigns have extended this utopianism to reject human and civil rights that offend and threaten a sentimental commitment to "bare life." The rhetorical and symbolic use of life—represented in Figure 12.5 through the answer to an unspoken question: "Because sex between a man and a woman makes babies, that's why . . ." (*sic*)— reinforces a topology of the visible. References to generative life fortify a naturalized set of social hierarchies, a "culturally specific normative superiority against others" (Douzinas and Nead 1999, 66). This establishment of hierarchy depends upon legality by paradoxically authorizing an exception over legal rules that favor an analogical growth of civil rights, an exception that reflects the sovereign power of electoral majorities.

Figure 12.5. Source: Family Research Council.

Butler's and Agamben's claim for a strong link between sovereign power and the war on terror, particularly the military prison at Guantanamo, strangely haunts this sovereign logic. For Butler, Guantanamo shows that "sovereignty denotes a form of power that is fundamentally lawless, and whose lawlessness can be found in the way in which law itself is fabricated or suspended at the will of a designated subject" (Butler 2004, 94). Seen in light of this sovereign empowerment through suspension, there is a homology between the limits to law that uphold the policy of detention without habeas and the limitations that amendments make by blocking challenges to marriage discrimination in the courts. As the state of exception "increasingly appear[s] as the dominant paradigm of government in contemporary politics" (Agamben 2005, 2), these instances of law's retreat both articulate and hold together the "threshold of undecidability . . . between life and law" (ibid., 86).

This boundary has an expressive dimension. The cultural connection between a war on terror and a war against life is sometimes made explicit, as when gay rights are said to be "in some ways worse than terrorism"[12] or when marriage is "defended" against in the same language or imagery as is used in urging support for "the homeland." The entanglement of gay rights and terrorism is also evident in the images from Abu Ghraib, where the revelations and depictions of torture reveal the contradictory amalgam of Orientalist ideas that Arabs are simultaneously

Figure 12.6. Source: Internet. Ad was composed by the same group that called itself the "Swift Boat Veterans for Truth" in an effort to weaken the AARP's rejection of Social Security reform in 2005.

vulnerable to (homo)sexual humiliation, that Arab men likely *are* homosexual because of their repressive relations with women, and that "terrorist" homophobia is more extreme than the enlightened American variety (Engle 2007; Puar 2004, 2005). In their articulation of the tolerances associated with Western civilization, these ways of reading the association of terrorism and sexuality dovetail with the conservative argument that civil rights for gays are not put in question by the amendments, only excessive legal claims for same-sex marriage.[13] The association between same-sex marriage and the war on terror is made visually explicit in the controversial advertisement represented in Figure 12.6 that suggests, in a seeming non sequitur to debates over social security reform, that support for equal rights to marriage *is* a rejection of a national commitment to war.

Zygmunt Bauman (1992, 7) has argued that life is a central theme in theories of citizenship and that challenges to the perpetuation of community often evoke the fear of death. The human response to death, in his understanding, is to commit to life, to perpetuation of the community. The juxtaposition of images in Figure 12.6 brings this specter of death much closer and implies the impossibility of turning away from violence in a vain pursuit of sexual rights. Numerous examples could be drawn from public rhetoric in the recent amendment campaigns that recapitulate the conservative idea that heterosexual marriage is special because, as one letter to the editor explained, "people of the same gender, regardless of how much they may love or care for each other, cannot engage in one of the most basic functions of marriage, procreation."[14] Remaining unsaid but implicit in this rhetoric is the idea that nongenerative sexuality is akin to death. The conservative religious leader Paul Cameron has made this explicit in a commonly quoted paragraph, which, for his supporters, plainly shows the affirmation of life in the nullification of the law.

> Homosexual marriage is a bad idea. While traditional marriage delivers benefits to its participants as well as to society, gay marriage harms everyone it touches especially homosexuals themselves. Not only does it place homosexuals at increased risk for HIV and other sexually transmitted diseases, but it also subjects them to an increased threat of domestic violence and early death. Homosexual marriage is nothing like traditional marriage.

The contrast between this attitude and the commitment to generative life epitomized by the heterosexual family is the boundary between law and the sovereign.

Can Civil Rights Advocates Embrace Life?

Carl Stychin (2003, 87) points out the vital relationship between health care rights and recognition of relationships in the United States, a link that has sometimes been used by conservatives to claim that gays value marriage for all the wrong reasons.[15] It is significant, I think, that so many opponents of the amendments that would have rolled back or occluded equal marriage rights frequently imitated biopolitical arguments in an effort to support and reinforce analogies to the civil rights movement. This language often went beyond the idea of benefits dependent on access to marriage, instead relying on the image of the injured person who could, in the register of the same conservative form of life, aesthetically conjure a *political* claim for rights. I illustrate some of these claims that appear in the 2004 Oregon Voters' Pamphlet.[16]

> Each of our children should be allowed to protect their loved ones in times of medical emergency, each of our children should be able to provide health insurance coverage for their spouse and their children, each of our children should know that if their spouse dies, they will not lose their nest egg or the family home.[17]
>
> If this amendment passes, countless Oregonians will be denied the right to make life-saving medical decisions for their loved ones. That's not healthy for families and it's not right for Oregon.[18]
>
> The constitution should give equal protection under the law. Measure 36 specifies different rights for Oregonians, forever. Victims of this amendment would be

children and families. Many families would be denied health care, inheritance rights and the ability to make decisions about their life. The amendment could restrict adoption policies, and could put children in jeopardy if a parent were to die.[19]

As nurses, we know Constitutional Amendment 36 will jeopardize the health of gay and lesbian couples and their families:

+ Constitutional Amendment 36 would deny many families the ability to quickly and easily make life-saving medical decisions in the case of an emergency.
+ While some insurers allow domestic partner access to their policies, many others do not. This lack of coverage leads to delayed treatment.[20]

I have two Moms that love me and want the best for me. But they are afraid, because Constitutional Amendment 36 would leave me without protections they say are important:

+ Being sure I can get on their health insurance coverage
+ Allowing both my parents to make decisions if I get hurt
+ Having both my parents be able to sign permission slips or deal with emergencies at school
+ Knowing that I'm going to stay with one Mom, should anything happen to the other. I'm just a kid and I just want the same protections that any other kid needs.

Please don't do something that will hurt my family and me. Don't Leave Kids Like Me Without Protections Vote "No" on Constitutional Amendment 36.

Henry P. Age 14[21]

The imagery of death, children's vulnerability, and the authority of health care professionals in place of or alongside the usual rights language suggests the importance paid to the vulnerable person in an effort to thwart constitutional action against civil rights. On the face of it, it is very difficult to see the difference between these appeals and those of conservatives who have called for the amendments as a way of enhancing the life of families and society generally. An important question is why this appeal to children and to health—two appeals that conservatives have successfully brought to bear on their own constructions of popular sovereignty—have seemingly had little effect. How does life within the conservative register work to recreate a status? The answer, I suggest, lies within the extended political logic of this new sovereignty, one handily glimpsed in the case of Terri Schiavo.

Terri Schiavo and the Limits of the Biopolitical

In early 2005, conservative leaders tried—unsuccessfully in fact as well as in popular opinion[22]—to broaden the icon of this bioethics to the unconscious in their media-saturated efforts to prevent the removal of a brain-dead woman's feeding tube. For Rancière, the visible and the sayable are intimately connected:

visibility should imply a language to tell what is sayable about the visible and who has the authority to see and tell what she has seen. Terri Schiavo seemed a useful icon for conservatives who continued to deplore the courts and to press for life, as she could not speak for herself, making the *police* function of configuring the sensible less amenable to the *politics* that could complicate and refigure it.

Lacking a living will and thus a clear legal position on her own fate, Terry Schiavo spent years receiving palliative care that came to an end with her husband's representation that she would not have wanted such a life for herself. Her parents contested their son-in-law's interpretation of their daughter's wishes and challenged him in various Florida and federal courts. In every case, they lost their arguments as judges ruled that Schiavo's husband could act as her legal guardian. Governor Jeb Bush intervened in the case several times, signing a law, in 2003, that allowed the governor to issue a one-time stay in certain cases. This law was ruled unconstitutional by the Florida Supreme Court in 2004, and again a trial court set a date for the removal of the feeding tube. In March 2005, while Schiavo lay in a hospice without food or hydration, Congress passed a bill designed to grant

> [t]he United States District Court for the Middle District of Florida . . . jurisdiction to hear, determine, and render judgment on a suit or claim by or on behalf of Theresa Marie Schiavo for the alleged violation of any right of Theresa Marie Schiavo under the Constitution or laws of the United States relating to the withholding or withdrawal of food, fluids, or medical treatment necessary to sustain her life.[23]

In his first-ever interruption of his frequent vacations, President Bush flew from his ranch in Texas to sign the bill in Washington amid much media fanfare, but the federal district and appeals courts refused to order the resumption of feeding. Schiavo died the morning after the sixth unsuccessful appeal to the Supreme Court in four years of litigation of the case.

The arguments arrayed in defense of Schiavo's continued feeding positioned the bare life of a person in a coma as a new biopolitical subject in need of broader legal protection than the Constitution could provide. For some, a discourse of human rights could be used to amplify legal protections. Republican Roscoe Bartlett of Maryland, for example, argued that legislation to protect Schiavo was necessary because "Life is sacred. . . . Many are galvanized by her cause because like me, they recognize that the right to life is one of our core fundamental human values."[24] President Bush simply argued that the law should "err on the side of life"[25] in an effort to "build a culture of life."[26] Representative David Weldon of Florida, who introduced the Incapacitated Persons' Legal Protection Act, made it clear that the matter of Schiavo was at the heart a sovereign power over life.

Figure 12.7. Terri Schiavo. Source: *Daily Catholic*, April 1, 2005.

Legislation was needed, he said, to "give[] incapacitated persons the same rights of due process available to death row inmates."[27]

The inmate on death row and the comatose person are, Agamben reminds us, intimately linked. Both are examples of the way that sovereign power is organized today around a control over life that it attempts to make sacred. The condemned and the comatose are both sacred lives lived beyond the nation but within the ambit of sovereignty.

This articulation of sovereignty and biopower is productive but complicated for civil rights doctrine. For one, it attempts to authorize an exception—even the individual exception of a "private bill" in the case of Terry Schiavo—that intervenes in commitments to federalism. Thus, like same-sex marriage, whose threat in insurgent states such as Hawai'i led to the first federal definition of marriage, Schiavo's care, which traditionally falls under the purview of state police powers, was transferred to the federal system. In a political environment where judges have been excoriated for their bias antagonistic to "the people" in these two areas of jurisprudence, both responses have been to strengthen the power of federal judges. But it also does more. For, while it bolsters and repositions legal authority, it also re-creates a sovereign community opposed to the given legal order, but not law as such.

In embracing the sacred life of the biopolitical, conservatives can reassert this commitment in new ways with important political consequences. For instance, this aesthetic form not only links to the exceptionality of Guantanamo prisoners and the war on terror that has mobilized many Republican activists but also reinforces a threatened religious identity embraced in the Catholic notion of a "culture of life." Attacks on Christians in Sudan, for example, have figured prominantly in conservative Christian discourse that repositions gay rights activists and their judicial supports as inappropriately using rights against more authentic civil rights subjects. The Sudanese "jihad" is used to argue not only that Christians are the true targets of terrorism but that Christians, linked to their African brothers and sisters in Sudan, are analogous to African Americans who appropriately fought for civil rights.

Perhaps the reason that the Schiavo case did not play as well as conservatives who relied upon these other resonances might have hoped is that it also repositioned sovereign communities against a notion of the "traditional" nuclear family that so much antigay rights rhetoric has upheld. By intervening in a decision that painfully pitted parental concerns that were legally trumped by those of Schiavo's husband, the legal maneuvers confused the cartography of private and public that the new aesthetics of the family developed in the same-sex-marriage controversy. The heterosexual family has been made iconic in conservative anti-same-sex-marriage discourse, and it is thereby rendered unavailable for inspection. This rhetoric has argued that the family is not a unit to be "known" in its separate elements but is best understood as an opaque tautology, an impenetrable center to this new sovereignty that sits like a black hole in the center of a spinning galaxy, organizing its shape through its tremendous gravity, unobserved and perhaps unobservable.

For this reason, arguments that filled the airwaves for weeks concerning the nature of Schiavo's caretakers—her family—made little difference to public opinion. Discussions centered on whether Michael Schiavo, the husband, was *really* a husband in the eyes of God (e.g., he had children with another woman, his interests were separate from his wife's) and whether the parents were greedy and fighting with Michael because they had not been given any of the proceeds of a civil settlement that he had won. These speculations encouraged people to *know* the family and, on that basis, to furnish assent to a Congress bent on bringing federal courts back into the family's tragic situation in an effort to render an abstract justice, to render life.

The political failures of the Schiavo private bill may offer some insight into why the biopolitical icons relied upon by many proponents of same-sex-marriage rights have not fared well. The iconography of family unavailable and impervious to legal inquiry makes it hard for alternative families to gain sympathy on the grounds that legal rights enhance their relationships. There is little cultural willingness to politically deconstruct the family—indeed, no language and no imagery that would make this a simple task fit for the imagery of campaign advertisements—and thus little opportunity to let law come inside. Civil rights may have a face, but it has become iconic and increasingly unavailable to those who need it most.

Conclusion

Two processes seem to be at stake in the creation and policing of a new distribution of the sensible. One is a materialization of rights by which pluralism is reworked from a politicized system of horizontal equality to one of hierarchy and status no longer under the control of courts. The second is a growing commitment to the biopolitical that encourages and is advanced by the retreat of law. These two processes are likely to become increasingly entangled through the iconography of the family, which also establishes the limit of this politics. The family is progressively understood through its generative capacities, while the biopolitical is used against gays who seek legal recognition. Whether this conservative biopolitics will begin to reassert control over the nonmarried gay lifestyle remains to be seen (see, for example, Katherine Franke 2004, 2006).

In many ways, what is happening in these conservative discourses can be understood as a return full circle to their origins following the U.S. Supreme Court's decision in *Roe v. Wade* (1973). Many years ago, Kristin Luker (1984) surmised that the Supreme Court's affirmation of abortion rights likely acted as a trigger that revealed to many that judges and modern progressive social movements did not share their commitments to the family and to fixed gender roles. Today, the right to life has become more broadly attached to the other pivot around which the institutional reaction to courts has been politicized: gay rights. As the two come together, they have created a powerful connection to other issues that operate under the same retreat-from-law logic of this popular sovereignty, especially the war on terror.

This does not mean that rights consciousness has entirely dissolved. Rights still provide a subjectivity for majorities imagining themselves to inhabit the equal rights side of the special rights/equal rights binary. These equal rights no longer facilitate the political analogies that Rancière sees to be intrinsic to political behavior; instead, they seek, often through silences and the creation of impermeable icons, to establish and police a hierarchy. It is for this reason that the war on terror may not produce the same commitment to civil rights that the Cold War likely did (Dudziak 2000; Skrentny 2002).

In the case of Terri Schiavo, conservative forces attempted to further distance the courts and judicial wisdom from control over life. Yet, here, the abstractions of life lived outside the family were unable to overcome the strong political commitment to the legally opaque heterosexual family, suggesting that the limits may now be found less in rights discourse than in the very icons that have enabled part of this political shift.

13 A Jury of One's Queers

Revisiting the Dan White Trial

Casey Charles

CRITICAL QUEER STUDIES examines the discursive formations through which sexual minorities continue to suffer, in the words of the late Justice Brennan, such a "pernicious and sustained hostility"—such an "immediate and severe opprobrium"—that their only counterparts in the United States are racial groups (*Rowland v. Mad River Local School District*, 470 U.S. 1009, 1014, 105 S.Ct. 1373 [1985] [opinion of Brennan, J., dissenting from a denial of certiorari]. As the legal scholar Mari Matsuda has declared, the "criminal justice system is a primary location of racist, sexist, homophobic, and class based oppression in this county" (Matsuda 1998, 319). This essay explores the methodology behind these trenchant assessments by revisiting perhaps the most notorious antigay crime in United States history, the assassination of Harvey Milk by the ex-policeman and San Francisco supervisor Dan White, who, after his manslaughter conviction, served a little over five years for the killings of Milk and Mayor George Moscone. Two dramatic reenactments of this famous trial—one an award-winning film, *The Times of Harvey Milk*, and the other a stage play entitled *The Execution of Justice*—provide the data and framework for my exploration of the way the criminal justice system perpetuates queer bias by sanctioning strategies of exclusion and erasure in almost all phases of trial—from jury selection to closing arguments, from expert testimony to pleas of diminished capacity.

The literature on the Dan White trial also dramatizes the larger social impact of this famous criminal proceeding, documenting the shock waves and riots the trial produced in a town that had become, in the space of a decade, the hub of a national gay rights movement, a mecca where, by 1979, one out of seven residents was gay or lesbian (Armstrong 2002, 115; FitzGerald 1981, 27). Taking place on the cusp of an incipient backlash that would soon usher Ronald Reagan into national office, the trial of Dan White continues to resonate as what Armstrong and Crage call a "commemorable event," in large part because it symbolizes a turning point in the history of a gay rights movement that would soon turn its attention from liberation to survival in the face of political conservatism and the AIDS epidemic (2006, 726). While the White Night Riots in San Francisco's City Hall, which followed the verdict, attest on one level to a dramatic disjunction between legal process and social advancement, the trial also continues to resonate in queer collective memory as a reminder of the deep-rooted homophobia within the criminal justice system, a prejudice evidenced by the long road to the defeat of sodomy laws, the continued use of the homosexual panic defense in some courts, and ongoing debates over adding sexual orientation to hate crimes legislation. The story of the rise and fall of the slain Harvey Milk achieved its commemorative status through a discursive explosion that started with the famous footage of now-Senator Dianne Feinstein announcing the murders on the morning of November 28, 1978, just days after 900 people from the People's Church had drunk lethal Kool Aid in Guyana: "As president of the Board of Supervisors," her shaky voice spoke into the microphones, "it is my duty to make this announcement: Mayor George Moscone and Supervisor Harvey Milk have been shot and killed. The suspect is Supervisor Dan White" (Mann 1997, 151–52). This television footage became the opening sequence of Epstein's famous film—a biography that reproduces the paradigmatic narrative of the fated queer by beginning with Milk's murder before documenting his amazing life story. Almost immediately after the shots rang out in City Hall that November morning, accounts of the homicides began to reverberate through channels of television coverage, newspapers, a recorded confession, courtroom sketches, trial transcripts, an opera, two major book-length accounts, a collection of poems, and, some five years later, two important documentaries that used these sources for their dramatic re-creations—Emily Mann's *Execution of Justice*, published in 1983, and the 1984 Academy-Award-winning documentary film *The Times of Harvey Milk*.[1]

These productions—one a film, the other a docudrama—not only cite trial transcripts, interviews, and newspapers; they also cite each other. Both have become part of a cultural commemoration that has incited the building of schools and centers, the creation of scholarships, the repeal of laws, and most recently, the production of a major motion picture, *Milk*, released after this chapter was written and garnering an Academy Award for Sean Penn.[2] These 1980s documentaries illustrate how the "difficult art" of the drama of the real, as Tony Kushner describes the documentary, undertakes cultural and historical critique as part of its generic structure (Kushner 1997).[3] In this essay, I explore first how jury selection in the Dan White case, as dramatized by Mann's docudrama, evidenced a form of homo-exclusion and erasure that led to a jury purged of queers, an audience already sympathetic to the defendant's tragic role before the trial started. Second, I examine the way Epstein's film transforms the trial's tragic narrative from the story of the heroic Dan White, who cracked under pressure, into a narration of the martyrdom of Harvey Milk. Both works use the tools of theater and film to critique even as they dramatize the defendant's audiotaped confession and his famous plea of diminished capacity, the so-called Twinkie defense, which alleged that the defendant's temporary mental illness resulted from an ingestion of large amounts of junk food.

Throughout my analysis, I rely on Victor Turner's notion that social conflict finds redress through a set of rituals that includes the analogous forums of courtroom and stage (1982, 12). For Turner, the trial acts form of social theater, a dramatic reenactment that replays original acts of violence through performances of confession, judgment, and punishment; it functions as a dramatic enactment that seeks to repair a rupture in the social fabric and return a community to a form of civil order (10). From the more specific perspective of Turner's analogy between social conflict and Aristotelian tragedy, the choral jury of Dan White's peers—removed chronologically and socially from the scene of the crime, sequestered, and cautioned—witnessed a legal reenactment of the 1978 killings, determining varying claims to truth, deciding the mode of redress they felt warranted, parceling out a remedy meant to return San Francisco to its status quo ante, an environment where Aristotelian justice might again prevail, where the laws made by those in power might again be obeyed (Boal 1985, 22–24; Turner 1982, 11). The commemorable resonance of the Dan White case, I will argue, arises in part because the elements of its narrative fit easily within the "existing genre" expectations of tragedy, replete with a protagonist who suffers from a mistake made in the face of misfortune (Armstrong and Crage 2006, 726). In many ways, the archive of the Dan White trial itself represents the first in a long line of dramatic retellings of this segment of gay history, though the defense in the Dan White trial uses the heteronormative criminal justice system to shift the focus from victim to defendant, to make White—not Harvey Milk—this tragedy's protagonist. In what follows, I first provide a historical context for the trial and then explore how subsequent dramatizations by Epstein and Mann retry the Dan White case even as they critique its discriminatory underpinnings. My final section brings critical queer studies to bear on the ideological strategies of these artistic commemorations, asking hard questions about how we can undertake a critique of this homophobic legal history without replicating the very demonization that these docudramas sometimes portray.

Of course, neither the social ritual of Dan White's trial nor the production of these documentaries took place in a historical vacuum. Both arose within a context of an increasing visible and vocal lesbian and gay presence in San Francisco; both narratives, moreover, still continue to function as forms of what Stuart Hall calls articulation and rearticulation—discursive events that transmit and produce power through a complex set of historical practices (Hall 1996; see also DeLuca 1999). These commemorative documentaries have become part of a collective consciousness that continues to influence social practice, as evidenced in the opening of schools, archives, and centers in Harvey Milk's name, as well as the continued push at local and national levels for legislation to protect the queer community. About the same time Dan White was released on parole from Soledad Prison, in 1984, after serving a sentence of about five years, Epstein's Oscar-winning film was released, reliving and retrying these events for thousands of viewers, celebrating Milk's life and martyrdom, and casting Dan White as homophobic antagonist. Was it pure coincidence that White was found dead in his car a year later, his lungs filled with carbon monoxide, a suicide note left for his estranged wife? Whether he ever watched Epstein's film is not known, but this uncanny intersection of culture and event at the very least had the "queer" effect of abrading the boundaries that some critics often draw between artistic representation and what has traditionally been called history.[4] In the early 1980s, White received a "new trial" in the unofficial courts of culture—in Epstein's film and Mann's docudrama, nonfiction accounts that sentenced this "gayslayer" to death by his own hand.

The Historical Context: A Policeman and His Target

This tape should be played only in the event of my death by assassination. . . . I fully realize that a person who stands for what I stand for—a gay activist—becomes a target for a person who is insecure, terrified, afraid or very disturbed themselves. . . . If a bullet should enter my brain, let that bullet destroy every closet door.
—Harvey Milk's Political Will, made on November 18, 1977[5]

Harvey Milk taped his prophetic will after he was elected to the Board of Supervisors, the governing body of San Francisco, in November 1977. The tenacious forty-eight-year-old owner of a camera shop on Castro Street had finally prevailed after three unsuccessful attempts to get elected, his victory attributable in part to a proposition passed the previous year that mandated district rather than city-wide elections for supervisors. As a result, the first African American, the first Asian American, the first single mother (Carol Ruth Silver), and the first "avowed homosexual" came to govern the city, along with Daniel James White, the thirty-year-old Irish Catholic ex-policeman from Visitation Valley, a working-class neighborhood in the southwest part of town.[6] White, a Democrat, had run a law-and-order campaign, framing his appearance with the theme from *Rocky* and big American flags, proclaiming, "I am not going to be forced out of San Francisco by splinter groups of radicals, social deviates, and incorrigibles" (Mann 1997, 164).[7] As part of his law-and-order platform, White opposed building a home for "troubled" youth in his district, but, as one of its first orders of business, the board voted in favor of it, Milk casting the deciding vote in favor after considerable deliberation. White never forgave Harvey for his vote. Though he opposed the Briggs Initiative (a failed 1978 proposition that would have mandated the firing of lesbian and gay teachers in the state), White found himself the lone dissenting vote against Milk's gay rights municipal law and street closings on Polk Street for the gay Halloween parade.

The simultaneous rise to political power of both Harvey Milk and Dan White pointed to a set of social contradictions that lay behind a remarkable decade of gay liberation in San Francisco. When 350,000 marchers participated in the Gay Freedom Day Parade on June 25, 1978, Harvey Milk addressing a rally in front of City Hall with the opening "I want to recruit you," the "new society" of the Castro reached what one historian calls "the high point of its development" (Stryker and Van Buskirk 1996, 70; FitzGerald 1981, 48). In the course of a decade, a plethora of gay bars, bathhouses, theaters, film festivals, newspapers, and political organizations had accompanied one of the most "miraculous" flourishings of culture in queer history (D'Emilio 1992, 87; Armstrong 2002, 113, 115). But the unprecedented turnout for the 1978 parade also reflected a reaction to a growing antigay political campaign, as evidenced by a California ballot measure that sought to keep lesbians and gay men out of public schools. Spawned by Anita Bryant's successful campaign to defeat Dade County's gay rights law a year earlier, the Briggs Initiative was defeated only after an arduous campaign led by Milk. Its viability pointed to an incipient backlash that would become a significant weapon in the Dan White trial.

What Stryker and Van Buskirk call the "cultural visibility" of the gay liberation movement had also made queers ready targets of an escalating incidence of violence in San Francisco (1996, 73). While police raids on lesbian and gay bars were commonplace in the 1950s and 1960s, that antagonism did not disappear in the 1970s, even with the political clout of the tavern owners. Gay murders, bombings of gay business, and arson continued in the 1970s, and the police were sometimes the perpetrators (77). Although Dan White was not openly homophobic, his campaign rhetoric employed terms like "malignancies of society" and social "blight" to code his distaste for public displays of affection and nudity in the queer community. White's disaffection with deviates and liberals, coupled with his allegiance to the police force, tapped into a growing frustration with the openness on Castro Street, a frustration backed by a long history of institutional erasure of and, in many cases, impunity for violent attack. The simultaneous political success of both Milk and White reflects a dialectic that still accompanies the struggle for queer civil rights, its detractors often growing more virulent in response to success, some, like Dan White, well aware of the law's history of unchecked oppression of sexual minorities.

On Friday, November 10, 1978, after ten months in office as a supervisor, Dan White resigned from the board, citing economic and family concerns. Pressured by his friends, he changed his mind a few days later and, on Tuesday, November 14, he asked the progressive mayor for his seat back. At first, Moscone said he would consider the resignation rescinded, but he later discovered the law required him to reappoint White formally. Milk lobbied against the reappointment, and, when Moscone met with White, he received no assurances that White would vote for any of Moscone's plans, including the settlement of an affirmative action lawsuit against the police department. On November 25, the mayor offered the job of supervisor to Don Horazney without informing White, who heard the news from a reporter on Sunday, November 26.

The next morning, White was driven to City Hall by his aide, carrying his loaded .38 in his suit's coat pocket along with a handful of extra shells in a handkerchief. Dropped off at the entrance, he noticed the new metal detectors in place as a result of the recent Jim Jones massacre. He decided to go around the corner and jump through an open window on the side of the building, running up to the mayor's office and asking the secretary if he could see the mayor. When he eventually gained entrance, White shot George Moscone five times, twice in the base of his skull (two so-called coup de grace shots). He then proceeded to his old office, reloaded his gun, and asked Harvey to talk to him, then shot Milk four times, twice in the head. White fled to St. Mary's Cathedral, called his wife, and turned himself in at Northern Station, where his close friend, Lieutenant Frank Falzon, allowed Dan to narrate his confession.

White was tried in San Francisco in May 1979, on two counts of first-degree murder. Lawyers impaneled an all-white jury with no gays and lesbians, and the defense built its defense on the doctrine of diminished capacity, a form of temporary insanity allegedly brought on by White's depression and junk-food binges. The jury found that White lacked the mental capacity to act with malice, convicted White of voluntary manslaughter, and sentenced him to seven years in prison. On May 21, 1979, the White Night Riots left 150 injured and caused millions of dollars in damage to cars and buildings near City Hall. Later the same night, police raids on Castro Street injured dozens of gay men. While commentators have noted that the riots resulted in little social change, given the incipient rise of the Moral Majority in the 1980s, the collective memory of this trial, I argue, has not gone unexpressed in film, theater, and nonfiction (D'Emilio 1992, 93; FitzGerald 1981, 79). These articulations have preserved a common heritage that still marks the bravery of both coming out and queer activism.

Ironically, Dan White received no psychiatric treatment while in prison and was paroled early in January 1984. He was found dead from carbon monoxide poisoning in the garage of his wife's house on October 21, 1985, a patriotic Irish ballad rolling on the cassette player in his car. Before his suicide, White invited his friend Frank Falzon to join him at the Olympics in Los Angeles in 1984. In an interview with the author Mike Weiss twenty years after the murders, Falzon divulged the content of his talks with White during the games. "I was on a mission," White had told his friend. "I wanted four of them. Carol Ruth Silver—she was the biggest snake of the bunch. And Willie Brown [a black Assemblymen and friend of Moscone], he was masterminding the whole thing." White confided to Falzon that his mission was to save San Francisco. During his 1998 interview with Weiss, the retired detective said he wanted finally to get White's confession off his chest (Weiss 1998, 32–33).

A Jury of His Peers

After the Stonewall Riots in New York in 1969, "coming out became a profoundly political act," John D'Emilio writes, one that promised "a huge step forward in shedding the self hatred and internalized oppression imposed by a homophobic society" (85). Ironically, this very same act resulted in disenfranchisement during jury selection in the Dan White trial. As Emily Mann details in her collage docudrama, defense counsel Doug Schmidt systematically asked prospective jurors in the case if they ever "supported controversial causes like homosexual rights," requesting that the judge dismiss for cause potential jurors who answered in the affirmative or suggested that they lived with someone of the same sex (157–58). As Mann dramatizes in Act I of her play, Judge Calcagno's rapid removal of any juror who mentioned even marching in the Gay Pride Parade highlights the court's prejudicial presumption that same-sex attraction was tantamount to bias in the case (157–58). In *Execution* as well in Epstein's film, we learn through the mouth of a TV reporter that the final jury contained no gays, no blacks, and no Asians; it consisted finally of one ex-policeman, the wife of an ex-county jailer, and four women old enough to be Dan White's mother (159). Most of the jurors were middle class, Catholic, and inhabitants of neighborhoods near White's district. As the docudrama's fast-moving montage jumps quickly from voir dire to the transcript of Joanna Lu's TV news report, it raises critical questions about how *coming out* in one venue of San Francisco in 1979 led to a *ruling out* of the constitutional right to participate in the process of trial by jury.

While prosecutor Tom Norman seemed pleased with the rapid impaneling of a law-and-order jury, seeking as he did the death penalty for the homicide of both Harvey Milk and Mayor Moscone, defense counsel Schmidt also expressed the same satisfaction, for he knew his client would "certainly be judged by a jury of his peers" (Mann 1997, 159). One of these attorneys was apparently making a major miscalculation. Both documentaries note the surprising alacrity with which the jury was selected. Judge Calcagno had sequestered more than a hundred prospective jurors and planned on a lengthy selection process, but the twelve were picked within a few days, and the prosecution raised no objection to its composition, in spite of recent California precedent for Sixth Amendment challenges to juries that failed to draw from a "representative cross-section of the community" without excluding any cognizable groups (*People v. Wheeler* 22 Cal.3rd 258, 583 P.2d 748 [1978]). Eight years later, the U.S. Supreme Court would follow *Wheeler's* lead by establishing the so-called *Batson* test, holding that jury composition could be challenged if one side shows a group bias in the selection process and the other is not able to rebut that presumption (*Batson v. Kentucky* 476 U.S. 79, 106 S.Ct. 1712 [1986]). Notably, most of these early cases involve the racial makeup of juries and involve challenges by defense counsel, so the absence of any challenge in the White case is in some ways explicable, but that absence also indicates a telling erasure of the queer community from the consciousness of what was considered a "representative cross-section" for purposes of jury makeup.

The Supreme Court extended the availability of *Batson* motions to the gender makeup of juries in 1994, and, in 2000, the California Court of Appeals in *People v. Garcia* (77 Cal.App.4th 1269, 92 Cal.Rptr. 339) ruled that gays and lesbians are a cognizable class for purposes of the rule that juries must be drawn from a representative cross-section of the community, stating that any exclusion based on their gay affiliation alone violates the state constitution of California. The court held that even though the U.S. Supreme Court does not give the heightened scrutiny afforded gender and race to laws that affect lesbians and gays, the California constitution requires courts to confront the "terra incognita" of sexual orientation. "Trial by jury presupposes a jury drawn from a pool broadly representative of the community as well as impartial in a specific case," Judge Bedsworth noted, and a "'representative cross-section of the community' is violated whenever a 'cognizable group' within that community is systematically excluded from the jury venire" (77 Cal.App.4th at 1275).

In *Garcia*, the California Court of Appeals held that gays and lesbians satisfy the criteria that establish a cognizable group for purposes of jury challenges, relying in part on *Wheeler*, the 1978 case that ironically was available to the bar at the time of the White trial. Cognizance, the *Garcia* court reiterated, comes first when a group "shares a common perspective arising from their life experience in the group, i.e. a perspective gained precisely *because* they are members of that group" (77 Cal.App.4th at 1276). Whereas common residency in a neighborhood for less than a year was insufficient to form a common perspective, in the case of gays and lesbians, the court reasoned, "it cannot seriously be argued in the era of 'don't ask; don't tell' that homosexuals do not have a common perspective. . . . They share a history of persecution comparable to that of blacks and women." The court dismissed the prosecution's argument on appeal that there was no common perspective "shared by Rep. Jim Kolbe (an Arizona Republican), RuPaul, poet William Alexander Percy, Truman Capote, and Ellen DeGeneres." In response to the appeal, Judge Bedsworth claimed that we should not confuse perspective with personality. "Commonality of perspective does not result in identity of opinion," the court stated; the whole point of the *Batson* challenge is to ensure that sexual minorities, "exposed to or fearful of persecution and discrimination," are included in the jury pool (77 Cal.App.4th at 1277). The second prong of the jury test was also met. Cognizance is not available if others in the community were able to represent the gay and lesbian perspective. The court could not see how any other group could understand the gay position, citing a *National Law Journal* poll (November 2, 1998) that found that 17.1 percent of prospective jurors admitted to a bias that "would make it impossible for them to be fair and impartial in a case in which one of the parties was homosexual" (4.8 percent admitted to the same bias against African Americans and 5 percent against women) (77 Cal.App.4th 1277).[8]

Relying on the 1978 *Wheeler* case, the *Garcia* decision provides a metaleptic commentary on the failure of the justice system to take cognizance of the inequity of the jury composition in the case of the People versus Dan White. In hindsight, this structural erasure seems almost willful, given the concurrent flourishing of a gay liberation movement that was commanding national attention. As both documentaries detail, Tom Norman, the veteran prosecutor, may never have even uttered the word "gay" during the entire 1979 trial, remaining silent while the defense lawyer, Doug Schmidt, used his challenges to dismiss every juror connected to "controversial homosexuals." When a young male prospective juror is questioned in Act I of *Execution*, the judge wastes no time in dismissing him for cause. "Do you live with anyone?" defense counsel queries. "A roommate," the juror responds. "What does he or she do?" Schmidt follows up. "*He* works at the Holiday Inn," the juror responds, the emphatic pronoun enough to convince the judge that this juror is too biased to hear the case. Another heterosexual woman is dismissed for cause when she admits to walking in the Gay and Lesbian Freedom Parade (Mann 1997, 158). In the end, Schmidt used his peremptory challenges to dismiss any juror who supported gay rights, and the defense faced no objection from the prosecutor, who seemed stubbornly ignorant of the role bias against queers would play in the case.

Instead, prosecutor Tommy Norman sought jurors who believed in the death penalty, oblivious to the social reality that those in favor of capital punishment are often aligned ideologically with social conservatives, many of whom might be empathetic to law officers who—in a fit of tragic diminished capacity—snap and shoot a homosexual and his gay-friendly mayor. Norman got his law-and-order jury, but it produced an audience for this courtroom drama that was predisposed to a public presumption about the deviance of queers and the innocence of law enforcement (See McMillen 1996, A10). One juror, himself an ex-cop, told the court during voir dire that he believed White had murdered Milk and Moscone because of "social pressure"—a metaphor for the tensions mounting in the city over gay migration. Even before any testimony, he articulated the exact argument defense counsel would use to excuse the actions of his client (Shilts 1982, 309, 324; Weiss 1984, 287).

Ironically, a *Wheeler* challenge to the jury makeup in the White case also depended on the public voice of the district attorney's office, a voice that was largely complicit in the defense strategy of queer exclusion. Most jury challenges come from minority defendants themselves, but in this case the man on trial was not only aligned with the DA's office as an ex-police officer; he was also part of a growing antiqueer faction in San Francisco. Through a successful backlash strategy, the defense argued for a jury of nonqueers, as if antihomosexuals were actually the cognizable minority for purposes of a constitutional challenge. If Harvey Milk's interest as a victim were to be represented, they would have to have come from a prosecution already infused with a structural bias, one that was loathe to recognize, much less argue, that one of San Francisco's finest might have committed a hate crime. While the prosecutor was also admittedly concerned about the interests of the slain mayor, the vigorous refusal to take cognizance of bias against queer perspectives in the jury manifested itself, paradoxically, as a virulent insistence that queer viewpoints were themselves inherently prejudicial in the case.

Defense counsel not only used the jury selection process to equate homosexual causes with controversy; he also convinced the judge that every member of this cognizable class was prima facie biased and therefore dismissible as a trier of fact in a case against the confessed murderer of a gay supervisor. The result was a jury of Dan White's peers—one not only without lesbians and gay men but one also resentful of any controversial queer presence—a jury in fact of antiqueers. The prosecution's decision to erase Milk's gayness in the case only facilitated the defense's exclusion of lesbian and gays from the jury. Under the ideological guise of impartiality, Judge Calcagno impaneled a jury partial to the heterosexual imperative, producing twelve angry straight whites ready to excuse Milk's killer for an act of violence they could understand if not publicly approve.

Emily Mann's collage documentary, *The Execution of Justice*, foregrounds jury venire early in Act I, featuring a screen behind the actors that reads "Jury Selection." The jury phase of the play follows the controversial counterpoint between Sister Boom Boom (a drag queen from the Order of Perpetual Indulgence) and a San Francisco cop who wears a Free Dan White t-shirt. Boom Boom reads from the Book of Dan, which tells the defendant to fear not, for the jury will give him "three to seven with time off for good behavior" while begging for "love, understanding, and forgiveness" when and if some crazy faggot inevitably kills Dan White after he serves time in prison for a few years (Mann 1997, 155). The policeman, on the other hand, is proud to say that Dan White showed "you could fight City Hall," especially a faggot-loving mayor who makes the police handle queers with "lavender gloves" in a city "stinkin' with degenerates" (153–55). The movement from dramatic street lingo to the microcosmic selection of jurors highlights the way the "conscience of the community," as Schmidt called it, has no room in its superego for either Boom Boom or queers closeted in a log cabin. "It appears the prosecution and the defense want the same jury," reporter Joanna Lu opines at the end of Mann's jury selection segment, her statement suggesting not so much collusion as an admixture of erasure and exclusion that left the panoptic space of the trial entirely normalized, absent any abnormal queer presence within the halls of justice (159).

A Man Among Men

> Good people, fine people, with fine backgrounds simply don't kill people in cold blood, it just doesn't happen, and obviously some part of them has not been presented thus far. Dan White was a native of San Francisco. He went to school here, went through high school here. He was a noted athlete in high school. He was an army veteran who served in Vietnam, and was honorably discharged from the army. He became a policeman thereafter, and after a brief hiatus developed, again returned to the police force in San Francisco, and later transferred to the fire department. He was married in December of 1976, and he fathered his son in July, 1978.
>
> —Doug Schmidt's Opening Statement, read by narrator Harvey Fierstein in *The Times of Harvey Milk*; also in Mann 1997, 162

Defense counsel's now-famous opening statement, replete with the implicit heterocentric codes of nativism, sports, militarism, and marriage, begins the trial's dramatization of the Dan White story, a narrative that demonstrates how social rituals reproduce the pervasive trajectory of the Aristotelian tragic paradigm, enacting what Victor Turner calls the "dynamic system of interdependence between social dramas and cultural performances," between—on another level—fiction and fact (1982, 107). Both documentaries incorporate Schmidt's opening statement into their script, illustrating the way trial practice has its roots of theater, in a social drama "that accords well with Aristotle's abstraction of dramatic form." Turner reminds us that social drama harbors "something of the investigative, judgmental and even punitive character of law-in-action, and something of the sacred, mythic, numinous, even 'supernatural' character of religious action—sometimes to the point of sacrifice" (108). Documentary, I have argued elsewhere in relation to *The Laramie Project*, also illustrates the converse; it exemplifies the ways the archives of social reality, including trial transcripts, often reenact the fictional structure of tragic narrative, the story of a hero's *hamartia* or mistake in the face of misfortune—a flaw with which juries can identify, pitying the fallen protagonist/defendant and fearing that circumstance might have driven them to the same violent catastrophe (Charles 2006). The Dan White jury, I have suggested previously, through a reactionary intersection between legal process and social movement, consisted of twelve citizens already predisposed to an antigay bias that they would "never recognize as the obvious prejudice it is" (Ingebretsen 2001, 163). An apt chorus was in place in the Dan White trial well before Schmidt's opening statement.

Augusto Boal calls the Aristotelian trajectory of social drama a theater of the repressed, a kind of homeopathic spectacle that allows an audience (and, by analogy, a jury) to experience an antisocial impulse vicariously, to enact a "purgation of all antisocial elements" through judgment, and then to return to a universe of defined and accepted values, a status quo ante that Aristotle calls the existing parameters of justice. The spectator "enjoys the pleasures and suffers the misfortunes of the character, to the extreme of thinking his thoughts," experiencing the "three changes of a rigorous nature: *peripeteia, anagnorisis,* and *catharsis*; he *suffers a blow* with regard to his fate (the action of the play), *recognizes the error* vicariously committed and *is purified of the antisocial characteristic* which he sees in himself" (1985, 40). For Boal, this process of empathy represents "a powerful system of intimidation," not because it deters viewers from acting immoderately but because it allows them to reenact violence and avoid confronting the social inequities that underlie the narrative (46). By enacting a process of punishment for disobedience to a legal system that itself remains unchanged, under the jurisdiction of those in power, tragedy itself, for Aristotle, represents a form of justice (24).

In a relevant adjustment to Aristotle's *Poetics,* Boal maintains that the classic American Western enlists our empathy not for the almost flawless good guy but for the "bad guy," who gains his admired power through hubris or ambition. Though this antihero often lacks recognition of his fault and feels little regret, the audience is still able to purge its aggressive tendencies by watching this hero's necessary punishment and then returning to its "square dances," to a system that functions conservatively "to diminish, placate, satisfy, eliminate all that can break the balance—all, including the revolutionary, transforming impetus" (Boal 1985, 47). I have argued elsewhere that Boal's revisionary poetics of tragedy applies to the Matthew Shepard murder and *The Laramie Project,* in which the killers McKinley and Henderson become the antiprotagonists in that legal drama. The Dan White trial, I think, pivots on an equally audacious defense strategy: the rewriting of this double assassination as the rise and fall of the All-American boy on the Barbary Coast, the story of a heroic but terribly beautiful young man born to root out the rottenness in the state of San Francisco, who must be punished for a fate that cried out to him, pressuring him to set right the strange queer eruption in the city. Aided by the exclusion and erasure of the love that dare not speak its name from the parameters of the courtroom, Schmidt's performance before the mute and expressionless White, who never testified in the trial, re-created the eponymous young supervisor as nostalgic and idealized heterosexual icon:

> Dan White came from a vastly different lifestyle than Harvey Milk, who was a homosexual leader and politician. Dan White was an idealistic young man, a working-class young man. He was deeply endowed with and believed very strongly in the traditional American values, family and home, like the district he represented. (*Indicates jury*) Dan White believed people when they said something. He believed that a man's word, essentially, was his bond. He was an honest man, and he was fair, perhaps too fair for politics in San Francisco. (Doug Schmidt's Opening Statement in Mann 1997, 163)

Mann's docudrama juxtaposes this transcript with an immediate flashback to an excerpt from one of White's own campaign speeches, in which the young politician details the recent "exodus from San Francisco by many of our family members, friends and neighbors. Alarmed by the enormous increase in crime, poor educational facilities and a deteriorating social structure, they have fled to temporary havens." White calls on the "thousands and thousands of angry frustrated people . . . to unleash a fury that can and will eradicate the malignancies which blight our beautiful city" (Mann 1997, 164). Both speeches work through metonymy and circumlocution to create links among families, honesty, and patriotism while aligning homosexuals with social deterioration and deceit. His proposed eradication of malignancies thinly veils the homo-hate that both the politician and his advocate would later successfully excuse, even justify, during a criminal trial for breach of the law's parameters—an "unleashing of fury" that a jury of White's peers would find entirely understandable.

Mann's juxtaposition of opening statement and stump speech also evinces an awareness of the acute sense of performance that White, the Jack London adventurer and lover of Irish literature, himself demonstrated through his silent composure during the trial and even, as we shall see, during his compelling confession. Mann's docudrama projects the cover of Leon Uris's Irish novel a *Terrible Beauty* during the recitation of Dan's confession in Act One (181), alluding to the defendant's interest in Irish history before and after his imprisonment. White identified with the IRA's Kevin Barry. He masked his savvy behind a "gee-whiz," play-ball front, a dumb-jock veneer that hid calculation within the nonchalant naiveté of a freshman idealist, even though Frank Falzon, who recruited Dan for the Police Officers Association softball team, testified that his best friend was an "exemplary individual" who was "outstanding in pressure situations" not only at bat but also on duty, revealing to an incredulous jury the degree to which White was never out of control of his performance as tragic victim of gay degeneracy (Mann 1997, 192–93).

Confession

By almost all accounts, the prosecution lost control of its case when it played for jurors the taped confession Dan White made after he arrived at Northern Station from the cathedral on the day of the murders. Part of that audiotape is spliced into the screenplay of Epstein's *Times of Harvey Milk*, a film that seeks to take back the social drama and to narrate its own tragic script—the rise and fall of Gimpy Milch, the Long Island Jew who came to San Francisco and fought his way onto the Board of Supervisors until the disturbed, repressed, and homophobic Dan White resorted to violence to sacrifice Holy Harvey. Unlike Mann's play, which primarily documents the trial in surreal pastiche even as it uses parts of Epstein's screenplay, *The Times* is a traditional film, playing on our emotions as it narrates through the crackling voice of Harvey Fierstein the inevitable catastrophe of the heroic Harvey, whose only flaw was his unwillingness to stay in the closet. Flaunt it he did once he left Wall Street. Footage of the gay politician's famous stump speech ("My name is Harvey Milk, and I'm here to recruit you") appears in the film's account of the supervisor's campaign against Proposition 6, the state-wide antigay initiative that was eventually defeated. Milk called himself a dreamer, "wearing the fabled helm of Mambrino" on his head, a reference to the barber's basin donned by Quixote in *Man of La Mancha*, a musical that Harvey claimed gave him his hope, even though he admitted to tilting at windmills with his dreams for a socialist city, hoping nonetheless he might slay "a dragon" in the bargain (Milk in Shilts 1982, 358). The film's depiction of the rise of the Mayor of Castro Street reaches its apogee in footage of the celebratory street fair, where Milk presides and Sylvester sings "You make Me Feel—Mighty Real," returning viewers to the pre-AIDS days of free gay love.

The Times of Harvey Milk starts with the newsreel of Dianne Feinstein's announcement of the murders in 1978, moving retrospectively to Milk's life story and reaching its catastrophe through a build-up to White's revenge on the liberals who were ruining his life. After presenting a biography of Milk and a social history of the rise of the Castro, the film presents footage of a disgruntled supervisor White, who slams his microphone during a hearing and descries the naked men on Market Street during the annual pride parade. Epstein's documentary then depicts the murder by splicing television clips of the chaos in the huge domed Civic Center after the shootings. Nowhere does the film play out its demonization of the disturbed assassin more mercilessly than in its replay of part of the antagonist's confession during the trial.[9] The technique speaks to one of the film's raisons d'être: the portrayal of the defendant's inner anger, his petty hatred for a system that refused to let him have his law-and-order way.

For many in the courtroom, the prosecution's replay of the scratchy audiotape was the cathartic turning point in the trial. It brought more than four jurors and many in the audience to tears of pity, just as Epstein's *Times* would re-create those tears five years later in theaters, this time in sympathy for the heroic victims, rather than for the assailant. White's confession was a twenty-five-minute monologue with few interruptions by the interrogators—a highly unorthodox ramble that included none of the usual probing by homicide investigators, who in this case were the defendant's friends on the force. It gave the prisoner a stage to perform his breakdown, to compose his emotional narrative of the good man making a mistake in the face of a sea of troubles, self-destructing in opposing them:

> We . . ., it's just that I've been under an awful lot of pressure lately, financial pressure, because of my job situation, family pressure, because of ah . . . not being able to have the time with my family. . . . It's just that I wanted to serve the people of San Francisco well and I did that. Then when the pressures got too great I decided to leave. After I left, my family and friends offered their support and said, whatever it would take to allow me to go back into office—well they would be willing to make that effort. And then it came out that Supervisor Milk and some others were working against me to get my seat back on the board. . . .
>
> I could see the game that was being played; they were going to use me as a *scapegoat*, whether I was a good supervisor or not, was not the point. This was a political opportunity and they were going to degrade me and my family. . . . The mayor told me he was going to call me before he made any decision, he never did that. I was troubled, the pressure, my family again, my, my son's out to a babysitter.
>
> (Epstein and Schmeichen, 1986; Mann 1997, 182–83)

In White's confessional mode, reminiscent of the Christian pastoral tradition explored by Foucault, the extraction of secret knowledge becomes isomorphic with presentation of truth, a moment of inward disclosure that awakens spirals of pleasure and power in listeners who gain access to the unfolding secret. Though Foucault elaborated the mechanisms of confession largely in relation to sexuality, in this case a kind *scientia criminalis* gives White's emotional words the prominence of a soliloquy in the dramatic trial, a moment when his inner truth is revealed, when the jurors, fascinated and excited by their access to knowledge, find out about the murderer's true motives (Foucault 1978, 47). The "excitation and incitement" that captured the courtroom, however, did have its sexual component; the words "family" and "pressure" are repeated over and over again as White's voice cracks, signaling in code the squeeze that gay migration had put on him. Even in 1978, "family" had already achieved its overgeneralized status as a semiotic

Figure 13.1. Medium shot of Dan White campaign poster.

banner for antigay crusaders, as White in his stump speeches knew only too well, the geographic and mental pressure he feels attesting to his own heightened sense of social and psychological friction with the growing queer community.

As the defendant's tone moves from whining to sudden composure, White speaks of the "game that was being played" with his future as the mayor vacillated and then decided not to reappoint him after he quit. "They were going to use me as a *scapegoat*," White tells his friend, Lieutenant Falzon. Even at this moment of intense disclosure, the defendant has the capacity to dip into the annals of social ritual to present himself as exemplar of the tragic scapegoat, the sacrificial lamb on whom the sins of society are heaped, his self-exculpation replacing any remorse for the violence done to the actual victims of his political crimes. Such "overriding feelings of victimization" have continued to this day as a frequent litany of right-wing conservatives, who feel vilified for their "moral" bias against homosexuals (Stein 2001, 116). White's 1979 confession shares a backlash rhetoric that has become commonplace in arguments against proposed hate crime and employment discrimination to protect sexual minorities.

In a remarkable cinematic reappropriation, Epstein's film captures White's successful "tragedization" of himself, even as it subverts the defense's version of the truth through its own idealization of the victim Milk. Employing a slow zoom on a black and white close-up of White's face during the tape's soundtrack, the sequence

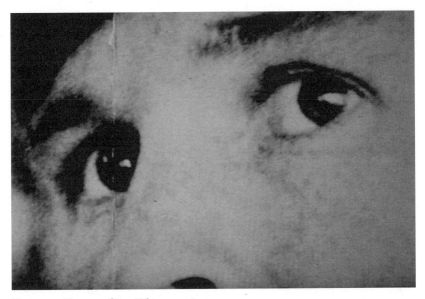

Figure 13.2. Close-up of Dan White campaign poster.

begins with a medium shot of candidate White's campaign poster, which depicts his tilted profile beside the blurred stars of an unfocused American flag (Figure 13.1).

As the tape plays, the crackly sound of the original worn cassette imitates the cracking of the defendant's voice while the prisoner recalls the mounting pressure that led to his reactionary violence. His wife working, his son at a babysitter, White moves his confessional narrative from event (the mayor's failure to call) to his assessment of his own version of "the troubles" via a non sequitur that moves from "troubled" to "the pressure, my family again"—as if he were reminding himself of key phrases. White's high-pitched complaint occurs in the film during a slow zoom into a head shot from the poster, eventually reaching the dark and frightening eyes of the assailant, which is eerily juxtaposed with his emotional confession (Figure 13.2).

The camera gives us an insight into an interior altogether more sinister than the sniffling sound effects that accompany White's story, the sounds the jury heard while the defendant sat quietly at trial, his wife in tears. "A certain glint in his eye that, ambiguous as Mona Lisa's smile, could have been determination or something darker; remorselessness, perhaps," one commentator noted about the poster used in the film, its grainy almost abstract zoom suggesting something awry, askance, almost menacing (Hinckle in Weiss 1984, 256–59).

By the end of the film's sequence, viewers are gazing at two eyes staring back at them, mirroring their own fascination with this glimpse into the unknown interior of the man on a mission.

In the final closeup, the great White hope becomes an abstract pair of eyes—a symbolic composite of black and white specks—the eyes of a man who, after shooting the mayor five times, was "struck by what Harvey had tried to do" and decided to go talk to him. The eyes are neither queer nor straight—just flat black specks on an empty forehead. Dan's disembodied voice continues as he describes his second murder. He had always been "honest" (straight) with Harvey, who was "devious" (queer): "I started to say how hard I worked for it and what it meant to me and my family an' then my reputation as, a hard worker, good honest person and he just kind of *smirked* at me as if to say, too bad an' then, an' then, I just go all flushed an', an' hot, and I shot him." Like his use of the word "scapegoat," White at this moment of supposed loss of control is still able to invoke one of the quintessential gestures that belongs to queer semiotics: the smirk, the simper, that affected manner and smile of the sardonic faggot mocking the tyranny of the All-American boy, who must react like any red-blooded American to such a challenge to his dominance.

Never mind that no prosecution witness was ever called to testify to the butt-patting and smirking with which several officers greeted Dan while they visited him at the police station on the day of the murders, as the documentaries note. In Dan's bless-me-father confessional, Milk's smirk represented a threat that suddenly forced him to take the law into his own hands. Unlike his reaction to the mayor, White gets "flushed" and "hot" before killing the smirker, using his "transitional object" (as one psychoanalyst called his loaded gun) to wipe the smirk off Harvey's insolent face (Epstein and Schmeichen 1986; Mann 1997, 208). White's description of his violent reaction to the smirking queer tapped into the rhetoric of the discredited but still extant homosexual panic defense, in which, even without sexual advance, the presence of a gay man may provoke a legally excusable overreaction in the straight assailant, whose masculinity is threatened (Charles 2006, 5; Chen 2000).

By the end of Dan's confession, the jury, as the film's narrator suggests, was putty in defense counsel's hands, the soliloquy having convinced the straight triers of fact that White was an honest, hard-working heterosexual, watching his city go "downhill" so far he "just couldn't take it anymore." His valiant crusade to save his family from an amalgamation of bleeding-heart liberals and smirking queers had brought a "pressure hitting" him so hard he felt his "skull's going to crack"—a tension the jury itself felt as it cathartically lived through the anguish of Dan White's *hamartia* (Epstein and Schmeichen 1986; Mann 1997, 186). Schmidt would argue in closing that Dan "will be punished. He's going to have to live with this for the rest of his life. His child will live with it and his family will live with it, and God will punish him" (Mann 1997, 233). Epstein's film transvalues this scenario by shifting judgment from the trial's mistaken jury to the filmgoing audience, leaving viewers of this confession scene staring into White's eyes of darkness, eyes that could belong to any frustrated good old boy, any angry American holding a gun without a permit. Harvey's prediction of assassination had come true, and his killer had emerged from the heart of the American dream—the film turning the tragic Danny Boy into a sinister hit man, transforming the protagonist of the trial into antagonist who sacrificed a gay man who had heroically blown open the closet door for a future of queer activism.

Insanity

Even with the evidentiary gift of the prosecution's backfired tape, defense counsel in this famous trial still had to overcome the substantial evidence of premeditation in the White case—the bullets, the window, the reloading, the shots to the skulls' base. The lapse of time between White's decision to visit his victims and the shootings rendered the heat-of-passion defense unviable, so Doug Schmidt had to find another argument to question the premeditation and deliberation needed for first-degree murder and/or the malice (intent to do an unlawful act) that was required to prove first- or second-degree murder, regardless of the evidence of deliberation.[10] To make his case, the young defense lawyer from Michigan turned to his favorite film, Otto Preminger's *Anatomy of a Murder*, for his strategy, adopting not only Jimmy Stewart's folksy aw-shucks act in the courtroom but also relying on the argument developed in Judge Voelker's 1957 novel of the same name (published under the pseudonym Robert Travers).[11] In the film, Lieutenant Manion (Ben Gazzara) escapes murder charges by pleading temporary insanity brought on by associative disorder and irresistible impulse. Schmidt, borrowing some frames from his favorite film, relied on California's diminished capacity law, which recognized temporary insanity as a legitimate defense to a charge of malice.

Although neither Mann nor Epstein cites the influence of Preminger's film on the defense strategy, both include segments about the trial's famous psychiatric testimony that was inspired in part by *Anatomy*. Mann's stage direction suggests a multiple series of witness stands that amalgamate all the defense psychologists. Under the heading "Psychiatric Defense," the docudrama reviews testimony from a handful of hired psychiatrists, Schmidt arguing that White suffered from a hidden case of depression, as evidenced by his periodic estrangement from his conjugal visits to his wife. The defendant was also binging on Hostess products, raising his blood sugar levels dangerously high and causing him to lose the superb definition he displayed in a famous shirtless photo of his shamrocked bicep. "Large quantities of what we call junk food," Dr. Blinder testified, "high-sugar-content food with lots of preservatives, can precipitate anti-social and even violent behavior" (Mann 1997, 214). For Dan White, the "American Dream" had become a "nightmare" because of Twinkies. When Mary Ann also testified that Dan had admitted to her that he didn't like himself, the jury wept again as she broke down on the stand, explaining her grief for her moody husband. One juror after the verdict said that she reached her decision in part because lengthy imprisonment would have left Mary Ann without her husband (Mann 1997, 204).

In an article published after the verdict, the renowned psychiatrist Thomas Szasz decried the defense's experts as "psychiatric perverters of our system of justice" who had perpetrated a "judicial crime" by becoming accomplices, lying through their teeth while the court legitimated their testimony and abrogated its duty to determine guilt and innocence. Szasz's attack on bought-and-sold psychiatrists in his field was coupled with a polemic against the "subtle but persistent appeal to the jury's anti-homosexual prejudice." For the fuming Szasz, "with great skill, Schmidt successfully replaced the reality of Dan White, the moral actor on the stage of life, with the abstractions of White's 'diminished capacity' and his 'background'—and then instructed the jury to focus on those fictions and ignore the facts." Instead of using Szasz's direct polemic, Mann imbeds her critique of the psychiatric defense in two characters: the sarcastic Sister Boom Boom, who reads from the Book of Dan (a mock-biblical tract), and Jim Denman, the defendant's jailer, whom the prosecution decided not to call as a witness. Denman's statements are woven into Mann's postmodern polyphony as a counterpoint to the psychiatric testimony. During the first days after White's arrest, Denman reveals that he saw no tears, shame, or remorse in the Dan White he watched in his cell; instead, he witnessed an inmate who was regularly visited by members of the force who patted him on the butt and stood around laughing (Mann 1997, 228). When the play's prose breaks into poetic form, as it often does, Denman concludes, "if Dan White was as depressed/ as the defense psychiatrists said he was before he went to City Hall,/ then shooting these people sure seemed to clear up his mind." In Execution, Mann exploits the unused testimony of Denman to undermine the credibility of the expert testimony on mental illness, contrasting the abstract expert testimony with the hands-on observation of White's jailer.

Mann's play also employs Sister Boom-Boom, San Francisco's famous Sister of Perpetual Indulgence, to provide a more satirical critique of the almost supernatural power of White's experts to magically recast him from premeditated murderer to unbalanced hero. Boom Boom, who read from the parodic Book of Dan at the beginning of the play, returns again to the testament at the end, raising a

Twinkie in her hands and intoning, "Take this and eat, for this is my defense," enacting a mock consecration that turns the sacred body of the defendant into a Hostess product, conflating religion and psychiatry in a way that comments on how the experts in the case were able to narrate a passion of White that turned him into a tragic scapegoat (Mann 1997, 245).

The science of psychiatry gave defense counsel a link to legal proof that made the narration of his client's "snap" under pressure more than a miraculous transformation. Schmidt's regular repetition of this aural metaphor signaled the un-seaming or "dividing practice" that allowed a jury to accept two diametrically opposed Dan Whites (Rabinow 1984, 11). The antithetical Most Valuable Player and junk-food depressive became linked and disconnected by an ideology of breaking or cracking that employed psychiatric truth to separate the tragic hero's *hamartia* from his *peripetaia*, his radical encounter with a destiny of misfortune. In classical tragedy, the very trait that brings about the hero's downfall is ironically instrumental in his rise to power. In Dan White's case, the same paradox was functioning: his hegemonic masculinity, his embodiment of the good, honest, hard-working white male, was intricately tied to the violence he perpetrated.

For the jury to explain this conjunction of American hero and violent homophobe, the discourse of psychology had to provide a theatrical, almost religious "magic" that could make the irrational rational in the court of law, where reason must appear to prevail. Dan's insanity—caused by what Boom Boom points to as the sacred Twinkie—thus provided the reasonable basis for an idealized subjectivity that was also disturbingly illegal. How else could such "a good policeman, good fireman" with so "much promise" also empty nine bullets into the bodies of two public officials? "Lord God! Nobody can say that the things that happened to him days or weeks preceding wouldn't make a reasonable and ordinary man at least mad, angry in some way," Schmidt argued in closing, invoking what Turner nominates as the "supernatural character" of social ritual, as he asked the jury to feel his client's pain (Mann 1997, 230). God, as Mann's Boom Boom suggests, had forced this reasonable man to snap under pressure, just as the jury of his peers would break down in pity for the destruction of their champion, unable to countenance his action, to understand and excuse it, without rendering this moral man temporarily immoral as a means of purging cathartically their own identificatory impulse. The defense, with the help of the prosecution's queer erasure, had produced the very subject the criminal system purported to denounce: a malicious, premeditated assassin whose identification with the ideals of the American way—including the law and order of criminal justice itself—showed the jury the violent and terrible core of their own ideals. The discourse of psychiatry provided the legal means to separate themselves from this homicidal product of their own ideology. In Mann's work, Sister Boom Boom, the drag queen who unabashedly mixes the sacred and profane, reveals the way religious belief combined with bias against sexual minorities was able to underwrite the "science" of the defendant's expert testimony.

The Queer Mirror

> The challenge of queer theorization, in my opinion, is to return often to those "sites of becoming," and more importantly, *un*becoming, wherein identity is temporarily constructed, solidified, and then threatened or rendered inadequate in its explanatory power.
> —Hall 2003, 109

The final zoom during Dan White's confession in Epstein's film puts us face-to-face with a fragmentary pair of eyes whose identity is finally as frightening in its mystery as it is in its archival context. Those large black dots on the page and screen belong to every viewer, including, I want to posit finally, the queer gaze. When Dan White committed suicide in his estranged wife's garage, in 1985, his death finished a life story that contained striking similarities to features of the archetypal gay narrative, still being enacted in towns everywhere across the country. White was beaten up and called a patsy as a kid; he overcompensated in high school by working out incessantly; he was subject apparently to depression; he was regularly estranged from his wife, whom he married only a few years before he was incarcerated. He was a man among men, an overachiever, at sports and at work. He was sensitive but regularly ridiculed by his fellow board members for his unwillingness to compromise. He hated himself. He was declared insane. He took his own life. These are the components of a pre-Stonewall novel, but they apply as well to a working-class Irish kid from the unglamorous side of a parochial town we idealize as beautiful San Francisco, a part of this city kids coming on a bus from Altoona, Pennsylvania, do not expect to find.

To suggest that this avowed political assassin of the first out elected official in the United States was a repressed gay man, as many, including Supervisors Milk and Silver, speculated, requires a leap of dubious faith I doubt few of us would want to take, but critical queer theory at the very least requires a recognition of the similarities between Sister Boom Boom and the Free Dan White cop protesting too much about having to walk the streets with "bald-headed, shaved-head men with those tight pants and muscles . . . putting their hands all over each other's asses" (Mann 1997, 154). The classification of White as either a latent queer or a homo-hater at some level engages in the very arbitrary construction of identity that has led to the marginalization of lesbian and gay men, establishing within

White's presupposed subjectivity an animus that to some extent justifies our own cognizance as a discrete group in need of a place in the jury pool. Cultural retrials of Dan White as closet case, gay-slayer, or antagonist in the production of the Harvey Milk legend are not immune from the practices of erasure, exclusion, and narrative catharsis that drove the original jury to a verdict of voluntary manslaughter.

How can we maintain the commemorative resonance of this famous case without replicating the practices of vilification that often mark strategies at work in the trial, Epstein's film, and Mann's play? Even as critical queer legal studies exposes the oppression and hostility of the criminal justice system, it must also search for explanations that move beyond the condemnation of homophobes toward a fuller understanding of the social structures that instantiate that bias. The satisfaction viewers of these artistic retellings find in the demonization of White often impedes the possible creation of what Augusto Boal calls a transformative theater as an alternative to Aristotelian tragedy: the promotion of a legislative stage that moves beyond the portrayal of individual heroes and demons towards dramas that call for change, enactments that are integrated into the social fabric and narrate stories of what Harvey Milk called the "only thing we have to look forward to: hope" (Mann 1997, 190). Though Mann's postmodern collage—with its intrinsic critique of jury selection and expert testimony—may do more to focus on the larger concerns of systemic bias than Epstein's film, which follows a traditional generic trajectory, *The Times of Harvey Milk*, through its biographical focus, presents a vision of a pre-AIDS and pre-backlash San Francisco that captures a transformative moment in social and political history.

When Harry Britt, Milk's successor on the Board of Supervisors, announces at the end of Mann's docudrama, "Our revenge is never to forget" (1977, 244), he reminds us that these cultural retellings of crucial events in the gay and lesbian archive act as vigilant reminders of the need to constantly forge new articulations that expose queer bias and call for its denunciation. But "what do you do with your need for retribution?" another character asks Britt, who replies, "We will never forget" (Mann 1997, 245). Mann's staging of the final scene as a stand-off between politicians and rioters outside City Hall anticipates the challenge for queer theorists, like Donald Hall, who envision a form of retribution that neither "solidifies" and therefore replicates violent bias nor avoids taking action against oppression. *The Times of Harvey Milk* captures one form of retribution in its archival compilation of the White Night Riots in City Hall after the verdict, footage of burning police cars and angry queers that can still shock audiences—gay and straight—into recognizing the consequences of social injustice. The film, replayed for new generations of students, acts not only as a part of a collective queer history but also as a social tool, a cultural force that inspires renewed commitment to activism, exemplifying the way artistic commemoration acts as an agent for political change.

By studying these documentaries from the standpoint of critical queer studies, we learn that there is no fixed form of justice, that "not forgetting" must take shape in ways that run the gamut from coming out to protest to making documentaries. Mann's play ends with a tableau reminiscent of both the Stonewall Riots and the encounter that opens her drama: we see Sister Boom Boom in City Hall taunting the police, who raise their shields during the White Night Riots—riots that gain compelling resonance in archival footage of *The Times of Harvey Milk*. These dramatic scenes, with their intermixing of confrontation and questioning about forms of retribution, seem to recognize that dramas of social injustice must be played out, as Victor Turner asserts, in the multifaceted acting of everyday life, whether those scenes take place in the theater, the courtroom, the streets, the classroom, or the bedroom. As the Harvey Milk legacy teaches, we all must struggle inside and outside the halls of justice to ensure that trials always impanel a jury of one's queers.

14 The Gay Divorcée

The Case of the Missing Argument

Ellen Ann Andersen

> Marriage is the first step on the road to divorce.
> —Raoul Felder, celebrity divorce lawyer

ARGUMENTS OVER THE propriety and wisdom of permitting same-sex couples to marry currently occupy a prominent place in the American landscape. The debate has played out in many venues, from courts to legislatures to ballots to books to blogs. No matter what the medium, a core argument advanced by marriage equality advocates has been that without the ability to marry, committed same-sex couples are denied access to a host of legal rights and responsibilities designed to promote familial and economic security. And, indeed, the list of legal rights and responsibilities attendant on marriage is a long one. A Government Accounting Office (GAO) report issued in 2004 itemized 1,142 separate federal benefits, rights, or privileges that depend on marital status. Hundreds of additional rights and responsibilities fall under the auspices of state law. One study of Washington state statutes itemized 423 separate provisions that convey rights or imposing obligations on the basis of marital status (Pederson 2004).

Some of these legislatively accorded rights are relatively trivial or narrowly focused. Under Washington law, for example, various fishing licenses pass automatically and without charge to the surviving spouses of license holders.[1] Others have much broader application. A small sampling of these rights includes the following: married couples may file tax returns jointly, inherit from each other automatically in the absence of a will, share income from governmental programs such as Social Security and Medicare, obtain wrongful-death benefits for a surviving partner, obtain joint insurance policies, and partake of employer-provided benefits such as access to health insurance and pension protections. They are treated as each other's next of kin for purposes of medical decision making, hospital visitation, and burial arrangements. They may take bereavement or sick leave to care for each other or for their children. Importantly, couples can obtain relatively few of these relationship-based rights in any way other than through marriage.[2]

The legal-harms argument can be found everywhere in right-to-marry advocacy. Its centrality is self-evident in litigation, where gay rights litigators such as GLAD

(Gay and Lesbian Advocates and Defenders) and Lambda Legal have taken pains to assemble groups of plaintiffs who have been demonstrably harmed by their inability to marry. In the words of Lambda Legal attorney Susan Sommer:

> The critical role that the client families play is to make real for the court and for the public that this is not just a fight about symbols and theories, that it's about concrete harms that hurt real people. . . . It's also important for us to have plaintiffs with children because the harms to those families are particularly poignant. (Pizer and Sommer 2006)

The eponymous Goodridges in the landmark case *Goodridge v. Department of Public Health* (2003) offer one illustration of the kinds of harms marriage advocates have sought to bring to the attention of courts. They ran into trouble during childbirth. Julie Goodridge had a complicated delivery, resulting in a caesarean section; their daughter was rushed to the neonatal intensive care unit. Even though Hillary Goodridge possessed a health care proxy naming her as the medical decision maker for her partner and their daughter, hospital personnel tried to prevent her from seeing either Julie or their newborn daughter.

The legal-harms argument has also been central to the advocacy of groups operating beyond the judicial arena. The Human Rights Campaign, for example, developed a "Top Ten Reasons for Marriage Equality" list of talking points for marriage activists. The GAO-identified federal rights and benefits of marriage occupy the number one spot, and three other talking points also invoke the legal disabilities faced by same-sex couples.[3] Talking points and persuasive essays authored by other advocacy organizations such as the National Gay and Lesbian Task Force (NGLTF) and Freedom to Marry likewise emphasize the legal rights, benefits, and privileges that are dependent on marital status.

But, for all their emphasis on the legal harms suffered by same-sex couples who cannot marry, advocates have largely ignored one of the most significant and commonly invoked legal consequences of marriage: access to the courts to determine the rights and responsibilities of each spouse after a relationship's dissolution. In a word, divorce. Advocates of marriage equality are all but silent on the subject, and, when they do discuss it, it is largely in a defensive posture as they seek to rebut opposition claims that permitting same-sex couples to marry will increase divorce rates.

It may seem unremarkable to you that proponents of marriage equality ignore or minimize the issue of divorce. After all, who argues that people should have the right to marry so that they can get divorced? Divorce is, after all, the symbolic opposite of marriage, marking its failure, with all the attendant social stigma such failure implies. My aim in this chapter, however, is to convince you that the deployment (or lack thereof) of divorce talk in the struggle over same-sex marriage is actually quite notable because it illustrates the constraints social movements face when they frame their arguments for sociolegal change. More specifically, the deployment of divorce talk speaks to the relationship between legal and cultural frames and the limits of legal arguments as a tool for advancing social movement aims.

I should note here that my interest is not in probing the capacity of the courts to effect progressive change, as important as that question is (see Andersen 2005; Horowitz 1977; McCann 1994; Rosenberg 1991; Scheingold 2004 [1974]). Rather I am interested in the *value of legal arguments as tools for effecting change*.

I proceed in several steps. I begin by briefly reviewing the social movement literature on frames and framing process and by discussing the relationship between legal and cultural frames. I turn then to an examination of the legal frames that construct divorce, showing how divorce is treated as a benefit of marriage and how same-sex couples—and their children—are harmed by their inability to employ divorce law when relationships end. Next, I examine the cultural frames that construct divorce, showing how divorce is treated as a threat to marriage and how opponents of same-sex marriage mobilize that frame to attack the concept of marriage equality. My core argument is that, while legal arguments can be a valuable resource for social movements, legal arguments that diverge too radically from prevailing cultural understandings are ineffective and perhaps even dangerous for movements to employ.

Cultural and Legal Frames

A frame, as Erving Goffman defined the term, is composed of the implicit rules that, by defining the situation, shape the meanings generated by that situation. It is an interpretive schematic permitting people to "to locate, perceive, identify and label" aspects of an event in ways that make them meaningful (Goffman 1974, 21).

In recent years, scholars have made extensive use of frames to explain the progress and outcomes of social movement claims. They have shown that the amalgam of preexisting images, beliefs, interpretive schemas, and values held by a society, that is, a society's *cultural* frames,[4] sets the parameters for the kinds of claims social movements can sensibly make. To be successful, movements must package their claims in a manner that resonates with extant cultural frames. David Snow and his colleagues (Snow et al. 1986) refer to the packaging of claims as the process of frame alignment. The contours of a society's cultural frames necessarily shape the kinds of claims that movements can make persuasively (Benford and Snow 2000; Jasper 1997; Swidler 1995). Mayer Zald (1996), for example, discusses how the feminist claim of a woman's right to her own body makes sense only in a cultural context that embodies notions of individual autonomy and citizen equality.

A central problem facing social movements as they engage in the frame align-ment process is that they are not the only actors on the field. As Robert Benford and David Snow have noted (2000, 626), the very existence of a social movement indicates a dispute within society over some aspect of reality. Those who mobilize in opposition to a movement also engage in frame alignment processes, this time with the specific goal of undermining the original movement's claims. Charlotte Ryan (1991) refers to these interactions as framing contests.

I have argued elsewhere that *legal* frames exist alongside cultural frames and may offer movements an alternative touchstone for persuasive claims-making (Andersen 2005). Legal frames are like cultural frames in that they both shape the meanings generated by a particular act or situation. But the meanings generated by legal and cultural frames may well differ because the categories established by the amalgam of existing constitutional, statutory, administrative, common, and case law (a.k.a. "the law") may differ from the categories established by the amal-gam of existing images, beliefs, interpretive schemas, and values (a.k.a. "culture"). The case of Colorado's Amendment 2 is illustrative of the different meanings that may be generated by cultural and legal frames, even when the conversation in both instances is about the "same" thing, namely civil rights.

In 1992, Colorado voters approved an amendment to their state constitution that repealed all existing gay rights laws and policies in the state and barred any government entity from enacting such laws or policies in the future.[5] Gay rights advocates immediately challenged the amendment in court, and the case made its way up to the U.S. Supreme Court, which struck the law down, finding that it violated the equal protection clause of the Fourteenth Amendment. The dif-ference between the electoral and the judicial outcomes had much to do with the framing of Amendment 2's meaning. During the campaign, opponents of Amendment 2 argued that existing antidiscrimination laws that provided protec-tion from discrimination based on sexual orientation conferred "special rights" on homosexuals on the basis of their "lifestyle choice," as opposed to giving rights to a "legitimate minority" such as African Americans. Phrases such as "protected class status" and "quota preferences" were tossed around liberally, invoking popu-lar confusion about whether existing antidiscrimination laws require preferential hiring and promotion.

The crux of pro-Amendment 2 arguments was that some groups in soci-ety receive rights that are unavailable to others and are therefore "special." Jane Schacter (1994) refers to this framing as the "discourse of equivalents." This approach fell on fertile ground because it tapped into antipathy toward civil rights laws, an antipathy largely based on the popular conflation of laws that pro-hibit discrimination and laws that mandate affirmative action in the context of race.[6] Amendment 2's opponents found themselves unable to defuse the cultural punch of the "special rights" frame within the confines of thirty-second television and radio spots.

When the forum switched from the ballot box to the courtroom, however, much of the persuasive power of the special rights framing dissipated. Although phrases like "special rights" and "protected class status" sound as though they are legal terms, they are legally meaningless—the legal equivalent of psychobabble. Instead, the courts variously examined Amendment 2 in light of equal protection and fundamental rights jurisprudence, requiring Colorado to articulate a rational basis—and at points a compelling purpose—for the law. Moreover, unlike the citizenry, the courts were not confused about the distinction between civil rights protections and affirmative action requirements. Civil rights protections have been used to stop state-sanctioned discrimination against disfavored groups. Affirmative action has been used to ameliorate the effects of past discrimination. From a legal perspective, the concepts are distinct, and the former does not imply the latter. Turning to the courts, then, permitted gay rights advocates to use the legal frames surrounding civil rights law as a way of trumping cultural frames surrounding civil rights law.

The strategy employed by gay rights advocates in the Colorado case is typical. Social change movements commonly turn to legal frames in an attempt to escape, or at least loosen, the straitjacket of cultural frames. Their success in doing so, however, depends on the relationship between cultural and legal frames. The two do not exist in isolation from each other, nor is there a clear hierarchy among them. Judges do not divest themselves of their cultural sensibilities when they don their robes, nor does the existence of those cultural sensibilities make legal doctrine irrelevant. Legal and cultural frames are mutually constitutive: cultural symbols and discourses influence legal understandings just as legal discourses and symbols influence cultural understandings (Andersen 2005, 13–14).

The mutually constitutive nature of legal and cultural frames means that social movements contemplating a turn to the courts must engage in a tricky calculus. When legal and cultural frames overlap completely, the invocation of law offers no comparative advantage to social movements seeking to destabilize cultural frames. But, when legal frames and cultural frames diverge too much, legal arguments may be either ineffective or unwise. Legal decisions are not immune to electoral and legislative backlash directed at reversing or undercutting their impact, a point amply illustrated by the passage of state-level constitutional bans on same-sex marriage in response to judicial rulings supporting marriage equality.

Legal arguments "work" for social movements only when there is a significant but incomplete overlap between legal and cultural frames. At those times, as with the Amendment 2 example, movements may be able to invoke useful legal frames that resonate sufficiently strongly with cultural frames to bring both judges and the general public along. The tricky part, of course, is figuring out where the "sweet spot" of frame overlap is and aligning one's arguments so as to hit that sweet spot. This task is made even more difficult by the ongoing counterframing efforts of opposing groups.

The Legal Context of Divorce

No one marries in order to get divorced, but many couples eventually come to the conclusion that they are unable or unwilling to continue their marriages. Accurate statistics are hard to come by for a variety of reasons, but one good guess is that 41 percent of first marriages in the United States end within the first fifteen years (Census Bureau 2002, 18).[7] The legal mechanism of divorce is designed to ensure that married couples dissolve their relationship in a manner that is reasonably equitable for both partners and in the best interest of any children.[8] It is accomplished through what is known as a separation agreement, which details the relative rights, roles, and responsibilities of each of the divorcing spouses vis-à-vis each other, third parties, and any children.

The great majority of separation agreements are arrived at through what Robert Mnookin and Tony Kornhouser (1979) call private bargaining, where the spouses and their lawyers come to a mutually satisfactory solution to the many issues raised by the dissolution of the relationship and turn to the court only to ratify the agreement. This bargaining is influenced by the prevailing statutory schemes that surround divorce in a given state. When couples are unable to reach a mutually acceptable agreement, the courts step in and set the terms of the divorce in matters ranging from child custody, visitation, and support, to property division, to allocation of other assets and debts, to spousal support, including continuation of spousal health care coverage.

Divorce laws vary widely from state to state, and so it is best to be cautious in summarizing them. That said, state laws can generally be divided into two camps for the purposes of determining what counts as a marital asset and three camps for the purposes of determining how those assets should be divided among the parties.

In the nine "community property" states, all assets accumulated by the couple during the course of the marriage are assumed to be jointly owned in the absence of specific evidence to the contrary and therefore subject to division during divorce.[9] Assets accumulated prior to the marriage are considered to be individually owned and not subject to division. In the forty-one "separate property" states, assets titled solely in one person's name are generally considered to be individual assets rather than marital assets no matter when they were acquired. However, individual assets are sometimes subject to division even if they were acquired prior to the marriage. The marital asset pool subject to division is thus heavily dependent on the state in which a divorcing couple resides.

If states differ in how marital assets are determined, they also differ with respect to the formula for distributing those assets between the parties. In three states, judges are required to divide marital assets equally between the divorcing spouses.[10] In eighteen states, equal division is the default presumption, but judges may deviate from a fifty-fifty split when sufficient equitable considerations warrant it.[11] In the remaining twenty-nine states, judges are given significant discretion to determine how to divide assets equitably. All states list specific factors that judges are to take into account when dividing assets. These factors commonly include the length of the marriage and the standard of living established within it, the relative earning powers, age, and health of the divorcing spouses, the standard of living established during the marriage, and the tangible and intangible contributions of each spouse to the accumulation of marital assets.

While states thus vary widely in the rules they employ to calculate and divide marital assets, all states share the same general goal: to ensure a *normatively just* division of assets that takes into account the myriad ways that each individual spouse contributed to the generation of marital assets, as well as the likely economic impact of the divorce on each spouse.

Generalizing about custody, visitation, and child support laws is as tricky as generalizing about asset allocation procedures, because every state has its own set of laws setting out the appropriate legal standards mediating outcomes in parenting cases. Moreover, because neither parent has a greater right to the care and custody of the children, judges have wide discretion in deciding how to allocate physical custody.[12] The emerging default is to award custody jointly, but judges often divide custodial time unevenly between parents and may even choose to grant one parent sole physical custody. Parents who do not receive physical custody have a fundamental constitutional right to visitation with their children, barring a showing of parental unfitness.

As with issues of asset allocation, judges across all states do share a common goal in custody, visitation, and support determinations, notwithstanding the variety of approaches to achieving that goal: to further the best interests of the child. The idea is that judges are supposed to take into consideration all the relevant circumstances of the particular case at hand and decide that case in the manner best calculated to secure the proper care, attention, and education for the children involved.

There have been many critiques of how divorce laws work in the United States. A number of scholars, for example, have argued that the current system systematically disadvantages women with children (see, e.g., Fineman 1991; Glendon 1987). Others have conversely lamented that the current system disadvantages fathers with children (Adams and Coltrane 2007; Coltrane and Hickman 1992). It takes nothing away from either of those claims to point out that the only system worse than getting divorced is breaking up *without* the ability to get divorced. Same-sex couples who decide to dissolve their relationships are generally not entitled to an equitable judicial determination of their rights and responsibilities under a state's divorce statutes, unless they live in one of the few states where they can marry or enter into a quasi-parallel relationship such as a civil union (Weinrib 2002, 228). Instead, they must turn to what Susan Hassan (2005) calls "piecemeal ways to untangle their lives." This is a difficult process, even for the most well-intentioned of couples. And, unfortunately, breaking up often brings out the worst in people, a phenomenon that is particularly problematic when there is a significant legal or economic asymmetry in the relationship: if only one of them has a legally recognized relationship to their children, for example, or if one partner has put his or her career on hold to raise the children, or one partner has put the other through school, or one partner holds most of the couple's assets in sole title. Under such circumstances, the "weaker" partner generally has little capacity to secure even a remotely equitable settlement in the absence of formal divorce. We turn now to an exploration of the problems of dissolving relationships without benefit of divorce.

Dissolution Without Divorce: On the Question of Property Division

While states have developed detailed statutory schemes for regulating property division at divorce, the rules that govern the dissolution of nonmarital relationships are considerably more ad hoc, varying widely across states and even across jurisdictions within a state. Ann Laquer Estin places the states on a spectrum (2001, 1383), and her categorization is useful here.[13]

Washington, Oregon, and Nevada anchor one end of the spectrum, taking the most equitable approach to allocating property in nonmarital dissolution proceedings. The three states will allocate property *as if* a divorce were occurring so long as the couple's relationship is sufficiently marriage-like.[14] On the other end of Estin's spectrum lie Illinois and Louisiana, whose courts have refused to enforce even written relationship contracts between unmarried couples, holding that to do so would contravene public policy favoring marriage and disfavoring cohabitation.[15]

The rest of the states fall somewhere between the two extremes. All enforce at least some written cohabitation contracts so long as the contract is based on something other than the provision of sexual services.[16] Courts in many states have also enforced oral or implied contracts, although the record here is spottier. In Texas and Minnesota, courts are statutorily prohibited from enforcing them.[17] Courts in at least seven other states have consistently refused to enforce them even though they are not statutorily prohibited from doing so.[18] Courts in twenty-two states have a clear record of enforcing oral contracts, and, of these, the few courts that have considered oral contracts in the context of same-sex relationship dissolutions have upheld them, as well.[19] The record in the remaining nineteen states is mixed or unknown.[20]

One obvious problem with the system as it stands is that the equitable remedies available to the "weaker" partner in nonmarital relationships vary enormously. In several states, couples without the foresight or financial wherewithal to draft written relationship contracts will discover that cohabitation creates no legal obligations regardless of the original intent or verbal agreement of the partners. In these instances, the dependent partner has no capacity to turn to the courts to secure even a remotely equitable division of property and must rely on the good will of the partner in the more secure financial position. Sadly, breaking up often brings out the worst in people. Divorce laws exist in part to ameliorate this tendency and to mitigate the financial losses suffered by the spouse less able to absorb them.

In the states where courts at least in principle recognize implied contracts between cohabiting partners, only Washington, Oregon, and Nevada presume their existence. In all other states, the burden of proof is on the party seeking the assistance of the court to prove that promises of mutual care and support existed. The default presumption is that the individual members of the couple remain independent economic units who may have pooled their resources for purposes of convenience and mutual gain but who did not intend to assume obligations of mutual care and support. Proving the contrary can be very difficult, especially when the respondent has every incentive to argue that an implied contract did not exist.[21] The default presumption about married couples, in contrast, is that they have become an interdependent economic unit; divorce law attempts to divide assets and impose support obligations in a manner that is fair and reasonable to both parties and is solicitous of the need of the more economically dependent of the two.

It is also worth noting that there are limits to the equitable remedies courts can order in the absence of a written contract, even in "good" states such as Washington, Oregon, and Nevada. For instance, judges are not permitted to award alimony to unmarried couples in the absence of a written agreement authorizing it, even though both states permit alimony awards in divorce proceedings.[22]

Couples who have drafted relationship contracts can avoid some of the problems of dissolution without divorce, but contracts, while useful, are no panacea. Like premarital agreements, they require that couples anticipate the possibility of relationship failure at a time when the relationship is strong, something that most couples, no matter what their sexuality, appear unwilling to do (Bowman 2004). They require a moderately high degree of sophistication about the legal consequences of cohabitation. They cost hundreds and sometimes thousands of dollars to draft. They may be radically incomplete, failing to anticipate changes in the couple's assets or economic roles after the arrival of children. They may be drafted sloppily and invalidated by the courts.

An even more significant problem, however, at least from the perspective of a dependent partner, is that contractual agreements are not subject to substantive fairness analysis in the way that separation agreements are. Suzanne Goldberg captures this difference between a contract law-based approach and a divorce law-based approach:

> At best the law treats a same-sex breakup as a business deal between two people about property. It's highly dependent on whatever separation agreement the couple may have. It's done without the complex background rules of divorce, which take into account the context of sacrifices and decisions two people make as a family unit. Divorce rules have evolved to ensure the partner in the weaker financial position is not left penniless. But when gay and lesbian couples separate, it boils down to who holds the purse strings. (quoted in Dahir 2001)

Relationship agreements do not even receive the same level of substantive fairness analysis as antenuptial (also known as premarital) agreements. When courts examine the latter, they generally look to whether the agreement is substantially fair at two distinct points at time: the time of drafting and the time of enforcement. If underlying circumstances have changed dramatically in the interim, judges may set aside certain provisions. Circumstances likely to trigger a court's concern about the substantive fairness of the agreement include unanticipated changes in the economic standing between the spouses (e.g., when one spouse leaves the workforce to care for children). The Minnesota Supreme Court's opinion in *McKee-Johnson v. Johnson* (1989) encapsulates the principle of time-of-enforcement review. Said the court, antenuptial agreements are not valid "if the premises upon which they were originally based have so drastically changed that enforcement would not comport with the reasonable expectation of the parties at the inception" and if enforcement of the agreement would therefore be "oppressive and unconscionable." Courts may also refuse to honor antenuptial agreements waiving spousal support if doing so would cause one party to become eligible for public assistance or otherwise cause substantial financial hardship to one party.

When courts examine cohabitation contracts, in contrast, they generally examine whether the contract is substantively fair at only one point in time: the time of the contract's creation. Changes in the interim are irrelevant. Even then, contracts do not need to be fair, except in the most rudimentary sense: there must be some consideration for both partners, and the contract must not be marred by fraud, misrepresentation, or other forms of dishonesty.

The breakup of Jennifer and Kathy Levinson illustrates the limitations of utilizing contracts to secure relationship rights. The California couple drafted a relationship contract in 1989 that articulated the financial responsibilities of each partner should the relationship end. At the time, the women were both working full time, had similar incomes, and had no children. By the time the couple split, in 2001, much had changed. The couple had two children. Jennifer had given up her job to run the household and raise the children. And Kathy had struck it rich in the dot-com boom. When she retired as the head of E*TRADE in 2000, her estimated net worth approached $40 million (Dahir 2001).

Had Kathy and Jennifer been able to marry or enter into a registered domestic partnership, Jennifer would have been entitled to half the assets acquired during the course of their legally recognized relationship.[23] Had the two drafted an antenuptial contract rather than a cohabitation contract, a judge might well have set aside its financial provisions given the substantial and unforeseen changes in the couple's circumstances. Under the terms of the cohabitation agreement, however, Jennifer had no claim to the lion's share of assets the couple had accumulated in the years between the agreement and the split.

In sum, to the extent that same-sex couples are precluded from marrying or entering into a quasi-parallel legal relationship, they cannot access a legal forum that married couples take for granted: divorce court. This inability to access divorce courts to resolve disputed claims arising from a relationship's dissolution causes precisely the kind of harms that modern divorce law attempts to avoid, allowing one partner to walk away substantially enriched from the relationship and leaving the other financially ruined. The extent of the damage depends on a number of factors, including the actions of the partners themselves, the nature of the economic relationship between them, and the extent to which alternative legal mechanisms such as contract law are available. But, even in the most progressive states vis-à-vis the recognition of nonmarital relationships, same-sex couples are systematically disadvantaged because of their inability to marry.

Dissolution Without Divorce: On the Question of Custody and Visitation

As a matter of long-standing law, a child born during a marriage is presumed to be the child of the mother's husband, whether or not he is the biological father. If the couple subsequently divorces, the ex-husband stands on equal legal footing with the child's mother with respect to all of the legal rights and responsibilities of parenthood, including custody, visitation, and child support. This presumption of legal fatherhood is so strong that even a DNA test establishing the impossibility of an (ex)husband's biological fatherhood does not necessarily release a man from the legal responsibility for child support or remove from him rights to custody and visitation.[24] As Rosato (2006, 83) has noted, justifications for the presumption have included a desire to promote family stability, give children two legal parents, and keep children off welfare.

States that permit same-sex couples to marry or to enter into quasi-parallel legal relationships have universally extended the parentage presumption to encompass the nonbiological parent of children born into the relationship.[25] These states also permit same-sex couples to adopt jointly so that both parents can establish a legal relationship to the child. Couples who subsequently divorce must agree to an equitable arrangement for visitation, custody, and child support or have one imposed on them by the courts.

In the absence of the parentage presumption imposed by marriage or its functional equivalent, same-sex couples who break up often face an entirely different set of legal presumptions when it comes to the care and custody of children born into the relationship. Same-sex couples form families in many different ways, but a common marker of these families is legal asymmetry with respect to children because only one parent has a legally recognized relationship with a given child. Female couples seeking to have children have two basic options: pregnancy or adoption. Male couples may choose adoption or surrogacy. In the context of pregnancy or surrogacy, only one parent will have a biological connection to the child.[26] In the context of adoption, generally one member of the couple formally adopts the child.[27]

The nonbiological/nonadoptive parent (co-parent, for short) may or may not be able to subsequently adopt the child, depending on the state in which the family resides. Eleven states plus the District of Columbia currently permit both members of a same-sex couple to establish parental ties as a matter of statute or authoritative judicial interpretation.[28] (This number includes the states that also permit same-sex couples to marry or form quasi-parallel legal relationships.) Individual judges have granted second-parent adoptions in at least sixteen other states.[29] But such adoptions are essentially prohibited as a matter of statute in four states[30] and have been ruled impermissible by appellate courts in another four.[31] Courts in other states have yet to issue rulings one way or the other.

Second-parent adoptions operate as a sort of surrogate for marriage in the context of relationship dissolution. Because both members of the couple have legal relationships to the child, courts will impose visitation, custody, and child support arrangements on those parents who are unable to reach and maintain a private agreement. But, when only one parent has a legally recognized relationship to the child, the traditional rules governing the care and custody of children break down. Parents have a constitutional right to the care and custody of their children.[32] Third parties do not. Parents have a legal responsibility to financially support their children. Third parties do not.

The only recourse co-parents have if their ex-partners refuse to allow them to share custody or even visit with children they may have raised from birth is to convince a court that they should be accorded "parental status" notwithstanding the absence of legal ties. Their lawyers have advanced a number of different legal theories to support this claim, including psychological, de facto, and equitable parenthood. Lawyers have also raised in loco parentis and equitable estoppel arguments. Each of these legal theories has unique features, but the commonality among them is the idea that if it walks like a duck, looks like a duck, and quacks like a duck, it's probably a duck. Likewise, if it *doesn't* walk/look/quack like a duck, it's probably not a duck. In other words, those who perform the functional role of parents ought to be treated by the courts as parents, because it is in the best interests of the child to do so.

Judicial reactions to these arguments have led to a patchwork quilt of outcomes (Rosato 2006, 76; see generally Miller 2005; Sherman 2005). Courts in Arizona, Florida, Illinois, New York, Ohio, Tennessee, and Utah have generally treated co-parents as legal strangers to their children, permitting the legally recognized parent to shut their ex-partners out.[33] Courts in a few other states, such as Missouri and Wisconsin, have granted co-parents visitation but not custody.[34] Courts in still other states, such as California, Colorado, Pennsylvania, and New Mexico, have held that co-parents have standing to pursue joint custody.[35] The Massachusetts Supreme Judicial Court has established *both* that co-parents without legal ties to children may receive visitation over the objections of their ex-partners *and* that co-parents without legal ties have no duty to support their children, even when they intentionally and purposefully work to bring a child into the world.[36]

In sum, the absence of the parentage presumption provided by marriage can create chaos if same-sex couples split up: chaos felt most acutely by the children but also by co-parents who find themselves shut out of parenting roles and by legally recognized parents who may be unable to secure child support from their ex-partners. Second-parent adoptions can immunize couples from these potential harms, but they are available only in scattered states. Moreover, they can be expensive, costing several thousand dollars to procure. Written parenting agreements are a secondary fallback option, but these too can be expensive and may not be enforceable. Litigation to establish parental rights and obligations in the absence of the parentage presumption is a third possibility in some states, but the costs, both financial and emotional, are tremendous and the outcome uncertain. These are precisely the sort of outcomes the parentage presumption is intended to avoid. And marriage is the mechanism through which the parentage presumption is vested.

Dissolution With Divorce: On the Problems With DOMA

It is worth noting that even in those few states that permit same-sex couples to marry or enter into quasi-parallel relationships, same-sex couples are legally disadvantaged when it comes to divorce. The culprit in this instance is the Defense of Marriage Act (DOMA). Passed in 1996, DOMA limits marriage to different-sex couples for all federal purposes.

Divorces proceed in state court, but they are intertwined with federal regulations. Federal law permits heterosexual couples who are divorcing to sell or transfer assets (such as title to a house) without incurring taxes but does not extend the same courtesy to same-sex couples, a disadvantage that can cost same-sex couples tens of thousands of dollars in additional taxes. Alimony is also treated differently. Payments are tax deductible only when they arise from the dissolution of a heterosexual marriage. Alimony income is taxed at different rates depending on whether the person receiving it left a same- or different-sex marriage.

DOMA also interferes with a couple's ability to divide what is often their largest asset: their retirement plans. Most retirement savings—IRAs, 401k's, 403b's, qualified pension plans, and the like—are regulated by the Employee Retirement and Income Security Act (ERISA). Under ERISA, these savings can be divided between divorcing heterosexual spouses without incurring a tax penalty.[37] Same-sex spouses face a 10 percent tax penalty for early withdrawal and lose the tax-deferred status of all the money that is reallocated. Same-sex couples with sufficient nonretirement assets may be able to trade off to avoid this hit (e.g., Mary gives Mona the house but keeps her retirement fund intact), but, for many couples, retirement savings are the sole form of savings accumulated.

DOMA harms same-sex couples in still other ways. Heterosexual couples can craft separation agreements that require one ex-spouse to continue coverage of the other in an employer-sponsored health care policy. Same-sex couples cannot. Heterosexual couples married for ten or more years prior to divorce are eligible to receive survivorship benefits from Social Security when their ex-spouse dies. Same-sex couples are not.[38]

DOMA can also cause harm in the context of children. *Miller-Jenkins v. Miller-Jenkins* illustrates this harm vividly. Lisa and Janet Miller-Jenkins entered into a civil union in Vermont in 2000, although they were then living in Virginia. In 2002, Lisa gave birth to their daughter in Virginia, and the couple relocated to Vermont. About a year after the couple moved, the relationship ended. Lisa moved back to Virginia with their daughter and petitioned for a dissolution of the civil union in Vermont family court. The court dissolved the union, awarding temporary custody to Lisa and giving Janet visitation rights.

Shortly thereafter, however, Lisa filed a petition in the Virginia legal system seeking a declaration that she was their daughter's only legal parent.[39] Virginia law limits marriage to different-sex couples and prohibits any legal contracts or partnerships that bestow marital rights on same-sex couples.[40] Relying on this law and on DOMA, which permits states to deny recognition of same-sex marriages and civil unions contracted in other states, a Virginia trial court declared Lisa to be their daughter's only legal parent and denied Janet visitation.

The situation then devolved into a series of competing court rulings. Lisa filed a motion with the Vermont court asking it to recognize the Virginia court ruling under the full faith and credit clause of the U.S. Constitution. The Vermont court refused. When Lisa continued to deny Janet visitation, the Vermont court held her in contempt. The Vermont Supreme Court upheld the lower court's ruling, holding that DOMA did not permit Virginia to ignore Vermont's custody determination and did not require Vermont to bow to Virginia's determination. Janet then filed an appeal of the Virginia lower court's decision, arguing that Virginia was required to uphold Vermont's custody determination under a federal law known as the Parental Kidnapping Prevention Act.[41] In November 2006, the Virginia Appeals Court agreed that the Vermont courts properly had jurisdiction in the case, vacating the lower court's ruling (*Miller-Jenkins v. Miller-Jenkins* 2006). The Virginia Supreme Court subsequently declined Lisa's appeal, as did the U.S. Supreme Court, ending the case.

Although Janet's access to her child was ultimately upheld by the courts of both Vermont and Virginia, the case took more than three years to work its way through two court systems, years in which Janet had little contact with her daughter. While *Miller-Jenkins v. Miller-Jenkins* is the first DOMA-based custody dispute to work its way through the courts, it will not be the last time a relationship ends badly and one parent attempts to use the law to shut the other out.

The Case of the Missing Argument

As the proceeding discussion has illustrated, same-sex couples—and their children—are seriously harmed by their inability to deploy divorce law to mitigate the financial and familial damage caused as they disentangle their lives. The American Law Institute (ALI) has recognized the severity of the problems facing same-sex and other unmarried couples who seek to dissolve their relationships. In 2002, it published the *Principles of Family Dissolution*, the product of a decade-long project to offer a unified vision for how states should approach the problems arising from relationship dissolutions. Among the *Principles'* recommendations are that states should accord unmarried couples in committed relationships the same rights as married couples with respect to property distribution, spousal support, and the care and custody of children.[42]

The ALI is an organization of some 1,500 legal scholars and practitioners whose work in drafting model laws has influenced the development of many different legal areas. Its publication of the *Principles* indicates widespread recognition within the legal community that the ability to divorce is a valuable legal consequence of marriage. From this perspective, the "problem" of divorce is not that it occurs too frequently but that only married people have access to it.

Yet, notwithstanding widespread legal recognition of the divorce problem, proponents of marriage equality are all but silent on the subject as they press their arguments for marriage reform. Why? Part of the answer has to do with the legal requirements of standing. As a rule, in order to obtain standing to challenge the legality of a law, would-be plaintiffs must show that they have suffered an actual or threatened injury large enough to give them a real and personal stake in the outcome. Couples who have been harmed because of their inability to divorce (that is, who have already broken up) simply do not have standing in a case seeking the right to marry (that is, the right to bind themselves together in a web of legal rights and responsibilities). However, the fact that the divorce problem cannot be embodied by the lived experiences of the actual plaintiffs does not preclude it from being raised during the course of a lawsuit. To the extent that same-sex couples mirror different-sex couples, some significant proportion will eventually split up, after all, and so face a threatened legal injury. Amici curiae also commonly raise legal issues that are not mentioned by the parties themselves.

The divorce problem could thus easily be raised in right-to-marry cases. And it could certainly be raised in advocacy materials aimed at legislative and popular audiences, such as the Human Rights Campaign's "Top Ten Reasons for Marriage Equality" list of talking points for marriage activists. It is not, however, because the cultural frames surrounding divorce diverge quite radically from the legal frames surrounding divorce. Raising the issue of divorce in such a circumstance would be akin to waving a red flag at a bull, because it would provide opponents with an opportunity to invoke cultural frames as a way of delegitimizing legal claims.

The Cultural Context of Divorce

The evolving cultural meaning of divorce in the United States has been contemplated by a broad array of scholars, pundits, pollsters, and activists (e.g., Basch 1999; Hackstaff 1999; Popenoe 1996; Whitehead 1997). My intent here is not to undertake a comprehensive examination of the cultural frames shaping the symbolic meaning of divorce. Instead, my more modest goal is to illuminate a central paradox in contemporary cultural understandings of divorce: its dual construc-

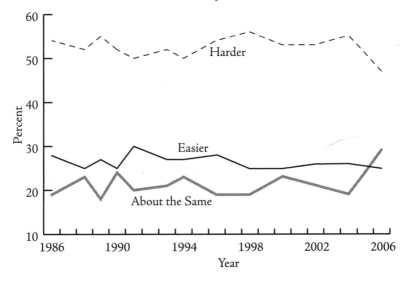

FIGURE 14.1
Should Divorce in This Country Be Easier or Harder?

tion as a morally acceptable individual choice and a pathological behavior that endangers children, the nuclear family, and perhaps even society itself.

Survey data illustrate this complicated cultural reaction to divorce. It is clear that Americans see divorce as an acceptable and sometimes preferable option. For example, two-thirds (67 percent) of adults surveyed in a 2006 Gallup Poll agreed that divorce was "morally acceptable."[43] A 2007 Pew Research Center survey similarly found that 58 percent of adults agreed with the following statement: divorce is painful but preferable to maintaining an unhappy marriage. A much lower percentage (38 percent) chose the alternate option: divorce should be avoided except in an extreme situation. The Pew survey respondents agreed by even more lopsided margins (67 percent to 19) that children are better off if parents who are very unhappy with each other get divorced rather than stay married.[44]

At the same time, Americans are clearly concerned about the prevalence of divorce. The General Social Survey has asked the following question periodically since 1974: "Should divorce in this country be easier or more difficult?" In 2006, 47 percent of respondents opted for "more difficult," while 25 percent chose "easier." An additional 29 percent stepped outside the format of the question to volunteer the response that divorce should remain about the same in terms of its difficulty. This ratio of responses has remained roughly stable over the past two decades (see Figure 14.1).[45]

A 1999 survey by the Pew Research Center revealed similar concerns about divorce. Respondents were read a list of "some changes that have taken place over the last 100 years" and asked to say whether "each one has been a change for the better, a change for the worse, or hasn't made much difference." Fifty-three percent indicated that increased acceptance of divorce was a change for the worse, while only 30 percent saw it as a change for the better.[46]

Contemporary concerns about divorce appear to stem from three premises: that lifelong marriage is both morally desirable and a core societal institution; that divorce is the antithesis of marriage, marking its failure; and that divorce harms children. The first two are long-standing cultural beliefs; the third a more recent phenomenon that draws on social science data indicating that children often experience long-term negative effects when their parents divorce, including increased rates of poverty, the loss or diminution of ties with one parent (usually the father), and an increased likelihood of psychological problems (see, e.g., Blankenhorn 1995; Popenoe 1996; Wallerstein, Lewis, and Blakeslee 2000; Whitehead 1997).

Whether or not these premises are correct is irrelevant. They are central to contemporary cultural conversations about marriage and divorce. Michele Adams and Scott Coltrane (2007) document this centrality in their study of media framing of divorce policy in recent years. They uncover the presence of three distinctive media frames. The first, which they title the *divorce reform* frame, discusses divorce in the context of making it easier or better for the participants, meaning divorcing couples and their children. The implicit assumption is that "access to divorce itself is good or at least preferable to not having such access" (26). This frame was predominant from the late 1960s through 1995 but was then supplanted by two other frames. The transitional *divorce repeal* frame casts divorce as a bad and/or morally evil institution, with the implication that it should be made more difficult to obtain, if not eliminated. The *marriage reform* frame incorporates the divorce repeal frame and adds a solution: "strengthening" marriage through government-sponsored programs offering premarital counseling, marriage education classes, and so on. The marriage reform frame became the predominant frame guiding discussions of divorce policy at the turn of the century, paralleling the Bush administration's efforts to promote two-parent, married, heterosexual families (26–28).

In this cultural context, the danger of linking the need for access to divorce to arguments for the right to marry is illustrated by the eagerness of those who oppose marriage equality to discuss the two concepts in the same breath. A significant strand of oppositional rhetoric expressly links same-sex marriage and divorce. This rhetorical strategy comes in two flavors.

The first is that permitting same-sex couples to marry will undermine marital stability by increasing divorce rates among heterosexuals. Stanley Kurtz is generally considered to be the standardbearer for this proposition. In a series of articles published in the *Weekly Standard* and the *National Review Online*, Kurtz drew on emerging data from the Netherlands, Denmark, Norway, and Sweden to argue that permitting same-sex couples to marry reinforces and accelerates the delinking of marriage and procreation because heterosexual couples in those nations are now less likely to marry and quicker to divorce, even when children are present (Kurtz 2004a–d). This, he argues, is particularly harmful to children but also damaging to familial and social stability in general (see also Fagan and Smith 2004).

The second flavor is that same-sex couples who marry will be much more likely to divorce than their heterosexual counterparts, an outcome that will also harm children, family, and social stability. Arguments about the perils of same-sex divorce appear in many different contexts. For example, opponents of marriage equality regularly file amicus briefs in right-to-marry cases that (mis)use social science data to claim that lesbians and gay men are inherently promiscuous people incapable of sustaining long-term relationships and thus likely to divorce at high rates.[47] Maggie Gallagher and Joshua Baker (2004) have argued that same-sex couples in Sweden divorce at rates far in excess of those of different-sex couples, as has Stanley Kurtz (2004a).[48] Most notoriously, the Reverend Louis P. Sheldon of the Traditional Values Coalition jumped all over Hillary and Julie Goodridge's announcement that they were separating after two years of marriage (and nineteen years as a couple prior to marrying). Here is what Sheldon had to say:

> It comes as no surprise to me that the two lesbians who were at the center of the gay marriage controversy in Massachusetts have now separated after only two years. Homosexual relationships are notoriously unstable—and many male homosexual activists openly admit they don't want monogamous marriages. . . .
>
> The separation of Julie and Hillary Goodridge is tragic not only for their daughter, but for our entire culture, which has been undermined by their successful lobbying efforts to have homosexual marriage legalized in Massachusetts. They have clearly shown just how little they value the institution of marriage and provide a chilling look into what our nation faces if homosexual marriage is legalized elsewhere.
>
> How many two-year-old homosexual marriage break ups will clog our courts and damage children who are caught in the crossfire of warring gay men and women who cannot remain faithful to each other? The institution of marriage is already fragile in America; it is likely that there will be an epidemic of homosexual divorces if widely sanctioned and children will be the primary victims of this dangerous social experiment. (Traditional Values Coalition)

The irony here is that from a legal perspective, the possibility that same-sex couples may split up is an argument *for* permitting them to marry rather than an argument *against* it, if only to give them access to the mechanism of divorce.

From a cultural perspective, however, the prospect that a couple may split up is an argument for preventing them from marrying in the first place. Divorce, from this perspective, symbolizes individual failure and societal degeneration.

As a result, to the extent that proponents of marriage equality have reacted to the divorce framing of their opponents, they have done so from a defensive posture. Several scholars, for example, have taken on Kurtz's analysis of Scandinavian divorce statistics, arguing that heterosexual divorce rates have declined or remained stable in the aftermath of partnership recognition laws and that heterosexual marriage rates have remained stable or increased (Badgett 2004; Eskridge and Spedale 2006; Eskridge, Spedale, and Yttering 2004). Eskridge, Spedale, and Yttering (2004) have also revisited claims about the rate of same-sex divorce, arguing that rates of partnership dissolution among same-sex couples have been relatively similar to, albeit higher than, those for heterosexual couples. Right-to-marry cases have likewise been the site of dueling amici as psychological associations submit briefs attesting to the desire and ability of same-sex couples to form enduring and committed relationships.[49]

Conclusion

The claim that same-sex couples are harmed by their inability to divorce makes good legal sense, and, were legal frames independent of cultural ones, we would expect marriage equality advocates to make it, in court if not more broadly. That this argument is missing reflects the fact that, for all its legal merits, linking marriage and divorce cuts completely against dominant cultural frames constructing divorce as a danger to marriage rather than a benefit of it. Indeed, the disjoint between the legal and the cultural framing of divorce is so large that opponents of marriage equality have been the ones to link marriage to divorce, invoking the specter of same-sex divorce as a reason to deny same-sex couples the right to marry.

The deployment of divorce talk in the battle over same-sex marriage illuminates two central constraints social movements face when they frame their arguments for sociolegal change. First, they must use the master's tools to disassemble (and rebuild) the master's house. How (and whether) they succeed in doing so is necessarily constrained by the nature of the tools in that toolkit (Swidler 1986). Legal frames exist alongside cultural frames in the toolkit and can sometimes offer an alternative touchstone for persuasive claims making. Their utility, however, is dependent on the relationship between the two frames. When legal frames mirror cultural frames perfectly, litigation is unlikely. To the extent that these mirror-image frames are aligned with social movement claims, there is little need to turn to the courts to work around political disadvantages. To the extent these mirror-image frames run counter to social movement claims, litigation is unlikely to be any more successful than other form of social movement activism.

But, when legal frames and cultural frames diverge too sharply, litigation may also be of minimal value because of the *second* constraint facing movements when they frame their arguments for sociolegal change: they do not operate in isolation. Instead, they share the field with opposing forces intent on undermining their claims. These opposing forces draw from the same toolkit. Movements engaged in frame alignment must therefore take into account the likely use opponents will make of specific claims.

In the case at hand, discussing the value of divorce in the context of marriage equality claims is legally sound but tactically foolish because of the distance between the legal and the cultural framing of divorce. I have probably persuaded you that access to divorce is indeed an important benefit of marriage, but I have had the luxury of making my case before an attentive and probably sympathetic audience willing to stick with me through a number of pages. Marriage equality advocates might well have similar success making the divorce-as-valuable claim in a court of law, where there is time to make complicated arguments and the immediate audience—judges—is schooled in the value of legal frames.

But, once an argument is made, anyone may draw on it. And, if legal and cultural frames are far enough apart, an argument that seems sensible in one context may seem outrageous in the other. Opponents would certainly jump all over any "divorce is good" claim by marriage equality advocates, if not in a court of law, then in the court of public opinion. There it would be used to reinforce stereotypes that lesbians and gay men are inherently promiscuous and have little interest in treating marriage as a lifelong commitment.

The danger here arises from the relationship among judicial, legislative, and electoral outcomes. Court cases do not proceed in a vacuum, and courtroom victories do not translate simplistically into more favorable public policies. Judicial decisions can be elided—and even subverted—by legislative and/or electoral responses. The history of right-to-marry litigation provides rich evidence of this process, as opposition forces have drawn on favorable right-to-marry decisions (and sometimes the mere possibility of such decisions) to foment electoral and legislative backlashes. For example, the initial success of an early right-to-marry case in Hawai'i, *Baehr v. Lewin*, was deployed by opposition forces as an argument for the necessity of state and federal statutes to mitigate *Baehr*'s potential impact. Results were impressive. During the course of *Baehr*'s litigation, Congress enacted DOMA, which (a) limited marriage to different-sex couples for all federal purposes and (b) permitted states to refuse recognition to same-sex marriages performed in other states. Thirty states enacted mini-DOMAs during the same time period.

Massachusetts's landmark right-to-marry case, *Goodridge v. Department of Public Health* offered similar ammunition for forces opposed to marriage equality. Within a year of the 2003 decision, thirteen states had amended their constitutions to limit marriage to opposite-sex couples. By the close of 2007, ten additional states had done so.[50]

Marriage equality advocates know that to win—and retain—the right to marry, they must craft legally persuasive arguments that are also culturally resonant, and so they largely ignore the subject of divorce in their discussion of the legal harms facing same-sex couples. They prefer to highlight instead the ways committed same-sex couples are forced to battle legal obstacles as they attempt to fulfill the cultural imperatives of marriage, including caring for each other in times of sickness and health and providing stable and nurturing homes for their children. This is entirely sensible from a pragmatic political perspective. The result, however, is that marriage equality advocates end up eliding the very real problems faced by same-sex couples whose relationships have ended.

There is a romantic view that holds that even the most politically disadvantaged people in society can bring a strong legal claim to court and prevail. The case of the missing divorce argument cuts directly against this notion. It suggests instead that the ability of disadvantaged groups to use the law to effect sociolegal change is subject to a condition we might refer to as the Goldilocks constraint. Sometimes legal and cultural frames are too close, so that litigation is unlikely to produce substantively better outcomes than any other form of social movement activism. Sometimes legal and cultural frames are too far apart, increasing the likelihood that legal "wins" will be undone by legislative and/or electoral responses. Only occasionally is the distance between legal and cultural frames ju-u-s-st right, creating a space for social movements to use legal arguments to advance their aims.

Notes

CHAPTER 1

1. We would like to thank Nancy Naples for comments on earlier drafts of this chapter. The California Supreme Court legalized same-sex marriages in *In re Marriage Cases* in 2008. However, later that year, the voters of California passed Proposition 8, a referendum that attempted to deny same-sex couples the right to marry. Proposition 8's passage throws *In re Marriage*'s effect into doubt. As of this writing, LGBT groups have mounted a legal challenge to Proposition 8.

2. Even today, while de jure segregation has been ruled unconstitutional, children in the United States still attend largely segregated schools (Kozol 2005), and the Supreme Court has recently drastically limited the availability of race-based plans to ameliorate those conditions.

3. As of this writing, same-sex couples are allowed to marry only in the states of Massachusetts, Connecticut, Iowa, Vermont, and Maine. New York has decided to recognize same-sex marriages performed in other states. So as far as state law is concerned, same-sex couples and different-sex couples are treated equivalently in these five states. However, the federal Defense of Marriage Act (DOMA) prohibits the federal government from recognizing same-sex marriages and thus same-sex couples are not treated as married couples for the purposes of the more than one thousand federal laws relating to marriage (Chambers 2001). In addition, DOMA allows other states not to recognize same-sex marriages performed in other states. Thus, a same-sex marriage that is recognized by law will not be considered valid by states other than New York and these five states.

CHAPTER 2

1. Ashley Currier (ashley.currier@gmail.com) is Assistant Professor of Sociology and Women's Studies at the Texas A&M University. This material is based on work supported by grants from the National Science Foundation under Sociology Program Doctoral Dissertation Improvement Grant No. 0601767, the Society for the Scientific Study of Sexuality Student Research Fund, and the University of Pittsburgh International Studies Fund. I would like to thank Scott Barclay, Mary Bernstein, and Kathleen M. Blee for their helpful revision suggestions.

2. I use the more inclusive terms "biracial" and "multiracial" instead of "coloured," though I recognize that the former terms are social constructions. "Coloured" is a "colonially created category for mixed race people" that still retains currency for Namibians (Hubbard and Solomon 1995, 165). Some members and staff of The Rainbow Project I interviewed stated that they did not like to define themselves in terms of racial and ethnic identities because it reminded them of how the apartheid regime structured social, political, and economic relations among Namibians. Despite members' and staff's statements, racial and ethnic differences erupted within the organization and contributed to the creation of schisms among members, leading to the exit of some members from the organization, which I analyze later.

3. In 2004, the Namibian Parliament replaced the Labour Act of 1992 with legislation that omitted the clause prohibiting discrimination on the basis of sexual orientation, which The Rainbow Project (TRP) did not publicly challenge (Fenwick 2005; *The Namibian*, May 7, 2004). I do not elaborate on TRP's lack

of mobilization around the new Labour Act legislation because I am still investigating this.

4. I do acknowledge the importance of ongoing discussions about the globalization of Western/Northern sexual and gender identity categories and their adoption by activists in the global South (Hoad 2007; Katyal 2002; Phillips 2001). African intellectuals have crafted their own complex responses to the use of Western/Northern identity categories, which range from rejection, to wariness, to an embrace of these categories (Massaquoi 2008; Muthien 2007; Nyeck 2008). However, it is beyond the scope of this chapter to review and nuance this debate with the insight it deserves.

5. Dianne Hubbard (2000, 11), a Legal Assistance Centre researcher, supported repealing the sodomy law because the Combating of Rape Act, which was passed in 2000, "expanded the definition of rape to include forcible sodomy."

6. "[A]ll laws in force at the date of independence remain in force until they are explicitly repealed or amended by Parliament, or declared unconstitutional by a competent court" (Hubbard 2000, 1).

7. Official discourse on toughening penalties for sodomy and expanding the criminalization of homosexuality resumed in May 2004, when Justice Minister Albert Kawana repeated that homosexuality was "illegal and criminal" during a parliamentary debate on whether to include a clause in the new Labour Bill prohibiting discrimination of sexual minorities (*The Namibian*, May 7, 2004). Namibian labor laws no longer protect workers from discrimination on the basis of sexual orientation (Fenwick 2005; Hubbard 2007).

8. Ekandjo later clarified that he "did not mean he wanted [gays and lesbians] killed. . . . '[E]limination does not only mean to kill. According to the dictionary meaning, elimination may also mean to ignore, to put aside and [get] rid of'" (*The Namibian*, November 3, 2000).

9. Opposition to the prominence of LGBT rights within the Namibian human rights sector is consistent with how "in most countries, LGBT concerns are ignored even by mainstream human rights groups, which may support them in private" but abstain from publicly embracing LGBT rights publicly as human rights (Ungar 2000, 73).

10. Racial and class differences also affect LGBT movements in other countries (Adam, Duyvendak, and Krouwel 1999; Armstrong 2002; Oswin 2007).

CHAPTER 3

1. Associate Professor, Pace Law School. J.D., B.A., University of Pennsylvania; M.I.A., Columbia University. I remain indebted to those who encouraged the first iteration of this article, Kendall Thomas, Ruthann Robson, and Susan Sturm. Thanks also to Scott Barclay, Mary Bernstein, and Anna-Maria Marshall for organizing this volume and for their many suggestions and to Christa D'Angelica, Michael A. Stevens, and Shamik Trivedi for their invaluable ideas and research support.

2. "The term 'queer,' juxtaposed to the 'lesbian and gay' of the subtitle, is intended to mark a certain critical distance from the latter, by now established and often convenient, formula" (de Lauretis 1991, iv). Section I will further develop the concept of "queer."

3. Anonymous Queers (1990) further describes queer identity: "Being queer means leading a different sort of life. It's not about the mainstream, profit margins, patriotism, patriarchy, or being assimilated. It's not about executive directors, privilege and elitism. It's about being on the margins, defining ourselves; it's about gender-fuck and secrets, what's beneath the belt and deep inside the heart; it's about the night. Being queer is 'grass roots' because we know that everyone of us, every body, every cunt, every heart, and ass and dick is a world of pleasure waiting to be explored. Everyone of us is a world of infinite possibility."

4. "To equate lesbian existence with male homosexuality because each is stigmatized is to erase female reality once again" (Rich 1993, 239). *See also* Ruthann Robson, who continues this critique, arguing that the focus by queer theory on men may perpetuate lesbian invisibility (Robson 1992).

5. In *Price Waterhouse*, the Supreme Court held that "[i]n forbidding employers to discriminate against individuals because of their sex, Congress intended to strike at the entire spectrum of disparate treatment of men and women resulting from sex stereotypes." 490 U.S. 228, 251 (1989) (internal citations omitted); *see also* Riccio v. New Haven Bd. of Educ., 467 F.Supp.2d 219 (D. Conn. 2006).

6. The New York Court of Appeals foolishly repudiated *Braschi*'s progressive legacy when it decided to maintain marriage discrimination in *Hernandez*. The court, using logic that has been ridiculed roundly and deservedly, argued that, for heterosexuals, children could result from "casual, even momentary intimate relationships" that required the "inducement" of marriage to promote family stability. The court distinguished same-sex couples' families as more stable "given the intrinsic differences in the assisted reproduction or adoption processes that most homosexual couples rely on to have children." Deploying reasoning stranger than fiction, the court rejected marriage equality because of heterosexuality's inherent fragility and the implicitly superior organization of same-sex couples' families.

7. I explore lesbian and gay voting rights in *Geographically Sexual?: Representing Lesbian and Gay Interests Through Proportional Representation*, in which I argue that the geographically based districting systems divide lesbian and gay communities that might, under a proportional system, constitute a formidable voting bloc (Rosenblum 1995; Rosenblum 1996).

CHAPTER 4

1. All that said, it is *not* my intent to determine whether or to what extent symbolic frames in LGBT amicus briefs influenced the outcome in the *Lawrence* case. Nor is my objective to generate and test formal hypotheses about the relationship between amicus briefs and Supreme Court decisions more generally. There is a substantial literature in political science and legal scholarship that explores this issue in depth (see Caldeira and Wright 1990; Kearney and Merrill 2000; Songer and Sheehan 1993). This body of scholarship treats amicus briefs as one variable among others— for example, the political and/or judicial philosophies of individual justices, public opinion, and precedent—that influence Supreme Court rulings. While I fully acknowledge and appreciate the insights of this research, it is beyond the scope of this study. Rather, my fundamental aim is to explore how legal briefs in Supreme Court cases serve as vehicles through which social movement activists (and specifically the LGBT movement) construct and deploy collective action frames around the discourse of legal rights.

2. Several recent studies, however, suggest that framing scholars are beginning to take legal institutions and courts more seriously. For example, in their book on abortion discourse, Ferree et al. (2002) acknowledge that the legal "forum" is a key component of the "discursive opportunity structure." Meanwhile, Saguy (2003) demonstrated the central roles played by American and French courts in shaping each society's distinctive concepts and discourses of sexual harassment. Another recent example most relevant to this article is Andersen's (2005) comprehensive analysis of the LGBT movement's litigation strategies at the state and national levels (including Supreme Court cases) that ties directly into the legal and cultural framing literatures.

3. Of course, legal rights frames and discourse are not limited to explicitly legal contexts

like court cases. As many sociolegal scholars have noted, rights discourse often permeates collective actors' identities outside formal legal settings, and even individuals in everyday life often interpret social relationships and conflicts through the symbolic prism of legal rights (see, e.g., Ewick and Silbey 1998; Marshall 2003; McCann 1994).

4. After their defeat in *Bowers*, activists challenged sodomy statutes largely on a state-by-state basis. As summarized by Andersen (2005), LGBT lawyers brought nearly two dozen such challenges in various states and Puerto Rico between 1992 and 2003, with varying degrees of success. Virtually all of them invoked the right to privacy under each state's own constitution; likewise, anywhere a sodomy law applied exclusively to homosexual conduct, equal protection challenges were brought, as well.

5. The Stonewall Law Association's amicus brief appears to be simply a condensed version of the longer and more comprehensive Human Rights Campaign's brief. In fact, five of the seven organizations listed on Stonewall's brief, including Stonewall itself, are also listed on HRC's brief. I thus merge the two under the rubric "Human Rights Campaign et al."

6. This list represents the sequential order in which each symbolic package was presented in HRC's brief.

7. In fact, appellate court evidence suggested that Lawrence was the *only* person in Texas to *ever* be prosecuted for engaging in private, consensual sodomy with another adult.

8. Minimum constitutional scrutiny in equal protection cases simply requires that the state show that the classification is rationally related to a legitimate government objective. However, for certain "suspect classifications" (e.g., those targeting racial minorities or women), the Court has applied "heightened" scrutiny that puts a greater burden on the state to justify the classification.

9. This is unsurprising, given that NLGLA is an organization made up almost exclusively of lawyers and legal professionals.

10. However, Justice O'Connor did write a concurring opinion that Texas's law *should have* been struck down on equal protection, not substantive due process grounds.

CHAPTER 5

1. The ACLU initially resisted requests for legal assistance from gays and lesbians and officially announced support for state sodomy statutes in the late 1950s. By the 1970s, however, the ACLU was actively supporting gay rights and litigating on behalf of these interests (Andersen 2005; Cain 2000).

2. Pinello (2003) included five major gay rights organizations in his analysis: the ACLU; Gay and Lesbian Advocates and Defenders; Lambda; the National Center for Lesbian Rights; and the Service Members Legal Defense Network.

3. Two organized interests were classified as libertarian—the Cato Institute and the Institute for Justice—because each participated in two cases and advanced a "liberal" position in one case and a "conservative" position in the other. In addition, both organized interests self-identify as libertarian organizations.

4. The following state and local lawyer and bar associations participated as liberal one-hit wonders in *Romer v. Evans* (1996): Colorado Bar Association; Connecticut Bar Association; Delaware State Bar Association; Florida Association for Women Lawyers; Gay and Lesbian Law Association of Florida; Illinois State Bar Association; Kansas Bar Association; Lawyers for Human Rights: The Lesbian and Gay Bar Association of Los Angeles; Maine State Bar Association; Massachusetts Bar Association; Minnesota State Bar Association; Minnesota Women Lawyers; National Bar Association; New Jersey State Bar Association; New Mexico Women's Bar Association; New York County Lawyers Association; Orange County Lawyers for Equality Gay and Lesbian; Oregon State Bar; State Bar of Arizona; State Bar of Montana Women's Law Section; State Bar

of Wisconsin Individual Rights Section; and Vermont Bar Association.

5. These membership organizations included the Intervarsity Christian Fellowship, Rejoyce in Jesus Campus Fellowship, the California State Club Association, the National Catholic Committee on Scouting, and the National Club Association.

6. These included the Church of Jesus Christ of Latter-Day Saints, the Ethics and Religious Liberty Commission of the Southern Baptist Convention, the Institute for Public Affairs of the Union of Orthodox Jewish Congregations in America, and the U.S. Catholic Conference.

7. The following one-hit wonders participated as amicus curiae in the Brief of the Alliance of Baptists et al. in Support of Petitioners in *Lawrence and Garner v. Texas* (2003): Alliance of Baptists; Al-Fatiha Foundation; Affirmation: Gay and Lesbian Mormons; American Jewish Committee; Association of Welcoming and Affirming Baptists; Commission on Social Action of Reform Judaism; Disciples Justice Action Network; Equal Partners in Faith; Fellowship of Reconciling Pentecostals International; Gay, Lesbian, and Affirming Disciples Alliance; General Synod of the United Church of Christ; Hadassah, the Women's Zionist Organization of America; Interfaith Alliance; Methodist Federation for Social Action; More Light Presbyterians; Northaven United Methodist Church; Reconciling Ministries Network; Seventh-Day Adventist Kinship International; Universal Fellowship of Metropolitan Community Churches; World Congress of Gay, Lesbian, Bisexual, and Transgender Jews: Keshet Ga'avah. They were joined by the following repeat players: Affirmation: United Methodists for Lesbian, Gay, Bisexual, and Transgendered Concerns; American Friends Service Committee; Axios USA; Brethren/Mennonite Council for Lesbian, Gay, Bisexual, and Transgender Interests; Dignity USA; Integrity; Lutherans Concerned/North America; and the Unitarian Universalist Association.

CHAPTER 6

1. I am grateful to Scott Barclay, Mary Bernstein, Anna-Maria Marshall, and Elizabeth Chambliss for comments on earlier drafts of this chapter. I am also grateful to the parents and lawyers who talked to me. Finally, an award from the University of Denver's PROF fund supported this research.

2. The Tenth Circuit Court of Appeals refused to grant standing to one of the families in *Finstuen v. Crutcher* (2007) because no one had refused to respect the second parent's claim to parenthood.

CHAPTER 7

1. For comments on earlier drafts of this chapter, we thank Mary Bernstein, Anna-Maria Marshall, John W. Meyer, and three anonymous reviewers. This project benefited from a grant to the first author from the Center for the Study of Democracy at the University of California, Irvine.

2. Sodomy laws come in several varieties. The broadest regulate all kinds of "unnatural carnal connections," including anal and oral sex between men, between women, between men and women, and between humans and animals. Most, however, are narrower, regulating hetero- and homosexual or just homosexual anal sex. We use LGB here instead of LGBT because the former is generally more appropriate for the global post–World War II context.

3. Recently, there have appeared several excellent quantitative analyses of different sex-law reforms in the 50 United States (Grattet, Jenness, and Curry 1998; Hawkins and Humes 2002; Kane 2003; Soule 2004).

4. The exact number of countries in the world depends on one's accounting. The year 1945 is our starting point because it marks the end of World War II and the founding of the United Nations. The larger study from which the data examined here are drawn examines global trends and cross-national variations in the criminal regulation of rape, adultery, sodomy,

and child sexual abuse, using both quantitative analyses and case studies of changes in Thailand, Egypt, and Poland (Frank 2008).

5. Most penal codes are written in one of the major colonial languages: English, French, or Spanish. The countries most likely to flout this rule are old and European—Denmark, for example, and Russia. To a great extent, translators helped us incorporate these cases.

6. These last countries, with the spottiest records, are disproportionately small, poor, and peripheral, which may imply that they are unusually likely to have idiosyncratic penal codes. Our experience, however, indicates otherwise. Such countries have little wherewithal for penal-code creativity, and thus they are highly likely to follow standardized world templates (with regard to both sex laws and others). Even for countries with incomplete data, we often have the most crucial information—marking penal-code reforms. Statutory revisions are public matters and thus tend to enter the public record.

7. In 1945, the Canadian law defined buggery or sodomy "as carnal copulation against nature by human beings with each other or with a beast. Since it is a form of carnal knowledge, there must . . . be penetration to some degree, and, where the offence is committed between humans, the penetration must be *per anum*" (Harvey 1944, 194). Thus, Canada's definition included male-male and male-female sex but not sex between women. A later 1985 reform (not shown) further shrank the scope of Canada's sodomy law, lowering the age of consent from 21 to 18.

8. Many nonreforming countries had no sodomy laws to begin with, as discussed later.

9. Table 7.3 shows that the target age of consent for homosexuals declined steadily over time, as youth were granted increasing sexual independence.

10. A growing number of scholars stress the global or transnational dimensions of social movements, including Ramirez (1987), Smith et al. (1997), Keck and Sikkink (1998), and Tarrow (1998).

11. The quotations in this section come from the papers of Robert Alan Roth (Robert Roth Papers, #7325, Division of Rare and Manuscript Collections, Cornell University Library). Roth was an activist and lawyer who lived in New York City. Beyond being involved in the Gay Activists Alliance, a pioneering gay group in the early 1970s, Roth devoted enormous energy to promoting gay groups and publications globally. He compiled voluminous data on the development of the gay movement internationally and published in the U.S. *Gay Yellow Pages* and in the London *Gay News*. Roth corresponded regularly with activists and gay men all over the world.

12. The Declaration notwithstanding, most Enlightenment philosophers continued to depict sodomy as a despicable vice. Nevertheless, they did not believe that penal laws should punish private behaviors, no matter how contemptible.

13. We were initially surprised to find that so few Catholic countries criminalized sodomy in the years 1945–2005. Contrary to our expectations, such laws appeared mainly in Protestant (and Protestant-colonized) lands, having spread through British colonial networks.

14. Berger (1970) posits a long-term shift from "family honor" to "individual dignity" over the whole course of modernity (expressed early on, for example, in France's 1789 Declaration of the Rights of Man). The individualizing impulses released by World War II turbocharged this older process.

15. Similarly, for example, "Nearly five years after the verdict from the European Court of Human Rights saying that the Cypriot law criminalizing sex between gay men [was] a violation of article 8 in the European Convention on Human Rights, the Cypriot parliament finally 21 May 1998 passed a new law that decriminalized gay sex. . . . The international pressure on Cyprus to repeal the ban on male homosexuality had increased up to the parliamentary debate. . . . The Council of Europe ha[d] (again) asked Cyprus to change the law . . . and also Amnesty International

ha[d] released a press statement" (Jensen 1998).

16. Some drafters of the Model Penal Code advocated the controversial notion that homosexuality was an illness and that sodomy was a victimless crime (Bernstein 2003). Of course, the notion of "victimless"-ness is extremely culturally variable.

17. Earlier attempts to form a transnational network of gay activists gave rise to the first International Gay Rights Congress, held in Edinburgh, Scotland, in 1974. The Congress discussed such issues as law, campaigns and publicity, the rights of gay women and young homosexuals, and counseling and befriending. Some participants deemed the Congress a failure, given the disagreement over the inclusion of lesbian issues on the agenda (Robert Roth Papers).

18. In repressed social and political contexts, LGB social movement organizations sometimes operate under the guise of human-rights or personal-rights organizations (see Currier, this volume).

CHAPTER 8

1. This chapter could not have been completed without financial support from the Sociology Department Dissertation Grant and Rackham Discretionary Funds at the University of Michigan. In addition, it benefited from the helpful feedback of Karin Martin, Antony Chen, Anna Kirkland, and Barry Adam.

2. I use "transgender" here as an umbrella term encompassing individuals who express identities such as transvestites, transsexuals, or bois; those who identify as no gender; and those who express multiple genders. I recognize the American and lesbian/gay bias of the use of "transgender"(Namaste 2005). My use of "transgender" in this research also suggests a clear dichotomy between transgender and LGB populations, even though there can be considerable overlap between the two. My grammatical use of "transgender" as an adjective rather than a noun reflects recent varia-

tions in usage (i.e., activists are transgendered individuals, not transgenders).

3. These ordinances usually penalize or discourage discrimination based on sexual orientation and/or gender identity in housing, employment, and/or accommodations. They can be amendments to the existing human or community relations ordinance or to a non-discrimination ordinance; requirements that sexual orientation be included in fair housing laws; or comprehensive nondiscrimination ordinances that includes sexual orientation and/or gender identity along with other protected categories. These ordinances are often called nondiscrimination, gay rights, human rights, or civil rights ordinances. They are frequently placed before the voters by public officials or members of the religious right in either a referendum or an initiative vote.

4. Congressman Barney Frank, one of the authors of the bill, was public about his reasons for refusing to include transgendered people in ENDA (Frank 2007). This transgender exclusion came over the strong and organized objections of almost all national LGBT organizations.

5. There is a growing body of literature on how to get these protections added or passed (Currah, Juang, and Minter 2006; Currah and Minter 2000, 2005).

6. This trend has changed, as sexual orientation language was used in only 16 percent of all transgender-inclusive ordinances between 2000 and 2007 (Transgender Law and Policy Institute and National Gay and Lesbian Task Force 2007).

7. Initially this group was a support group, formed by local lesbian, gay, bisexual, and heterosexual ally activists, that called itself Citizens for Community (C4C). C4C was influential during the subcommittee meetings in the summer of 1997 but renamed itself Campaign for Equality, a ballot campaign committee, in the fall of 1997 when it became clear that the ordinance would pass and be challenged with a referendum or initiative. Until the referendum campaign began, C4C and YCFE were virtually interchangeable organizations, so for the sake of brevity I will refer to both as YCFE.

8. Elsewhere I give a detailed comparison of lesbian, gay, bisexual, queer, and heterosexual allies' attitudes toward transgender inclusion, including the development of these attitudes and their consequences for LGBT organizations created to pass or defend local nondiscrimination ordinances (Stone 2006).

CHAPTER 9

1. But this figure now vastly underestimates the number of local governments that provide such benefits, because in states that have adopted statewide partnership-recognition laws, (e.g., "domestic partnerships" in California, Washington, and New Jersey, "civil unions" in Vermont and Connecticut, and "reciprocal beneficiary" rights in Hawai'i), all local governments must treat such relationships as they treat marriages.

2. Cases where the challenge to the domestic-partnership ordinance did not focus on the authority of the local government to provide the benefits were not included. This exception includes two cases, Oakland, California, and the Chicago, Illinois, Board of Education, where the issue was discrimination against opposite-sex couples because only same-sex couples were eligible for the benefits. In Cleveland Heights, Ohio, the case concerned the acceptance of petition signatures in support of a referendum on the domestic-partnership benefits program, and, in Missoula, Montana, the issue concerned insufficient public notice before adoption of the program. In Anchorage, Alaska, the Alaska Civil Liberties Union sued both the state government and the municipality of Anchorage on equal protection grounds, saying that the denial of domestic-partnership benefits to same-sex couples was discriminatory. The challenge to San Francisco's ordinance requiring contractors with the city to provide their employees with domestic-

partnership benefits or the equivalent is not included because (1) it did not involve the benefits provided to city employees, and (2) the case was heard in federal court and, although there are some claims being made that San Francisco exceeded its authority by regulating contractors in this way, the principal claim is that the city's action is preempted by the *federal* Employment and Retirement Income Security Act (ERISA), not by state law. The issue of federal preemption was never in question in the cases selected for study. A similar case involving city contractors arose in Portland, Maine, where Catholic Charities filed suit (Kesich 2004).

3. The Kalamazoo case, which is pending before the state supreme court, already involves the appellate court overturning the lower court.

4. "Marriage in the state of Louisiana shall consist only of the union of one man and one woman. No official or court of the state of Louisiana shall construe this constitution or any state law to require that marriage or the legal incidents thereof be conferred upon any member of a union other than the union of one man and one woman. A legal status identical or substantially similar to that of marriage for unmarried individuals shall not be valid or recognized. No official or court of the state of Louisiana shall recognize any marriage contracted in any other jurisdiction which is not the union of one man and one woman"(Louisiana Constitution, Article XII, section 15, Defense of Marriage).

CHAPTER 10

1. The term "transgender" in this chapter refers to a person whose gender identity is not congruent with biological birth markers, including chromosomes, gonads, internal and external morphology, hormones, and phenotype. An intersex person is someone whose biological markers are not all clearly male or clearly female (See Blackless et al. 2000, 151).

1. Family Research Council, May 15, 2008, Press Release: "CA Supreme Court Imposes Same-Sex 'Marriage,' Overturning Prop. 22.'"

2. Lambda Legal, May 15, 2008, Press Release: "Lesbian and Gay Couples Win Freedom to Marry in California."

3. "Pivotal Day for Gay Marriage in U.S. Nears; Massachusetts Move to Legalize Weddings May Intensify Backlash in Other States" *San Francisco Chronicle*, May 2, 2004, p. A1.

4. "N.J. Ruling Mandates Rights for Gay Unions," *The Washington Post*, October 26, 2006, p. A1.

5. Related to the more specific legal "naming, blaming, and claiming" associated with disputing and legal mobilization scholarship (Felstiner, Abel, and Sarat 1980–81).

6. While the founder of the AFA is an ordained minister and the group incorporates biblical values into its goals, it does not self-identify as a predominantly religious organization. See http://www.afa.net.

7. Both AFA and TVC have legal divisions, the Center for Law and Policy and the Traditional Values Coalition Education and Legal Institute, respectively, that provide legal representation. While an examination of those groups that have grown out of anti-same-sex-marriage initiative campaigns and/or whose main purpose is to oppose same-sex marriage would be useful, these groups are often particular to specific states and tend to be small and newly formed.

8. The search was performed for all available dates through 2007.

9. Published back to back in a Fall 1989 issue of OUT/LOOK National Gay and Lesbian Quarterly were articles by Tom Stoddard and Paula Ettelbrick arguing for and against prioritizing marriage. The first efforts to force states to legally recognize same-sex marriage actually took place in the early 1970s, in *Baker v. Nelson* (1971) in Minnesota, *Jones v. Hallahan* (1973) in Kentucky, and *Singer v. Hara* (1974) in Wash-

ington (Chambers 2000, 282–88; Eskridge 2002, 4–9). However, each was filed with independent counsel, and same-sex marriage would not reemerge as an issue until the early 1990s with the filing of Baehr in Hawai'i.

10. This is consistent with the coding method adopted by Katherine Stenger in her dissertation *Voices Crying Out in the Wilderness* (2005). Also note that I independently constructed a list of argument frames that is quite similar to the list she developed (Appendix D, 173).

11. From Senator Nickles's testimony at the hearing of the Senate Judiciary Committee on the Defense of Marriage Act on July 11, 1996:

> It has become clear that advocates of same-sex unions intend to win in the lawsuit in Hawaii and then invoke the Full Faith and Credit Clause to force the other 49 states to accept same-sex unions.
>
> Many States are justifiably concerned that Hawaii's recognition of same-sex unions will compromise their own laws prohibiting such marriages. Legislators in over 30 States have introduced bills to deny recognition to same-sex unions ... This bill would address this issue head-on, and it would allow each State to make the final determination for itself.
>
> It seems to me, that the strategy of those advocating same-sex unions is profoundly undemocratic. I cannot envision a more appropriate time for invoking our constitutional authority to define the nature of the States' obligations to one another.

12. On appeal, the state supreme court reversed the trial court's decision in light of the passage of a state constitutional amendment granting the legislature the power to reserve marriage to opposite-sex couples (*Baehr v. Miike* 1999, 92 Haw. 634).

13. See the Web site for the National Conference of State Legislatures at http://www.ncsl.org for information on state initiatives and referenda.

14. Georgia, Kentucky, Mississippi, Okla-homa, Utah, Arkansas, Michigan, Montana, North Dakota, Ohio, and Oregon.

15. "Maybe Same Sex Marriage Didn't Make the Difference," *New York Times*, November 7, 2004, Section 4, p. 5.

16. The state legislature quickly chose the lat-ter, passing a civil union law in December.

17. "In Boston, Community Responds With Anger," *Boston Globe*, September 11, 1996, p. A10.

18. "Protests Oppose Gay Marriages; Pastors Rally as 2 Groups File Suit Against Nickels," *Seattle Times*, March 12, 2004, p. B1.

19. "Courts Could Make Parallels With Old Racial Laws; Deciding on Legality of Same-Sex Unions Raises Similar Issues," *San Francisco Chronicle*, February 29, 2004, p. A11.

20. There is a single institution argument frame attributed to a pro-same-sex-marriage group. "Marriage is the central social and legal institution of our society. As long as gay people are told we cannot marry, we are being told that we are second-class citizens." Evan Wolfson, senior staff attorney for Lambda, in conjunction with a status frame, quoted in "The Right to Marry; Allderdice High School Graduate Is Leading the Way in the Battle to Win Legal Recognition for Same-Sex Mar-riage," *Pittsburgh Post-Gazette*, March 11, 1997, p. F1.

21. "Some States Trying to Stop Gay Mar-riages Before They Start," *New York Times*, March 15, 1995, p. A18, emphasis added.

22. "Gay Rights Affirmed in Historic Ruling; 6-3 Decision: Supreme Court Throws Out Sodomy Law," *San Francisco Chronicle*, June 27, 2003, p. A1.

23. "Legal Gay Marriage on the Nation's Hori-zon; Hawai'i May Be 1st State to Take Step," *USA Today*, January 2, 1996, p. A6.

24. "Bush's Comments Put Ban on Gay Mar-riage on Hold," *Houston Chronicle*, January 25, 2004, P. A6.

25. "On Washington; Barr Spars With Gay Advocate," *Atlanta Journal and Constitution*, December 5, 1996, p. A8.

26. "Pivotal Day for Gay Marriage in U.S. Nears; Massachusetts Move to Legalize Wed-dings May Intensify Backlash in Other States," *San Francisco Chronicle*, May 2, 2004, p. A1.

27. "Backers of Gay Marriage Ban Find Tepid Response in Pews," *New York Times*, May 16, 2004, p. A1.

28. There are two statements coded as hetero-family attributed to pro-same-sex-marriage groups. These are both from Carol Speser, the director of Rainbow Spirit Rising, and reflect the hesitation of some LGBT groups to pursue marriage precisely because of its history as a heterosexual institution. These statements are a clear example of the fact that grassroots organizations can have very different ideas about framing than national organizations (Javors 2001): "While a lot of us feel it's important to validate our relationships, a lot of people don't want to mirror a heterosexual relationship, because there's a lot of inequity there. A lot aren't sure this is the model they want to use." Quoted in "Ontario Precedent Sharpens Focus on Issue of Same-Sex Marriage," *Buffalo News*, June 23, 2003, p. A1.

29. "Children: A Pivotal Issue in Gay Mar-riage Ruling; Judge Stays Decision as Debate Intensifies," *Washington Post*, December 5, 1996, p. A3.

30. "Family Values Groups Gear Up for Battle Over Gay Marriage," *Washington Post*, August 17, 2003, p. A6.

31. "Folksy Grandma Battles Gay Marriage; As Religious Right Musters in Central Valley, Jody Hutchens Emerges as an Unlikely Leader," *San Francisco Chronicle*, April 11, 2005, p. A1.

32. "House Panel Approves 'Defense of Marriage'; Bill Would Restrict Homosexual Unions," *Houston Chronicle*, June 13, 1996, p. A18.

33. "New Jersey Is Likely to Be Gay Marriage Battleground," *New York Times*, June 26, 2002, p. B5.

34. "Gays Seek Right to Marry: Mass. Lawsuit Goes Beyond Civil Unions," *Boston Globe*, April 12, 2001, p. A1.

35. "New Jersey Is Likely to Be Gay Marriage Battleground," *New York Times*, June 26, 2002, p. B5.

36. "Gay Marriage Foes Push Amendment Coalition Formed to Fight SJC Ruling," *Boston Globe*, January 8, 2004, p. B1.

37. "Hawaii Judge Ends Gay-Marriage Ban," *New York Times*, December 4, 1996, p. A1.

38. "Mass. About to Alter Gay-Marriage Debate," *USA Today*, December 26, 2003, p. A3.

39. "GOP Senators Rush to Ban Gay Nuptials in Constitution; Proposal Might Be Ready for Debate Before Election Day," *Houston Chronicle*, March 4, 2004, p. A6.

40. "Gay Rights Battle Not Just About Marriage; State-Backed Civil Unions a Major Step," *Houston Chronicle*, March 8, 2004, p. A1.

41. "Gay Marriage Foes Push Amendment Coalition Formed to Fight SJC Ruling," *Boston Globe*, January 8, 2004, p. B1.

42. This measure of dispersion is equal to $1 - H$, where H is a Herfindahl index,

$$H = \prod_{k=1}^{K} p_k^2$$

and where p is the fraction of the total frames for a given year that each argument frame represents and K is the total number of frames, 21. In other words, the Herfindahl index is the sum of the squared proportions or fractions for each year in the sampled time period.

43. One might expect greater dispersion with higher counts. The correlation between this dispersion measure and count of frames for total frames is 0.51, for frames attributed to pro-same-sex-marriage groups 0.58, and for frames attributed to anti-same-sex-marriage groups 0.64.

CHAPTER 12

1. For example, the Harris Poll, June 13, 2001, found two-to-one support for employment nondiscrimination regulations that cover sexual orientation, from 61 percent to 20 percent to 58 percent to 29 percent, depending on the specific questions asked. Referenda in Hawai'i and Alaska in 1998 showed that 69 percent of voters were opposed to same-sex marriage, a figure roughly equivalent to that found in national polls since then.

2. *Baehr v. Lewin*, 74 Haw 530 (1993) at 567 ff. See also Andrew Koppelman (1988) and Cass Sunstein (1994).

3. Michel Foucault writes that "for millennia, man remained what he was for Aristotle: a living animal with the additional capacity for political existence; modern man is an animal whose politics calls his existence as a living being into question" (1978, 143). Foucault argues that this modern biopolitical preoccupation competes with sovereign power without fully replacing it; he has urged us to "see things not in terms of the replacement of a society of sovereignty by a disciplinary society by a society of government; in reality one has a triangle, sovereignty-discipline-government" (1991, 102). This triangular metaphor suggests that the biopolitical can be seen to coexist with the sovereign, that it need not be read as a replacement of one epoch with another. I argue that this co-extensiveness is critical to understanding the politics of sovereignty today.

4. This advertisement was in support of a measure to repeal Article XII of the Cincinnati charter. That article prohibits the application of nondiscrimination measures to cases of employment discrimination based on sexual orientation.

5. "Bigot Label Fitting for Tucker, Too," *Atlanta Journal Constitution*, October 31, 2004, p. D9.

6. Testimony of Reverend Richard Richardson, U.S. Senate Committee on the Judiciary, "A Proposed Constitutional Amendment to Preserve Traditional Marriage," March 23, 2004.

7. *Salt Lake City Tribune*, October 31, 2004, p. A20.

8. Senator Wayne Allard of Colorado, 150 Cong Rec S7871 (2004).

9. Representative Tom DeLay, 150 Cong Rec H7890 (2004).

10. Bill Lewis, Letter to the Editor, *Portland Oregonian*, October 31, 2004, p. B5.

11. Senator Bill Stephens, "Marriage Law Needs Added Protection," *Atlanta Journal Constitution*, October 31, 2004, p. D11.

12. Statement of Gary Bauer, conservative presidential candidate, in response to the Supreme Court of Vermont decision that recognized the legal rights of same-sex couples. Associated Press, December 27, 1999.

13. In similar ways, Duggan's (2003) notion of "homonormativity" and Yoshino's (2006) idea of a "covering regime" both recognize the cultural value of extreme models of homosexuality for the normative imagination of citizenship today. See also Puar (2006).

14. Bill Lewis, Letter to the Editor, *Portland Oregonian*, October 31, 2004, p. B5.

15. For example, according to one letter writer, pro-amendment forces in Oregon sent a mailer arguing that "gay marriage is more about 'two adults wanting benefits' than 'a husband and wife raising a family.'" Letter of Shirley Catterall, *Portland Oregonian*, October 31, 2004, p. B5. This argument has a genealogy reaching to the original contest of this sort in Hawai'i in the mid-1990s. Eight Hawai'ian legislators argued, in an amicus brief to the court as part of an effort to derail the pending marriage case, "If the State of Hawai'i permits same-sex couples to marry, marriage will be reduced to an entity formed by persons wishing to exploit its tax advantages and other benefits." Posttrial brief, *Baehr v. Miike*, 1996, filed by Representatives Abinsay, Kahikina, Kanoho, Meyer, Stegmaier, Swain, Cachola, and Ward, p. 9.

16. The vote on Oregon's Measure 36 was always expected to be close, and the state experienced a great deal of advocacy on both sides of the issue. The Voters Pamphlet was given to all voters for free by the state; since it did not censor or edit submissions, this document provides a very useful gauge of the rhetorical nature of the campaign.

17. Jim and Elise Self, Eugene, On behalf of their children, in the Oregon Voters Pamphlet, 2004, p. 89.

18. Chris B. and David B., Portland, in the Oregon Voters Pamphlet, 2004, p. 89.

19. Board of Directors of the YWCA of Greater Portland, in the Oregon Voters Pamphlet, 2004, p. 90.

20. Kathleen Sheridan, R.N., in the Oregon Voters Pamphlet, 2004, p. 100.

21. Sue Kaufman and Laura Schulz, Henry's moms, in the Oregon Voters Pamphlet, 2004, p. 101.

22. Polls suggested that the congressional attempt to have courts intervene in a decision that had already been handed to her legal guardian played very poorly indeed. In many polls over the past few years, the vast majority of Americans have answered that the spouse should have final say on matters of the final right-to-die decision. Examples include ABC News/*Washington Post* poll, 65 percent to 25 percent; Fox News, 50 percent to 31 percent; KING-TV, Seattle, 67 percent to 19 percent; *St. Petersburg Times* (Florida), 75 percent to 13 percent.

23. Pub. L. 109-3, passed March 20, 2005.

24. *Congressional Record*, March 20, 2005, H1734.

25. *New York Times*, March 24, 2005.

26. White House press release, March 17, 2005.

27. *Congressional Record*, March 3, 2005, p. H972.

CHAPTER 13

1. Mann's play begins with the same television coverage. Other retellings of these murders include Shilts 1982; Weiss 1984; Wallace and Korie 1994 (opera); *I Promise You This: Collected Poems in Memory of Harvey Milk* 1979; Hinckle 1985. This essay examines as its primary data Mann's *Execution of Justice*, which premiered in 1984, and Epstein and Schmeichen's film *The Times of Harvey Milk* (1986). For a partial transcript of the trial, see

Salter 1991. For background, see FitzGerald 1981, 25–119; D'Emilio 1992, 57–94; Armstrong 2002; and Stryker and Van Buskirk 1996. Gus Van Sant's feature-length film *Milk* (2008) opened to critical acclaim in fall, 2008, after this essay was written. The film, based on the story of Harvey Milk's life and ending with the vigil after his death, does not depict the trial of Dan White.

2. For the Harvey Milk legacy, see Shilts 1982, 347–38. The diminished- capacity defense was repealed by the California legislature after the White verdict.

3. Kushner (1997) is quoted in Dawson 1999, xii. Mann's docudrama has become one of the "exemplar[s] of the staged oral history," a fast-growing body of American docudramas that compile interviews, court transcripts, and other documents to create on-stage dialogue. Anne Deavere Smith, Tony Kushner, and Moises Kaufman have published in this genre (see Claycomb 2003, 99). Because these documentaries incorporate archival materials into their scripts, my reading of this play and film often leads to examination of the historical documents that Mann and Epstein have integrated into their creative productions.

4. "Abrade" is Donald Hall's verb for the way queer studies questions discursive categories, in this particular case, the differentiation between a prevailing notion of ineffectual "art" and the privileged stature of "reality." I follow Hall's universalizing position in this essay. While queer studies, he states, has as its primary focus "putting pressure on simplistic notions of identity and in disturbing the value systems that underlie designations of normal and abnormal identity, sexual identity in particular" (Hall 2003, 14), it also has as its broader scope the intent "to abrade the classifications, to sit athwart conventional categories or traverse several" (13).

5. Portions of Milk's tape appear in Mann 221–22; a full transcript of one of the tapes of the will is transcribed in Shilts 1982, 372–75. Only one copy of the tape contains the famous bullet sentence.

6. Milk followed his lover Jack McKinley to San Francisco in 1968. He grew up on Long Island, living the life of a closeted Goldwater Republican and Wall Street analyst before migrating to San Francisco (see Shilts 1982, 12 ff).

7. White grew up as one of eight children in Visitation Valley, a working-class neighborhood south of downtown. At ten, he was a skinny, crew-cut kid whose round face made him a "patsy" in the eyes of other boys in the neighborhood. Dan's father, Charlie, trained his boy to fight back. White became quarterback at Riordan High and an MVP on the police softball league (Weiss 1984, 49).

8. The *Garcia* court's distinction between commonality of perspective and identity of opinion raises important theoretical questions about the imprecision of ascribing value to minority status, even as Judge Bedsworth's progressive ruling, more than twenty years after the White trial, evidences the law's intransigence in taking judicial notice of what Justice Brennan called queer "opprobrium." Without positing the existence of an essential queer identity, the *Garcia* decision found that J. Edgar Hoover and James Baldwin share a common heritage of persecution sufficient to make them cognizable, if not to themselves, then at least to a court seeking an impartial cross-section of the community for purposes of jury selection. The real existence of past and present homo-exclusion proved convincing and efficacious for Judge Bedsworth, a fact that cannot be overlooked by those critical legal studies scholars who have recently questioned the efficacy of rights claims (see Polletta 2000). For the *Garcia* majority, even the availability of passing in the closet— which widens the philosophical gaps between queers in the world—could not obviate the history of sodomy laws, shock therapy, and, most recently, constitutional amendments. (In 2004 elections, eleven states adopted constitutional amendments prohibiting same-sex marriage. On November 4, 2008, California voters approved Proposition 8, a ballot initiative that amended Article 7.5 of the state constitution to make only "marriage between a man or woman" valid or recognized. Litigation is currently under way to challenge Proposition 8.

9. The film includes parts of the audiotaped confession. A complete transcript is available in Weiss's *Double Play*, 262–70. Mann excerpts it under a banner called "The Confession" (181–87).

10. Mann includes the jury instruction in her play. "In the crime of murder of the first degree, the necessary concurrent mental states are: malice aforethought, premeditation and deliberation. In the crime of murder of the second degree, the necessary concurrent mental state is: malice aforethought. In the crime of voluntary manslaughter, the necessary mental state is: an intent to kill. . . . There is no malice aforethought if the evidence shows that due to diminished capacity caused by illness, mental defect, or intoxication, the defendant did not have the capacity to form the mental state constituting malice aforethought, even though the killing was intentional, voluntary, premeditated and unprovoked" (1997, 240). Though a vexed term, malice is often understood as *knowledge* of an intention to commit an unlawful act. The jurors decided that White's diminished capacity due to mental illness (depression and diet) vitiated his malice.

11. *Anatomy of a Murder* was an immediate success, spending sixty-one consecutive weeks on the bestseller list after St. Martin's published it in 1957. Judge Voelker based the novel he called "pure fiction" on the real-life slaying at the Lumberjack Tavern in Big Bay, Michigan, north of Marquette, in 1952. After Otto Preminger bought the rights, his film opened in 1959, grossing $5.5 million and garnering seven Academy Award nominations. Preminger hired the famed Boston attorney Joseph N. Welch—who had come to fame in the McCarthy hearings—to play the judge in the film.

CHAPTER 14

1. Revised Code of Washington §§ 77.65–77.70 (2004).

2. Under the Defense of Marriage Act (1996), married same-sex couples do not qualify for any of the 1,142 federal benefits. Pub. L. 104–199, 100 Stat. 2419 (Sep. 21, 1996), codified at 1 U.S.C. § 7 (1997).

3. Item #4 expounds on the "hundreds of ways in which state laws take marital status into account, including some of the most basic of human rights." Item #5 discusses the ways in which children with only one legally-recognized parent are legally disadvantaged. Item #8 argues that civil unions are not the legal equivalent of marriages for purposes of the federal rights and responsibilities described in item #1. The entire list is available online at http://www.hrc.org/.

4. The construct I title a society's cultural frames has been referred to by other scholars variously as its myths (Campbell 1988), domain assumptions (Gouldner 1970), or cultural stock (Zald 1996).

5. Colorado's Amendment 2 states: "NO PROTECTED STATUS BASED ON HOMOSEXUAL, LESBIAN OR BISEXUAL ORIENTATION. Neither the State of Colorado, through any of its branches or departments, nor any of its agencies, political subdivisions, municipalities or school districts, shall enact, adopt or enforce any statute, regulation, ordinance or policy whereby homosexual, lesbian, or bisexual orientation, conduct, practices, or relationships shall constitute or otherwise be the basis of or entitle any person or class of persons to have or claim any minority status, quota preferences, protected status or claim of discrimination. This Section of the Constitution shall be in all respects self-executing."

6. For extended discussions of attitudes toward civil rights laws in the context of gay rights see Andersen (2005), Button, Wald, and Rienzo (1997), and Schacter (1994). Similar framing

battles over the meaning of civil rights laws in the context of gay rights occurred in several other states and localities during the same time period. See Herman (1996), Wiethoff (2003), and Witt and McCorkle (1997).

7. For an accessible explanation of the difficulty of calculating divorce rates, see Dan Hurley's article "Divorce Rate: It's Not as High as You Think," *New York Times*, April 19, 2005, p. F7.

8. The process also provides therapeutic benefits, including a legally created and culturally accepted forum for closure as well as a standard nomenclature (DiFonzo 2003, 54–55).

9. Arizona, California, Idaho, Louisiana, Nevada, New Mexico, Texas, Washington, and Wisconsin.

10. California, Louisiana, and New Mexico.

11. Alaska, Arizona, Arkansas, Florida, Hawai'i, Idaho, Illinois, Indiana, Michigan, Nevada, New Hampshire, North Carolina, Ohio, Oregon, Texas, Washington, West Virginia, and Wisconsin.

12. There used to be a tender-years doctrine that favored the mother over the father where young children were involved, but that doctrine has fallen out of legal favor in recent years. See Benkov (1994) and Hitchens (1996).

13. In most jurisdictions that have decided cases, courts now treat same-sex relationships as though they are analogous to unmarried heterosexual relationships for purposes of property division, and so much of the following discussion is applicable to different-sex as well as same-sex couples. It is worth noting, though, that heterosexual couples have the choice whether or not to marry, while same-sex couples usually do not. Moreover, a number of states still recognize common-law marriages, allowing different-sex couples—but not same-sex couples—to divorce even when they never formally married.

14. Among the factors judges utilize to determine the status of the relationship in both states are the intent of the parties, the duration of the relationship, and the pooling of resources and services for joint projects.

Joint assets of couples who meet the criteria are divided equitably upon the relationship's dissolution. Nevada has not yet dealt specifically with the issue of same-sex couples, while Washington and Oregon have.

15. See *Hewitt v. Hewitt* (Illinois 1979) and *Schwegman v. Schwegman* (Louisiana 1983). Several analysts include Georgia in this category although in at least one instance a Georgia court upheld a written contract between cohabitants for the joint ownership and division of property (*Crooke v. Gilden* 1992). Note that all states allow unmarried partners to file petition for partition to divide property held in joint title.

16. Only a handful of states have dealt with written agreements involving same-sex couples, but those have been enforced, as well. See *Estate of Reaves v. Owen* (Mississippi 1999); *Silver v. Starrett* (New York 1998); *Posik v. Layton* (Florida 1997); *Crooke v. Gilden* (Georgia 1992).

17. Tex. Bus. & Com. Code Ann. 26.01(b)(3) and Minn. Stat. Ann. 513.075.

18. Kentucky, Massachusetts, New Hampshire, New Mexico, New York, and North Dakota. Because same-sex couples can now marry in Massachusetts, that state's refusal to enforce implied contracts is less problematic for same-sex couples.

19. See, e.g., Anderson v. Anderson (Indiana 1992), holding that a lesbian couple who had totally commingled their property and otherwise evidenced an intent to function as a single economic unit should be treated in the same fashion as a married heterosexual couple with respect to the equitable division of property. See also Ireland v. Flanagan (Oregon 1981) and Whorton v. Dillingham (California 1988).

20. It may seem odd that a state's policy about enforcing oral contracts could be unknown. However, unless a case is heard at the appellate level, it is usually invisible to researchers, because trial court judgments are not reported in any regular format. In states there is no appellate record concerning the enforceability of oral agreements.

21. See, e.g., *Boone v. Howard* (1989), where a Delaware court rejected a lesbian woman's claim that she and her partner had entered into an oral agreement to live together for business, social, and personal purposes and to pool all of their assets and earnings together.

22. Awards of alimony have declined throughout the United States in recent years, although such awards are still granted in proceedings where one spouse is caring for young children, has limited employment possibilities, or will otherwise suffer severe financial hardship postdivorce.

23. Registered domestic partnerships did not become available in California until 2001 and did not contain a divorce provision until 2005. In 2008, California became the second state to permit same-sex couples to marry. California voters, however, quickly passed a constitutional amendment that restricted marriage to opposite-sex couples. The constitutionality of that vote has been challenged in court.

24. See, e.g., *Love v. Love* (Nevada 1998), finding a husband liable for child support notwithstanding a DNA test establishing that he was not the child's father.

25. For example, 15 Vt. Stat. Ann. tit. 15, § 1204 (2004) states: "The rights of parties to a civil union, with respect to a child of whom either becomes the natural parent during the term of the civil union, shall be the same as those of a married couple, with respect to a child of whom either spouse becomes the natural parent during the marriage."

26. It is possible for one woman to donate an egg and the other to carry the child to term. In these instances, the child will have both a biological mother and a gestational mother.

27. In eleven states plus the District of Columbia, the couple may adopt the child jointly. The states currently permitting joint adoption are listed in the following footnote.

28. The states are California, Connecticut, Illinois, Indiana, Massachusetts, Maine, New Jersey, New York, Oregon, Pennsylvania and Vermont.

29. Alabama, Alaska, Delaware, Georgia, Hawai'i, Iowa, Maryland, Michigan, Missouri, Minnesota, Nevada, New Hampshire, New Mexico, Rhode Island, Texas and Washington. It is possible that trial courts in other states have also granted such second-parent adoptions. Records of family court proceedings are sometimes sealed. For regularly updated information about adoption laws, see the Lambda Legal Defense and Education Fund (www.lldef.org) or the Human Rights Campaign (www.hrc.org).

30. Arkansas and Utah prohibit all cohabitating couples who are unmarried from adopting. Mississippi specifically prohibits same-sex couples from adopting. Florida prohibits all lesbians and gay men from adopting. The legal status of Florida's law, however, is unclear. In late November 2008, as this book was going to press, a Miami-Dade Circuit Court judge ruled that the law violated the Florida constitution's guarantee of equal protection. The state has announced its attention to appeal the ruling. See Almanzar (2008).

31. In re Adoption of *T.K.J. and K.A.K,* 931 P.2d 488 (Colorado 1996); *In re Adoption of Luke* (Nebraska 2002); *In re Adoption of Doe* (Ohio 1998); *Interest of Angel Lace M.* (Wisconsin 1994).

32. See *Stanley v. Illinois* (1972), in which the Supreme Court held that the right to raise one's children was an essential and basic civil right. See also *Santosky v. Kramer* (1982), finding a fundamental liberty interest of parents in the care, custody, and management of their children.

33. See *Janis C. v. Christine T.* (New York 2002); *In re Cheyenne Madison Jones* (Ohio 2002); *In re the Matter of Visitation with C.B.L.* (Illinois 1999); *Kazmierazak v. Query* (Florida 1999); *Thomas v. Thomas* (Arizona 2002).

34. *Matter of T.L.* (Missouri 1996); *In re Custody of HSH-K* (Wisconsin 1995).

35. For example, a Colorado appellate court recently held that the former same-sex partner of an adoptive parent had standing to seek

custody and visitation rights as a psychological parent given the duration, closeness, and
continuation of her relationship with the
child and evidence that emotional harm to
the child would accrue if the relationship was
terminated (*In re E.L.M.C.*, 2004).

36. See *E.N.O. v. L.M.M.* (Massachusetts
1999) and *T.F. v. B.L.* (Massachusetts 2004).

37. 29 U.S.C. 1001 et seq.; 26 U.S.C. 401(a)(11),
414(p) (qualified plans); 5 U.S.C. 8339(j),(i)
(Federal Civil Service).

38. Wyatt Buchanan (*San Francisco Chronicle*,
September 25, 2006, p. B1, provides a useful
summary of the many problems faced by
divorcing same-sex couples because of the
federal government's refusal to recognize
same-sex marriages.

39. Apparently, Lisa had renounced her homosexuality by this point. She was represented by
the American Center for Law and Justice.

40. Va. Code § 20-45.3.

41. 28 U.S.C. § 1738A.

42. For an extended discussion of the
Principles of Family Dissolution, see the *Duke
Journal of Family Law*'s special edition on the
subject (2001). No state has adopted the ALI's
Principles as of this writing.

43. Gallup Poll, May 8–11, 2006. N = 1,002
nationwide. Margin of error ±3%.

44. Pew Research Center for the People and
the Press survey. February 16–March 14, 2007.
N = 2,020 adults nationwide. Margin of
error±3%.

45. Teenagers report even higher levels of
discomfort with the incidence of divorce. The
Gallup Youth Survey has asked the following
question since 1977: "Generally speaking, do
you think it is too easy or not easy enough
for people in this country to get divorced?" In
recent years, the percentage of teens who think
that it is too easy to get divorced has hovered
around 75 percent.

46. Pew Research Center for the People and
the Press survey conducted by Princeton Survey Research Associates. April 6–May 6, 1999.
N = 1,546 adults nationwide. Margin of error
±3%. Each question in the "better or worse"
battery was asked of half the respondents.

47. See, e.g., Brief of the Family Research
Council as Amicus Curiae in Support of
Defendants-Appellants, *Conaway v. Deane*
(2006, 35–37) and Brief of the Family
Research Council as Amicus Curiae in Sup-
port of Defendants-Respondents, *Lewis v.
Harris* (14–19).

48. The data employed by these authors come
from an academic paper prepared by the
demographer Gunnar Andersson and his colleagues for presentation at the 2004 Annual
Meeting of the Population Association of
America. See Noack, Seierstad, and Weedon-
Fekjær (2005) for an analysis of divorce rates
in Norway.

49. See, e.g., Friend-of-the-Court Brief of
the American Psychological Association, the
American Psychiatric Association and Other
Mental Health Organizations in Support of
Equal Treatment for Same-Sex Couples and
their Children, *Deane & Polyak v. Conaway*,
Maryland Court of Appeals, September
2006 Term, Docket No. 44, 14–17. See also
Brief of American Psychological Association
and New Jersey Psychological Association
as Amici Curiae in Support of Plaintiffs-
Appellants, *Lewis v. Harris*, Superior Court
of New Jersey, Docket No. A-2244-03T5,
16–19.

50. These states joined the four that had
amended their constitutions prior to the
Goodridge decision.

References

365Gay.com Newscenter Staff. 2008, January 24. "Court Upholds New Orleans Same-Sex Partner Benefits." Available at from http://365gay.com/Newscon08/01/012408nola.htm (accessed June 25, 2008).

Adam, Barry D. 2002. "Theorizing the Globalization of Gay and Lesbian Movements." *Sociological Views on Political Participation in the 21st Century* 10: 123–37.

Adam, Barry, D., Jan Willem Duyvendak, and André Krouwel (eds.). 1999. *The Global Emergence of Gay and Lesbian Politics: National Imprints of a Worldwide Movement.* Philadelphia: Temple University Press.

Adams, Michele, and Scott Coltrane 2007. "Framing Divorce Reform: Media, Morality, and the Politics of Family." *Family Process* 46: 17–34.

Agamben, Giorgio. 1998. *Homo Sacer: Sovereign Power and Bare Life.* Palo Alto, CA: Stanford University Press.

Agamden, Giorgio. 2005. *State of Exception.* Chicago: University of Chicago Press.

Alliance Defense Fund Media Relations. 2008, March 7. "ADF Attorneys Appeal Domestic Partnership Case." Available at http://www.alliancedefensefund.org/news/pressrelease.aspx?cid=4419 (accessed January 8, 2009).

Almanzar, Yolanne. 2008. "Florida Gay Adoption Ban Is Ruled Unconstitutional," *New York Times*, November 26.

Altman, Dennis. 2001. *Global Sex.* Chicago: University of Chicago.

Amenta, Edwin, Kathleen Dunleavy, and Mary Bernstein. 1994. "Stolen Thunder? Huey Long's Share Our Wealth, Political Mediation, and the Second New Deal." *American Sociological Review* 59: 678–702.

Amenta, Edwin, and Michael P. Young. 1999. "Democratic States and Social Movements." *Social Problems* 46(2): 153–68.

American Law Institute. 2002. *Principles of the Law of Family Dissolution: Analysis and Recommendations.* Philadelphia: ALI.

American Psychological Association and New Jersey Psychological Association. "Brief of American Psychological Association and New Jersey Psychological Association as Amici Curiae in Support of Plaintiffs-Appellants, *Lewis v. Harris.*" Superior Court of New Jersey, Docket No. A-2244-03T5: 16–19. Available at http://data.lambdalegal.org/pdf/543.pdf.

American Psychological Association et al. 2006. "Friend-of-the-Court Brief of the American Psychological Association, the American Psychiatric Association and Other Mental Health Organizations in Support of Equal Treatment for Same-Sex Couples and Their Children, *Deane & Polyak v. Conaway.*" Maryland Court of Appeals, September 2006 Term, Docket No. 44: 14–17. Available at http://www.aclu.org/images/asset_upload_file725_27253.pdf.

Andersen, Ellen Ann. 2005. *Out of the Closets and Into the Courts: Legal Opportunity Structure and Gay Rights Litigation.* Ann Arbor: University of Michigan Press.

Andersen, William R. 1980. "Resolving State/Local Governmental Conflict—A Tale of Three Cities." *Urban Law Annual* 18: 129–52.

Andersson, Gunnar, et al. 2004. "Divorce-Risk Patterns in Same-Sex 'Marriages' in Norway and Sweden." Paper presented at the annual meeting of the Population Association of America, April 1–3, in Boston, Massachusetts.

Anonymous Queers. 1993 (1990). "Queers Read This." In *Lesbians, Gay Men, and the Law*, ed. William B. Rubenstein, pp. 45–47. New York: New Press.

Anonymous Queers. 1997. "Queers Read This: I Hate Straights." In *Sexual Orientation and the Law*, ed. W. B. Rubenstein, pp. 79–81. St. Paul, MN: West.

Armstrong, Elizabeth A. 2002. *Forging Gay Identities: Organizing Sexuality in San Francisco, 1950–1994*. Chicago: University of Chicago Press.

Armstrong, Elizabeth A., and Mary Bernstein. 2008. "Culture, Power, and Institutions: A Multi-Institutional Politics Approach to Social Movements." *Sociological Theory* 26(1): 74–99.

Armstrong, Elizabeth A., and Suzanna M. Crage. 2006. "Movements and Memory: The Making of the Stonewall Myth." *American Sociological Review* 17: 724–51.

Avery, Alison, et al. 2007. "America's Changing Attitudes Toward Homosexuality, Civil Unions, and Same-Gender Marriage: 1977–2004." *Social Work* 52: 71–79.

Babbie, Earl. 2001. *The Practice of Social Research* (9th ed.). Belmont: Wadsworth.

Backer, Larry Cata. 1993. "Exposing the Perversions of Toleration: The Decriminalization of Private Sexual Conduct, the Model Penal Code, and the Oxymoron of Liberal Toleration." *Florida Law Review* 45(5): 755–802.

Badgett, Lee. 2004. "Will Providing Marriage Rights to Same-Sex Couples Undermine Heterosexual Marriage? Evidence from Scandinavia and the Netherlands." *Institute for Gay and Lesbian Strategic Studies*. Available at http://www.iglss.org/media/filed/briefing.pdf.

Bailey, Robert W. 1999. *Gay Politics, Urban Politics*. New York: Columbia University Press.

Barclay, Scott, and Shauna Fisher. 2006. "Cause Lawyers in the First Wave of Same Sex Marriage Litigation." In *Cause Lawyers and Social Movements*, ed. Austin Sarat and

Stuart Scheingold, pp. 84–100. Stanford: Stanford University Press.

Barclay, Scott, and Anna-Maria Marshall. 2005. "Supporting a Cause, Developing a Movement, and Consolidating a Practice: Cause Lawyers and Sexual Orientation Litigation in Vermont." In *The Worlds Cause Lawyers Make*, ed. Stuart Scheingold and Austin Sarat, pp. 171–202. Palo Alto: Stanford University Press.

Barkan, Steven E. 1984. "Legal Control of the Southern Civil Rights Movement." *American Sociological Review* 49: 552–65.

Baron, Jonathan. 2000. *Thinking and Deciding*. New York: Cambridge University Press.

Bartholet, Elizabeth. 1999. *Nobody's Children: Abuse and Neglect, Foster Drift, and the Adoption Alternative*. Boston: Beacon Press.

Basch, Norma. 1999. Framing American Divorce: From the Revolutionary Generation to the Victorians. Berkeley: University of California Press.

Bauman, Richard W. 2002. *Ideology and Community in the First Wave of Critical Legal Studies*. Toronto: University of Toronto Press.

Bauman, Zygmunt. 1992. Mortality, Immortality, and other Life Strategies. Cambridge/Oxford: Polity Press.

Baumgartner, Frank R., and Bryan D. Jones. 1993. *Agendas and Instability in American Politics*. Chicago: University of Chicago Press.

Baumgartner, Frank R., and Beth L. Leech. 1998. *Basic Interests: The Importance of Groups in Politics and in Political Science*. Princeton: Princeton University Press.

Bayse, Chad. 2004. "Pulling the Lilly From the Pond? Minneapolis Wades Into Domestic Partner Benefits Legislation Once Again." *William Mitchell Law Review* 30: 931–68.

Bell, Derrick. 1993. *Faces at the Bottom of the Well: The Permanence of Racism*. New York: Basic Books.

Benford, Robert D. 1993. "Frame Disputes Within the Nuclear Disarmament Movement." *Social Forces* 71: 677–701.

Benford, Robert D., and David A. Snow. 2000. "Framing Processes and Social Movements: An Overview and Assessment." *Annual Review of Sociology* 26: 611–39.

Benkov, Laura. 1994. *Reinventing the Family: The Emerging Story of Lesbian and Gay Parents.* New York: Crown.

Benton, Lauren. 2001. *Law and Colonial Cultures: Legal Regimes in World History, 1400–1900.* Cambridge: Cambridge University Press.

Berger, Peter L. 1970. "On the Obsolescence of the Concept of Honor." *Archives Européenes de Sociologie* 11: 339–47.

Berlant, Lauren. 1997. *The Queen of America Goes to Washington City: Essays on Sex and Citizenship.* Durham, NC: Duke University Press.

Berland, Lauren. 1999. "The Subject of True Feeling: Pain, Privacy and Politics." In *Cultural Pluralism, Identity Politics and the Law,* ed. Austin Sarat and Thomas Kearns, pp. 49–84. Ann Arbor: University of Michigan Press.

Berman, David R. 1995a. "State-Local Relations: Patterns, Problems, and Partnerships." In *The Municipal Yearbook 1995.* Washington, DC: ICMA.

Berman, David R. 1995b. "Takeovers of Local Governments." *Publius: The Journal of Federalism* 25(3): 55–70.

Bernstein, Mary. 1997. "Celebration and Suppression: The Strategic Uses of Identity by the Lesbian and Gay Movement." *American Journal of Sociology* 103(3): 531–65.

Bernstein, Mary. 2001. "Gender, Queer Family Policies and the Limits of Law." In *Queer Families, Queer Politics: Challenging Culture and the State,* ed. Mary Bernstein and Renate Reimann, pp. 420–446. New York: Columbia University Press.

Bernstein, Mary. 2002. "Identities and Politics: Toward a Historical Understanding of the Lesbian and Gay Movement." *Social Science History* 26: 531–81.

Bernstein, Mary. 2003. "Nothing Ventured, Something Gained?: Conceptualizing Social Movement 'Success' in the Lesbian and Gay Movement." *Sociological Perspectives* 46: 353–79.

Bernstein, Mary. 2005. "Liberalism and Social Movement Success: The Case of the United States Sodomy Statutes." In *Regulating Sex: The Politics of Intimacy and Identity,* ed. E. Bernstein and L. Schaffner, pp. 2–18. New York: Routledge.

Bernstein, Mary, and Mary C. Burke. "What Happened to Queer?: Cultural Outcomes and the Same-Sex Marriage Movement in Vermont." Unpublished manuscript.

Bernstein, Mary, and Renate Reimann. 2001. "Queer Families and the Politics of Visibility." In *Queer Families, Queer Politics,* ed. Mary Bernstein and Renate Reimann, pp. 1–20. New York: Columbia University Press.

Berry, Mary Frances. 1993. *The Politics of Parenthood: Child Care, Women's Rights and the Myth of the Good Mother.* New York: Viking Press.

Beyond Marriage. 2008. Available at http://www.beyondmarriage.org/ (accessed February 4, 2008).

Birkland, Thomas. 1997. *After Disaster: Agenda Setting, Public Policy and Focusing Events.* Washington, DC: Georgetown University Press.

Birkland, Thomas. 1998. "Focusing Events, Mobilization, and Agenda Setting." *Journal of Public Policy* 18(1): 53–74.

Blackless, Melanie, et al. 2000. "How Sexually Dimorphic Are We?" *American Journal of Human Biology* 12: 151–66.

Blankenhorn, David. 1995. *Fatherless America: Confronting Our Most Urgent Social Problem.* New York: Basic Books.

Blue Ribbon Committee. 1999. Handout. "Rights Afforded and Areas." May 20, 1999, Sean Drate Files. Private Collection.

Boal, Augusto. 1985. *Theatre of the Oppressed.* Trans. Charles A. and Maria-Odilia Leal McBride. New York: Theatre Communications Group.

Bob, Clifford. 2005. *The Marketing of Rebellion: Insurgents, Media, and International*

Activism. New York: Cambridge University Press.

Boggis, Terry. 2001. "Affording Our Famlies: Class Issues in Family Formation." In *Queer Families, Queer Politics: Challenging Culture and the State*, ed. Mary Bernstein and Renate Reimann, pp. 175–181. New York: Columbia University Press.

Boli-Bennett, John, and John W. Meyer. 1978. "Ideology of Childhood and State-Rules Distinguishing Children in National Constitutions, 1870–1970." *American Sociological Review* 43: 797–812.

Borowski, Greg J. 1999. "City OKs Same-Sex Registry," *Milwaukee Journal-Sentinel*, July 13, p. 1.

Boswell, John. 1982. "Revolutions, Universals, and Sexual Categories." *Salmagundi* 89: 58–59.

Boswell, John. 1988. *The Kindness of Strangers: The Abandonment of Children in Western Europe From Late Antiquity to the Renaissance*. New York: Pantheon Books.

Bower, Lisa. 1997. "Queer Problems/Straight Solutions: The Limits of 'Official Recognition.'" In *Playing With Fire: Queer Politics, Queer Theories*, ed. Shane Phelan, pp. 267–91. New York: Routledge.

Bowman, Cynthia Grant. 2004. "Legal Treatment of Cohabitation in the United States." *Law and Policy* 26(1): 119–51.

Boyle, Elizabeth Heger, and John W. Meyer. 1998. "Modern Law as a Secularized and Global Model: Implications for Sociology of Law." *Soziale Welt* 49: 213–32.

Brewer, Sarah E., David Kaib, and Karen O'Connor. 2000. "Sex and the Supreme Court: Gays, Lesbians and Justice." In *The Politics of Gay Rights*, ed. Craig A. Rimmerman, Kenneth D. Wald, and Clyde Wilcox, pp. 377–408. Chicago: University of Chicago Press.

Briffault, Richard. 1990a. "Our Localism: Part I —The Structure of Local Government Law." *Columbia Law Review* 90 (January): 1–115.

Briffault, Richard. 1990b. "Our Localism: Part II—Localism and Legal Theory." *Columbia Law Review* 90: 346–454.

Broad, K. L. 2002. "GLB+T?: Gender/Sexuality Movements and Transgender Collective Identity (De)Constructions." *International Journal of Sexuality and Gender Studies* 7(4): 241–64.

Brodzinsky, David. 2003. "Adoption by Lesbians and Gays: A National Survey of Adoption Agency Policies, Practices, Attitudes." New York: Evan Donaldson Institute.

Brooks, Thomas. 2006. *A Wealth of Family: An Adopted Son's International Quest for Heritage, Reunion, and Enrichment (Family Success)*. New York: Alpha Multimedia.

Brown, Michael P. 2000. *Closet Space: Geographies of Metaphor From the Body to the Globe*. New York: Routledge.

Brunsson, Nils, and Bengt Jacobsson. 2002. *A World of Standards*. Oxford: Oxford University Press.

Burchell, Jonathan, and John Milton. 1994. *Principles of Criminal Law*, rev. ed. Cape Town, South Africa: Juta.

Burgess, Diane, and Eugene Borgida. 1999. "Who Women Are, Who Women Should Be: Descriptive and Prescriptive Gender Stereotyping in Sex Discrimination." *Psychology, Public Policy, and Law* 5: 665–92.

Burstein, Paul. 1991. "Legal Mobilization as a Social Movement Tactic: The Struggle for Equal Employment Opportunity." *American Journal of Sociology* 96(5): 1201–25.

Butler, Judith. 2004. *Precarious Life: The Powers of Mourning and Violence*. London: Verso.

Button, James W., Barbara A. Rienzo, and Kenneth D. Wald. 1997. *Private Lives, Public Conflicts*. Washington, DC: Congressional Quarterly.

Cable, Sherry, Donald W. Hastings, and Tamara L. Mix. 2002. "Different Voices, Different Venues: Environmental Racism Claims by Activists, Researchers, and Lawyers." *Human Ecology Review* 9: 26–42.

Cain, Patricia A. 1993. "Litigating for Lesbian and Gay Rights: A Legal History." *Virginia Law Review* 79: 1551–1641.

Cain, Patricia A. 2000. *Rainbow Rights: The Role of Lawyers and Courts in the Lesbian and Gay Civil Rights Movement.* Boulder, CO: Westview Press.

Caldeira, Gregory, and John Wright. 1988. "Organized Interests and Agenda Setting in the U.S. Supreme Court." *American Political Science Review* 82: 1109–1127.

Caldeira, Gregory A., and John R. Wright. 1990. "Amici Curiae Before the Supreme Court: Who Participates, When and How Much?" *Journal of Politics* 52: 782–806.

Calhoun, Cheshire. 1993. "Denaturalizing and Desexualizing Lesbian and Gay Identity." *University of Virginia Law Review* 79: 1859–75.

Campbell, Joseph. 1988. The Power of Myth. New York: Doubleday.

Cameron, Paul. "Same Sex Marriage: Tiel Death Do Us Part?" Available at http://www.familyresearchinst.org/fri_eduPamplhet7.html.

Carbone, J. 2006. "Wells Conference on Adoption Law: The Role of Adoption in Winning Public Recognition for Adult Partnerships." *Capital University Law Review* 35: 341–98.

Carp, E. Wayne. 1996. *Family Matters.* Cambridge, MA: Harvard University Press.

Carp, E. Wayne. 2004. *Adoption Politics: Bastard Nation and Ballot Initiative 58.* Lawrence: University of Kansas Press.

Census Bureau. 2002. Current Population Reports, Number, Timing, and Duration of Marriages and Divorces: 1996. Washington, DC: U.S. Department of Commerce.

Chabot, Sean, and Jan Willem Duyvendak. 2002. "Globalization and Transnational Diffusion Between Social Movements: Reconceptualizing the Dissemination of the Gandhian Repertoire and the "Coming Out" Routine." Theory and Society 31(6): 697–740.

Chambers, David L. 2000. "Couples: Marriage, Civil Union, and Domestic Partnership." In Creating Change: Sexuality, Public Policy, and Civil Rights, ed. John D'Emilio et al, pp. 281–304. New York: St. Martin's Press.

Chambers, David L. 2001. "'What If?' The Legal Consequences of Marriage and the Legal Needs of Lesbian and Gay Male Couples." In *Queer Families, Queer Politics: Challenging Culture and the State,* ed. Mary Bernstein and Renate Reimann, pp. 306–37. New York: Columbia University Press.

Charles, Casey. 2005. "Queer Writes." Women's Studies in Communication 28 (Spring): 32–57.

Charles, Casey. 2006. "Panic in the Project: Critical Queer Studies and the Matthew Shepard Murder." Law and Literature 18 (Summer): 225–52.

Chen, Christina Pei-Lin. 2000. "Provocation's Privileged Desire: The Provocation Doctrine, 'Homosexual Panic,' and the Non–violent Unwanted Sexual Advance Defense." *Cornell Journal of Law and Public Policy* 10: 195–235.

Chong, Dennis. 1991. *Collective Action and the Civil Rights Movement.* Chicago: University of Chicago Press.

Chong, Dennis, and James N. Druckman. 2007. "Framing Theory." *Annual Review of Political Science* 10: 103–26.

Christ, P. Daniel. 1999. Memorandum, "Re: Proposed Human Rights Ordinance." July 29. Rudy Serra Files. Private Collection.

Clark, Gordon L. 1985. *Judges and the Cities: Interpreting Local Autonomy.* Chicago: University of Chicago Press.

Claycomb, Ryan M. 2003. "(Ch)oral History: Documentary Theatre, the Communal Subject and Progressive Politics." *Journal of Dramatic Theory and Criticism* 17 (Spring 2003): 95–119.

Cmiel, Kenneth. 1995. *A Home of Another Kind: One Chicago Orphanage and the Tangle of Child Welfare.* Chicago: University of Chicago Press.

Cohen, Cathy. 1999. *The Boundaries of Blackness: AIDS and the Breakdown of Black Politics.* Chicago: University of Chicago Press.

Cohen, Jean. 1985. "Strategy or Identity: New Theoretical Paradigms and Contemporary Social Movements." *Social Research* 52: 663–716.

Cole, James D. 1991. "Local Authority to Supersede State Statutes." *New York State Bar Journal* 63 (October): 34–38.

Collins, Paul M. 2004. "Friends of the Court: Examining the Influence of Amicus Curiae Participation in U.S. Supreme Court Litigation." *Law and Society Review* 38: 807–32.

Coltrane, Scott, and Neal Hickman. 1992. "The Rhetoric of Rights and Needs: Moral Discourse in the Reform of Child Custody and Child Support Laws." *Social Problems* 39: 400–20.

Connolly, Catherine. 2002. "The Voice of the Petitioner: The Experiences of Gay and Lesbian Parents in Successful Second–Parent Adoption Proceedings." *Law and Society Review* 36(2): 325–46.

Coombs, Mary. 2001. "Transgenderism and Sexual Orientation: More Than a Marriage of Convenience." In *Queer Families, Queer Politics: Challenging Culture and the State,* ed. Mary Bernstein and Renate Reimann, pp. 397–419. New York: Columbia University Press.

Coontz, Stephanie. 2005. *Marriage, a History: From Obedience to Intimacy, or How Love Conquered Marriage.* New York: Viking Adult.

Coutin, Susan B. 1998. "From Refugees to Immigrants: The Legalization Strategies of Salvadoran Immigrants and Activists." *International Migration Review* 32(4): 901–25.

Coutin, Susan B., W. Maurer, and Barbara Yngvesson. 2002. "In the Mirror: The Legitimation Work of Globalization." *Law and Social Inquiry* 27(4): 801–46.

Crenshaw, Kimberle. 1989. "Demarginalizing the Intersection of Race and Sex: A Black Feminist Critique of Antidiscrimination Doctrine, Feminist Theory, and Antiracist Politics." *University of Chicago Legal Forum* 189: 139–68.

Crenshaw, Kimberle, Neil Gotanda, Gary Peller, and Kendall Thomas, eds. 1995. *Critical Race Theory: The Key Writings That Formed the Movement.* New York: New Press.

Crimp, Douglas. 1988. "How to Have Promiscuity in an Epidemic." In *AIDS: Cultural Analysis, Cultural Activism,* ed. Douglas Crimp, pp. 237–53. Cambridge, MA: MIT Press.

Croucher, Sheila. 2002. "South Africa's Democratisation and the Politics of Gay Liberation." *Journal of Southern African Studies* 28(2): 315–30.

Currah, Paisley, Richard M. Juang, and Shannon Price Minter. 2006. *Transgender Rights.* Minneapolis: University of Minnesota Press.

Currah, Paisley, and Shannon Minter. 2000. *Transgender Equality: A Handbook for Activists and Policymakers.* Washington DC: The Policy Institute of the National Gay and Lesbian Task Force and National Center for Lesbian Rights.

Currah, Paisley, and Shannon Minter. 2005. "Unprincipled Exclusions: The Struggle to Achieve Judicial and Legislative Equality for Transgender People." In *Regulating Sex: The Politics of Intimacy and Identity,* ed. Elizabeth Bernstein and Laurie Schaffner, pp. 35–50. New York: Routledge.

Dahir, Mubarek. 2001. "Breaking Up Is Hard to Do." *The Advocate,* September 11. Available at http://www.thefreelibrary.com/Breaking+up+is+hard+to+do-a078265975.

Dalton, Susan E. 2000. "Nonbiological Mothers and the Legal Boundaries of Motherhood: An Analysis of California Law." In *Ideologies and Technologies of Motherhood: Race, Class Sexuality, Nationalism,* ed. Helena Ragone and France Winddance Twine, pp. 191–232. New York: Routledge.

Dalton, Susan E. 2001. "Protecting Our Parent-Child Relationships: Understanding the

Strengths and Weaknesses of Second Parent Adoption." In *Queer Families, Queer Politics: Challenging Culture and the State*, ed. Mary Bernstein and Renate Reimann, pp. 201–21. New York: Columbia University Press.

Dang, Alain and Somjen Frazer. 2005. "Black Same-Sex Households in the United States." *National Gay and Lesbian Task Force Policy Institute*. Available at www.Thetaskforce.org.

Daughter From Danang. Directed by Gail Dolgin and Vicente Franco. PBS Home Video, 2002. DVD

Daum, Courtenay. 2006a. "Sex, Laws, and Cyberspace: Organized Interest Litigation Before the U.S. Supreme Court." *Justice System Journal* 27: 302–22.

Daum, Courtenay. 2006b. "Not in My Back-yard: Conservative Organized Interests and Gay Rights Litigation Before the U.S. Supreme Court." Paper presented at the annual meeting of the Western Political Science Association, March 17 Albuquerque, NM.

DeBoer, Robby. 1994. *Losing Jessica*. New York: Doubleday.

de la Dehesa, Rafael. 2007. *Sexual Modernities: Queering the Public Sphere in Latin America*. Unpublished book manuscript, Department of Sociology, CUNY-Staten Island.

De Lauretis, Teresa. 1991. "Queer Theory: Lesbian and Gay Sexualities. An Introduction." *Differences: A Journal of Feminist Cultural Studies* 3, pp. iii–xviii.

DeLeon, Richard. 1999. "San Francisco and Domestic Partners: New Fields of Battle in the Culture War." In Culture Wars and Local Politics, ed. Elaine B. Sharp, pp. 117–36. Lawrence: University of Kansas Press.

Delgado, Richard, and Jean Stefancic. 2001. *Critical Race Theory: An Introduction*. New York: New York University Press.

DeLuca, Kevin. 1999. "Articulation Theory: A Discursive Grounding for Theoretical Practice." Philosophy and Rhetoric 32 (1999): 334–48.

D'Emilio, John. 1983. Sexual Politics, Sexual Communities: The Making of a Homosexual *Minority in the United States, 1940–1970*. Chicago: University of Chicago.

D'Emilio, John. 1992. *Making Trouble: Essays on Gay History, Politics, and the University*. New York: Routledge.

D'Emilio, John. 1997. "Back to Basics: Sodomy Law Repeal." Washington, DC: National Gay and Lesbian Task Force. Available at http://legalminds.lp.findlaw.com/list/queerlaw–edit/msg00258.html.

Diescho, Joseph. 1994. *The Namibian Constitution in Perspective*. Windhoek, Namibia: Gamsberg Macmillan.

DiFonzo, James Herbie. 1997. Beneath the Fault Line: The Popular and Legal Culture of Divorce in Twentieth-Century America. Charlottesville: University of Virginia Press.

DiFonzo, James Herbie 2003. "Unbundling Marriage." *Hofstra Law Review* 32: 31–70.

DiMaggio, Paul J., and Walter W. Powell. 1983. "The Iron Cage Revisited: Institutional Isomorphism and Collective Rationality in Organizational Fields." American Sociological Review 48: 147–60.

Donovan, Todd, and Shaun Bowler. 1998. "Direct Democracy and Minority Rights: An Extension." *American Journal of Political Science* 42: 1020–24.

Douzinas, Costas, and Lynda Nead. 1999. *Law and the Image: The Authority of Art and the Aesthetics of Law*. Chicago: University of Chicago Press.

Dowd, N. 1996. "Rethinking Fatherhood." *Florida Law Review* 48: 523–37.

Drucker, Peter. 1996. "In the Tropics There Is No Sin": Sexuality and Gay–Lesbian Movements in the Third World." *New Left Review* 218: 75–101.

Dudas, Jeffrey. 2003. "Rights, Resentment, and Social Change: Treaty Rights in Contemporary American." Ph.D. dissertation, University of Washington.

Dudas, Jeffrey. 2005. "In the Name of Equal Rights: 'Special' Rights and the Politics of

Resentment in Post–Civil Rights America."
Law and Society Review 39: 723–57.

Dudziak, Mary L. 2000. *Cold War Civil
Rights: Race and the Image of American
Democracy.* Princeton: Princeton University
Press.

Dugan, Kim. 2005. *The Struggle Over Gay,
Lesbian, and Bisexual Rights: Facing Off in
Cincinnati.* New York: Routledge.

Duggan, Lisa. 2003. *The Twilight of Equality?: Neoliberalism, Cultural Politics, and the
Attack on Democracy.* Boston: Beacon Press.

Duggan, Lisa, and Richard Kim. 2005.
"Beyond Gay Marriage." *The Nation,* July
18, 25.

Duina, Francesco G. 1999. *Harmonizing
Europe: Nation–States Within the Common
Market.* Albany: SUNY Press.

Dunlap, Mary C. 1991. "The Lesbian and Gay
Marriage Debate: A Microcosm of Our
Hopes and Troubles in the Nineties." *Law
and Sexuality* 1: 63–96.

Dupuis, Martin. 2002. *Same–Sex Marriage,
Legal Mobilization, and the Politics of Rights.*
New York: Peter Lang.

Earl, Jennifer. 2003. "Tanks, Tear Gas, and
Taxes: Toward a Theory of Movement
Repression." *Sociological Theory* 21(1):
45–68.

Edelman, Lauren B. 1992. "Legal Ambiguity
and Symbolic Structures: Organizational
Mediation of Civil Rights Law." *American
Journal of Sociology* 97: 1531–76.

Edelman, Lauren B., and Mark Suchman.
1997. "The Legal Environment of Organizations." *Annual Review of Sociology* 23:
479–515.

Edelman, Lee. 2004. *No Future: Queer Theory
and the Death Drive.* Durham, NC: Duke
University Press.

Edelman, Murray J. 1995. *From Art to Politics:
How Artistic Creations Shape Political Con-
ceptions.* Chicago: University of Chicago
Press.

Ehrenreich, Nancy 2002. "Subordination and
Symbiosis: Mechanisms of Mutual Support
Between Subordinating Systems." *Univer-

sity of Missouri Kansas City Law Review* 71:
251–67.

Ellingson, Stephen. 1995. "Understanding
the Dialectic of Discourse and Collective Action: Public Debate and Rioting in
Antebellum Cincinnati." *American Journal
of Sociology* 101(1): 100–44.

Emens, Elizabeth F. 2004. "Monogamy's Law:
Compulsory Monogamy and Polyamorous
Existence." *New York University Review of
Law and Social Change* 29: 277–81.

Eng, David. 2003. "Transnational Adoption
and Queer Diasporas." *Social Text* 21(3): 1–38.

Eng, David L., Judith Halberstam, and Jose
Estaban Muñoz. 2005. "What's Queer
About Queer Studies Now?" Social Text
23(3–4): 84–85.

Engel, David. 1984. "The Oven Bird's Song:
Insiders, Outsiders, and Personal Injuries in
an American Community." *Law and Society
Review* 18: 551–82.

Engel, David, and Frank Munger. 2003. *Rights
of Inclusion: Law and Identity in the Life Stories of Americans With Disabilities.* Chicago:
University of Chicago Press.

Engle, Karen. 2007. "The Face of a Terrorist."
Cultural Studies = Critical Methodologies
7(4): 397–424.

Entman, Robert M. 1993. "Framing: Toward
Clarification of a Fractured Paradigm."
Journal of Communication 43(4): 51–58.

Epp, Charles. 1998. *The Rights Revolution:
Lawyers, Activists and Supreme Courts in
Comparative Perspective.* Chicago: Univer-
sity of Chicago Press.

Epprecht, Marc. 2004. *Hungochani: The
History of a Dissident Sexuality in Southern
Africa.* Montréal, Canada: McGill–Queen's
University Press.

Epstein, Lee. 1985. *Conservatives in Court.*
Knoxville: University of Tennessee Press.

Epstein, Robert, and Richard Schmeichen.
1986. *The Times of Harvey Milk* (film).
Cinecom International.

Eskridge, William N., Jr. 1993. "A History of
Same-Sex Marriage." *University of Virginia
Law Review* 79: 1419–1513.

Eskridge, William N., Jr. 1999. *Gaylaw: Challenging the Apartheid of the Closet.* Cambridge, MA: Harvard University Press.

Eskridge, William N., Jr. 2002. *Equality Practice: Civil Unions and the Future of Gay Rights.* New York: Routledge.

Eskridge, William N., Jr., and Nan D. Hunter. 2004. *Sexuality, Gender and the Law.* New York: Foundation Press.

Eskridge, William N., Jr., and Darren R. Spedale. 2006. *Gay Marriage: For Better or for Worse?: What We've Learned From the Evidence.* Oxford: Oxford University Press.

Eskridge, William N., Jr., Darren R. Spedale, and Hans Ytterberg. 2004. "Nordic Bliss: Scandinavian Registered Partnerships and the Same-Sex Marriage Debate." *Issues in Legal Scholarship, Single-Sex Marriage: Article 4.* Available at http://www.bepress.com/ils/iss5/art4.

Estin, Ann Laquer. 2001. "Unmarried Partners and the Legacy of *Marvin v. Marvin*: Ordinary Cohabitation." *Notre Dame Law Review* 76: 1381–408.

Ethics Committee of the American Society for Reproductive Medicine. 2004. "Informing Offspring of Their Conception by Gamete Donation." *Fertility and Sterility* 81(3): 527–31.

Ettlebrick, Paula L. 1989. "Since When Is Marriage a Path to Liberation?" *OUT/LOOK* (Autumn): 8–12.

Evans, Murray. 2003. "Lexington Vote Rescinds Domestic Partnership Benefits." *Louisville Courier-Journal*, November 7, p. 1.

Ewick, Patricia. 2004. "Consciousness and Ideology." In *The Blackwell Companion to Law and Society*, ed. Austin Sarat, pp. 80–94. Malden, MA: Blackwell.

Ewick, Patricia, and Susan S. Silbey. 1998. *The Common Place of Law: Stories From Everyday Life.* Chicago: University of Chicago Press.

Fagan, Patrick F., and Grace Smith. 2004. "The Transatlantic Divide on Marriage: Dutch Data and the U.S. Debate on Same-Sex Unions." WebMemo #577, *National Review Online*, September 29. Available at http://www.heritage.org/Research/Family/wm577.cfm.

Family Research Council. 2006. "Brief of the Family Research Council as Amicus Curiae in Support of Defendants-Appellants, *Conaway v. Deane.*" Maryland Court of Appeals, September Term, Docket no. 44: 35–37. Available at http://www.frc.org/get.cfm?i=CB06I01&f=WA06K63.

Family Research Council. 2006. "Brief of the Family Research Council as Amicus Curiae in Support of Defendants-Respondents, *Lewis v. Harris.*" Superior Court of New Jersey, Docket No. A-2244-03T5: 14–19. Available at http://domawatch.org/cases/newjersey/lewisvharris/SupremeCourt/CoalitionAmicus_FRC.pdf.

Farole, Donald J. 1999. "Reexamining Litigant Success in State Supreme Courts." *Law and Society Review* 33: 1043–1058.

Feldblum, Chai. 1999. "The Desexing of Gay Rights." *Harvard Gay and Lesbian Review* 6(3)(Summer): 22–24.

Felstiner, William L. F., Richard L. Abel, and Austin Sarat. 1980–81. "The Emergence and Transformation of Disputes: Naming, Blaming, Claiming." *Law and Society Review* 15: 631–54.

Fenwick, Colin. 2005. "Labour Law in Namibia: Towards an 'Indigenous Solution.'" *University of Melbourne Legal Studies Research Paper* No. 133. Available at http://ssrn.com/abstract=815305 (accessed September 23, 2006).

Ferree, Myra Marx, William Gamson, Jürgen Gerhards, and Dieter Rucht. 2002. *Shaping Abortion Discourse: Democracy and the Public Sphere in Germany and the United States.* Cambridge: Cambridge University Press.

Fineman, Martha. 1995. *The Neutered Mother, the Sexual Family, and Other Twentieth Century Tragedies.* New York: Routledge.

Fineman, Martha Albertson. 1991. *The Illusion of Equality: The Rhetoric and Reality of Divorce Reform.* Chicago: University of Chicago Press.

First Person Plural. 2000. Directed by Deann Borshay Liem. PBS. P.O.V.

Fiss, Owen M. 1978. "Foreword: The Forms of Justice." *Harvard University Law Review* 93: 1–281.

FitzGerald, Frances. 1981. *Cities on a Hill: A Journey Through Contemporary American Cultures.* New York: Simon and Schuster.

Fleischmann, Arnold, and Jason Hardman. 2004. "Hitting Below the Bible Belt: The Development of the Gay Rights Movement in Atlanta." *Journal of Urban Affairs* 26: 407–26.

Fortin, A. J. 1995. "AIDS, Surveillance, and Public Policy." *Research in Law and Policy Studies* 4: 173–97.

Fortun, Kim. 2001. *Advocacy After Bhopal: Environmentalism, Disaster and New Global Orders.* Chicago: University of Chicago Press.

Foucault, Michel. 1978. *The History of Sexuality. Vol. 1: An Introduction.* Trans. Robert Hurley. New York: Vintage.

Foucault, Michel. 1989. *Foucault Live.* Ed. Sylvère Lotringer. Trans. John Johnston. Los Angeles: Semiotext(e).

Foucault, Michel. 1991. "Governmentality." In *The Foucault Effect: Studies in Governmentality,* ed. Graham Burchell, Colin Gordon, and Peter Miller, pp. 87–104. Chicago: University of Chicago Press.

Foucault, Michel. 2003. *Society Must Be Defended: Lectures at the College de France, 1975–76.* New York: Picador.

Franco, Vicente, and Gail Dolgin. 2002. *Daughter From DaNang.* New York: PBS.

Frank, Barney. 2007. Statement of Barney Frank on ENDA. Available at http://www.house.gov/frank/ENDASeptember2007.html (accessed June 20, 2008).

Frank, David John. 2008. "Criminal Sex: Global Trends and Cross-National Variations in Laws Regulating Sexual Activity." Unpublished project prospectus, Department of Sociology, University of California, Irvine.

Frank, David John, Tara Hardinge, and Kassia Wosick-Correa. 2009. "The Global Dimensions of Rape-Law Reform: A Cross-National Study of Policy Outcomes." *American Sociological Review* 74: 272–90.

Frank, David John, Wesley Longhofer, and Evan Schofer. 2007. "World Society, NGOs, and Environmental Policy Reform in Asia." *International Journal of Comparative Sociology* 48: 275–95.

Frank, David John, and Elizabeth H. McEneaney. 1999. "The Individualization of Society and the Liberalization of State Policies on Same-Sex Sexual Relations, 1984–1995." *Social Forces* 77: 911–44.

Frank, David John, and John W. Meyer. 2002. "The Profusion of Individual Roles and Identities in the Post-War Period." *Sociological Theory* 20: 86–105.

Frank, Liz. 2000. "Namibia." In *Lesbian Histories and Cultures: An Encyclopedia,* ed. Bonnie Zimmerman, pp. 531–32. New York: Garland.

Frank, Liz, and Elizabeth Khaxas. 1996. "Lesbians in Namibia." In *Amazon to Zami: Towards a Global Lesbian Feminism,* ed. Monika Reinfelder, pp. 109–17. London: Cassell.

Frank, Thomas. 2004. *What's the Matter With Kansas?: How Conservatives Won the Heart of America.* New York: Metropolitan Books.

Franke, Katherine M. 2004. "The Domesticated Liberty of *Lawrence v. Texas.*" *Columbia Law Review* 104: 1399–426.

Franke, Katherine M. 2006. "Sexuality and Marriage: The Politics of Same-Sex Marriage Politics." *Columbia Journal of Gender and Law* 15: 236–248.

Freundlich, Madelyn. 2007. *For the Records: Restoring a Legal Right for Adult Adoptees.* New York: Evan B. Donaldson Institute.

Friedman, Lawrence. 1965. *Contract Law in America: A Social and Economic Case Study.* Madison: University of Wisconsin Press.

Frug, Gerald. 1980. "The City as a Legal Concept." *Harvard Law Review* 93(6): 1057–54.

Frug, Gerald. 1999. *Citymaking: Building Communities without Building Walls*. Princeton: Princeton University Press.

Frye, Phyllis Randolph, and Alyson Dodi Meiselman. 2001. "Same Sex Marriages Have Existed in the United States for a Long Time Now." *Albany Law Review* 64: 1031–71.

Galanter, Marc. 1974. "Why The 'Haves' Come Out Ahead: Speculation on the Limits of Legal Change." *Law and Society Review* 9: 95–160.

Gallagher, Maggie, and Joshua K. Baker. 2004. "Same-Sex Unions and Divorce Risk: Data From Sweden." *iMAPP Policy Brief*, May 3. Available at http://www.marriagedebate.com/pdf/SSdivorcerisk.pdf.

Gamble, Barbara S. 1997. "Putting Civil Rights to a Popular Vote." *American Journal of Political Science* 41: 245–69.

Gamson, Joshua. 1997. "Messages of Exclusion: Gender, Movements and Symbolic Boundaries." *Gender and Society* 11: 178–99.

Gamson, Joshua. 1998. *Freaks Talk Back: Tabloid Talk Shows and Sexual Nonconformity*. Chicago: University of Chicago Press.

Gamson, William. 1992. *Talking Politics*. New York: Cambridge University Press.

Gay and Lesbian Advocates and Defenders. 2007. Available at http://www.glad.org (accessed June 2007).

General Accounting Office. 2004. GAO-04-353R: Defense of Marriage Act: Update to previous report. Available at www.gao.gov/new.items/D04353r.pdf.

Gerstmann, Evan. 1999. *The Constitutional Underclass: Gays, Lesbians, and the Failure of Class-Based Equal Protection*. Chicago: University of Chicago Press.

Gevisser, Mark. 1995. "A Different Fight for Freedom: A History of South African Lesbian and Gay Organisation From the 1950s to the 1990s. In *Defiant Desire: Gay and Lesbian Lives in South Africa*, ed. Mark Gevisser and Edwin Cameron, pp. 14–88. New York: Routledge.

Gibson, Alan J. 1999. *San Francisco's 1996–97 Equal Benefits Ordinance—A Case Study*. Unpublished MPA thesis, San Francisco State University.

Gillette, Clayton P. 1997. "The Allocation of Government Authority: The Exercise of Trumps by Decentralized Governments." *Virginia Law Review* 83 (October): 1347–417.

Glendon, Mary Ann. 1987. *Abortion and Divorce in Western Law: American Failures, European Challenges*. Cambridge, MA: Harvard University Press.

Glendon, Mary Ann. 1997. *The Transformation of Family Law: State, Law and Family in the United States and Western Europe*. Chicago: University of Chicago Press.

Go, Julian. 2003. "A Globalizing Constitutionalism? Views From the Postcolony, 1945–2000." *International Sociology* 18: 71–95.

Goddard, Keith. 2004. "A Fair Representation: GALZ and the History of the Gay Movement in Zimbabwe." *Journal of Gay and Lesbian Social Services* 16(1): 75–98.

Goffman, Erving. 1974. *Frame Analysis: An Essay on the Organization of the Experience*. New York: Harper Colophon.

Goldberg-Hiller, Jonathan. 2002. *The Limits to Union: Same-Sex Marriage and the Politics of Civil Rights*. Ann Arbor: University of Michigan Press.

Goldberg–Hiller, Jonathan, and Neal Milner. 2003. "Rights as Excess: Understanding the Politics of Special Rights." *Law and Social Inquiry* 28: 1075–118.

Goldsmith, Mike. 1995. "Autonomy and City Limits." In *Theories of Urban Politics*, ed. David Judge, Gerry Stoker, and Harold Wolman, pp. 282–52. Thousand Oaks, CA: Sage.

Goluboff, Risa Lauren. 2003. "The Work of Civil Rights in the 1940s: The Department of Justice, the NAACP, and African American Agricultural Labor." Ph.D. dissertation, Princeton University.

Gomez, Mario. 1995. "Social Economic Rights and Human Rights Commissions." *Human Rights Quarterly* 17(1): 155–69.

Goodman, Ryan, and Derek Jinks. Forthcoming. Socializing States: Promoting Human Rights Through International Law. Oxford: Oxford University.

Gordon, Jennifer. 2005. "Law, Lawyers, and Labor: The United Farm Workers' Legal Strategy in the 1960's and 1970's and the Role of Law in Union Organizing Today." *Pennsylvania Journal of Labor and Employment Law* 8: 1–72.

Gordon, Rachel. 2004, February 15. "The Battle Over Same-Sex Marriage." San Francisco Chronicle, p. A-1.

Gossett, Charles W. 1994. "Domestic Partnership Benefits: Public Sector Patterns." *Review of Public Personnel Administration* 14(1)(Winter): 64–84.

Gossett, Charles W. 1999. "Dillon's Rule and Gay Rights: State Control Over Local Efforts to Protect the Rights of Lesbians and Gay Men." In *Gays and Lesbians in the Democratic Process: Public Policy, Public Opinion and Political Representation*, ed. Ellen Riggle and Barry Tadlock, pp. 62–88. New York: Columbia University Press.

Gouldner, Alvin W. 1970. *The Coming Crisis in Western Sociology.* New York: Basic Books.

"Governor Signs 26 Bills Into Law Today." 2007, May 14. Available at http://www.colorado.gov/cs/Satellite?c=Page&cid=11 89240278740&pagename=GovRitter%2F GOVR.

Grattet, Ryken, Valerie Jenness, and Theodore Curry. 1998. "Innovation and Diffusion in U.S. Hate Crime Law." *American Sociological Review* 76: 1174–85.

Gray, Virginia and David Lowery. 1996. *The Population Ecology of Interest Representation: Lobbying Communities in American States.* Ann Arbor: University of Michigan Press.

Greenberg, David F. 1988. *The Construction of Homosexuality.* Chicago: University of Chicago Press.

Greenberg, Jack. 1974. "Litigation for Social Change: Methods, Limits, and Role in Democracy," *Rec. Ass'n B. N.Y.* 29: 320, 331.

Greenberg, Julie A. 1999. "Defining Male and Female: Intersexuality and the Collision Between Law and Biology." *Arizona Law Review* 41: 265–328.

Greenberg, Julie A., and Marybeth Herald. 2005. "You Can't Take It With You: Constitutional Consequences of Interstate Gender-Identity Rulings." *Washington Law Review* 80: 819–885.

Grossman, Joel, Herbert Kritzer, and Stewart Macaulay. 1999. "Do The 'Haves' Still Come Out Ahead?" *Law and Society Review* 33: 803–10.

Guigni, Marco, Doug McAdam, and Charles Tilly (eds.). 1999. *How Social Movements Matter.* Minneapolis: University of Minnesota.

Gurr, T., and T. King. 1987. *The State and the City.* Chicago: University of Chicago Press.

Gutis, Phillip S. 1991. "New York Court Defines Family to Include Homosexuals," *New York Times,* July 7.

Guthrie, Chris, et al. 2001. "Inside the Judicial Mind." *Cornell Law Review* 86: 777–830.

Hackstaff, Karla B. 1999. *Marriage in a Culture of Divorce.* Philadelphia: Temple University Press.

Haider-Markel, Donald. 1998. "The Politics of Social Regulatory Policy: State and Federal Hate Crime Policy and Implementation Effort." *Political Research Quarterly* 51: 69–88.

Haider-Markel, Donald. 1999. "Creating Change—Holding the Line: Agenda Setting on Lesbian and Gay Issues at the National Level." In *Gays and Lesbians in the Democratic Process: Public Policy, Public Opinion and Political Representation*, ed. Ellen D. B. Riggle and Barry L. Tadlock, pp. 242–68. New York: Columbia University Press.

Haider-Markel, Donald, Alana Querze, and Kara Lindaman. 2007. "Lose, Win or Draw? A Reexamination of Direct Democracy and Minority Rights." *Political Research Quarterly* 60(2): 304–14.

Haider-Markel, Donald P., and Kenneth J. Meier. 1996. "The Politics of Gay and Lesbian Rights: Expanding the Scope of the Conflict." *Journal of Politics* 58: 332–49.

Haider-Markel, Donald P., Mark R. Joslyn, and Chad J. Kniss. 2000. "Minority Group Interests and Political Represenation: Gay Elected Officials in the Policy Process." *Journal of Politics* 62(2): 568–77.

Hall, Donald E. 2003. *Queer Theories*. New York: Palgrave.

Hall, Stuart. 1996. "On Postmodernism and Articulation: An Interview With Lawrence Grossberg." In *Critical Dialogues in Cultural Studies*, ed. David Morley and Kuan-Hsing Chen. New York: Routledge.

Halley, Janet E. 1989. "The Politics of the Closet: Towards Equal Protection for Gay, Lesbian, and Bisexual Identity." *University of California-Los Angeles Law Review* 36: 915–76.

Halley, Janet E. 1994. "Reasoning About Sodomy: Act and Identity in and After *Bowers v. Hardwick*." *Virginia Law Review* 79: 1721–80.

Halley, Janet E. 1998. "Gay Rights and Identity Imitation: Issues in the Ethics of Representation." In *The Politics of Law: A Progressive Critique*, ed. David Kairys, pp. 115–46. New York: Basic Books.

Halley, Janet E., and Wendy Brown, eds. 2003. *Left Legalism/Left Critique*. Durham, NC: Duke University Press.

Halperin, David M. 1986. "One Hundred Years of Homosexuality." *Diacritics* 16: 34–45.

Haltom, William, and Michael McCann. 2004. *Distorting the Law: Politics, Media, and the Litigation Crisis*. Chicago: Chicago University Press.

Handler, Joel F. 1978. *Social Movements and the Legal System: A Theory of Law Reform and Social Change*. New York: Academic Press.

Harcout, Bernard E. 2004. "Foreword to 'You Are Entering a Gay and Lesbian Free Zone': On the Radical Dissents of Justice Scalia and other (Post-) Queers. [Raising Questions about *Lawrence*, Sex Wars, and the Criminal Law]." *Journal of Criminal Law and Criminology* 94: 503–49.

Harper, Phillip Brian. 1990. "Multi/Queer/Culture." *Radical America* 4: 24–30.

Harvey, Alan Burnside (ed.). 1944. *Tremeear's Annotated Criminal Code of Canada*, 5th edition. Calgary, Alberta: Burroughs & Company.

Hassan, Susan H. 2005. Testimony Before State of New Hampshire SB 427 Study Commission to Study All Aspects of Same-Sex Civil Marriage and the Legal Equivalents Thereof, Whether Referred to as Civil Unions, Domestic Partnerships, or Otherwise. September 15. Available at http://NH.Glad.org/SusanHassanS-B427Testimony.pdf.

Hawkins, Darren, and Melissa Humes. 2002. "Human Rights and Domestic Violence." *Political Science Quarterly* 117: 231–57.

Heinz, John P., Edward Laumann, Robert Nelson, and Robert Salisbury. 1993. *The Hollow Core: Private Interests in National Policy Making*. Cambridge, MA: Harvard University Press.

Henley, Kyle. 2004. "Lesbian Custody Case Not Enough to Impeach Judge." *Colorado Springs Gazette*, April 12, p. 1.

Herald, Marybeth. 2004. "A Bedroom of One's Own: Morality and Sexual Privacy After *Lawrence v. Texas*." *Yale Journal of Law and Feminism* 16: 1–40.

Herman, Didi. 1996. "(Il)legitimate minorities: The American Christian Right's –Antigay Rights Discourse." *Journal of Law and Society* 23: 346–63.

Hernández-Truyol, Berta E. 2004. "Querying Lawrence." *Ohio State University Law Journal* 65: 1151–1228.

Hinckle, Warren. 1985. *GaySlayer!* Silver Dollar Books.

Hirschl, Ran. 2004. *Towards Juristocracy: The Origins and Consequences of the New Constitutionalism*. Cambridge, MA: Harvard University Press.

Hitchens, Donna J. 1996. "Family Law." In *Sexual Orientation and the Law*, Release #9, ed. Roberta Achtenberg. New York: Clark, Boardman, Callaghan.

Hoad, Neville. 2007. *African Intimacies: Race, Homosexuality, and Globalization.* Minneapolis: University of Minnesota Press.

Hojnacki, Marie. 1997. "Interest Groups' Decisions to Join Alliances or Work Alone." *American Journal of Political Science* 41: 61–87.

Hollinger, Joan Heifetz. 2004. "Note on the Revised Uniform Parentage Act (UPA) of 2002." In *Families by Law,* ed. Naomi Cahn and Joan Heifetz Hollinger, pp. 294–97. New York: New York University Press.

hooks, bell. 1981. *Ain't I a Woman: Black Women and Feminism.* Cambridge, MA: South End Press.

Horowitz, Donald L. 1977. *The Courts and Social Policy.* Washington, DC: Brookings Institution.

Howard, Jeanne. 2006. "Expanding Resources for Children: Is Adoption by Gays and Lesbians Part of the Answer for Boys and Girls Who Need Homes?" New York: Evan B. Donaldson Adoption Institute.

Hubbard, Dianne. 2000. "Gender and Law Reform in Namibia: The First Ten Years." Available at http://www.lac.org.na/grap/Pdf/1sttenyr.pdf (accessed April 19, 2007).

Hubbard, Dianne. 2007. "Gender and Sexuality: The Law Reform Landscape." In *Unravelling Taboos: Gender and Sexuality in Namibia,* ed. Suzanne LaFont and Dianne Hubbard, pp. 99–128. Windhoek, Namibia: Legal Assistance Centre.

Hubbard, Dianne, and Collette Solomon. 1995. "The Many Faces of Feminism in Namibia." In *The Challenge of Local Feminisms: Women's Movements in Global Perspective,* ed. Amrita Basu, pp. 163–86. Boulder, CO: Westview Press.

Huffstutter, P. J. 2007. "Laws Against Marriage Threatening Benefits for Domestic Partners." *Los Angeles Times,* July 8.

Hull, Kathleen. 2001. "The Political Limits of Rights Frames: The Case of Same-Sex Marriage in Hawaii." *Sociological Perspectives* 44: 207–32.

Hull, Kathleen. 2006. *Same-Sex Marriage: The Cultural Politics of Love and Law.* New York: Cambridge University Press.

Human Rights Campaign. 2003. "Amicus Brief to the Supreme Court of the United States, *Lawrence v. Texas.*" 2003 U.S. S. Ct. Briefs LEXIS 37.

Human Rights Campaign. 2009. *Top Ten Reasons for Marriage Equality.* Available at http://www.hrc.org/issues/5491.htm (accessed May 22, 2009).

Human Rights Campaign Foundation. 2006. *The State of the Workplace for Gay, Lesbian, Bisexual, and Transgender Americans 2005–06.* Washington, DC: HRC Foundation. Downloaded on 8/17/06 from http://www.hrc.org/Template.cfm?Section = Get_Informed2&CONTENTID=32936 &TEMPLATE=/ContentManagement/ContentDisplay.cfm.

Human Rights Watch (HRW) and the International Gay and Lesbian Rights Commission (IGLHRC). 2003. *More Than a Name: State-Sponsored Homophobia and Its Consequences In Southern Africa.* Available at http://www.iglhrc.org/files/iglhrc/reports/safriglhrc0303.pdf (accessed May 18, 2007).

Hunt, Alan. 1993. *Explorations in Law and Society: Toward a Constitutive Theory of Law.* New York: Routledge.

Hunt, Gerald. 1999. Laboring for Rights: Unions and Sexual Diversity Across Nations. Philadelphia: Temple University Press.

Hunter, Nan D. 1991. "Marriage, Law, and Gender: A Feminist Inquiry." *Law and Sexuality* 1(9) (1991): 9–69.

Hurst, James W. 1955. *Law and the Conditions of Freedom in Nineteenth Century United States.* Madison: University of Wisconsin Press.

Hutchinson, Darren L. 2000. "'Gay Rights' for 'Gay Whites'?: Race, Sexual Identity, and Equal Protection Discourse." *Cornell Law Review* 85: 1358–91.

I Promise You This: Collected Poems in Memory of Harvey Milk. 1979. In the Gay and Lesbian Archives, San Francisco Public Library.

Ingebretsen, Edward. 2001. *At Stake: Monsters and the Rhetoric of Fear in Public Culture.* Chicago: University of Chicago Press.

International Gay and Lesbian Rights Commission (IGLHRC). 2001. "Sexual Minorities and the Work of the United Nations Special Rapporteur on Torture." Available at http://www.iglhrc.org/files/iglhrc/reports/torturereport.pdf (accessed June 22, 2007).

Isaacks, Madelene. 2005. "'I Don't Force My Feelings for Other Women, My Feelings Have to Force Me': Same-Sexuality Amongst Ovambo Women in Namibia." In *Tommy Boys, Lesbian Men, and Ancestral Wives: Female Same-Sex Practices in Africa,* ed. Ruth Morgan and Saskia Wieringa, pp. 77–120. Johannesburg, South Africa: Jacana Media.

Ivers, Gregg, and Karen O'Connor. 1987. "Friends as Foes: The Amicus Curiae Participation and Effectiveness of the American Civil Liberties Union and Americans for Effective Law Enforcement in Criminal Cases, 1969–1982." *Law and Policy* 9(2): 161–78.

Jacob, Herbert. 1988. *The Silent Revolution: The Transformation of Divorce Law in the United States.* Chicago: University of Chicago Press.

Jasper, James. 1997. *The Art of Moral Protest.* Chicago: University of Chicago Press.

Javors, Irene, and Renate Reimann. 2001. "Building Common Ground: Strategies for Grassroots Organizing on Same-Sex Marriage." In *Queer Families, Queer Politics: Challenging Culture and the State,* ed. Mary Bernstein and Renate Riemann, pp. 293–305. New York: Columbia University Press.

Jenness, Valerie. 2004. "Explaining Criminalization: From Demography and Status Politics to Globalization and Modernization." *Annual Review of Sociology* 30: 147–71.

Jensen, Steffen. 1998. "Cyprus—Law 'Reform.'" *Euro-Letter* 60: 2.

Jepperson, Ronald. 2002. "The Development and Application of Sociological Neoinstitutionalism." In *Contemporary Sociological Theories,* ed. J. Berger and M. Zelditch, pp. 229–66. Lanham, MD: Rowman and Littlefield.

Johnston, Hank. 2005. "Comparative Frame Analysis." In *Frames of Protest: Social Movements and the Framing Perspective,* ed. Hank Johnston and John A. Noakes, pp. 237–60. New York: Rowman and Littlefield.

Jones, Bryan D. 1994. *Reconceiving Decision-Making in Democratic Politics: Attention, Choice, and Public Policy.* Chicago: University of Chicago Press.

Jones, Bryan D. 2001. *Politics and the Architecture of Choice: Bounded Rationality and Governance.* Chicago: University of Chicago Press.

Jones, Bryan D., and Frank R. Baumgartner. 2005. *The Politics of Attention: How Government Prioritizes Problems.* Chicago: University of Chicago Press.

Jones, Lynn C. 2005. "Exploring the Sources of Cause and Career Correspondence Among Cause Lawyers." In *The Worlds Cause Lawyers Make,* ed. Stuart Scheingold and Austin Sarat, pp. 203–38. Palo Alto: Stanford University Press.

Jones, Lynn C. 2006. "The Haves Come Out Ahead: How Cause Lawyers Frame the Legal System for Movements." In *Cause Lawyers and Social Movements,* ed. Austin Sarat and Stuart Scheingold, pp. 182–96. Palo Alto: Stanford University Press.

Kahneman, Daniel, Jack L. Knetsch, and Richard H. Thaler. 1991. "Anomalies: The Endowment Effect, Loss Aversion, and Staus Quo Bias." *Journal of Economic Perspectives* 5: 193–206.

Kahneman, Daniel, et al. (eds.). 1982. *Judgment Under Uncertainty: Heuristics and Biases.* New York: Cambridge University Press.

Kane, Melinda D. 2003. "Social Movement Policy Success: Decriminalizing State Sodomy Laws, 1969–1998." *Mobilization* 8: 313–34.

Kane, Melinda D. 2007. "Timing Matters: Shifts in the Causal Determinants of Sodomy-Law Decriminalization, 1961–1998." *Social Problems* 54: 211–39.

Kantorowicz, Ernst Hartwig. 1957. *The King's Two Bodies: A Study in Mediaeval Political Theology*. Princeton: Princeton University Press.

Kass, John, and Nancy Ryan. 1997. "Partners Plan Shows New Daley." *Chicago Tribune*, March 20.

Katyal, Sonia. 2002. "Exporting Identity." *Yale Journal of Law and Feminism* 14(1): 97–176.

Katyal, Sonia. 2006. "Sexuality and Sovereignty: The Global Limits and Possibilities of Lawrence." *College of William and Mary Bill of Rights Journal* 14: 1429, 1435.

Katzenstein, Mary Fainsod. 1990. "Feminism Within American Institutions: Unobtrusive Mobilization in the 1980s." *Signs: Journal of Women in Culture and Society* 16(1): 27–54.

Katzenstein, Mary Fainsod. 1995. "Discursive Politics and Feminist Activism in the Catholic Church." In *Feminist Organizations: Harvest of the New Women's Movement*, ed. by Myra Marx Ferree and Patricia Yancey Martin, pp. 35–52. Philadelphia: Temple University Press.

Katzenstein, Mary Fainsod. 1998. *Faithful and Fearless: Moving Feminist Protest Inside the Church and Military*. Princeton: Princeton University Press.

Kearney, Joseph D., and Thomas W. Merrill. 2000. "The Influence of Amicus Curiae Briefs on the Supreme Court." *University of Pennsylvania Law Review* 148: 743–835.

Keck, Margaret E., and Kathryn Sikkink. 1998. *Activism Beyond Borders: Advocacy Networks in International Politics*. Ithaca, NY: Cornell University Press.

Keen, Lisa, and Suzanne B. Goldberg. 1998. *Strangers to the Law: Gay People on Trial*. Ann Arbor: The University of Michigan Press.

Kelman, Mark. 1987. *A Guide to Critical Legal Studies*. Cambridge, MA: Harvard University Press.

Kennedy, Elizabeth Lapovsky, and Madeline D. Davis. 1993. *Boots of Leather, Slippers of Gold*. New York: Penguin.

Kersch, Ken I. 1997. "Full Faith and Credit for Same Sex Marriages?" *Political Science Quarterly* 112(1): 117–37.

Kesich, Gregory. 2004. "Catholic Charities, City Claim Victory." *Portland [ME] Press Herald*, February 7, p. 1A.

Kinder, Donald R. 1998. "Communication and Opinion." *Annual Review of Political Science* 1: 167–97.

Kingdon, John W. 1995. *Agendas, Alternatives, and Public Policies*. New York: Longman.

Kirkland, Anna. 2003. "Victorious Transsexuals in The Courtroom: A Challenge for Feminist Legal Theory." *Law and Social Inquiry* 28(1): 1–37.

Kitschelt, Herbert. 1986. "Political Opportunity Structures and Political Protest: Anti-Nuclear Movements in Four Democracies." *British Journal of Political Science* 16: 57–85.

Klarman, Michael. 2006. *From Jim Crow to Civil Rights: The Supreme Court and the Struggle for Racial Equality*. New York: Oxford University Press.

Kobylka, Joseph. 1987. "A Court-Created Context for Group Litigation: Libertarian Groups and Obscenity." *Journal of Politics* 49: 1061–78.

Kobylka, Joseph. 1991. *The Politics of Obscenity*. Westport, CT: Greenwood Publishing Group.

Koppelman, Andrew. 1988. "The Miscegenation Analogy: Sodomy Law as Sex Discrimination." *Yale Law Journal* 98: 145–64.

Korobkin, Russell. 1998. "The Status Quo and Contract Default Rules." *Cornell Law Review* 83: 608–87.

Koshner, Andrew J. 1998. *Solving the Puzzle of Interest Group Litigation*. Westport, CT: Greenwood Press.

Kozol, Jonathan. 2005. *The Shame of the Nation: The Restoration of Apartheid Schooling in America*. New York: Crown.

Krane, Dale, and Platon N. Rigos. 2000. "Municipal Power and Choice: An Examination of Frug's 'Powerlessness' Thesis." Paper presented at the Annual Meeting of the American Political Science Association, Washington, DC., August 31–September 3, 2000.

Kriesi, Hanspeter, and Dominique Wislet. 1999. "The Impact of Social Movements on Political Institutions: A Comparison of the Introduction of Direct Legislation in Switzerland and the United States." In *How Social Movements Matter*, ed. M. Guigni, Doug McAdam, and Charles Tilly, pp. 42–66. Minneapolis: University of Minnesota.

Kritzer, Herbert M., and Susan S. Silbey. 2003. *In Litigation: Do the Haves Still Come Out Ahead?* Palo Alto: Stanford University Press.

Kulick, Don, and Charles H. Klein. 2003. "Scandalous Acts: The Politics of Shame Among Brazilian Travesti Prostitutes." In *Recognition Struggles and Social Movements: Contested Identities, Agency, and Power*, ed. Barbara Hobson, pp. 215–38. New York: Cambridge University Press.

Kurtz, Stanley. 2004a. "The End of Marriage in Scandinavia." *Weekly Standard* 9(20), February 2.

Kurtz, Stanley. 2004b. "Unhealthy Half Truths: Scandinavian Marriage Is Dying." *National Review Online*, May 25. Available at www.Nationalreview.com.

Kurtz, Stanley. 2004c. "Going Dutch: Lessons of the Same-Sex Marriage Debate in the Netherlands." *Weekly Standard* 9(36), May 31.

Kurtz, Stanley. 2004d. "No Explanation: Gay Marriage Has Sent the Netherlands the Way of Scandinavia." *National Review Online*, June 3. Available at www.Nationalreview.com.

Kushner, Tony. 1997. "The Art of the Difficult." *Civilization* (August–September): 62–67. Reprinted in Gary Fisher Dawson (1999), *Documentary Theatre in the United States:* *An Historical Survey and Analysis of Its Content, Form, and Stagecraft*. Westport, CT: Greenwood Press.

LaFont, Suzanne. 2007. "Decolonising Sexuality." In *Unravelling Taboos: Gender and Sexuality in Namibia*, ed. Suzanne LaFont and Dianne Hubbard, pp. 245–60. Windhoek, Namibia: Legal Assistance Centre.

Lahey, Kathleen A., and Kevin Alderson. 2004. *Same–Sex Marriage: The Personal and the Political*. Toronto, Ontario: Insomniac Press.

Lambda Legal Defense and Education Fund. 1985. "Amicus Curiae Brief in *Bowers v. Hardwick*." 1985 U.S. Briefs 140. LexisNexis Academic (accessed February 2, 2005).

Lambda Legal Defense and Education Fund. 1999. "Groups Issue Standards for Custody Disputes in Same Sex Relationships." Available at http://www.lambdalegal.org/news/pr/groups-issue-standards-for.html (accessed November 7, 2007).

Lambda Legal Defense and Education Fund. 1999. "*Jacks v. City of Santa Barbara*." Available at .

Lambda Legal Defense and Education Fund. 2009. "Overview of State Adoption Statutes." Available at http://www.lambdalegal.org/our-work/issues/marriage-relationships-family/parenting/overview-of-state-adoption.html (accessed January 2, 2009).

Lau, Richard R., and Mark Schlesinger. 2005. "Policy Frames, Metaphorical Reasoning, and Support for Public Policies" *Political Psychology* 26: 77–114.

Letellier, P. 2001. "The Delightful and Rocky Road of Lesbian and Gay Parenting." *Lesbian News* 26(11).

Levit, Nancy. 1998. *The Gender Line: Men, Women, and the Law*. New York: New York University Press.

Levitsky, Sandra R. 2006. "To Lead With Law: Reassessing the Influence of Legal Advocacy Organizations in Social Movements." In *Cause Lawyers and Social Movements*, ed. Austin Sarat and Stuart

Scheingold, pp. 182–96. Palo Alto: Stanford University Press.

Lewis, Gregory B., and Charles W. Gossett. 2008. "Changing Public Opinion on Same-Sex Marriage: The Case of California." *Politics and Policy* 36(1): 4–30.

Liem, Deann Borshay. 2000. *First Person Plural*. New York: PBS.

Löfström, Jan. 1998. "A Premodern Legacy: The 'Easy' Criminalization of Homosexual Acts Between Women in the Finnish Penal Code of 1889." *Journal of Homosexuality* 35: 53–79.

Lorway, Robert. 2006. "Dispelling 'Heterosexual African AIDS' in Namibia: Same-Sex Sexuality in the Township of Katutura." *Culture, Health, and Sexuality* 8(5): 435–49.

Lorway, Robert. 2007. "Breaking a Public Health Silence: HIV Risk and Male-Male Sexual Practices in the Windhoek Urban Area." In *Unravelling Taboos: Gender and Sexuality in Namibia*, ed. Suzanne LaFont and Dianne Hubbard, pp. 276–95. Windhoek, Namibia: Legal Assistance Centre.

Luker, Kristin. 1984. *Abortion and the Politics of Motherhood*. Berkeley: University of California Press.

MacKinnon, Catherine A. 1989. *Toward a Feminist Theory of the State*. Cambridge, MA: Harvard University Press.

Mahood, Harold R. 1990. *Interest Group Politics in America: A New Intensity*. Englewood Cliffs, NJ: Prentice-Hall.

Malawi Law Commission. 2000. *Law Commission Report on Review of the Penal Code*. Zomba, Malawi: Government Printer.

Mann, Emily. 1997. *The Execution of Justice, in Testimonies: Four Plays*. New York: Theatre Communications Group.

Marks, T. C., Jr., and J. F. Cooper. 1988. *State Constitutional Law*. St. Paul, MN: West.

Marotta, Toby. 1981. *The Politics of Homosexuality*. Boston: Houghton-Mifflin.

Marshall, Anna-Maria. 2003. "Injustice Frames, Legality and the Everyday Construction of Sexual Harassment." *Law and Social Inquiry* 28: 659–89.

Massaquoi, Notisha. 2008. "The Continent as a Closet: The Making of an African Queer Theory." *Outliers* 1(1): 50–60. Available at http://www.irnweb.org/siteFiles/Publications/3475FB49E91EA345023F0FC29F259DDC.pdf (accessed June 15, 2008).

Matsuda, Mari J. 1998. "Crime and Affirmative Action." *Georgetown Journal of Gender, Race and Justice* 1: 309–23.

McAdam, Doug. 1999. Political Process and the Development of Black Insurgency, 1930–1970. Chicago: University of Chicago Press.

McAdam, Doug, Sidney Tarrow, and Charles Tilly 2001. *Dynamics of Contention*. New York: Cambridge University Press.

McCammon, Holly J. 1998. "Using Event History Analysis in Historical Research: With Illustrations From a Study of the Passage of Women's Protective Legislation." *International Review of Social History* 34: 33–55.

McCann, Michael. 1994. *Rights at Work: Pay Equity Reform and the Politics of Legal Mobilization*. Chicago: University of Chicago Press.

McCann, Michael. 2004. "Law and Social Movements." In *The Blackwell Companion to Law and Society*, ed. Austin Sarat, pp. 506–22. Malden, MA: Blackwell.

McGuire, Kevin. 1990. "Obscenity, Libertarian Values and Decision Making in the Supreme Court." *American Politics Quarterly* 18: 47–67.

McGuire, Kevin, and Gregory Caldeira. 1993. "Lawyers, Organized Interests, and the Law of Obscenity: Agenda Setting in the Supreme Court." *American Political Science Review* 87: 717–26.

McIntyre, Lisa. 1994. *Law in the Sociological Enterprise: A Reconstruction*. Boulder, CO: Westview.

McMillen, Liz. 1996. "The Importance of Storytelling: A New Emphasis by Law Scholars." *Chronicle of Higher Education* (July 26): A10.

McVeigh, Rory, Michael R. Welch, and Thoroddur Bjarnason. 2003. "Hate Crime

Reporting as a Successful Social Movement Outcome." *American Sociological Review* 68: 843–67.

Méchoulan, Eric. 2004. "On the Edges of Jacques Rancière." *SubStance* 33(1): 3–9.

Meier, Kenneth J. 1994. *The Politics of Sin: Drugs, Alcohol, and Public Policy.* Armonk, NY: M. E. Sharpe.

Melber, Henning. 2003. "Limits to Liberation: An Introduction to Namibia's Postcolonial Political Cultures." In *Re-Examining Liberation in Namibia: Political Culture Since Independence,* ed. Henning Melber, pp. 9–24. Uppsala, Sweden: Nordic Africa Institute.

Melucci, Alberto. 1985. "The Symbolic Challenge of Contemporary Movements," *Social Research* 52: 789–816.

Melucci, Alberto. 1989. *Nomads of the Present.* London: Hutchinson Radius.

Melucci, Alberto. 1996. *Challenging Codes: Collective Action in the Information Age.* Cambridge: Cambridge University Press.

Merry, Sally Engle. 1990. *Getting Justice and Getting Even: Legal Consciousness Among Working-Class Americans.* Chicago: University of Chicago Press.

Meyer, David, and Nancy Whittier. 1994. "Social Movement Spillover." *Social Problems* 41: 277–98.

Meyer, David S. 2002. "Opportunities and Identities: Bridge–Building in the Study of Social Movements." In *Social Movements: Identity, Culture and the State,* ed. David S. Meyer, Nancy Whittier, and Belinda Robnett, pp. 3–24. New York: Oxford University Press.

Meyer, David S., and Suzanne Staggenborg. 1996. "Movements, Countermovements, and the Structure of Political Opportunity." *American Journal of Sociology* 101(6): 1628–60.

Meyer, John W., John Boli, George M. Thomas, and Francisco O. Ramirez. 1997. "World Society and the Nation-State." *American Journal of Sociology* 103: 144–81.

Meyer, John W., and Brian Rowan. 1977. "Institutionalized Organizations: Formal Structure as Myth and Ceremony." *American Journal of Sociology* 83: 340–63.

Meyerowitz, Joanne. 2002. *How Sex Changed: A History of Transsexuality in the United States.* Cambridge, MA: Harvard University Press.

Miller, Robin Cheryl 2005. "Child Custody and Visitation Rights Arising From Same-Sex Relationship." *A.L.R. 5th* 80: 1.

Milner, Neal. 1989. "The Denigration of Rights and the Persistence of Rights Talk: A Cultural Portrait." *Law and Social Inquiry* 14: 631–75.

Minter, Shannon Price. 2006. "Do Transsexuals Dream of Gay Rights? Getting Real About Transgender Inclusion." In *Transgender Rights,* ed. Paisley Currah, Richard M. Juang, and Shannon Price Minter, pp. 141–70. Minneapolis: University of Minnesota Press.

Mnookin, Robert, and Tony Kornhauser. 1979. "Bargaining in the Shadow of the Law." *Yale Law Journal* 88: 950–97.

Modell, Judith S. 1994. *Kinship With Strangers: Adoption and Interpretations of Kinship in American Culture.* Berkeley: University of California Press.

Modell, Judith S. 2001. "Open Adoption: Extending Families, Exchanging Facts." In *New Directions in Anthropological Kinship,* ed. Linda Stone, pp. 246–63. Lanham, MD: Rowman and Littlefield.

Moe, Terry M. 1980. *The Organization of Interests.* Chicago: University of Chicago Press.

Murray, Stephen O., and Will Roscoe (eds.). 1998. *Boy-Wives and Female Husbands: Studies of African Homosexualities.* New York: Palgrave MacMillan.

Muthien, Bernadette. 2007. "Queerying Borders: An Afrikan Activist Experience." *Journal of Lesbian Studies* 11(3–4): 321–30.

Namaste, Viviane. 2005. *Sex Change, Social Change: Reflections on Identity, Institutions and Imperialism.* Toronto: Women's Press.

Naples, Nancy. 1998. *Grassroots Warriors: Activist Mothering, Community Work, and the War on Poverty.* New York: Routledge.

National Lesbian and Gay Law Association. 2003. "Amicus Brief to the Supreme Court of the United States, *Lawrence v. Texas*." 2003 U.S. S. Ct. Briefs LEXIS 40.

National Gay and Lesbian Task Force. 2007. "Relationship Recognition for Same-Sex Couples in the U.S. as of July 2007)." Available at http://thetaskforce.org/downloads/reports/issue_maps/relationship_recognition_7_07.pdf (accessed August 25, 2007).

Neal, Ordeana R. 1996. "The Limits of Legal Discourse: Learning From the Civil Rights Movement in the Quest for Gay and Lesbian Civil Rights." *New York Law School Law Review* 40: 679.

Nice, David C., and Patricia Fredericksen. 1995. *The Politics of Intergovernmental Relations*. 2nd edition. Chicago: Nelson-Hall.

Nielsen, Laura Beth. 2004. "Law and Rights." In *The Blackwell Companion to Law and Society*, ed. Austin Sarat, pp. 63–79. Malden, MA: Blackwell.

Noack, Turid, Ane Seierstad, and Harald Weedon-Fekjær. 2005. "A Demographic Analysis of Registered Partnerships (Legal Same-Sex Unions): The Case of Norway." *European Journal of Population* 21: 89–109.

Noakes, John A., and Hank Johnston. 2005. "Frames of Protest: A Road Map to a Perspective." In *Frames of Protest: Social Movements and the Framing Perspective*, ed. Hank Johnston and John A. Noakes, pp. 1–29. New York: Rowman and Littlefield.

Nyeck, Sybille N. 2008. "Impossible Africans." *Outliers* 1(1): 5–7. Available at http://www.irnweb.org/siteFiles/Publications/3475FB49E91EA345023F0FC29F259DDC.pdf (accessed June 15, 2008).

O'Connor, Karen, 1980. *Women's Organizations' Use of the Courts*. Lexington, MA: Lexington Books.

O'Connor, Karen. 1997. "Lobbying the Justices or Lobbying for Justice." In *The Interest Group Connection*, ed. Paul Herrnson, Ronald Shaiko, and Clyde Wilcox, pp. 267–88. New Jersey: Chatham House.

O'Connor, Karen, and Lee Epstein. 1981–82. "Amicus Curiae Participation in U.S. Supreme Court Litigation: An Appraisal of Hakman's 'Folklore.'" *Law and Society Review* 16: 311–21.

O'Connor, Karen, and Lee Epstein. 1983. "The Rise of Conservative Interest Group Litigation." *Journal of Politics* 45: 479–89.

O'Connor, Karen, and Lee Epstein. 1984. "The Role of Interest Groups in Supreme Court Policymaking." In *Public Policy Formulation*, ed. Robert Eyestone, pp. 63–82. Greenwich, CT: JAI Press.

Oliver, Pamela E., and Hank Johnston. 2005. "What a Good Idea!: Ideologies and Frames in Social Movement Research." In *Frames of Protest: Social Movements and the Framing Perspective*, ed. Hank Johnston and John A. Noakes, pp. 185–203. New York: Rowman and Littlefield.

Olson, Mancur, Jr. 1965. *The Logic of Collective Action*. Cambridge, MA: Harvard University Press.

Olson, Susan. 1984. *Clients and Lawyers: Securing the Rights of Disabled Persons*. Westport, CT: Greenwood Press.

Olson, Susan. 1990. "Interest Group Litigation in Federal District Court: Beyond the Political Disadvantage Theory." *Journal of Politics* 52: 854–882.

Oswin, Natalie. 2007. "Producing Homonormativity in Neoliberal South Africa: Recognition, Redistribution, and the Equality Project." *Signs: Journal of Women in Culture and Society* 32(3): 649–69.

Padgug, Robert. 1979. "Sexual Matters: Rethinking Sexuality in History." *Radical History Review* 20: 3–23.

Palmberg, Mai. 1999. "Emerging Visibility of Gays and Lesbians in Southern Africa." In *The Global Emergence of Gay and Lesbian Politics: National Imprints of a Worldwide Movement*, ed. Barry D. Adam, Jan Willem Duyvendak, and André Krouwel, pp. 266–92. Philadelphia: Temple University Press.

Pankratz, Howard. 2004. "Psychological Parent Prevails." *Denver Post*, July 2, p. B1.

Passavant, Paul. 2007. "The Contradictory State of Giorgio Agamben." *Political Theory* 35: 147–74.

Patterson, Thomas. 1993. *Out of Order*. New York: Vintage Books.

Patton, Cindy. 1995. "Refiguring Social Space." In *Social Postmodernism: Beyond Identity Politics*, ed. Linda Nicholson and Steven Seidman, pp. 216–49. Cambridge: Cambridge University Press.

Patton, Cindy. 1997. "Queer Space/God's Space: Counting Down to the Apocalypse." *Rethinking Marxism* 9(2): 1–23.

Pederson, Jamie D. 2004. "An Analysis of the Benefits and Burdens of Marriage Contained in the Revised Code of Washington." Available at http://www.lmaw.org/freedom/docs/WA-RCWProj.htm.

Pedriana, Nicholas. 2006. "From Protective to Equal Treatment: Legal Framing Processes and Transformation of the Women's Movement in the 1960s." *American Journal of Sociology* 111: 1718–61.

Pedriana, Nicholas, and Robin Stryker. 1997. "Political Culture Wars 1960s Style: Equal Employment Opportunity/Affirmative Action Law and the Philadelphia Plan." *American Journal of Sociology* 103: 633–91.

Phillips, F., and A. Estes. 2007. "Right of Gays to Marry Set for Years to Come—Vote Keeps Proposed Ban Off 2008 Ballot." *Boston Globe*, June 15, p. A1.

Phillips, Oliver. 2001. "Constituting the Global Gay: Issues of Individual Subjectivity and Sexuality in Southern Africa." In *Law and Sexuality in the Global Arena*, ed. Carl Stychin and Didi Herman, pp. 17–34. Minneapolis: University of Minnesota Press.

Pierceson, Jason. 2005. *Courts, Liberalism and Rights*. Philadelphia: Temple University Press.

Pinello, Daniel R. 2003. *Gay Rights and American Law*. Cambridge: Cambridge University Press.

Pinello, Daniel R. 2006. *America's Struggle for Same Sex Marriage*. New York: Cambridge University Press.

Piven, Frances Fox, and Richard Cloward. 1977. *Poor People's Movements*. New York: Pantheon Books.

Pizer, Jenny, and Susan Sommer. 2006. "Fighting Marriage Discrimination: The Litigators' Perspective." *Of Counsel* 2(5). Available at http://ga4.org/lambdalegal/notice-description.tcl?newsletter_id=3757295.

Plous, Scott. 1993. *The Psychology of Judgment and Decision Making*. New York: McGraw-Hill.

Polikoff, Nancy D. 1993. "Will We Get What We Ask For: Why Legalizing Gay and Lesbian Marriage Will Not 'Dismantle the Legal Structure of Gender in Every Marriage.'" *University of Virginia Law Review* 79: 1535–50.

Polikoff, Nancy D. 2008. *Beyond (Straight and Gay) Marriage: Valuing All Families Under the Law*. Boston: Beacon Press.

Polletta, Francesca. 2000. "The Structural Context of Novel Rights Claims: Southern Civil Rights Organizations 1961–66." *Law and Society Review* 34: 367–406.

Polletta, Francesca. 2006. *It Was Like a Fever: Storytelling in Protest and Politics*. Chicago: University of Chicago Press.

Popenoe, D. 1996. *Life Without Father: Compelling New Evidence That Fatherhood and Marriage Are Indispensable for the Good of Children and Society*. New York: Martin Kessler/Free Press.

Posner, Richard A. 1994. *Sex and Reason*. Cambridge, MA: Harvard University Press.

Post, Robert, ed. 2001. *Prejudicial Appearances: The Logic of American Antidiscrimination Law*. Durham, NC: Duke University Press.

Preminger, Otto. 1959. *Anatomy of a Murder* (film). Columbia Pictures.

Puar, Jasbir K. 2004. "Abu Ghraib: Arguing Against Exceptionalism." *Feminist Studies* 30(2): 522–34.

Puar, Jasbir K. 2005. "Queer Times, Queer Assemblages." *Social Text* 23(3–4): 121–39.

Puar, Jasbir K.. 2006. "Mapping U.S.-Homonormativities." *Gender, Place and Culture* 13(1): 67–88.

Rabinow, Paul. 1984. Introduction to the Foucault Reader. New York: Pantheon Books.

Rahami, Mohsen. 2005. "Development of Criminal Punishment in the Iranian Post Revolutionary Penal Code." European Journal of Crime, Criminal Law and Criminal Justice 13: 585–602.

Rainbow Project (TRP). 1998. "The Way Forward: Strategic Planning Workshop of the Rainbow Project." Meeting minutes.

Ramirez, Francisco O. 1987. "Comparative Social Movements." In Institutional Structure: Constituting State, Society and the Individual, ed. G. M. Thomas, J. W. Meyer, F. O. Ramirez, and J. Boli, pp. 261–78. London: Sage.

Rancière, Jacques. 1999. Disagreement: Politics and Philosophy. Minneapolis: University of Minnesota Press.

Rancière, Jacques. 2004a. "The Politics of Aesthetics." Kein Theatre (kein.org). Available at http://theater.kein.org/node/view/99 [accessed February 12, 2006].

Rancière, Jacques. 2004b. The Politics of Aesthetics: The Distribution of the Sensible. London: Continuum.

Randolph, Elizabeth. 2001. "Family Secrets, or . . . How to Become a Bisexual Alien Without Really Trying." In Queer Families, Queer Politics: Challenging Culture and the State, ed. Mary Bernstein and Renate Reimann, pp. 104–11. New York: Columbia University Press.

Readler, Chad. 1998. "Local Government Anti-Discrimination Laws: Do They Make a Difference?" University of Michigan Journal of Law Reform 31 (Spring):777–813.

Reich, Jennifer A. 2005. Fixing Families: Parents, Power and the Child Welfare System. New York: Routledge.

Reid-Pharr, Robert F. 2007. Once You Go Black: Desire, Choice and Black Masculinity in Post-War America. New York: New York University Press.

Rich, Adrienne. 1993. "Compulsory Heterosexuality and Lesbian Existenc." In The Lesbian and Gay Studies Reader, ed. Henry Abelove, Michèle Aina Barale, and David M. Halperin, pp. 227–54. New York: Routledge.

Richards, David. 1998. Women, Gays, and the Constitution : The Grounds for Feminism and Gay Rights in Culture and Law. Chicago: University of Chicago Press.

Richards, David. 1999. Identity and the Case for Gay Rights: Race, Gender, Religion as Analogies. Chicago: University of Chicago Press.

Richman, Kimberly. 2002. "Lovers, Legal Strangers and Parents: Negotiating Parental and Sexual Identity in Family Law." Law and Society Review 36(2): 285–325.

Richman, Kimberly. 2005. "(When) Are Rights Wrong?: Rights Discourse and Indeterminacy in Gay and Lesbian Parents' Custody Cases." Law and Social Inquiry 30: 137–76.

Richman, Kimberly D. 2009. Courting Change: Queer Parents, Judges and the Transformation of American Family Law. New York: New York University Press.

Riggle, E. D. B., S. S. Rostosky and R. A. Prather. 2006. "Advance Planning by Same-Sex Couples." Journal of Family Issues 27(6): 758–76.

Riggle, E. D. B., and B. L. Tadlock (eds.). 1999. Gays and Lesbians in the Democratic Process. New York: Columbia University Press.

Rimmerman, Craig A. 2002. From Identity to Politics: The Lesbian and Gay Movements in the United States. Philadelphia: Temple University Press.

Robson, Ruthann. 1992. Lesbian Out Law: Survival Under the Rule of Law. Ann Arbor, MI: Firebrand Books.

Robson, Ruthann. 2006. "Reinscribing Normality? The Law and Politics of Transgender Marriage in Transgender Rights." In Transgender Rights, ed. Paisley Currah, Richard M. Juang, and Shannon P. Minter, pp. 299–309. Minneapolis: University of Minnesota Press.

Rodriguez, Cindy. 2004. "Child Wins in Mommy vs. Mommy." Denver Post, July 8, p. F1.

Rosato, Jennifer, 2006. "Children Of Same-Sex Parents Deserve the Security Blanket of the Parentage Presumption." *Family Court Review* 44(1): 74–86.

Rosenberg, Gerald, N. 2008 [1991]. *The Hollow Hope: Can Courts Bring About Social Change?* Chicago: University of Chicago Press.

Rosenblum, Darren. 1995. "Overcoming 'Stigmas': Lesbian and Gay Districts and Black Electoral Empowerment." *Howard University Law Journal* 39: 149–200.

Rosenblum, Darren. 1996. "Geographically Sexual?: Advancing Lesbian and Gay Interests Through Proportional Representation." *Harvard University Civil Rights-Civil Liberties Law Review* 31: 119–54.

Rosenblum, Darren. 2007. "Internalizing Gender: Why International Law Theory Should Adopt Comparative Methods." *Columbia University Journal of Transnational Law* 45: 759–828.

Ross, J. O. 1999. "A Legal Analysis of Parenthood by Choice, Not Chance." *Texas Journal of Women and the Law* 9: 29–52.

Rothschild, Cynthia. 2005. *Written Out: How Sexuality Is Used to Attack Women's Organizing.* New York: International Gay and Lesbian Human Rights Commission.

Rubin, Gayle. 1984. "Thinking Sex: Notes for a Racial Theory of the Politics of Sexuality." In *Pleasure and Danger: Exploring Female Sexuality*, ed. Carol S. Vance, pp. 267–81. New York: HarperCollins.

Rubin, Henry. 2003. *Self-Made Men: Identity and Embodiment Among Transsexual Men.* Nashville: Vanderbilt University Press.

Rubenstein, William B. (ed.). 1993. *Lesbians, Gay Men, and the Law.* New York: New Press.

Ruskola, Teemu. 2005. "Gay Rights Versus Queer Theory: What Is Left of Sodomy After *Lawrence v. Texas?*" *Social Text* 23: 235–49.

Ryan, Charlotte. 1991. *Prime Time Activism: Media Strategies for Grassroots Organizing.* Boston: South End.

Saguy, Abigail. 2003. *What Is Sexual Harassment: From Capitol Hill to the Sorbonne.* Berkeley: University of California Press.

Salisbury, Robert. 1984. "Interest Representation: The Dominance of Institutions." *American Political Science Review* 78: 64–76.

Salter, Kenneth W. 1991. *The Trial of Dan White.* El Cerrito, CA: Market and Systems Interface Publications.

Sanday, Peggy Reeves. 1981. "The Socio-Cultural Context of Rape: A Cross-Cultural Study." *Journal of Social Issues* 37: 5–27.

Santora, T. 2001. "What's Good for the Goose: A Critical Review of Unions as Employers and the Continuing Struggle Toward Equal Benefits in the Workplace." *Working USA* 4(4): 98–123.

Santoro, Wayne A., and Gail M. McGuire. 1997. "Social Movement Insiders: The Impact of Institutional Activists on Affirmative Action and Comparable Worth Policies." *Social Problems* 44(4): 503–19.

Sarat, Austin. 1990. "'The Law Is All Over': Power, Resistance, and the Legal Consciousness of the Welfare Poor." *Yale Journal of Law and the Humanities* 2(2): 343–80.

Savage, Dan. 1999. *The Kid: What Happened After My Boyfriend and I Decided to Go Get Pregnant.* New York: Plume.

Schacter, Jane S. 1994. "The Gay Civil Rights Debate in the States: Decoding the Discourse of Equivalents." *Harvard Civil Rights-Civil Liberties Law Review* 29: 283–317.

Schattschneider, E. E. 1960. *The Semisovereign People.* New York: Holt, Rinehart, and Winston.

Scheingold, Stuart. 2004 [1974]. *The Politics of Rights: Lawyers, Public Policy, and Political Change.* Ann Arbor: University of Michigan Press.

Schlag, Pierre. 2002. "The Aesthetics of American Law." *Harvard Law Review* 115: 1047–1118.

Scott, James C. 1998. *Seeing Like a State: How Certain Plans to Improve the Human Condition Have Failed.* New Haven: Yale University Press.

Schlozman, Kay Lehman and John Tierney. 1986. *Organized Interests and American Democracy.* New York: Harper and Row.

Schneider, Anne, and Helen Ingram. 1993. "Social Construction of Target Populations: Implications for Politics and Policy." *American Political Science Review* 87(2): 334–47.

"Second Parent Adoptions: A Snapshot of Current Law." Available at http://www.nclrights.org/publications/2ndparentadoptions.htm (accessed May 6, 2005).

Seidman, Steven. 1993. "Identity and Politics in a 'Postmodern' Gay Culture: Some Historical and Conceptual Notes." In *Fear of a Queer Planet*, ed. Michael Warner, pp. 105–42. Minneapolis: University of Minneapolis.

Seidman, Steven. 1997. *Difference Troubles: Queering Social Theory and Sexual Politics.* New York: Cambridge University Press.

Seidman, Steven. 2002. *Beyond the Closet: The Transformation of Gay and Lesbian Life.* New York: Routledge.

Sewell, William H. 1992. "A Theory of Structure: Duality, Agency and Transformation." *American Journal of Sociology* 98: 1–29.

Shamir, Ronen, and Sara Chinski. 1998. "Destruction of Houses and Construction of a Cause: Lawyers and Bedouins in the Israeli Courts." In *Cause Lawyering: Political Commitments and Professional Responsibilities*, ed. Austin Sarat and Stuart Scheingold, pp. 227–59. New York: Oxford University Press.

Shanley, M. L. 1995. "Unwed Fathers' Rights, Adoption and Sex Equality: Gender-Neutrality and the Perpetuation of Patriarchy." *Columbia Law Review* 95: 60–103.

Sharp, Elaine B. (ed.). 1999. *Culture Wars and Local Politics.* Lawrence: University of Kansas Press.

Sharpe, Andrew. 2007. "Endless Sex: The Gender Recognition Act of 2004 and the Persistence of a Legal Category." *Feminist Legal Studies* 15: 57.

Sharpe, Andrew. 2007. "A Critique of the Gender Recognition Act 2004." *Bioethical Inquiry* 4: 33–42.

Sheehan, Reginald S., William Mishler, and Donald R. Songer. 1992. "Ideology, Status and the Differential Success of Direct Parties Before the Supreme Court." *American Journal of Political Science* 86: 464–71.

Sherman, Donald 2005. "Sixth Annual Review of Gender and Sexuality Law: V. Family Law chapter: Child Custody and Visitation." *Georgetown Journal of Gender & Law* 6: 691.

Sherrill, Kenneth. 1999. "The Youth of the Movement: Gay Activists in 1972–1973. In *Gays and Lesbians in the Democratic Process: Public Policy, Public Opinion and Political Representation*, ed. Ellen D. B. Riggle and Barry L. Tadlock, pp. 269–96. New York: Columbia University Press.

Shilts, Randy. 1982. *The Mayor of Castro Street.* New York: St. Martin's.

Silverstein, Helena. 1996. *Unleashing Rights: Law, Meaning, and the Animal Rights Movement.* Ann Arbor: University of Michigan Press.

Silverstein, Helena. 2007. *Girls on the Stand: How Courts Fail Pregnant Minors.* New York: New York University Press.

Skocpol, Theda. 1985. "Bringing the State Back In: Strategies of Analysis in Current Research." In *Bringing the State Back In*, ed. P. B. Evans, D. Rueschemeyer, and T. Skocpol, pp. 3–43. Cambridge: Cambridge University Press.

Skrentny, John D. 2002. *The Minority Rights Revolution.* Cambridge, MA: Belknap Press of Harvard University Press.

Skrentny, John D. 2006. "Policy-Elite Perceptions and Social Movement Success: Understanding Variations in Group Inclusion in Affirmative Action." *American Journal of Sociology* 11(6): 1762–1815.

Smart, Carol. 1989. *Feminism and the Power of Law.* London: Routledge.

Smith, Jackie, Charles Chatfield, and Ron Pagnucco (eds.). 1997. *Transnational Social Movements and Global Politics: Solidarity beyond the State.* Syracuse: Syracuse University Press.

Smith, Mark. 2000. *American Business and Political Power: Public Opinion, Elections, and Democracy*. Chicago: University of Chicago Press.

Smith, Susan. 2006. *Safeguarding the Rights and Well-Being of Birthparents in the Adoption Process*. New York: Evan B. Donaldson Institute. Available at http://www.adoptioninstitute.org/publications/2006_11_Birthparent_Study_All.pdf (accessed January 5, 2009).

Snow, David A. 2004. "Framing Processes, Ideology, and Discursive Fields." In *The Blackwell Companion to Social Movements*, ed. David A. Snow, Sarah A. Soule, and Hanspeter Kriesi, pp. 380–412. Malden, MA: Blackwell.

Snow, David A., and Robert D. Benford. 1992. "Master Frames and Cycles of Protest." In *Frontiers in Social Movement Theory*, ed. Aldon D. Morris and Carol McClurg Miller, pp. 133–55. New Haven: Yale University Press.

Snow, David, E. Burke Rochford, Jr., Steven K. Worden, and Robert D. Benford. 1986. "Frame Alignment Processes, Micromobilization, and Movement Participation." *American Sociological Review* 51: 464–81.

Somerville, Siobhan B. 2000. *Queering the Color Line: Race and the Invention of Homosexuality in American Culture*. Durham, NC: Duke University Press.

Songer, Donald R., and Reginald S. Sheehan. 1992. "Who Wins on Appeal? Upperdogs and Underdogs in the United States Courts of Appeals." *American Journal of Political Science* 36: 235–58.

Songer, Donald R., and Reginald S. Sheehan. 1993. "Interest Group Success in the Courts: Amicus Participation in the Supreme Court." *Political Research Quarterly* 46: 339–60.

Songer, Donald R., Reginald S. Sheehan, and Susan Brodie Haire. 1999. "Do the 'Haves' Come Out Ahead Over Time? Applying Galanter's Framework to Decisions of the U.S. Courts Of Appeals, 1925–1988." *Law and Society Review* 33: 811–32.

Sorauf, Frank. 1976. *The Wall of Separation*. Princeton: Princeton University Press.

Soule, Sarah A. 2004. "Going to the Chapel? Same-Sex Marriage Bans in the United States, 1973–2000." *Social Problems* 5: 453–77.

Spurlin, William J. 2001. "Broadening Postcolonial Studies/Decolonizing Queer Studies: Emerging 'Queer' Identities and Cultures in Southern Africa." In *Postcolonial, Queer: Theoretical Intersections*, ed. John C. Hawley, pp. 185–205. Albany: SUNY Press.

Staggenborg, Suzanne. 1988. "The Consequences Of Professionalization and Formalization In The Pro-Choice Movement." *American Sociological Review* 53(4): 585–605.

Stallsmith, Pamela. 2006. "Same Sex Marriage Ban." *Richmond Times Dispatch*, November 8, p. A1.

Stein, Arlene. 2001. *The Stranger Next Door: The Story of a Small Community's Battle over Sex, Faith, and Civil Rights*. Boston: Beacon Press.

Stein, Arlene. 2006. *Shameless: Sexual Dissidence in American Culture*. New York: New York University Press.

Steinberg, Marc. 1999. "The Talk and Back Talk of Collective Action." *American Journal of Sociology* 105(3): 736.

Steinberg, Marc W. 1995. "The Roar of the Crowd: Repertoires of Discourse and Collective Action Among the Spitalfields Silk Weavers in Nineteenth-Century London." In *Repertoires and Cycles of Collective Action*, ed. Mark Traugott, pp. 57–87. Durham, NC: Duke University Press.

Steinmetz, George. 2007. *The Devil's Handwriting: Precoloniality and German Colonial State in Qingdao, Samoa, and Southwest Africa*. Chicago: University of Chicago Press.

Stenger, Katherine, E. 2005. *Voices Crying Out in the Wilderness: Religious Groups and Media Coverage of National Policy Debates*. Ph.D. dissertation, University of Washington.

Sterett, Susan M. 1998. "Caring About Individual Cases: Immigration Lawyering in Britain." In *Cause Lawyering: Political Commitments and Professional Responsibilities,* ed. Stuart Scheingold and Austin Sarat, pp. 112–30. New York: Oxford University Press.

Stone, Amy L. 2006. "More Than Adding a T: Transgender Inclusion in Michigan Gay Rights Ordinances, 1992–2000." Ph.D. dissertation, University of Michigan.

Stone, Deborah A. 1989. "Causal Stories and the Formation of Policy Agendas." *Political Science Quarterly* 104(2): 281–300.

Strang, David, and John W. Meyer. 1993. "Institutional Conditions for Diffusion." *Theory and Society* 22: 487–511.

Stryker, Robin. 1994. "Rules, Resources, and Legitimacy Processes: Some Implications for Social Order, Conflict, and Change." *American Journal of Sociology* 99: 847–910.

Stryker, Susan, and Jim Van Buskirk. 1996. *Gay by the Bay: A History of Queer Culture in the San Francisco Bay Area.* San Francisco: Chronicle Books.

Sturm, Susan P. 1993. "The Legacy and Future of Corrections Litigation." *University of Pennsylvania Law Review* 142: 639.

Stychin, Carl F. 2003. *Governing Sexuality: The Changing Politics of Citizenship and Law Reform.* London: Hart.

Suarez, David F., and Francisco O. Ramirez. 2007. "Human Rights and Citizenship: The Emergence of Human Rights Education." In *Critique and Utopia: New Developments in the Sociology of Education,* ed. C. A. Torres and A. Teodoro, pp. 43–64. Oxford: Rowman and Littlefield.

Sullivan, Maureen. 2004. *Family of Woman: Lesbian Mothers, Their Children, and the Undoing of Gender.* Berkeley: University of California Press.

Sunstein, Cass R. 1993. "On Analogical Reasoning." *Harvard Law Review* 106(3): 741–91.

Sunstein, Cass R . 1994. "Homosexuality And The Constitution." *Indiana Law Journal* 70(1): 1–28.

Sunstein, Cass R. 2004. "Moral Heuristics and Moral Framing." *Minnesota Law Review* 88: 1556–97.

Swidler, Ann. 1986. "Culture in Action: Symbols and Strategies." *American Sociological Review* 51: 273–86.

Swidler, Ann. 1995. "Cultural Power and Social Movements." In *Social Movements and Culture,* ed. Hank Johnston and Bert Klandermans, pp. 25–40. Minneapolis: University of Minnesota Press.

Syed, Anwar H. 1966. *The Political Theory of American Local Government.* New York: Random House.

Szasz, Thomas. 1979. "'J'Accuse': Psychiatry and the Diminished American Capacity for Justice." In the Mike Weiss Papers, San Francisco Public Library.

Tarrow, Sidney. 1992. "Mentalities, Political Cultures, and Collective Action Frames: Constructing Meaning Through Action." In *Frontiers in Social Movement Theory,* ed. Aldon D. Morris and Carol McClurg Miller, pp. 174–202. New Haven: Yale University Press.

Tarrow, Sidney. 1993. "Cycles of Collective Action: Between Moments of Madness and the Repertoire of Contention." *Social Science History* 17(2): 281–307.

Tarrow, Sydney. 1998. *Power in Movement* (2nd ed.). New York: Cambridge University Press.

Tatchell, Peter. 1992. *Europe in the Pink.* London: Gay Men's Project.

Taylor, Verta. 1989. "Social Movement Continuity: The Women's Movement in Abeyance." *American Sociological Review* 54(5): 761–75.

Taylor, Verta, and Nella Van Dyke. 2004. "Get Up, Stand Up": Tactical Repertoires of Social Movements." In *The Blackwell Companion to Social Movements,* ed. David A. Snow, Sarah A. Soule, and Hanspeter Kriesi, pp. 262–93. Malden, MA: Blackwell.

Thomas, Kendall. 1992. "Beyond the Privacy Principle." *Columbia University Law Review* 92: 1431–1516.

Thomson, Linda. 2006. "Salt Lake Can Offer Benefits to More Than Spouses." *Deseret Morning News* [Salt Lake City, UT], May 13.

Tilly, Charles. 1978. *From Mobilization To Revolution*. Reading, MA: Addison-Wesley.

Touraine, Alain. 1981. *The Voice and the Eye: An Analysis of Social Movements*. Cambridge: Cambridge University Press.

Traditional Values Coalition. 2006. "Separation of 'Goodridge' Lesbians Confirms TVC Fears About 'Gay' Marriage." July 21. Available at http://www.traditionalvalues.org/modules.php?sid=2802.

Transgender Law and Policy Institute and National Gay and Lesbian Task Force. 2007. *Scope of Explicitly Transgender-Inclusive Anti-Discrimination Laws*. Available at http://www.transgenderlaw.org (accessed June 18, 2008).

Travers, Robert. 1957. *Anatomy of a Murder*. New York: St. Martin's.

Tribe, Laurence H. 2004. "*Lawrence v. Texas*: The 'Fundamental Right' That Dare Not Speak Its Name." *Harvard Law Review* 117: 1894–955.

Truman, David. 1951. *The Governmental Process*. New York: Knopf.

Tsutsui, Kiyoteru, and Christine Min Wotipka. 2004. "Global Civil Society and the International Human Rights Movement: Citizen Participation in Human Rights International Nongovernmental Organizations." *Social Forces* 83: 587–620.

Turner, Victor. 1982. *From Ritual to Theatre: The Human Seriousness of Play*. New York: Performing Arts Journal Publications.

Tushnet, Mark. 1987. *The NAACP's Legal Strategy Against Segregated Education, 1925–1950*. Chapel Hill: University of North Carolina Press.

Ungar, Mark. 2000. "State Violence and Lesbian, Gay, Bisexual, and Transgender (LGBT) Rights." *New Political Science* 22(1): 61–75.

Unger, Roberto. 1983. "The Critical Legal Studies Movement." *Harvard Law Review* 96: 561–675.

Vaid, Urvashi. 1995. *Virtual Equality: The Mainstreaming of Gay and Lesbian Liberation*. New York: Anchor Books.

Valdes, Francisco. 1995. "Queers, Sissies, Dykes, and Tomboys: Deconstructing the Conflation of 'Sex,' 'Gender,' and 'Sexual Orientation' in Euro-American Law and Society." *California Law Review* 83: 1.

Valdes, Francisco. 2004. "Anomalies, Warts and All: Four Score of Liberty, Privacy and Equality." *Ohio State Law Journal* 65: 1341–1400.

Valocchi, Steve. 1996. "The Emergence of the Integrationist Ideology in the Civil Rights Movement." *Social Problems* 43: 116–30.

Van Sant, Gus. 2008. *Milk*. Focus Features Films.

van Zyl, Mikki. 2005. "Shaping Sexualities— Per(trans)forming Queer." In *Performing Queer: Shaping Sexualities, 1994–2004, Vol. 1*, ed. Mikki van Zyl and Melissa Steyn, pp. 19–38. Roggebaai, South Africa: Kwela Books.

Verhovek, Sam Howe. 1993. "Michigan Court Says Adopted Girl Must Be Sent to Biological Parents." *New York Times*, July 3, section 1, p. 5.

Vose, Clement. 1959. *Caucasians Only*. Berkeley: University of California Press.

Waldman, Ellen, and Marybeth Herald. 2005. "Eyes Wide Shut: Erasing Women's Experiences from the Clinic to the Courtroom." *Harvard Journal of Law and Gender* 28: 285.

Wallace, Stewart, and Michael Korie. 1994. *Harvey Milk: Opera in Three Acts*. In the Gay and Lesbian Archive, San Francisco Public Library.

Wallerstein, Judith, Julia Lewis, and Sandra Blakeslee. 2000. *The Unexpected Legacy of Divorce: A 25–Year Landmark Study*. New York: Hyperion.

Walters, Suzanna Danuta. 2001. "Take My Domestic Partner, Please: Gays and Marriage in the Era of the Visible." In *Queer Families, Queer Politics: Challenging Culture and the State*, ed. Mary Bernstein and Renate Reimann, pp. 338–57. New York: Columbia University Press.

Warner, Michael. 2000. *The Trouble With Normal: Sex, Politics and the Ethics of Queer Life*. Cambridge, MA: Harvard University Press.

Washington, Ray. 2000. "Domestic Partners Policy Case Dismissed." *Gainesville[FL] Sun*, November 16.

Weber, David, and Laurel Sweet. 2000. "Judge KO's Domestic Partner Ordinance." *Boston Herald*, November 3, p. 1.

Weeks, Jeffrey. 1989. *Sex, Politics, and Society: The Regulation of Sexuality Since 1800* (2nd ed.). London: Longman.

Weeks, Jeffrey. 1996. "The Construction of Homosexuality." In *Queer Theory/ Sociology*, ed. S. Seidman, pp. 41–63. Malden, MA: Blackwell.

Weigel, David C. 1997. "Proposal for Domestic Partnership in the City of Detroit: Challenges Under the Law." *University of Detroit Mercy Law Review* 74(4) (Summer): 825–49.

Weinrib, Laura. 2002. "Reconstructing Family: Constructive Trust at Relational Dissolution. *Harvard Civil Rights-Civil Liberties Law Review* 37: 207–47.

Weinstein, Jami, and Tobyn DeMarco. 2004. "Challenging Dissent: The Ontology and Logic of Lawrence v. Texas." *Cardozo Women's Law Journal* 10: 423.

Weiss, Jillian Todd. 2003. "GL vs. BT: The Archaeology of Biphobia and Transphobia Within the U.S. Gay and Lesbian Community." In *Bisexuality and Transgenderism: Intersexions of the Others*, ed. Jonathan Alexander and Karen Yescavage, pp. 25–56. New York: Harrington Park Press.

Weiss, Jillian Todd. 1984. *Double Play: The City Hall Killings*. Menlo Park, CA: Addison-Wesley.

Weiss, Mike. 1998. "Dan White's Last Confession." *San Francisco* (1998): 32–33.

West, Robin L. 2003. Re-Imagining Justice: Progressive Interpretations of Formal Equality, Rights, and the Rule of Law. Burlington, VT: Ashgate.

Weston, Kath. 1997. Families We Choose: Lesbians, Gays, Kinship. New York: Columbia University Press.

Wheeler, Stanton, Bliss Cartwright, Robert Kagan, and Lawrence Friedman. 1987. "Do the Haves Come Out Ahead? Winning and Losing in State Supreme Courts, 1870–1970." *Law and Society Review* 21: 403–45.

Whitaker, Brian. 2006. *Unspeakable Love: Gay and Lesbian Life in the Middle East*. Berkeley: University of California Press.

Whitehead, Barbara Defoe 1997. *The Divorce Culture: Rethinking Our Commitments to Marriage and Family*. New York: Knopf.

Whittier, Nancy. 2002. "Meaning and Structure in Social Movements." In *Social Movements: Identity, Culture and the State*, ed. David S. Meyer, Nancy Whittier, and Belinda Robnett, pp. 289–308. New York: Oxford University Press.

Widmer, Eric D., Judith Treas, and Robert Newcomb. 1998. "Attitudes Toward Nomarital Sex in 24 Countries." *Journal of Sex Research* 35: 349–57.

Wiethoff, Carolyn. 2003. "Naming, Blaming, and Claiming in Public Disputes: The 1998 Maine Referendum on Civil Rights Protection for Gay Men and Lesbians." *Journal of Homosexuality* 44: 61–82.

Williams, Joan C. 2003. "The Social Psychology of Stereotyping: Using Social Science to Litigate Gender Discrimination Cases and Defang the 'Cluelessness' Defense." *Employee Rights and Employment Policy Journal* 7: 40.

Williams, Lena. 1993. "Blacks Rejecting Gay Rights as a Battle Equal to Theirs," *New York Times*, June 28, 1993, p. A1.

Williams, Patricia. 1991. *The Alchemy of Race and Rights*. Cambridge, MA: Harvard University Press.

Willoughby, Kimberly R. 2003. *Ordinary Issues, Extraordinary Solutions: A Legal Guide for the GLBT Community in Colorado*. Denver: Bradford.

Wilson, James Q. 1995. *Political Organizations.* Princeton: Princeton University Press.

Witt, Stephanie L., and Suzanne McCorkle (eds.). 1997. *Anti-gay Rights: Assessing Voter Initiatives.* Westport, CT: Praeger.

Wolfe, Alan. 1998. *One Nation, After All : How Middle-Class Americans Really Think About: God, Country, Family, Racism, Welfare, Immigration, Homosexuality, Work, the Right, the Left, and Each Other.* New York: Viking.

Wolfson, Evan. 1994. "Crossing the Threshold: Equal Marriage Rights for Lesbians and Gay Men, and the Intra-Community Critique." *New York University Review of Law and Social Change* 21: 567–615.

Wolfson, Evan. 2004. *Freedom to Marry: About Us* (May 7, 2004). Available at http://freedomtomarry.org/about.asp (accessed November 27, 2007).

Woodhouse, B. 1993. "Hatching the Egg: A Child-Centered Perspective on Parents' Rights." *Cardozo Law Review* 14: 1747–865.

Wood, Michael A. 2003. "Comment: The Propriety of Local Government Protections of Gays and Lesbians from Discriminatory Employment Practices." *Emory Law Journal* 52 (Winter): 515–54.

Woodhull, Victoria. 1872, 1873. "A Speech on the Principles of Social Freedom in New York City" (November 20, 1871) and Boston (January 3, 1872). In Ellen Carol DuBois. 1988. "Outgrowing the Compact of the Fathers: Equal Rights, Woman Suffrage, and the United States Constitution, 1820–1878." In *The Constitution and American Life*, ed. David Thelen. Ithaca, NY: Cornell University Press, 176–96.

Yeoman, Barry. 1997. "The Real State Takeover." *The Nation* 264(7) (February 24): 21–24.

Yngvesson, Barbara, and Susan B. Coutin. 2006. "Backed By Papers: Undoing Persons, Histories, and Return." *American Ethnologist* 33(2): 177–90.

Yoshino, Kenji. 2006. *Covering : The Hidden Assault On Our Civil Rights.* New York: Random House.

Zald, Mayer N. 1996. "Culture, Ideology and Strategic Framing." In *Comparative Perspectives on Social Movements: Political Opportunities, Mobilizing Structures, and Cultural Framings*, ed. Doug McAdam, John D. McCarthy, and Mayer N. Zald, pp. 261–74. New York: Cambridge University Press.

Zald, Mayer N., and Roberta Ash. 1966. "Social Movement Organizations: Growth, Decay, and Change." *Social Forces* 44(3): 327–41.

Zimmerman, Joseph F. 1995. *State-Local Relations: A Partnership Approach* (2nd ed.). Westport, CT: Greenwood Press.

CASES CITED

Andersen v. King County 158 Wn. 2d 1 (2006)

Anderson v. Anderson, No. 43CO1-9105-CP-269 (Kosciusko Cir. Cr., Indiana, 1992).

Andrew White et al. v. Arlington County et al. 1999. Final Order, Chancery No. 98-144, March 22, 1999, Judge Benjamin N. A. Kendrick.

Anglin v. City of Minneapolis. 1992. Findings of Fact, Conclusions of Law, and Order for Judgment, Minneapolis Commission on Civil Rights, File No. 88180-EM-12, November 17.

Anonymous v. Anonymous, 325 N.Y.S.2d 499, 500 (N.Y. Sup. Ct. 1971)

Arlington County v. White. 2000. 2000 Va. LEXIS 71.

Attorney General for the Commonwealth v. Kevin, 30 Fam. L. R. 1 (Austl. 2003).

Attorney-General v. Otahuhu Family Court, 1 N.Z.L.R. 603, 606 (H.C. 1991).

Baehr v. Lewin, 852 P.2d 44 (Hawai'i 1993), clarified on grant of reconsideration in part, 852 P.2d 74 (Hawai'i 1993), aff'd and remanded for trial, sub nom *Baehr v. Miike*, 910 P.2d 112 (Hawai'i 1996), dismissed 994 P.2d 566 (Hawai'i 1999).

Baker, et al. v. State of Vermont, et al., 170 Vt. 194, 744 A.2d 864 (1999).

Boone v. Howard, 1989 WL 124898 (Delaware Super. Ct. 1989)

Bottoms v. Bottoms, 457 S.E.2d 102 (VA 1995).

Bowers v. Hardwick, 478 U.S. 1039 (1986).

Boy Scouts of America v. Dale, 530 U.S. 640 (2000).

Braschi v. Stahl Assoc., 543 N.E.2d 49 (N.Y. 1989).

Brown v. Bd. of Educ., 347 U.S. 483 (1954).

Buckner v. City of Kansas City. 2004. Complaint filed in Circuit Court, Jackson County, Missouri, downloaded on 8/25/07 from http://www.alliancedefensefund.org/userdocs/BucknervKansasCityComplaint.pdf.

Buckner v. City of Kansas City. 2007. Declaratory Judgment and Order Granting Summary Judgment in Favor of Defendant City of Kansas City, Missouri. Division 14, Circuit Court of Jackson County, Missouri, Judge John M. Torrance, November 13.

Burlington Industries v. Ellerth, 524 U.S. 742 (1998).

C. (L.) v. C. (C.), (1992) 10 O.R.3d 254 (Can.)

Catavalo v. City of Cambridge. 2000. "Findings of Fact, Conclusions of Law and Order for Judgment," Middlesex Superior Court, Civil Action No. 00-1319, October 30, 2000, Judge James McHugh.

City of Atlanta v. McKinney. 1995. 265 Ga. 161; 454 S.E.2d 517.

City of Atlanta v. Morgan. 1997. 268 Ga. 586; 492 S.E.2d 193.

Connell v. Francisco, 898 P.2d 831 (Washington 1995)

Connors vs. City of Boston. 1999. 1999 Mass. LEXIS 482.

Conaway v. Deane and Polyak, 932 A.2d 571 (Maryland 2007)

Corbett v. Corbett 2 All E.R. 33 (P. 1970).

Cossey v. United Kingdom, 13 Eur. Ct. H.R. 622 (1991).

Crawford et al. v. City of Chicago et al. 1999. 1999 Ill. Appl. LEXIS 211, March 31.

Crawford et al. v. City of Chicago et al. 1999. 185 Ill. 2d 621; 720 N.E.2d 1090; 1999 Ill.

LEXIS 1083; 242, Ill. Dec. 135, October 6, 1999 (petition for leave to appeal denied).

Crooke v. Gilden, 414 S.E.2d 645 (Georgia 1992).

Cruzan v. Missouri Dept. of Health, 497 U.S. 261 (1990).

Dallas v. England, 846 S.W.2d 957 (Tx. Court of Appeals 1993).

Davenport et al. v. Little-Bowser, et. al., 269 Va. 546 (2005).

Devlin et al. v. City of Philadelphia. 2000. 48 Pa. D. and C.4th 86; 2000 Pa. D. and C. LEXIS 150, October 5, 2000.

Devlin et al. v. City of Philadelphia. 2002. 2002 Pa. Commw. LEXIS 683, August 29, 2002.

Devlin et al. v. City of Philadelphia. 2004. 2004 Pa. LEXIS 3059.

Dobre v. Nat'l R.R. Passenger Corp., 850 F. Supp. 284 (E.D. Pa. 1993).

Eileen F. Slattery et al. v. City of New York et al., 179 Misc. 2d 740; 686 N.Y.S.2d 683; 1999 N.Y. Misc. LEXIS 35, February 8, 1999.

Eisenstadt v. Baird, 405 U.S. 438 (1972).

E.N.O. v. L.M.M., 711 N.E.2d 886 (Massachusetts 1999), cert. denied, 528 U.S. 1005 (1999).

Estate of Reaves v. Owen, 744 So. 2d 799 (Mississippi Ct. App. 1999)

Finstuen v. Crutcher, 496 F. 3 1139 (2007).

Finstuen v. Edmondson, 497 F. Supp. 2d 1295 (2006).

Goodridge v. Department of Public Health, 440 Mass. 309 (2003).

Goodwin v. United Kingdom, 35 Eur. Ct. H.R. 18 (2002).

Griswold v. Connecticut, 381 U.S. 479 (1965).

Heinsma v. City of Vancouver. 2001. 2001 Wash. LEXIS 549, August 23.

Hernandez v. Robles, 855 N.E. 2d 1 (2006).

Hewitt v. Hewitt, 77 Ill. 2d 49, 394 N.E.2d 1204 (Illinois 1979).

Holloway v. Arthur Anderson & Co., 566 F.2d 659 (9th Cir. 1977).

Hurley v. Irish-American Gay, Lesbian, and Bisexual Group of Boston, 515 U.S. 557 (1995).

In re Adoption of Doe, 719 N.E.2d 1071 (Ohio Ct. App. 1998).

In re Adoption of Luke, 640 N.W.2d 374 (Nebraska 2002).

In re Adoption of R.B.F., 569 Pa. 269 (2002).

In re Adoption of T.K.J. and K.A.K., 931 P.2d 488 (Colorado 1996)

In re Bonfield, 96 Ohio St. 3 218 (2002).

In re Cheyenne Madison Jones, 2002 WL 940195 (Ohio Ct. App. May 10, 2002).

In re Custody of HSH-K, 193 Wisc. 2d 649 (Wisconsin 1995).

In re E.L.M.C., 100 P.3d 546 (Colorado Ct. App. 2004).

In re Estate of Gardiner, 22 P.3d 1086 (Kan. Ct. App. 2001) (Gardiner I).

In re Estate of Gardiner, 42 P.3d 120 (Kan. 2002) (Gardiner II).

In re Heilig, 372 Md. 692, 723, 816 A.2d 68 (2003).

In re Ladrach, 513 N.E.2d 828 (Ohio Prob. Ct. 1987).

In re Marriage Cases, 183 P.3d 384 (Cal. 2008).

In re Marriage License for Nash, Nos. 2002-T-0149, 2002-T-0179, 2003 WL 23097095 at *6 (Ohio Ct. App. Dec. 31, 2003).

In Re Marriage of Simmons, 355 Ill.App.3d 942, 825 N.E.2d 303 (2005).

In re the Matter of Visitation with C.B.L., 723 N.E.2d 316 (Ill. App. Ct. 1999).

In re Nicholas H., 28 Cal. 4th 56 (2002) .

In re Opinions of the Justices to the Senate, 802 N.E.2d 565 (Mass. 2004).

In the matter of the custody of C.C.R.S., 892 P. 2d 246 (1995).

In the matter of E.L.M.C., 100 P.3d 546 (Colo. App. 2004).

In the matter of Infant Girl, W. 845 N.E. 2d 229 (2006).

In the Matter of the Utah State Retirement Board's Trustee Duties and Salt Lake City Ordinance No. 4 of 2006. 2006. Utah Third District Court, Salt Lake County, Civil No. 050916879, May 11, downloaded on 8/18/06 from http://www. acluutah.org/normanruling.pdf.

Interest of Angel Lace M., 516 N.W.2d 678 (Wisconsin 1994).

Ireland v. Flanagan, 627 P.2d 496 (Oregon Ct. App. 1981).

Jack H. Godley et al. vs. Town of Carrboro and Town of Chapel Hill. 2000. Order, File No. 99-CVS 844, May 16, 2000, Judge Orlando F. Hudson, Jr.

James H.K. Bruner and Gretchen Bruner v. City of Albany, Common Council, Mayor Gerald Jennings. 1996. Decision and Order, Index #3444-96, Supreme Court, Albany County. October 18, 1996.

James v. Ranch Mart Hardware, 881 F. Supp. 478 (D. Kan. 1995).

Janis C. v. Christine T., 742 N.Y.S.2d 381 (App. Div. 2002).

Johnson v. Calvert, 5 Cal. 4th 84 (1993).

Kantaras v. Kantaras, 884 So. 2d 155 (Fla. Dist. Ct. App. 2004).

Kazmierazak v. Query, 736 So.2d 106 (Fla. Ct. App. 1999).

LaWall v. Pima County. 1998. Arizona Superior Court, Pima County, Case No. C-320550, Minute Entry, March 13.

Lawrence and Garner v. Texas, 539 U.S. 558 (2003).

Lawrence Lowe v. Broward County. 1999. Final Judgment, April 30, 1999; Case No. 99-2775 (09), Judge Robert L. Andrews.

Ledbetter v. Goodyear Tire and Rubber, 127 S.Ct. 2162 (2007).

Lowe v. Broward County. 2000. 2000 Fla. App. LEXIS 11893, September 20.

Lowe v. Broward County. 2001. 2001 Fla. LEXIS 819, April 4, 2001 (petition for review denied).

Lewis v. Harris, 908 A.2d 196 (New Jersey 2006).

Lilly v. City of Minneapolis. 1995. 527 N.W.2d 107; 1995 Minn. App.

Lilly v. City of Minneapolis. 1995. 1995 Minn. LEXIS 264, March 29, 1995 (denial of review).

Lim Ying v. Hiok Kian Ming Eric, 1 S.L.R. 184 (Sing. 1991).

Littleton v. Prange, 9 S.W.3d 223 (Tex. App. 1999).

Love v. Love, 959 P.2d 523, 527 (Nevada 1998).

Loving v. Virginia, 388 U.S. 1 (1967).

M.T. v. J.T., 355 A.2d 204 (N.J. Super. Ct. App. Div. 1976).

Martin v. City of Gainesville. 2000. "Order Granting Motion to Dismiss," 8th Judicial Circuit Court, Case No. 2000 CA 1814, November 12, 2000, Judge Stan R. Morris.

Martin v. City of Gainesville. 2001. 2001 Fla. App. LEXIS 16945.

Matter of T.L., 1996 WL 393521 (Missouri Cir.1996).

McKee-Johnson v. Johnson, 444 N.W.2d 259 (Minnesota 1989).

Miller-Jenkins v. Miller-Jenkins, 912 A.2d 951 (Vermont 2006).

Miller-Jenkins v. Miller-Jenkins, 49 Va. App. 87, (Virginia Ct. App. 2006).

Morrison v. Sadler, 821 N.E.2d 15 (Indiana Court of Appeals, 2005).

National Pride at Work et al. v. Granholm and City of Kalamazoo. 2005. Opinion and Order, Case No. 05-368-CZ, Circuit Court for the County of Ingham, State of Michigan, Judge Joyce Draganchuk, downloaded on 8/25/07 from http://www.aclumich.org/pdf/briefs/dplawsuitdecision.pdf.

National Pride at Work et al. v. Governor of Michigan and City of Kalamazoo. 2007. 2007 Mich. App. LEXIS 240.

National Pride at Work et al. v. Governor of Michigan and City of Kalamazoo. 2008. 748 N.W.2d 524; 2008 Mich. LEXIS 915.

Order on City's Demurrer to First Amended Complaint, Motion for judgment on the Pleadings and Requests for Judicial Notice, January 13, 1999; Case No. 223122, Judge Thomas P. Anderle.

Parents Involved in Community Schools v. Seattle School District No. 1, 127 S.Ct. 2738 (2007).

Perez v. Sharp, 198 P.2d 17 (Cal. 1948)

Planned Parenthood v. Casey, 505 U.S. 833 (1992)

Posik v. Layton, 695 So.2d 759 (Florida Dist. Ct. App. 1997).

Price Waterhouse v. Hopkins, 490 U.S. 228 (1989).

Pritchard v. Madison Metropolitan School District. 2001. 2001 Wisc. App. LEXIS 141, February 8.

Pritchard v. Madison Metropolitan School District. 2001. 2001 WI 88; 246 Wis. 2d 166; 630 N.W.2d 220; 2001 Wisc. LEXIS 505, May 8, 2001 (petition for review denied).

Pulsifer v. City of Portland (ME). 2004. Superior Court, Cumberland County, No. CV-03-448, April 27, 2004.

Ralph et al. v. City of New Orleans. 2006. 928 So.2d 537; 2006 La. LEXIS 1431.

Rees v. United Kingdom, 9 Eur. Ct. H.R. 56 (1987).

Riccio v. New Haven Bd. of Educ., 467 F. Supp. 2d 219 (D. Conn. 2006).

Roe v. Wade, 410 U.S. 113 (1973).

Romer v. Evans, 517 U.S. 620 (1996).

Roni Heinsma vs. City of Vancouver. 2000. Court's Decision, No. 99-2-00772 1, June 26, 2000, Judge John F. Nichols.

Santosky v. Kramer, 455 U.S. 745 (1982).

Schaefer and Tader v. City and County of Denver. 1998. 973 P.2d 717; 1998 Colo. App. LEXIS 255.

Schaefer and Tader v. City and County of Denver, 1999 Colo. LEXIS 361, April 12, 1999 (petition for leave to appeal denied).

Schwegman v. Schwegman, 441 So. 2d 316 (Louisiana Ct. App. 1983).

Shahar v. Bowers, 70 F.3d 1218 (1995).

Sheffield and Horsham v. United Kingdom, 27 Eur. Ct. H.R. 163 (1999).

Silver v. Starrett, 674 N.Y.S.2d 915 (New York Sup. Ct. 1998).

Singer v. Hara, 1974 Wash. LEXIS 846 (October 10, 1974).

Slattery et al. v. City of New York et al. 1999. 1999 N.Y. App. Div. LEXIS 11158, November 4, 1999.

Slattery et al. v. City of New York et al. 2000. 2000 N.Y. LEXIS 231, February 29, 2000 (appeal dismissed).

Smith v. City of Salem, 369 F.3d 912 (6th Cir. 2004).

Sommers v. Budget Marketing, 667 F.2d 748 (8th Cir. 1982).

Stanley v. Illinois, 405 U.S. 645 (1972).

Steve Tyma et al. v. Montgomery County Council et al. 2000. Order, Civil No. 211250, October 30, 2000.

Teri Rohde et al. v. Ann Arbor Public Schools et al. 2005. 265 Mich. App. 702; 698 N.W.2d 402; 2005 Mich. App. LEXIS 910.

Teri Rohde et al. v. Ann Arbor Public Schools et al. 2007. 2007 Mich. LEXIS 1630.

T.F. v. B.L., 442 Mass. 522 (Massachusetts 2004).

Thomas S. v. Robin Y., 209 A.D. 2d 298 (New York Supreme Court Appellate Division, 1994).

Thomas v. Thomas, 49 P.3d 306 (Ariz. Ct. App. 2002).

Turner v. Safley, 482 U.S. 78 (1987).

Tyma v. Montgomery County. 2002. 2002 Md. LEXIS 345, June 14.

Ulane v. Eastern Airlines, Inc., 742 F.2d 1081 (7th Cir. 1984).

Vasquez v Hawthorne, 33 P3d 735 (Washington 2001).

Wheeler v. Wheeler, 281 Ga. 838 (2007).

Whorton v. Dillingham, 248 Cal. Rptr. 405 (California Ct. App. 1988).

STATUTES

Title VII, 42 U.S.C. § 2000e-2(a)

Gender Recognition Act, 2004, Eliz. II, 7 (Eng.).

TREATY

Hague Convention on Protection of Children and Cooperation in Respect of Intercountry Adoption. Available at http://hcch.e-vision.nl/index_en.php?act=conventions.text&cid=69 (accessed December 4, 2007).

Contributors

ELLEN ANN ANDERSEN is an associate professor of political science at the University of Vermont. She is the author of *Out of the Closets and into the Courts: Legal Opportunity Structure and Gay Rights Litigation.* She has also authored a series of articles on AIDS activism together with M. Kent Jennings. Andersen is currently working with a collaborator, Verta Taylor, on a study of the same-sex couples who married in California, Oregon, and Massachusetts during 2004.

SCOTT BARCLAY is an associate professor of political science at the University at Albany: State University of New York. His recent research has focused on the political, demographic, and social movement factors that influence the legislative and judicial response of individual U.S. states to same-sex marriage. He has also considered the long-term role of the print media in shaping public opinion on this issue. He has published in a variety of journals, including recently in *Law and Social Inquiry, Law and Policy,* and *Policy Studies Journal.*

MARY BERNSTEIN is an associate professor of sociology at the University of Connecticut. Her scholarship seeks to understand the role of identity in social movements, how movement actors interact with the state and the law, and what factors influence sexual citizenship in social institutions. Her recent publications include "Identity Politics" (*Annual Review of Sociology*, 2005); "Paths to Homophobia" (*Sexuality Research and Social Policy*, 2004); "Nothing Ventured, Nothing Gained? Conceptualizing Social Movement 'Success' in the Lesbian and Gay Movement" (*Sociological Perspectives*, 2003); and "Identities and Politics: Toward a Historical Understanding of the Lesbian and Gay Movement" (*Social Science History*, 2002). She is also coeditor (with Renate Reimann) of *Queer Families, Queer Politics: Challenging Culture and the State* (Columbia University Press, 2001).

STEVEN A. BOUTCHER is a doctoral candidate in the department of sociology at the University of California, Irvine. He is currently working on his dissertation, which examines the institutionalization of pro bono legal work within elite law firms.

BAYLISS CAMP is a lecturer in sociology at California State University, Sacramento. His research focuses on political sociology and civic engagement. His most recent work looks at how "Defense of Marriage" ballot referendums potentially reconfigure traditional partisan loyalties and interparty competition at the state level (forthcoming in *Sociological Perspectives*).

CASEY CHARLES is a professor and chair of English at the University of Montana, Missoula, where he teaches law and literature, gay and lesbian studies, and Shakespeare. *The Sharon Kowalski Case: Lesbian and Gay Rights on Trial* (University of Kansas, 2003) was nominated for a Publishing Triangle Award in 2004, and his poetry chapbook, *Controlled Burn* (2007), was named as one of the ten best Montana publications of the year by the *Missoula Independent*. Portions of his new critical manuscript have appeared in *Law and Literature* and *Women's Studies in Communication*. He is one of the founders of the University of Montana's Outfield Alliance and the Western Montana Gay and Lesbian Community Center.

ASHLEY CURRIER is an assistant professor of sociology and women's studies at Texas A&M University. She is currently working on a book project, *Becoming Visible: LGBT Organizing in Namibia and South Africa*, which explores how Namibian and South African lesbian, gay, bisexual, and transgender (LGBT) organizations work to overcome their political and social invisibility. Her current research examines the origins and persistence of homophobia(s) in southern African political discourse.

COURTENAY W. DAUM received her Ph.D. from Georgetown University and is an assistant professor of political science at Colorado State University. Her research interests include organized interest mobilization and litigation at the U.S. Supreme Court, feminist legal theory, gender and politics, and judicial behavior.

SHAUNA FISHER is a graduate student in political science at the University of Washington. Her research has focused on the role of courts in social change and the activities of social movements in multiple venues in the pursuit of rights claims. Specifically, she has focused on various aspects of lesbian and gay rights, with particular emphasis on the politics of same-sex marriage.

DAVID JOHN FRANK is an associate professor of sociology and, by courtesy, education at the University of California, Irvine. His research centers on world society and global social institutions, especially in the realms of environmental protection, higher education, criminal sex, and individual personhood. Most recently, he published *Reconstructing the University* (Stanford University Press, 2006, coauthored with Jay Gabler) and "University Expansion and the Knowledge Society" (*Theory and Society*, 2007, coauthored with John W. Meyer).

JONATHAN GOLDBERG-HILLER (Ph.D., University of Wisconsin-Madison, political science) is an associate professor and chair of the political science department at the University of Hawai'i -Mānoa. His recent research explores the ways postwar forms of identity, nationalism, political authority, and political economy have modulated the mobilization of rights in various empirical contexts. His book, *The Limits to Union: Same-Sex Marriage and the Politics of Civil Rights* (University of Michigan Press, 2004), explores the thematic prominence of sexuality in contemporary national and international rights politics. He has published articles on special rights discourse, indigenous rights politics, international human rights law, labor law, and other topics in *Law and Social Inquiry, Social and Legal Studies, Studies in Law Politics and Society, Theory and Event,* and other journals, and he serves on the international editorial board of *Social and Legal Studies* and the editorial board of *Studies in Law Politics and Society.* He has been appointed Fulbright Senior Specialist candidate, 2006-2011, and has won university-wide teaching awards twice.

CHARLES W. GOSSETT is professor and chair of political science at California State Polytechnic University, Pomona. His research and publishing are in the areas of public personnel management and gay and lesbian politics at the state and local level.

MARYBETH HERALD is a professor at Thomas Jefferson School of Law in San Diego, California. She graduated from Harvard Law School and joined the faculty at Jefferson in 1991 and served as associate dean from 1994 to 2002. She teaches constitutional law and an advanced constitutional law seminar. Herald writes and speaks in the areas of gender and transgender discrimination issues, among other constitutional law topics. Her recent work (with coauthor Julie Greenberg) describes the contradictory state approaches to defining male and female that create bizarre and confusing results as transgender persons cross state lines.

ANNA-MARIA MARSHALL is an associate professor of sociology at the University of Illinois, Urbana-Champaign. Her research focuses on the relationships among law, social movements, and everyday life. In particular, she has studied how women use law and politics to understand their experiences with sexual harassment, the role of cause lawyers in the Vermont campaign for civil unions, and, most recently, the role of law and lawyers in the environmental justice movement. Her book, *Confronting Sexual Harassment: The Law and Politics of Everyday Life* (2005), was published by Dartmouth Ashgate. Her articles have appeared in *Law and Society Review, Law and Social Inquiry,* and various edited volumes.

NICHOLAS PEDRIANA is currently an adjunct instructor at Northwestern University. His research interests are law, politics, and social movements, primarily in the context of civil rights policies and constitutional law involving the rights and opportunities of disadvantaged groups. He is especially interested in how and under what conditions social movement mobilization of law and legal institutions can reduce social inequality and foster progressive change for racial minorities, women, and gays and lesbians.

DARREN ROSENBLUM is an associate professor of law at Pace University Law School in New York. His publications focus on sexual minority rights and international arbitration, and his current scholarship focuses on comparative law issues related to women's political representation and antidiscrimination law.

SUSAN M. STERETT is chair and professor of the political science department at the University of Denver. She is the author of *Creating Constitutionalism? The Politics of Legal Expertise and Administrative Law in England and Wales* (1997) and *Public Pensions: Gender and Civic Service in the States, 1850s–1937* (2003), as well as articles in journals including *Comparative Political Studies, Law and Social Inquiry*, and *Studies in American Political Development*. She is currently working on two projects. One concerns legal formations of family and the other focuses on displacement and documentation after Hurricane Katrina.

AMY L. STONE is an assistant professor of sociology and anthropology at Trinity University in San Antonio, Texas. Her research examines gender, sexuality, and strategy within social movements. Her chapter is part of a larger project on transgender inclusion in the LGBT movement. She is currently working on a comprehensive study of strategic diffusion of antigay initiatives in the Religious Right and LGBT movement from 1975 to 2005

Index

anti-same-sex marriage campaigns (*continued*):
children's vulnerability, imagery of, 251;
common sense arguments, 246–247;
death, imagery of, 250–251; domestication,
239–240; entanglement of gay rights
and terrorism, 248–249; generative life,
references to, 247; groups supporting, 212;
inversion, 240–244; nongenerative sexuality,
images of, 250; politics of distancing, 232;
popular sovereignty, mobilization for, 232–
238, 246, 256; rights-harassed majority,
images of, 240–244; Shuttlesworth, Fred,
244; special rights arguments, 239–240;
suspicion of judges, legislators, 244–245
Anzaldua, Gloria, 110
appellate courts, 109–111, 115
Aristotle, 259, 267–268
Arizona: dissolution of nonmarital
relationships, 293; domestic partnerships,
165, 166, 174; Pima County, 163, 166–168,
176–177, 186
Arkansas, 165, 318n30
Arlington County, Virginia, 163, 168, 173,
175–176, 184
Arlington County v. White, 175
Armstrong, Elizabeth A., 257
Atlanta, Georgia, 163, 168, 184
Attorney Gen. v. Kevin (Australia), 195
Attorney-General v. Otahuhu Family Court (New
Zealand), 190–191
Australia, transgender(ed) in, 195

Backer, Larry Cata, 9, 72
backlash: against civil rights claims by gays and
lesbians, 218, 239–240, 245–246, 250–
251, 254; against *Lawrence v. Texas*, 225;
politics of, 211; in trial of Dan White, 261,
266, 272. *See also* countermobilization
Baehr v. Lewin, 83, 216, 301
Baehr v. Miike, 83, 222
Baker, Joshua, 299
Baker v. Nelson, 212
Baker v. Vermont, 83
Bartlett, Roscoe, 252
Batson test, 264–265
Bauer, Gary, 222–223
Bauman, Zygmunt, 249
Baumgartner, Frank R., 229

Bay Area Lawyers for Individual Freedom, 89
Beckel, David, 207
Bedsworth, William, 264–265, 315n8
Benford, Robert D., 209, 284
Berlant, Lauren, 243, 246
Bernstein, Mary, 32, 159
biopolitical discourse, 234–236, 251–255
Birkland, Thomas, 215
birth certificates, 103–119; appellate courts,
109–111; challenges to, 107–108; claims
to state and family recognition, 111–112;
Colorado, 104–108, 118; custody and
visitation, 114; custody disputes, 114;
early twentieth century, 111; emergent
legality, 104; facts made by, 111; family
law, changes in, 111–113; interest group
victories, 110; Lambda Legal Defense
and Education Fund (LLDEF), 103, 104;
law's authority, 107; National Center for
Lesbian Rights (NCLR), 103; recognition
of parenthood, 114; recognition of same-sex
families, parenting, 114–115; reproductive
technology, 111–112; requirements for,
110; responsibilities associated with, 116–
117; in same-sex parent cases, 104–108,
111–112; for transgender(ed), 191–192,
197–198 (see also *Cossey v. United
Kingdom*; *Rees v. United Kingdom*); Uniform
Parentage Act (UPA, 1973), 106–108
Blanchard, Leslie, 45
Boal, Augusto, 268, 279
Boston, Massachusetts, domestic-partnership
ordinance, 163, 173, 176, 178, 184
Bottoms v. Bottoms, 9
Bowers v. Hardwick: American Civil Liberties
Union (ACLU), 86; amicus curiae briefs,
88, 96; due process, 58; initiation of,
81; interest group participation, 92–96,
98–100; interests of gays and lesbians, 77;
privacy rights, 58, 81; reversal of, 38, 68 (see
also *Lawrence v. Texas*)
Boy Scouts of America, 13–14, 84, 87, 97
Boy Scouts of America v. Dale: amicus curiae
briefs, 88, 96–97; First Amendment
rights, 81; initiation of, 81; interest group
participation, 86, 92–94, 96, 98–100;
interests of gays and lesbians, 77
Brandeis, Louis, 183

Colorado Supreme Court, 107
Coltrane, Scott, 298
coming out (tactic), 263
common-law marriages, 169, 317n12
Concerned Women for America, 102, 213
Connecticut: civil unions, 46; domestic
partnerships, 165; *Kerrigan v. Commission of
Public Health*, 38, 51, 217; marriage equality,
44; same-sex marriage, 303n3
Connor, Ken, 220
Connors et al. v. City of Boston, 163, 184
Corbett v. Corbett: filtering out of science, 189;
gender of postoperative person, 193–194;
immutability of sex assigned at birth,
188–189; influence, 188, 190, 191, 197,
198; reconstructed vaginas, 190; rejection in
Australia, 195
Cossey v. United Kingdom, 190, 192
countermobilization: attention paid to, 229;
by interest groups, 80; same-sex marriage,
208–209, 226–227; school segregation, 5;
special rights, 210–211. *See also* backlash
Coutin, Susan, 115–116
Covey, Craig, 152
Crage, Suzanne M., 257
Craig, Larry, 50
Crawford et al. v. City of Chicago, 184
Crenshaw, Kimberle, 40
Crews, Ronald A., 225
criminal justice system: queer bias, perpetuation
of, 257–258
criminal/penal codes: French Penal Code,
136; global institutionalization of, 136;
Malawi, 136; Napoleonic Code, 48. *See also*
nondiscrimination ordinances
criminal sex laws: in Cyprus, 308n15
criminalization of homosexuality: justification
of discrimination against gays and lesbians,
60–61, 69, 70; Namibia, 23, 26, 28. *See also*
homophobia
critical legal studies movement: protection of
privileges of the powerful, 4
Critical Race Theory (CRT), 39, 42–43
Cruzan v. Missouri Department of Health, 58
Curry, Robert, 241–242
custody and visitation, 9, 114, 287, 291–293
Cuthbert, Pam, 150
Cyprus, 308n15

Dallas v. England, 9
Davenport et al v. Little-Bowser et al., 103
Davids, Laurencia, 26
Declaration of the Rights of Man, 136
decriminalization of sodomy: The Rainbow
Project (TRP, Namibia), 27–29; in United
States (see *Lawrence v. Texas*); worldwide
pattern of, 129, 133, 136, 138, 308n15
Defense of Marriage Act (DOMA): debates
surrounding, 222–223; Nickles's Senate
testimony, 311n11; passage, context of,
301; portability of marriage benefits, 44;
provisions, 301; retirement benefits, 294;
same-sex marriage, 44, 215–216, 228–229,
294–295, 303n3; state versions of, 169 (see
also marriage amendments)
deferral of legal tactics, 21, 23, 25–37
Delaware, domestic partnerships, 165
D'Emilio, John, 138, 263
Denman, Jim, 276
Denver, Colorado: domestic-partnership
ordinance, 162, 168, 176, 184; second-
parent adoption, 105
Deo, Len, 223
"dependent," definition of, 171, 172–173, 177–178
Devlin et al. v. City of Philadelphia, 163, 173,
177, 185
Dillon, John F., 159
Dillon's Rule, 159–162, 175–176, 179
discourse: biopolitical discourse, 234–236,
251–255; collective action discourse, 53;
public persuasiveness of legal discourse,
11, 17; rights discourse, 52; U. S. Supreme
Court as a discursive field, 53, 56, 71–72
discrimination: on basis of sexual orientation
(Namibia), 304n7; on basis of sexual
orientation (South Africa), 27; on basis
of sexual orientation (United States),
305n5; marriage discrimination (New York
State), 305n6. *See also* nondiscrimination
ordinances
distribution of the sensible, 239, 245, 255
District of Columbia, 181, 292
divorce, 281–302; acceptability of, 297–298;
alimony, 289, 294, 318n22; antenuptial
(premarital) agreements, 290; breaking up
without ability to, 288 (see *also* nonmarital
relationships, dissolution of); children, care

and custody of, 287; children, effect on, 297–298; community property states, 286; context, cultural, 296–300; context, legal, 286–288; custody and visitation, 291–293; division of assets, 286–287; Felder on, Raoul, 281; Illinois, 288; incidence, prevalence of, 297, 319n45; Louisiana, 288; marriage equality, 282–283, 296, 301; oral contracts, 289; parentage presumption, 291–293; private bargaining in, 286; property division, 288–291, 317n12; same-sex couples, 114; same-sex marriage, 298–299; separate property states, 286–287; separation agreements, 286, 291; state law, 286; visitation, 287; Washington State, 288

divorce reform frame, 298

divorce repeal frame, 298

Dobre v. National Railroad Passenger Corporation, 201

domestic-partnership ordinances, 158–186; "adult designee" ordinances, 180–182; American Civil Liberties Union (ACLU), 166, 168; cases, 162–168, 310n2; cases, affirmed, 179; cases, arguments in, 168–173, 177; cases, judicial responses to arguments, 173–179; cases, overturned, 179; *City of Atlanta v. McKinney*, 162, 173, 175, 176, 178, 179, 183, 184; *City of Atlanta v. Morgan*, 162, 175, 178, 179, 184; Colorado initiative, 111; conservative public interest law organizations, 166; definition of "dependent," 171, 172–173, 177–178; Dillon's Rule, 159–162, 175–176, 179; employee benefits, 158–159, 310n2; health benefits, 65; home rule, 159–160; initial court rulings, statewide effect of, 164; Lambda Legal Defense and Education Fund (LLDEF), 164, 166; limiting by rewriting laws, 182; local government's authority to offer benefit programs, 159–162, 165, 171, 175–179, 182–183, 310n2; "morality politics," 179; preemption cases, 161, 178; private challengers to, 160; standards for, 49; state law, 161, 176, 177, 178–179, 182

domestic partnerships, 111, 165–167, 174, 180–182

domestic partnerships, registered, 318n23

domestication, 239–240

Douzinas, Costas, 234–235, 236–237

due process, 57, 58, 68, 81–82

Duggan, Lisa, 47

economic rights, 55

Edelman, Murray, 237–238

Eisenstadt v. Baird, 57

Ekandjo, Jerry, 28, 29, 30, 304n8

emergent legality, 104

employee benefits: definition of "dependent," 171, 172–173, 177–178; domestic-partnership ordinances, 158–159, 310n2. *See also* domestic-partnership ordinances

Employee Retirement and Income Security Act (ERISA), 294, 310n2

employment discrimination: sodomy laws, 9; transgender(ed), 187, 196–197, 202; wage discrimination, 3

Employment Nondiscrimination Act (ENDA), 143, 309n4

England. See *Corbett v. Corbett*

Epstein, Rob, 258, 259

equal protection: Amendment 2 (Colorado, 1992), 80, 94, 284; Anchorage suit, 310n2; government classifications, 58; group classifications, assumption of, 73; *Lawrence v. Texas*, 53, 59–61, 67, 68, 71; LGBT movement, 57; as master frame, 57, 66; privacy rights, 59–61; *Romer v. Evans*, 58–59, 80, 81; Social Security, 11; sodomy laws, 57

Eskridge, William, 118, 300

essentialism constructs, 39–40

Estin, Ann Laquer, 288

Europe, 131–132, 188, 195

European Convention on Human Rights, 190, 192–193

European Court of Human Rights (ECHR): Cypriot law criminalizing sex between gay men, 308n15; *Goodwin v. United Kingdom*, 191, 193–194; privacy rights, 194; sodomy laws, invalidation of, 70; transgender(ed), 190, 191–194, 199

European Union: Charter of Fundamental Rights, 191, 192; reform of sodomy laws, 138, 139

Evan B. Donaldson Institute, 117

Ewick, Patricia, 107

Execution of Justice (Mann), 276–280; citation of *Times of Harvey Milk* film, 258; defense's opening statement, 267; diminished-capacity defense (Twinkie defense), 316n10; ending, 279–280; jury instructions, 316n10; jury selection, 263, 266–267; juxtaposition of transcripts and White's speeches, 269; psychiatric testimony, 275, 276–277; Sister Boom Boom, 266, 276–277, 280
expert testimony in trial of Dan White, 276

Falzon, Frank, 262–263, 269, 272
family law, 111–113, 115–116
Family Research Council (FRC), 102, 207, 219, 222, 244
fathers' rights cases, 112
Federal Marriage Amendment (FMA), 216, 237, 248
Feinstein, Dianne, 258, 270
Felder, Raoul, 281
feminism, Black women and, 40
Ferndale, Michigan, 143, 147, 152–156
Ferndale Blue Ribbon Ad Hoc Committee, 152–153
Ferndale Friends and Neighbors (FANS), 152
Finsteun v. Crutcher, 103
Finsteun v. Edmundson, 103
First Amendment, 78, 81, 90
Florida: adoption by gays and lesbians, 106, 318n30; Broward County, 163, 164, 176, 184; dissolution of nonmarital relationships, 293; domestic partnerships, 165, 166, 174; Gainesville, 162, 164, 184; *Kantaras II*, 198, 199; *Kantaras v. Kantaras*, 199; same-sex marriage, 169; transgender(ed), 199
Florida Supreme Court, 252
Focus on the Family, 213
focusing events, 215–217
Foreman, Matt, 221
Foucault, Michel, 235–236, 239, 313n3
Fourteenth Amendment. *See* due process; equal protection
frames (framing), 53–57, 208–230, 283–286; agenda setting, effects on, 208–209, 210; antitax and antipoverty movements, 55; binary categories, 202; civil rights law,

285; collective action frames, 53–54, 209; common sense argument, 246–247; cultural frames, 283–286, 300; definition, 209, 283; dispersion over time, 227–229; divorce reform frame, 298; divorce repeal frame, 298; family and children-related frames, 221–223, 227; frame alignment, 283–284, 301; framing contests, 211, 284; issue framing, 210, 229; judges frame, 224–226; legal frames, 54–55, 284, 300; marriage reform frame, 298; master frames, 54, 55, 57, 62, 66, 70–71; meanings generated by, 284–285; mirror-image frames, 300–301; morality frame, 230; movement-specific frames, 55; oppositional frames, 1; overlap of, 285–286, 302; policymaking, 229; pro-choice *vs.* pro-life movements, 55; public vote frame, 223–225, 227, 230; rights-based frames, 218–219, 227, 230; same-sex marriage debate, 208–230; selective attention, 210; slippery slope frame, 220, 230; social movements, 209–210, 229, 283–284, 285–286; threat frames, 219–222, 227; U. S. Supreme Court as a discursive field, 53, 56, 71–72; variety of, 227. *See also* anti-same-sex marriage campaigns
France, 136
Frank, Barney, 309n4
Frank, Liz, 30, 31
Frank, Thomas, 243
Freedom to Marry, 282
French Penal Code, 136

Gainesville, Florida, 162, 164, 184
Galanter, Marc: interests of the powerful, 41; one-shot players, 110; repeat players, 4–5, 78–79, 83, 110
Gallagher, Maggie, 299
Gardiner, J'Noel, 197–198
Gardiner I, 197
Gardiner II, 198, 199
Gawanas, Bience, 26
Gay and Lesbian Advocates and Defenders (GLAD): founder, 86; founding, 79, 212; gay rights litigation, 84, 89, 91, 97; *Hurley v. Irish-American Gay, Lesbian, and Bisexual Group of Boston*, 86, 97; legal harms argument by, 281–282; same-sex marriage cases, 213

Massachusetts Lesbian and Gay Bar
Association, 89
Massachusetts Supreme Judicial Court:
accusations against judges on, 225;
centrality of marriage, 203–204; civil rights
paradigm for LGBT struggle for equal
rights, 45–46, 51; dissolution of nonmarital
relationships, 293; same-sex marriage, 217
MassEquality, 226
McAdam, Doug, 207, 209
McCann, Michael, 6
McKee-Johnson v. Johnson, 290
Méchoulan, Eric, 238, 244–245
Mexico, 134
Michigan, 146–157; Ann Arbor, 184; domestic
partnerships, 165, 167, 174; Ferndale,
143, 147, 152–156; Kalamazoo (*see*
Kalamazoo); nondiscrimination ordinances,
146; same-sex marriage, 162; transgender
inclusion, 146–157; Ypsilanti, 143, 147–
152, 156
Milk, Harvey: assassination of, 257–258; City
Hall stump speech (1978), 261, 270; early
life, 315n6; legacy of, 280; White, Dan,
260–262
Miller-Jenkins v. Miller-Jenkins, 294–295
Milner, Neal, 240
minimum constitutional scrutiny, 306n8
Minneapolis, Minnesota, domestic-partnership
ordinance, 162, 163, 168, 173, 178, 180,
185
Minnesota: antenuptial (premarital)
agreements, 290; definition of "dependent,"
171, 173; dissolution of nonmarital
relationships, 289; domestic partnerships,
165, 167, 174; *McKee-Johnson v. Johnson*,
290
Minnesota Supreme Court, 290
Mississippi, 165, 318n30
Missoula, Montana, 310n2
Missouri: dissolution of nonmarital
relationships, 293; domestic partnerships,
165, 167, 174, 182; Kansas City, 163, 180,
185; marriage amendment, 217
Mnookin, Robert, 286
Model Penal Code (1955), 56–57, 138–139,
309n16
Montana, 165, 310n2

Montgomery County, Maryland, 163, 176, 185
"morality politics," 179
Morrison v. Sadler, 111
Moscone, George, 257, 258, 261–262
motherhood, biological *vs.* gestational, 113–114
M.T. v. J.T., 190–191, 200–201
Mugabe, Robert, 24
Muslim countries, sodomy laws in, 123–124,
130, 131

NAACP Legal Defense and Educational Fund,
78, 86, 87
Nambinga, Jeremiah, 28
Namibia, 21–37; Combating of Rape
Act (2000), 304n5; constitution, 23;
criminalization of homosexuality, 23,
26, 28; discrimination on basis of sexual
orientation, 304n7; homophobia, 22–23,
29, 30–31, 304n8; immigration rights for
same-sex couples, 30; labor laws, 304n7;
Labour Act (1992), 23, 26, 27, 303n3;
laws in force at independence, 304n6;
LGBT movement (*see* The Rainbow
Project); marginalization of sexual and
gender minorities, 21–22; Office of the
Ombudsman, 26–27; Ovambo ethnic
group, 29; repression by the state, 24, 26–
32; sodomy laws, 27–29, 304n5, 304n7
Namibian Non-Governmental Organisation
Forum (1999), 31–32
Napoleonic Code, 48
National Association of Social Workers, 89
National Center for Lesbian Rights (NCLR),
103, 104, 108, 115
National Gay and Lesbian Task Force
(NGLTF), 57, 73, 213, 221, 282
National Law Journal poll (1998), 265
National Lesbian and Gay Law Association
(NLGLA), 66–68, 73, 306n9
*National Pride at Work et al. v. Granholm and
City of Kalamazoo*, 163, 176, 185
National Society for Human Rights (Namibia),
31
Nead, Lynda, 234–235, 236–237
Nebraska, domestic partnerships, 165
neo-institutionalism, 135
Nevada, 165, 288, 289, 317n14
New Hampshire, domestic partnerships, 165

Philadelphia, Pennsylvania, 163, 168, 176, 185
Pierceson, Jason, 6
Pima County, Arizona, 163, 166–168, 176–177, 186
Pinello, Daniel R., 80
Pizer, Jennifer, 207
Planned Parenthood v. Casey, 58
Pohamba, Hifikepunye, 23
policy elites. *See* political elites
policymaking, frames (framing) and, 229
Polikoff, Nancy, 47
political elites: court decisions, 10; movement activists, 10, 144–146, 156–157; perception of transgender issues, 144, 151, 156; understandings of minority groups, 156
political mobilization, 6, 49–50, 109
politics: aesthetics of, 234; of backlash, 211; of distancing, 232; local politics, 146; "morality politics," 179; Rancière on, 233–234, 235, 238, 244–245; rights-based politics, 109
popular sovereignty, 232–238, 246, 256
Portland, Maine, 163, 168, 176–177, 186
preemption, 161, 178
Price Waterhouse v. Hopkins, 201–202, 305n5
Principles of Family Dissolution (American Law Institute), 295–296
Pritchard et al. v. Madison Metropolitan School District, 163, 177, 185
privacy rights: in *Bowers v. Hardwick*, 58, 81; due process, 57; equal protection, 59–61; European Court of Human Rights (ECHR), 194; *Goodwin v. United Kingdom*, 194; international norms, 44; *Lawrence v. Texas*, 9, 43–44, 53, 59–61, 68–69; LGBT movement, 13–14, 57; as master frame, 57; same-sex couples, 9; sodomy laws, 57; transgender(ed), 9–10, 194; U. S. Supreme Court, 9, 57
procreation, 137, 299
property division, 288–291, 317n12
Public Employees Health Program (PEHP), 180–181
publicity from legal campaigns, 6
Pulsifer et al. v. City of Portland, 163, 186

"queer" (the term), 39–40
queer activists, 47–48
queer continuum, 40–41
queer theorists, 47–48, 51

Rainbow Project. *See* The Rainbow Project
Ralph et al. v. City of New Orleans, 163, 185
Rancière, Jacques: on aesthetics, 231; on *police* function, 233–234, 238; on politics, 233–234, 235, 238, 244–245; the visible and the sayable, 251–252
reassignment surgery, 153, 190, 191
Rees v. United Kingdom, 190, 192
repertoire, tactical, 21, 23–25
repression by the state, 24, 26–32
reproductive technology, 111–114
Rhode Island, domestic partnerships, 165
Riccio v. New Haven Board of Education, 42
Rich, Adrienne, 39, 40–41, 305n4
right-to-die decisions, 314n22
right-to-marry litigation. *See* marriage equality
rights: of birth parents *vs.* adoptive parents, 113; Charter of Fundamental Rights of the European Union, 191; civil rights (*see* civil rights movement); custody and visitation, 9, 114, 287, 291–293; Declaration of the Rights of Man, 136; economic rights, 55; fathers' rights, 112; human (*see* human rights); immigration, 30; local power structures, 109; materiality of, 233; privacy (*see* privacy rights); right to enjoy life, 193–194; right to marry someone of different race, 58; right to refuse life-saving medical treatment, 58; right to terminate pregnancy, 57–58; right to use contraception, 57; rights-harassed majority, 240–244; social movements, 3–7, 12; special (*see* special rights); Women's Rights Project, 87
rights-based politics, 109
rights discourse, 52
Ritter, Bill, 119
Roberts, John G., 101
Robson, Ruthann, 198
Roe v. Wade, 57–58, 256
Romer v. Evans: Amendment 2 (Colorado, 1992), 10, 58–59, 80, 105; American Civil Liberties Union (ACLU), 86; amicus curiae briefs, 88, 96; equal protection, 58–59, 80, 81; initiation of, 81; interest group participation, 93–94, 98–100; interests of gays and lesbians, 77; Kennedy, Anthony McLoed, 59; Lambda Legal Defense and Education Fund (LLDEF), 86;

Romer v. Evans (continued): liberal one-hit wonders in, 305n4; O'Connor, Sandra Day, 59; In re T.K.J., 105–106

Roni Heinsma v. City of Vancouver, 186

Rosato, Jennifer, 292

Rosenberg, Gerald, 5

Roth, Robert, 134, 308n11

Rowland v Mad River Local School District, 257

Rubenstein, Bill, 45

Rubin, Gayle, 41

Ryan, Charlotte, 284

Salt Lake City, Utah: domestic-partnership ordinance, 162, 168, 176–177, 180–181, 186; marriages in, 169–170

same-sex couples: adoption, 112–113, 318n30; custody and visitation, 114; custody battles, 114; Defense of Marriage Act (DOMA), 294–295; divorce, 114; eligibility for domestic-partnership benefits, 310n2; employee benefits, 158–159, 310n2; immigration rights in Namibia, 30; Nevada, 317n14; partnership dissolution, rate of, 300; privacy rights, 9; second-parent adoption, 103–104; survivorship benefits from Social Security, 294; Washington State, 317n14. See also nonmarital relationships

same-sex marriage, 207–230; 1996, 228–229; 2003 and 2004, 229; agenda setting in debates about, 226–227, 230; Anderson v. King County, 217; Baehr v. Lewin, 83, 216, 301; California, 303n1, 318n23; children born into the relationship, 292; city officials, 217; civil disobedience by mayors (2004), 51; civil rights analogies, 218, 239–240, 245–246, 250–251, 254; civil rights protections, 235; Connecticut, 303n3; custody and visitation, 292; Defense of Marriage Act (DOMA), 44, 215–216, 228–229, 294–295, 303n3; delinking of marriage and procreation, 299; divorce, 298–299; Florida, 169; focusing events in, 215–217; frames (framing), 208–230; Goodridge v. Department of Public Health, 38, 45–46; harmfulness, 208; hesitation in pursuing, 47–48, 312n28; heterosexual marriage, similarity to, 47; judges, courts, 207, 224–226, 244–246;

Lewis v. Harris, 217; local government, 217; Massachusetts, 217, 229, 303n3; Michigan, 162; mobilization and countermobilization around, 208–209; New York State, 303n3; newspaper coverage of, 212–213, 217; opposition to, 313n1 (see also anti-same-sex marriage campaigns); parentage presumption, 292; portability of marriage benefits, 44; pro-same-sex marriage groups, 212; Proposition 8 (California), 303n1; queer activists, 47–48; queer theorists, 47–48, 51; In re Marriage Cases, 303n1; recognition of marriages performed in other states, 303n3; special rights, 218; state constitutional amendments prohibiting (see marriage amendments); transgender(ed), 198, 203; Utah, 168; Vermont, 44; war on terror, association with, 249. See also marriage equality

San Francisco, California, 257, 262, 279, 310n2

Santa Barbara, California, 163, 176–177, 186

Scalia, Antonin, 44, 216, 220

Schacter, Jane, 284

Schaefer and Tader v. City and County of Denver, 163, 184

Scheingold, Stuart, 3, 42, 49–50

Schiavo, Michael, 255

Schiavo, Terri, 232, 251–255, 256

Schmidt, Doug, in trial of Dan White, 263, 265, 267, 269, 274, 275, 276–277

school segregation: available remedies, 3; countermobilization, 5; Parents Involved in Community Schools v. Seattle School District No. 1, 3; persistence after Brown v. Board of Education, 4, 5; U. S. Supreme Court, 303n2

second-parent adoption: Colorado, 105, 108; legal recognition, 103–104, 318n29; nonmarital relationships, 292

secondary marginalization, 144–145

selective attention, 210

Sex Panic!, 50

sex stereotyping, 188, 201–202

sexual harassment, 3

sexual orientation: discrimination on basis of (Namibia), 304n7; the term, 40; transgender(ed) parallels with, 145, 147–148, 149, 151, 156

"sexual preference" (the term), 40

sexual reassignment surgery, 153, 190, 191

sexual subversives, 41, 42, 44

Shahar v. Bowers, 9

Shanghala, Sakeus, 26

Sharpe, Andrew, 191

Sheffield and Horsham v. United Kingdom, 190, 192

Sheldon, Louis P., 221, 299

Shuttlesworth, Fred, 239–240, 244

Silbey, Susan, 107

Silver, Carol Ruth, 260, 263, 278

Singapore, 190

Singer v. Hara, 44

Sister Boom Boom, 266, 276–277, 278, 280

Sister Namibia, 22, 30, 31

Skrentny, John, 143, 144, 145, 156

Slattery et al. v. City of New York et al., 163, 177, 185

Smith v. City of Salem, 201

Snow, David A., 209, 283–284

social change: law, 3–12, 39, 49; legal arguments as a tool, 283, 285–286; legal victories, 43; litigation, 42, 49, 72, 109; political mobilization, 49–50, 109; social movements, 300

social justice, local government and, 183

social movements, 3–12, 208–211, 283–286; aesthetics, 231–232; agenda setting by, 208; cause lawyers, 10; dynamics of, 208; frames (framing), 209–210, 229, 283–284, 285–286; holy grail of political battle, 56; interest groups, 76; law, 7, 8–9, 11, 109–110; legal arguments as a tool, 283, 285–286; litigation, value of, 301; litigation-based strategies, 50; local politics, 146; mobilization, 209; movement activists and political elites, 10, 144–146, 156–157; perceptions about the world, 209; political elites, 10; political mobilization, 6; rights, 3–7, 12; rights-based strategies, 6; scholarship about, 211; social change, 300; state, 145–146, 157

Social Security, 11, 294

Social Security Administration, 108

social-service provision *vs.* legal tactics, 25, 33–34, 36–37

sodomy: consensual sodomy, 137; decriminalization (*see* decriminalization of sodomy); definitions, 308n7; to

Enlightenment philosophers, 308n12; procreation, 137; punishment for, 70; as Western practice, 22, 70, 130

sodomy laws: Catholic countries, 308n13; constitutional claims against, 57; custody and visitation, 9; custody rights, denial of, 9; employment discrimination, 9; equal protection, 57; European Court of Human Rights (ECHR), 70; Georgia, 58, 81; Lambda Legal Defense and Education Fund (LLDEF), 57, 80; Lesbian and Gay Rights Project, 80; Namibia, 27–29, 304n5, 304n7; New York State, 57; overturning of (*see* *Lawrence v. Texas*); Pennsylvania, 57; privacy rights, 57; Protestant countries, 308n13; reform of (*see* sodomy laws, reform of); repeal of, 56–57, 60–61; South Africa, 27; state-by-state challenges, 56–57, 80, 306n4; Texas, 62–64, 66, 67, 70–71; unconstitutionality of, 9; varieties of, 307n2

sodomy laws, reform of, 123–141; 1970s, 134; American Law Institute Model Penal Code (1955), 138–139; case coverage, 125; colonies, former British, 136; colonies, former French, 132, 136; colonies, former Spanish, 132, 136; cross-national variations in timing, 140–141; Declaration of the Rights of Man, 136; decriminalization (*see* decriminalization of sodomy); diffusion, 139; diversity of affected countries, 130–132, 141; domestic LGB social movements, 123, 133–135, 140; English-speaking and Western Germanic countries, 134; Europe, 131–132; European Union, 138, 139; everyday practices *vs.* official policies, 140; French Penal Code, 136; fundamentalist regimes, 123–124; individualism/individualization, 137–138; mechanisms of change, 138–139; Muslim countries, 123–124, 130, 131; neo-institutionalism, 135; patterns, 126–132, 126–133, 141; post-World War II period, 130, 131; pre-1975 reforms, 134; punishment of offenders, 124, 125, 130; reduction in homosexual age of consent, 129; regime change, 130; scope of laws, 124, 125–126, 133; state-centric explanations, 123, 132–135, 140; United States, 138–139; world-society perspective, 123, 135–136